THE COMPLETE MAHABHARATA

Udyoga Parva

THE COMPLETE MAHABHARATA

Volume 4

Udyoga Parva

Jayashree Kumar

RUPA

Published by
Rupa Publications India Pvt. Ltd 2013
7/16, Ansari Road, Daryaganj
New Delhi 110002

Sales centres:
Allahabad Bengaluru Chennai
Hyderabad Jaipur Kathmandu
Kolkata Mumbai

Copyright © Jayashree Kumar 2013

All rights reserved.
No part of this publication may be reproduced, transmitted, or stored in a retrieval system, in any form or by any means, electronic, mechanical, photocopying, recording or otherwise, without the prior permission of the publisher.

ISBN: 978-81-291-2459-3

10 9 8 7 6 5 4 3 2 1

The moral right of the author has been asserted.

Printed at Thomson Press India Ltd., Faridabad

This book is sold subject to the condition that it shall not, by way of trade or otherwise, be lent, resold, hired out, or otherwise circulated, without the publisher's prior consent, in any form of binding or cover other than that in which it is published.

for my mother

Contents

A Brief Introduction ix
Acknowledgements xi

Canto 1–19	Senodyoga Parva	1–51
Canto 20–32	Sanjaya-yana Parva	52–92
Canto 33–40	Prajagara Parva	93–141
Canto 41–46	Sanat Sujata Parva	142–168
Canto 47–71	Yanasandhi Parva	169–243
Canto 72–150	Bhagavad-yana Parva	244–460
Canto 151–160	Sainya Niryana Parva	461–487
Canto 161–165	Uluka Duta Gamana Parva	488–509
Canto 166–173	Rathatiratha Sankhyana Parva	510–530
Canto 174-199	Ambopakhyana Parva	531–596

A Brief Introduction

The last complete version of the Mahabharata to be written in India in English prose was the translation by Kisari Mohan Ganguli in the late 19th century. He wrote it between 1883 and 1896. To the best of my knowledge, it still remains the only full English prose rendering of the epic by any Indian.

More than a hundred years have passed since Ganguli achieved his monumental task. Despite its closeness to the original Sanskrit and its undeniable power, in more than a hundred years the language and style of the Ganguli translation have inevitably become archaic.

It seemed a shame that this most magnificent of epics, a national treasure, an indisputable classic of world literature, believed by many to be the greatest of all books ever written, is not available in complete form to the Indian (or any) reader in modern, literary and easily accessible English: as retold by Indian writers.

So we, a group of Indian writers and editors, warmly and patiently supported by our publisher Rupa Publications India, undertook a line-by-line retelling of the complete Mahabharata, for the contemporary and future reader. Our aim has not been to write a scholarly translation of the

Great Epic, but an eminently readable one, without vitiating either the spirit or the poetry of the original, and without reducing its length.

This is not a translation from the Sanskrit but based almost entirely on the Ganguli text, and he himself did use more than one Sanskrit version for his work. However, as will be obvious, the style of this new rendering is very much our own, and our hope is to bring as much of the majesty and enchantment of this awesome epic to you as is possible in English.

Ramesh Menon
Series Editor

Acknowledgements

My thanks go, again, to Ramesh Menon for having given me the opportunity to be involved in this project; and to my mother, my son and my daughter for their love and support throughout the making of this volume.

CANTO 1

SENODYOGA PARVA

AUM! I bow down to Narayana and Nara, the most exalted Purusha, and to the Devi Saraswati and invoke the spirit of *Jaya!*

Vaisampayana said, "After the joyful celebrations of Abhimanyu's wedding, the Kurus of the wedding party rest that night and present themselves in the morning before Virata in his sabha. King Virata's court is full of treasures, the choicest vaiduryas and other precious stones; exquisitely wrought thrones and deep silk-covered armchairs are carefully laid out and the great hall is fragrant with the scent of a wealth of garlands.

The visiting kings are all present, when Virata and Drupada, the eldest among them, enter and occupy the thrones at the head of the sabha. Balarama, Krishna and their father Vasudeva are present. Satyaki, great Kshatriya of the Sini vamsa, and Rohini's son Balarama sit beside the Panchala king. Krishna and Yudhishtira sit beside the king of the Matsyas and with them are all the sons of Drupada, Bhima and Arjuna, Madri's sons, Virata's princes, and Pradyumna, Samba, Abhimanyu. Draupadi's sons, young lions who rival their fathers in courage, grace and prowess, are there as well, and they sit upon rich, gold-inlaid seats.

All these glittering heroes in their resonant ornaments and grand attire make that sabha of kings sparkle like the star-filled sky. Greetings exchanged all round and pleasantries done with, the assembled Kshatriyas fall quiet, their pensive gazes fixed on Krishna. And rising, he calls their attention to the circumstances of the Pandavas. The sabha is hushed and the Kshatriyas are absorbed by what he says, which is grave and profound.

Krishna says, 'You all know how Yudhishtira was deceitfully defeated at dice by Subala's son, and how his kingdom was stolen from him. You also know of his oath to live in exile in the forest. Although Pandu's sons can conquer the very Earth, they kept the oath they had sworn and those incomparable princes fulfilled the cruel conditions imposed on them. This last, thirteenth year, was the most trying for them, but they have endured their ajnatavasa, disguised, suffering silently and unrecognised. You are all aware of these things.

These illustrious men spent that thirteenth year doing menial service. You must take all this into consideration and decide what course is best, and fair to both Yudhishtira and Duryodhana. What you decide about the Kauravas and the Pandavas must be in keeping with dharma and must have your unanimous approval.

Yudhishtira would not want even Devaloka if he violated dharma to gain the realm of the gods; he would gladly accept a single small village for his kingdom if that was righteous. All you kings and noble princes know how the sons of Dhritarashtra robbed Yudhishtira of the kingdom that was his birthright, and how he has suffered untold adversity. Although Dhritarashtra's sons cannot hope to resist Arjuna's prowess, Yudhishtira and his brothers still wish their cousins well; they wish for peace.

These matchless sons of Kunti and Madri only ask for what is theirs—what they won by vanquishing other kings in battle. When they were mere boys, you know how, many a time and using diverse methods, Duryodhana, his brothers and Sakuni plotted to kill the sons of Pandu, because Duryodhana always wanted the kingdom for himself. Consider how greedy those twisted, evil men are and how virtuous Yudhishtira.

Consider deeply the relationship between them. I beseech you all to consult together and to decide on which side dharma lies.

The Pandavas have always been devoted to truth. They have fulfilled their oath faithfully. If the sons of Dhritarashtra do not give them justice now, and their kingdom back, the sons of Pandu will kill them all. When kings friendly to the Pandavas hear about the long suffering inflicted on them, they will all rally behind them and risk their very lives to see their tormentors punished, to see them die. Do not presume that the Pandavas are too few or too weak to prevail over their enemies. United, and with the support of their allies, they will destroy those who oppose them.

However, we do not know Duryodhana's mind, or what he might do. How can we form any opinion about what is best for both the Pandavas and the Kauravas without knowing what Dhritarashtra's son intends? So, let an able ambassador—a high-born man who is virtuous, honest and alert—go to Duryodhana and persuade him to give half the kingdom to Yudhishtira.'

Full of wisdom and dharma, Krishna's words hang over the hushed sabha; he speaks impartially and for peace. His elder brother listens and then Balarama rises to addresses the gathering of kings."

CANTO 2

SENODYOGA PARVA CONTINUED

"Baladeva says, 'You have all heard Krishna. What he says is in keeping with dharma, prudent and impartial, and equally beneficial for both Yudhishtira and Duryodhana. The sons of Kunti are prepared to give up half their kingdom to Duryodhana; the sons of Dhritarashtra should be willing to do the same. The Kurus should be grateful to us and rejoice that the conflict between them has been so amicably resolved. The Pandavas will be content with this arrangement, provided their cousins do the honourable thing. And the satisfaction of the Pandavas is conducive to the welfare of all mankind.

I would be happy if one amongst us, committed to pacifying both the Kurus and the Pandavas, goes as a duta to Hastinapura, taking Yudhishtira's thoughts with him, and also to discover Duryodhana's intentions. This man must pay his respects to the noble Bhishma, to Dhritarashtra, to Drona and his son Aswatthama, to Vidura and Kripa, to Sakuni prince of Gandhara and to the Sutaputra Karna. Let him also pay his respects to the other sons of Dhritarashtra, who are all renowned for their strength and learning, who know dharma well, who are brave and aware of all that has happened, and who read the signs of the times.

When all these and the elders are assembled, let our messenger speak with humility, since this will best serve the interests of Yudhishtira.

While it is true that Dhritarashtra's sons took the kingdom with some deceit, our messenger must spare no effort to avoid provoking them. When Yudhishtira had his throne he forgot himself; he gambled wildly at dice and lost his kingdom.

Yudhishtira was never adept at dice-play, and despite his brothers and friends trying to dissuade him, he foolishly challenged Sakuni, who is a master gambler. Hundreds of other dice-players were present, whom Yudhishtira could have beaten, but he ignored them and, of all men, he challenged Sakuni. Naturally, he lost game after game but he still refused to play anyone but Sakuni, who easily routed him and took everything he owned. How can Sakuni be blamed for this?

Therefore, our messenger must employ the utmost humility and first placate Dhritarashtra, who might then persuade Duryodhana to deal in peace. We must not incite a war with the Kurus, but approach Duryodhana in conciliation. War can never achieve what a peaceful agreement would, an enduring result.'

While the great and ponderous Balarama is still speaking, suddenly Satyaki, prince of the Sinis, jumps up and, his face red with indignation, roundly condemns what Baladeva advocates."

CANTO 3

SENODYOGA PARVA CONTINUED

"Satyaki says, 'What a man says reflects what is in his heart; as do your words. Men are either brave or cowardly; of two branches of the same tree, only one might bear fruit; in the same dynastic line, there may be foolish men as well as those who have great strength of character.

O you whose banner bears the image of a plough, it is not what you say that I condemn, but those who listen to you. How can they allow a man who dares blame virtuous Yudhishtira to speak in this sabha? Clever dice-players challenged Yudhishtira even though he had little skill and, trusting in their integrity, he was vanquished. Can such men be said to have won honourably?

If they had come to Yudhishtira in his own house, whilst he played dice with his brothers, and bested him there, their victory would have been righteous. They challenged him, who was bound by Kshatriya dharma, and they won by deceit. How can what they did be called dharma? Having agreed to what they made the stakes in the game, a life in the forests, how could Yudhishtira demean himself by asking to be freed from his wager, even if he was beaten with cunning sleight of hand? Even if, by rights, Yudhishtira still owned his ancestral kingdom, it would have been beneath him to beg.

How can the Kauravas be termed righteous and their intentions honourable when they accused the Pandavas of having been discovered, although the sons of Pandu had completed their ajnatavasa unrecognised? Bhishma and Drona begged them to return the Pandavas' rightful throne, but they refused.

I would use arrows rather than words to convince them. I would use force to make them prostrate at Yudhishtira's feet. They and their allies must bow before him, or they must die. When I, Yuyudhana, am provoked by anger to fight, they will not resist me, even as mountains cannot withstand a striking thunderbolt.

Who can withstand Arjuna in fight? Who can resist him who has the discus for his weapon? Who can stand against me? Who can face the inexorable Bhima? And who that values his life would come near the sons of Madri, whose bows are firmly held and who are like twin embodiments of Yama?

Who would dare face Drupada's son Dhrishtadyumna, or these five sons of Pandu, who glorified Draupadi's name, who rival their father in valour and in every other way, and who are full of Kshatriya pride? Who would ride against Subhadra's son, whose mighty bow neither the Devas, nor Gada, nor Pradyumna, nor Samba can resist, and who is like Death himself, or like the very Vajra, or like Agni?

We will kill Duryodhana, Sakuni and Karna in battle and install Yudhishtira on the Kuru throne. There is no sin in slaying those who are intent on killing us, but to beg from our enemies is both adharma and shameful.

I ask you to do what Yudhishtira wants. Let Pandu's son regain the kingdom that Dhritarashtra surrenders. If Yudhishtira does not get his kingdom today, I will mow down our enemies.' "

CANTO 4

SENODYOGA PARVA CONTINUED

"Drupada says, 'Mahabaho, it will be as you say. Duryodhana will never give up the kingdom peacefully; his doting father Dhritarashtra will go along with him; Bhishma and Drona will, too, from helplessness and loyalty, and Karna and Sakuni from bravado. I like what Baladeva said; we must do as he advises, but only if we want peace.

We should not speak to Duryodhana with mild words. He has a vicious nature, and temperance will not persuade him to see reason. Gentleness is appropriate for dealing with a donkey, but only firmness for cattle. If we speak leniently to Duryodhana, that evil one will think we are fools and presume that he has won.

Let us make preparations and send word to our friends, asking them to gather an army for us. Let swift messengers go to Salya and Dhrishtaketu, to Jayatsena and the prince of the Kekayas. Duryodhana will also send word to these kings. By dharma, men will respond to the first one who asks them. So make haste to reach out to your friends.

A great undertaking awaits us. Send word quickly to Salya and to the kings loyal to him, to Bhagadatta of immeasurable valour who rules the eastern coast, to fierce Hardikya and Andhaka, to the brilliant king of the Mallas and to Rochamanas. Summon Brihanta and Senabindu; Senajit, Prativindhya and Chitravarman; Bahlika, Munjakesa and the ruler of the Chedis; Suparsva, Subahu and that Maharatha Paurava. Call the kings of the Sakas, the Pahlavas, the Daradas; call Surari, Nadija and Karnaveshta, Neela and Bhumipala Viradharman; call Durjaya and Dantavaktra, Rukmi and Janamejaya, Ashada, Vayuvega and Purvapali; call Bhuritejas, Devaka, Ekalavya and his sons. Send also for the Karushaka kings and the valiant Kshemadhurti, and for the kings of the Kamboja and the Rishika tribes of the west coast; send for Jayatsena and the king of Kasi, for the rulers of the land of the five rivers, and for the son of Kratha; send for the rulers of the mountain realms, for Janaki and Susarman and Maniman, for Yotimatsaka and Dhrishtaketu, for the kings of Pansu, Tunda and Dandadhara, and for Brihatsena. Summon Aparajita, Nishada, Sreniman and Vasuman; call Brihadbala of untold might, Bahu the conqueror of hostile cities and the warlike Samudrasena and his valiant son; summon Udbhava and Kshemaka, Vatadhana, Srutayu and Dridhayu; summon the gallant son of Salva, the king of the Kalingas, and the unconquerable Kumara. Speedily send word to all these men. Yes, this plan appeals to me.

And let this learned Brahmana, my priest, be the messenger who goes to Dhritarashtra. Tell him what he must say to Duryodhana, how to address Bhishma, that noblest of warriors and what to say to Drona, that greatest of Maharathas.'"

CANTO 5

SENODYOGA PARVA CONTINUED

"Krishna says, 'What you counsel surely befits the king of the Panchalas, for your deep kinship and allegiance towards Pandu's son. Yet, we want to adopt a wise course of action, and that is our first duty; it would be foolish to do otherwise. Our relationship to the Kauravas and the Pandavas is equal, regardless of their own inclinations towards each other. You and all of us were invited for a wedding. The marriage has been celebrated; let us go home happily.

You are the first of all the kings here, both in age and learning, and the rest of us are like sishyas to you. Dhritarashtra has always had great respect for you; and you are also a friend of the acharyas Drona and Kripa. So, I ask you to send a message to the Kurus on behalf of the Pandavas. We are unanimously resolved that you should be our duta.

If the Kuru king makes peace on equitable terms, the cordial, brotherly feelings between the Kauravas and Pandavas will be restored. If, on the other hand, Duryodhana takes a haughty stand and refuses peace, send for the others first and then summon us as well.

The wielder of the Gandiva will be ignited with anger; the dull-headed, evil Duryodhana, his kinsmen and his friends will meet their fate.'"

Virata pays homage to Krishna, bids farewell to him, and Krishna sets off home with his kinsmen. After Krishna leaves for Dwaraka, Yudhishtira and his followers join Virata and begin to prepare for war.

Virata and Drupada send messengers to all the other monarchs, and at their request many powerful kings gladly arrive to join them. The sons of Dhritarashtra hear that the Pandavas have amassed a great army and they, too, muster a force of many rulers of the Earth. O king, quickly the world teems with warriors galvanised to the cause of either the Kurus or the Pandavas. Armies composed of the four kinds of forces pour in from all sides and fill the land; and Bhumi Devi, with her mountains and forests, seems to tremble beneath their tread.

The king of the Panchalas consults Yudhishtira and sends his wise and learned priest to the Kurus."

CANTO 6

SENODYOGA PARVA CONTINUED

"Drupada says to his priest, 'Of all beings, those endowed with life are superior to the inert; of living beings, those endowed with intelligence are superior to the others; of intelligent creatures, men are foremost; of men, Dvijas are the highest; of the twice-born, students of the Vedas are the best; of Vedic students, those of refined minds are first; of cultured men, the practical are the best; and of practical men, those who know Brahman, the Supreme Being, are the highest.

You are at the very apex of this pyramid of beings. Distinguished by your age and learning, you are equal in intellect to Indra or Brihaspati. You know what kind of man the king of the Kurus is, and you know what Yudhishtira is. It was with Dhritarashtra's knowledge that the Kauravas deceived the Pandavas and, despite Vidura's counsel, that king follows his son.

On behalf of the Kurus, Sakuni challenged Yudhishtira to a game of dice, although the Pandava was as a callow beginner while he himself was an expert. Unskilled in play, and guileless, Yudhishtira adhered strictly to rules of Kshatriya dharma. The ruthless Kurus cheated and won Yudhishtira's kingdom from him, and they are not going to give it up voluntarily.

If you speak words of dharma to Dhritarashtra, you will certainly gain the hearts of his warriors. Vidura will support what you say and, thereby, antagonise Bhishma, Drona, Kripa and the others. When the enemy commanders are alienated from their simple-minded fighting men, they will need to regain the confidence of their soldiers. In the meantime, the Pandavas will prepare their armies and gather their supplies, while, with you lingering in their midst and sowing subtle discord in the hearts of their men, the enemy will not be able to make adequate preparations for war. This plan of action seems the best.

It is possible that Dhritarashtra might agree to your proposal and do as you ask. You, being virtuous, must behave toward them with dharma. Win the hearts of the compassionate by discoursing at length on the trials that the Pandavas have endured and convince the elderly by reminding them about the customs of their forefathers.

I have no doubts in this regard, nor do you need to be apprehensive of any danger. You are a Brahmana, well versed in the Vedas; and you are going there as a duta; furthermore, you are elderly. So, old friend, set out at once for Hastinapura to promote the cause of the Pandavas. Set out on the day of the Pushyami nakshatra, during that part of the day called Jaya.'

The priest sets out for Hastinapura, mindful of Drupada's instructions. That learned man, who has a deep knowledge of the Artha Shastra, goes with a retinue of disciples towards the city of the Kurus, to advance the welfare of Pandu's sons."

CANTO 7

SENODYOGA PARVA CONTINUED

Vaisampayana said, "After the Pandavas send the priest to Hastinapura, they send other messengers to the kings of various kingdoms, and Arjuna sets out for Dwaraka. After Krishna and Baladeva leave for Dwaraka with all the Vrishnis, the Andhakas and hundreds of Bhojas, Dhritarashtra's son sends out spies to garner information about what the Pandavas are doing.

Duryodhana hears that Krishna is on his way home and goes at once to Dwaraka, riding on fine horses swift as the wind, and taking a small troop of warriors with him. He and Arjuna arrive on the same day in the beautiful city of the Anarta realm. On reaching there, those two lions of Kuru vamsa find that Krishna is sleeping, and they go to his bedchamber.

Krishna is still asleep when Duryodhana enters the chamber and sits on a fine seat at the head of the bed. Arjuna enters behind him and stands at the foot of the bed, his head bent and hands folded. When Krishna awakes his gaze falls first on Arjuna. He greets both him and Duryodhana, and after asking if they had a safe journey, mildly enquires why they have come to see him.

Duryodhana says, 'You must help me in the impending war. Arjuna and I are both your friends, Madhusudana, and you are related to both of us in the same way. Today, it is I who petitions you first. Men of dharma take up the cause of the one who approaches them first. This is the way of the ancients.

Krishna, you are the first of all men of dharma, and everyone respects you, at all times. I ask you to follow dharma and do what is right.'

Krishna replies, 'That you have come first, O king, I do not doubt in the least. But, it is Arjuna that I saw first. Because you were the first to approach me and because Arjuna was the first one I saw, I shall help you both. It is said that those who are younger should choose first. That gives Dhananjaya the first choice.

There exists a vast force of Yadavas, numbering ten crores, known as the Narayanas. Each of them is stronger than me and each one can fight in the very thick of any battle. One of you can have these irresistible soldiers. The other will have me; but I will bear no arms and neither will I fight on the field.

Arjuna, you decide first which you will choose, because law dictates that you have the first choice.'

Arjuna chooses Krishna, who will not fight on the battlefield, who is Vishnu himself, creator, preserver and slayer of men, the uncreated one, born among men of his own will, foremost of all Kshatriyas, beyond all the Devas and Danavas. Duryodhana gladly accepts the Yadava army of Narayanas and, though he knows that Krishna will not be with him, he is thrilled at having acquired the massive force. Having secured that awesome army, Duryodhana goes in some delight to his old master, Rohini's son Balarama, to tell him of the reason for his visit and its outcome.

Baladeva says to Duryodhana, 'Remember all that I said at Virata's daughter's wedding. It is for your sake that I spoke against Krishna there and contradicted him. Again and again, I spoke of the equality of our relationship to both sides. However, Krishna did not adopt my views, and I cannot separate myself from Krishna for even a moment. Since I cannot go into battle against him, I have resolved not to fight, either for Kunti's sons or for you.

O Bharatarishabha, born as you are into the noble race of Bharata, go bravely into battle and fight with Kshatriya dharma.'

Duryodhana embraces that hero whose weapon is the plough and, despite being aware that Krishna is not on his side, he still considers Arjuna and the Pandavas as having already been defeated. He then goes to Kritavarman, who gives him an akshauhini of troops. And surrounded by that terrifying host, he rides forth, to the great joy of his friends.

After Duryodhana has left, Krishna says to Arjuna, 'Why did you choose me, when you knew that I will not fight at all?'

Arjuna answers, 'I have no doubt that you will slay all our enemies, even without fighting yourself. I, too, can kill them all, by myself, Purushottama. You are the most illustrious being in this world, and your renown and honour will come with you. I wish for that, and that is why I chose you. I have always wanted to have you for my sarathy, and I ask you now to fulfil my long-cherished desire.'

Krishna says with a deep smile, 'I am glad that you chose me, son of Kunti. As for your wish, yes, I will be your charioteer.'

His heart full of joy, Arjuna returns with Krishna to where Yudhishtira waits."

CANTO 8

SENODYOGA PARVA CONTINUED

Vaisampayana said, "O king, Salya hears the news that the messengers bring and, accompanied by his sons and a teeming legion of soldiers, every man mighty in battle, he sets out to come to the Pandavas.

His encampment extends over one and a half yojanas, so vast is Salya's force. Rajan, this most powerful king commands an entire akshauhini. In his army are heroes wearing armour of different colours, carrying a myriad of banners and all sorts of bows, adorned with diverse ornaments, garlands and jewellery, and wearing beautiful clothing. Hundreds of thousands of the foremost Kshatriyas are the leaders of his troops, and they are clothed and decorated, each in the tradition of his native land.

Salya moves slowly, majestically, toward the Pandava camp, frequently giving his men time to rest. The Earth's little creatures are crushed and the ground trembles under the tread of his legions. Hearing that the great and mighty warrior is on the march, Duryodhana makes all haste to win him over to his side. He swiftly has finely-decorated, palatial pavilions erected at many enchanting sites for Salya's comfort and pleasure, and sends performers to entertain that king.

The first of these retreats is adorned with garlands and stocked with meat and the choicest delicacies and refreshments. There are fine pools and tanks of different shapes, all delightful to see; there is plentiful food, and there are spacious apartments. Salya arrives at the first exotic pavilion, and Duryodhana's best servants wait upon him as if he is a Deva.

Salya reaches another hall of entertainment that is as resplendent as an arbour of the gods. And there, luxuriating in comforts fit for any celestial, he thinks himself superior to the lord of the Devas and even thinks of Indra as being shabby in comparison.

The delighted Salya asks the servants, 'Where are Yudhishtira and the others who have arranged for these lavish mansions? Bring the men who built them before me; they deserve to be richly rewarded. I must acknowledge their work. I hope Kunti's son will approve.'

The surprised servants inform Duryodhana, who stays hidden until Salya's pleasure is so great that he is ready to grant even his life, and then he comes forward and reveals himself to his uncle. The king of the Madras sees him and understands that it is Duryodhana who has taken all these pains to fete him.

And Salya embraces Duryodhana and says, 'I want to give you something that you truly want.'

Duryodhana says, 'Auspicious one, let it be as you say, and grant me this boon: I ask you to lead my armies in battle.'

Salya says, 'So be it. What do I need to do?'

The son of Gandhari cries again and again, 'It is done! It is done!'

And Salya says, 'O best of men, go back to your city. I must pay Yudhishtira a visit. I will do that first and come to you very soon.'

Duryodhana says, 'O Bhumipala, come quickly indeed after seeing the Pandava. I depend on you entirely, so remember the boon you have granted me.'

Salya says, 'Blessings upon you! I will hasten back. Go in peace to your city, O protector of men.'

The two kings, Salya and Duryodhana, embrace and Duryodhana

returns to his capital. Salya goes to inform the sons of Kunti of what has happened.

When he reaches Upaplavya and enters the encampment there, Salya sees all the sons of Pandu before him. The mighty-armed Salya meets them and accepts the customary courtesies—water to wash his feet with and honourable gifts, including a cow. The king of the Madras asks how they are and, with great joy, embraces Yudhishtira, Bhima, Arjuna and his sister's twin sons.

When they are all seated, Salya says to Yudhishtira, 'Naravyaghra, is all well with you? How fortunate it is that you have completed your exile. Such a difficult task you, your brothers and the princess have accomplished by living in the wilderness! No less trying was the year of your ajnatavasa.

When a man has his throne taken from him, there is nothing but hardship to look forward to. Rajan, what happiness is there for such a one? But after killing your enemies you will gain as much, no, a hundredfold more, felicity and joy than the torment that Dhritarashtra's son inflicted on you.

You are wise in the ways of the world and, so, my son, you never do anything out of avarice. You walk in the footsteps of the ancient Rajarishis. You must remain firmly on your path of generosity, selflessness and truth. Mercy, self-control, truth, universal compassion and every other wonderful quality present in this world are also present in you.

You are mild, generous, devout and large-hearted; and you look on virtue as the highest good. Many are the laws of dharma that prevail amongst men, and you know them all. In fact, you know everything there is to know of this world of ours.

Bharatottama, how great it is that you have emerged from your travails. How fortunate I am to see you, who are a treasure-house of dharma, now free and among your followers.'

Then, Bhaarata, the king tells Yudhishtira of his meeting with Duryodhana, and about the boon he granted him.

Yudhishtira says, 'Pledging your allegiance to Duryodhana out of heartfelt gratitude is dharma indeed. But, Bhumipala, I ask you to do one thing for me. Even if what I ask is not dharma, you must do it for my sake. Listen to my plea.

On the battlefield you are Krishna's equal as a charioteer. When Karna and Arjuna come face to face in a mortal duel, I have no doubt that you will be Karna's sarathy. At that time, I beg you, protect Arjuna, even while you are his enemy's sarathy. You must dampen the Sutaputra's spirits, for his lack of confidence is his only weakness, and only through that can Arjuna prevail over him. Uncle, you must do this, even though it is unseemly. For if Karna is not slain, we will lose the war.'

Salya says, 'Bless you, Pandava, and now listen to me. You ask me to dispirit Karna in battle. Yes, I am sure I will become his charioteer, for he does consider me equal to Krishna. When he prepares to fight Arjuna, I will point out the dangers he faces. I will extol Arjuna and convince Karna that he is no match for your brother. Shorn of courage and pride, he will be easy to kill.

I swear that I am determined to do what you ask. Whatever else I may be able to do for your good, I will do as well. The anguish you suffered along with Draupadi during the game of dice; the savage words that the Suta's son spoke then; the misery that Jatasura and Kichaka inflicted on you; Draupadi's torment, which was like Damayanti's—this will all end in joy, O Kshatriya.

Do not grieve over what happened, for destiny is inexorable. From time out of mind, the noblest men have endured all manner of suffering; why, even the Devas have found grave misfortunes, Rajan. It is told that Indra and his wife had to endure great grief once, and were plunged in black despair.'"

CANTO 9

SENODYOGA PARVA CONTINUED

"Yudhishtira says, 'Best of kings, how did Devendra and his queen come to endure such torment?'

Salya says, 'Listen, and I will tell you this ancient itihasa. Hear, Bhaarata, how affliction befell Indra and his consort.

Once, Tvashtri, the lord of creatures and among the foremost of Devas, sat in austere tapasya, and out of his rancour against Indra, created a son with three heads. That lustrous being of universal form, Viswarupa, hankered after Indra's throne. He had three awesome faces that resembled the Sun, the Moon and Fire. With one he read the Vedas, with one he drank wine and his gaze from the third seemed to imbibe the whole world. With unflinching tapasya, this imperturbable and self-controlled being lived a life of devout spiritual discipline. Severe and terrible was his penance.

Observing the sternness, courage and truthfulness of this being of immeasurable tejas, Indra worried that he would take his place as the lord of the Devas.

Indra thought to himself, "How can this one be made addicted to sensual pleasures? How can he be made to forsake his tapasya? If he grows any stronger, he will absorb the entire universe."

Having pondered thus within himself, Indra sent Apsaras from Devaloka to tempt the son of Tvashtri.

He commanded them, saying, "Hurry! Go and tempt the three-headed one to plunge deep into pleasures of the senses. You, who are blessed with captivating hips, adorn yourselves in provocative attire, deck yourselves in fine necklaces and employ passionate gestures and language. My lovely ones, my heart is perturbed; distract him and alleviate my dread. Beautiful nymphs, avert this peril that hangs over me. May well-being be yours."

The Apsaras said, "O slayer of Bala, have no fear, we will seduce him. Together, we will tempt this rishi who sits in tapasya so fearful that his eyes seem to scorch everything they see. We will bring him under our control and put an end to your fears."

They went to the three-headed one and, arriving there, those exquisite temptresses teased him with gestures of love and their beautiful bodies. Absorbed in deep tapasya, he looked at them but was unmoved. With subdued senses he was like the ocean, full to the brim and unshakeable.

Their efforts were to no avail. The Apsaras came back to Indra and, with hands joined, said, "O, we could not shake that tranquil one. Now do whatever you must."

Indra honoured the Apsaras and dismissed them, thinking all the while about other ways of destroying his enemy. He soon lit upon a way to be rid of the three-headed one.

He said to himself, "Today, I will cast my thunderbolt at him, and he will die. Even the most powerful man must not take a nascent enemy lightly, of little account though he may yet be."

And so, with the exhortations of the Shastras in mind, he decided to kill the three-headed being and hurled his Vajra at him. It was terrible to see, such a fire, and struck dread into the heart. Struck by that all-powerful thunderbolt, the three-headed one died, and as he fell he loosened the summit of a mountain.

The lord of the Devas saw that he was dead and lay still, like a mountain, but Indra found no peace. Instead, he was scalded by the effulgence of that being, who blazed in death as he had in life. Lying on the field, his three heads seemed eerily alive. Overawed and in fear of that dazzling lustre, Indra was plunged in dismay.

Just then, he saw a carpenter walking through the forest with an axe on his shoulder.

Indra said to him, "I ask a favour of you. Cut off this dead one's heads."

The carpenter said, "His shoulders are broad, and my axe is not big enough. Also, I will not do this sinful thing."

Indra said, "Have no fear but quickly do as I say. At my command your axe will be as powerful as a thunderbolt."

The carpenter said, "Who are you, who have done this dreadful thing? Tell me the truth, I want to know."

Indra said, "Then know this: I am Indra, the lord of the Devas. Now do as I tell you. Do not hesitate, carpenter."

The carpenter said, "O Indra, why are you not ashamed of your bestial crime? How it is that you do not dread the sin of killing a Brahmana, particularly this son of a Mahamuni?"

Indra said, "I will perform rigorous atonement to purify myself of these sins. He whom I killed with my Vajra was a powerful enemy. I am still uneasy; I fear him even now. Waste no time; cut off his heads and I shall bestow my favour upon you. I grant that in all sacrifices, you will get the head of the sacrificial beast as your share. Now do what I ask!"

Hearing this, the carpenter cut off the heads of the three-headed one with his axe. When the heads were severed, partridges, quails, pigeons and all kinds of birds flew out from the naked throats. From the head which the three-headed one used to recite the Vedas and drink Soma nectar, partridges flew out in a flock. From the head with which he looked at the cardinal points as if to absorb them all, quails emerged. From that head which he used to drink wine came sparrows and hawks.

With the heads removed, Indra's trepidation left him. He returned to Devaloka with a light heart, and the carpenter went home. Indra was pleased that he had accomplished his objective.

When Tvashtri heard that Indra had killed his son, his eyes reddened, and he said, "Indra has killed my son, who was innocent of any offence, who was absorbed in constant tapasya, who was merciful, who was self-controlled and who had subdued his senses. To destroy Indra, I will create Vritra.

Let the Lokas behold my power; let the worlds see my tapasyashakti; let that inhuman, evil-minded Deva see what I do."

With these words, the furious Tvashtri, famed for his tapasya, washed his mouth with water in achamana, offered oblations to the fire and created the dreadful Vritra. He spoke to the Asura he had made, saying, "O Vritra, who are destined to slay Indra, may your might swell by the power of my tapasya."

And that Asura grew prodigiously in strength. Born of fire, like Agni's son, he towered towards the sky.

He said, "I have risen like the apocalyptic Sun; tell me what am I to do."

"Kill Indra," said Tvashtri, and left for the celestial realms.

A great battle ensued between Vritra and Indra. Both were fired with wrath, and the duel between them was terrible. The heroic Vritra seized the lord of gods and whirled him round and threw him into his open maw.

The Devas were terrified to see how easily Vritra had swallowed Indra, and they created Jrimbhika to kill Vritra. Waiting his chance, Indra drew his body into itself and flew out when Vritra opened his mouth to yawn. It is since then that the yawn became a characteristic of living beings in the three worlds. Great was the joy of the Devas at Indra's escape. And the furious battle between Indra and Vritra resumed.

They fought for a long, long time and, finally, Indra could not withstand Vritra, who was infused by the power of Tvashtri's tapasya; the Deva king fled and the Asura prevailed. In disarray after Indra's retreat, all the other Devas were easily overpowered by Tvashtri.

O Bhaarata, they consulted the greatest rishis and deliberated on the proper thing to do. Seized with dread, they sat on the top of the Mandara Mountain and invoked the indestructible Vishnu,' says Salya."

CANTO 10

SENODYOGA PARVA CONTINUED

"Salya continues, 'Indra said, "O Devas, Vritra has consumed the universe, and no-one can withstand him. Once I could have vanquished him, but not any more. What can I do now? He is unassailable: he has inexorable tejas; he is a Mahatman; victory will always be his in battle; he can swallow the three worlds with its Devas, Manavas and Asuras.

Swargavasis, I have decided that we must go to Vishnu and seek his counsel. He will help us find a way to kill this evil one.

At Maghavat's word, all the Devas and the Rishis went to the omnipotent Vishnu, to place themselves under the protection of that protector of all.

They said to the Supreme God, "O Narayana, it was you who once covered the three worlds in three strides. It was you who procured the Amrita and quelled the Asuras in battle. It was you who restrained the Asura Bali and placed Sakra on the throne of Devaloka. You are the Lord of the gods and the Soul of the universe. You are the almighty God whom all beings worship.

Best of Gods, be the means of our salvation, of all the Devas and Indra. O Asurasudana, all creation is pervaded by Vritra."

Vishnu said, "It is my dharma to do what benefits you. I will tell you how Vritra can be killed. Go with the Rishis and the Gandharvas to Vritra, who has absorbed the universe into himself. Go in an attitude of conciliation and win him over with feigned humility.

By virtue of my power, Indra will be victorious, for I shall invisibly enter his Vajra. Go now, all of you, with the Rishis and the Gandharvas, and make peace between Sakra and Vritra."

When he had spoken, the Rishis and the Devas, with Indra at their head, left all together. As they approached, they saw Vritra's splendour, ablaze as if to incinerate the ten cardinal points and consume the three worlds; and glorious, like the Sun or the Moon.

The Rishis came up to Vritra and said to him in a soothing tone, "O unconquerable one, your energy has consumed the universe. However, you have not vanquished Indra, although you have fought him for so long. All beings, including gods, men and demons, suffer from your conflict. Let there be peace between you and Sakra. You will be happy and live forever in Indra's realm."

The mighty and noble Vritra heard what they said and, bowing his head to them, said, "Great ones, I hear you and the Gandharvas clearly. Now listen to what I have to say. How can there be friendship between Indra and me? How can there be amity between two inveterate enemies?"

The Rishis said, "Concord between righteous beings happens at a single meeting and is always desirable. After that first contact, whatever is destined will happen. One should not lose the opportunity of forming an alliance with a man of dharma. Indeed, one should actively seek the friendship of the righteous. Wise men say that friendship with a good man is like wealth in a time of poverty, for the friend will give sage advice when it is needed. The friendship of a good person is of great benefit and, so, a wise man should never want to kill a righteous being.

Indra is honoured by the just; he is the refuge of the magnanimous; he speaks the truth, always; he is without blame; he knows what dharma is; and his judgment is refined. Let there be eternal friendship between you and Indra. Have faith in him and let your heart not be otherwise inclined."

The illustrious Asura said, "I revere you Rishis who are endowed with supernatural powers. Do as I say, exactly as I say, and then, Devas, I will do everything these Brahmanottamas advise.

My condition is: I shall not be killed with anything that is wet or dry, with anything made of stone or wood, with a weapon used in close combat or with an astra, neither during the day nor at night, not even by Indra himself or any of the gods. On these terms I will make eternal peace with Indra."

The Rishis agreed. Peace was restored, and Vritra was glad. Indra, too, was pleased, but thoughts of killing Vritra continued to fill his mind. The lord of the Devas passed his time, always uneasy and looking for a chink in the compact he had made with Vritra.

One day, in the eerie twilight of evening, Indra caught sight of the mighty Asura on the sea shore. He thought of the boon that had been granted to the Asura, and he thought, 'It is evening now—neither day nor night. I must kill Vritra, my enemy, who has stripped me of my power. Unless I slay this mighty Asura, even if I have to use deceit, I will not prosper."

At that moment, thinking these thoughts and bearing Vishnu's promise to him in mind, Indra saw a mass of foam in the sea, as big as a hill, and he said, "This is neither dry, nor wet, nor is it a weapon. Let me cast it at Vritra, and he will die."

And he infused that mountain of foam with the Vajra and cast it. Vishnu entered the foaming Vajra and sloughed off Vritra's head, and the matchless demon fell onto white, damp sands, his bare throat spouting a rill of blood. With the Asura's death, the universal pall of darkness lifted and the cardinal points shone again; fragrant breezes blew; and gladness filled all the living. The Devas, with the Gandharvas, Yakshas and Rakshasas, and with the great Nagas and Rishis, glorified Indra with hymns in his praise; and all of them bowed to him.

Indra and the Devas were happy, and Indra spoke soul-stirring words in joy at having killed his enemy. Ever conscious of dharma, Indra worshipped Vishnu, the most praiseworthy One of all.

However, having killed Vritra, bane of the gods, Indra was overcome by his crime of deceit, and black dejection seized his very soul. Terrorised by his sin of Brahmahatya, for he had killed a Brahmana when he slew Tvashtri's three-headed son, he withdrew from the world. He became like one who had lost his very mind. Haunted constantly by his sins, he was unrecognisable. He hid under water, writhing like a snake and, bereft of his presence, the Earth looked as if she had been devastated by a storm of the pralaya.

Bhumi became treeless, and her forests withered; rivers stopped in their courses, and lakes and even seas dried up; and animals were stricken because it never rained and a drought without remit gripped the world. The Devas and all the great Rishis were seized in fear; the world, without a king, was wracked by cataclysms of every kind. With no lord, panic took the Devas and the Devarishis. They wondered desperately who could replace Indra, but none amongst them had any inclination to be the king of the gods.'"

CANTO 11

SENODYOGA PARVA CONTINUED

"Salya says, 'Then all the Rishis and Devas said, "Let us crown the radiant Rajarishi Nahusha as king of the Devas. He is strong and famed, and always devoted to dharma."

They went to him and said, "O Bhumipala, we want you to be our king."

Nahusha, with self-interest at heart, said to the Devas, Rishis and Pitrs, "I am feeble and cannot protect you. You need a powerful god to be your king. Only Indra always owned that prowess."

The Devas with the Rishis at their head said, "It is true that we all have weaknesses. Rule the realms of Devaloka with the help of our tapasya. Rajarajan, accept the crown of heaven and this boon from us: whatever being stands within your sight—be he a Deva, an Asura, a Yaksha, a Rishi, a Pitr or a Gandharva—you shall absorb his power. Thereby your own power will be enhanced and you will grow in strength. Be guided only by dharma and rule the worlds. Protect the Brahmarishis and the Devas."

Nahusha was crowned king of Devaloka and, placing dharma before everything else, he became sovereign of all the worlds. Nahusha had led a virtuous life, but when he obtained the precious boon and reign over Devaloka, his mind began to turn to sensual thoughts.

He surrounded himself with Apsaras and other celestial nymphs. He began to enjoy myriad pleasures in the Nandana vana, on Mount Kailasa, upon the crest of Himavat, on the Mandara Mountain, on the slopes of the Sweta, Mahendra and Malaya mountains, and in the oceans and rivers. He listened to captivating stories and enjoyed the sweet strains of musical instruments and divine voices singing. Viswavasu and Narada, bevies of Apsaras, bands of Gandharvas and the six seasons embodied attended upon him. Scented breezes wafted around him, cool and refreshing.

Once, while the profligate king was enjoying himself in this way, he caught sight of Sachi Devi, Indra's favourite queen. He looked at her, and his soul in the grip of lust, he said to his courtiers, "Why does this Devi, Indra's queen, not minister to me? I am the lord of the Devas and the ruler of all the worlds. Let Sachi come to me at once."

Saddened when she heard this, Sachi said to Brihaspati, "O Brahmana, protect me from Nahusha. I take refuge with you. You have always said that I bear auspicious marks, being the favourite of the lord of the Devas; that I am chaste, devoted to my lord and destined never to become a widow. You say all this repeatedly; now let your words be proven true. You have never said anything in vain; therefore, Brahmanottama, all that you have said must come to pass."

Brihaspati said to Sachi, who was beside herself with fear, "What I have said will come true, Devi. It will not be long before you see the return of Indra. Truly, you have nothing to fear from Nahusha, and I shall unite you with Indra very soon."

Nahusha heard that Indra's queen had taken refuge with Brihaspati, the son of Angiras, and he was furious.'"

CANTO 12

SENODYOGA PARVA CONTINUED

"Salya says, 'Seeing that Nahusha was angry, the Rishis and Devas said to their king, who looked so fearsome now, "O Devaraja, shed your rage. When you are angry, the entire universe trembles, with its Asuras, Gandharvas, Kinnaras and Nagas. Let go of this wrath, righteous one. A man like you should not lose his equanimity.

Devi Sachi is another man's wife. Calm yourself. Turn your mind away from the sin of ravishing another's wife. You are the king of the Devas, and may you prosper! Protect your subjects with dharma."

Nahusha was mindless with desire and paid no heed to what they said. Accusing Indra, he said, "Ahalya of the blemishless reputation was the wife of a Muni. Indra ravished her while her husband still lived. Why did you not stop him? Many were the deeds of inhumanity, of unrighteousness and of deceit that Indra committed in times past. Why did you not prevent him?

Let the Devi serve my pleasure; it will do her good and will protect you all, as well."

The Devas said, "We will bring Indra's queen to you, as you command. Set aside your anger and be at peace."

The Devas and Rishis went to inform Brihaspati and Sachi about what had transpired. They said, "Brahmanottama, we know that Sachi Devi has come to you for refuge and that you have promised to protect her. But we, the Devas, Gandharvas and Rishis, beg you to give her up to Nahusha. The lustrous Nahusha is now the king of the Devas and is above Indra. Let the beautiful Devi accept him as her lord."

Hearing this, Sachi began to sob pitifully, and she said to Brihaspati, "O best of Devarishis, I do not want Nahusha for my lord. I have placed myself in your protection; save me from this calamity."

Brihaspati said, "I am resolved not to abandon you. You of the blemishless life, I shall not forsake you, for you are virtuous and devoted to truth. I do not want to commit a sin, especially since I am a Brahmana who knows dharma, for I worship the truth and am aware of all the dictates of dharma. No, I will never betray you. Go your ways, Devas. But first, hear what Brahma has said about this:

He who surrenders to a foe the terrified person who has asked for protection will not find refuge when he himself is in need of it. The seeds he plants will not grow, and rains will fail.

He who gives up to an enemy the terrified one who has asked for his protection never succeeds in anything that he undertakes. He will lose his senses and fall stricken from heaven. The gods refuse the offerings he makes. His progeny die untimely deaths, and his Pitrs fight among themselves. The Devas with Indra at their head will cast the Vajra at such a one.

Know this to be true. I shall not give up Sachi, who is Indra's queen and his favourite. I, Brihaspati, tell you this, which is for her good and mine. I will never surrender Sachi."

Then the Devas and the Gandharvas said, "Acharya Brihaspati, think of a solution."

Brihaspati said, "Let this auspicious Devi ask Nahusha for some time before she decides what to do. This will be to her advantage and ours, for Kaala might create many obstacles in Nahusha's way while we wait. Only Time knows the future. Nahusha has become powerful and haughty because of the boon you granted him."

Brihaspati's words pleased the Devas, who said, 'You have spoken well, O Guru. This is, without doubt, for the good of all the Devas. However, we must pacify this Devi."

Then the Devas led by Agni spoke soothingly to Indra's queen, saying, "You are the holder of the universe of mobile and immobile things. You are chaste and true. Go to Nahusha. That degenerate who lusts after you will fail to have what he wants, and Indra will regain sovereignty over Devaloka."

Indra's queen went bashfully to Nahusha of the dreadful mien, but to attain her end, not his. Struck mindless with lust, Nahusha saw her, how young and lovely she was, and was ecstatic.'"

CANTO 13

SENODYOGA PARVA CONTINUED

"Salya says, 'Nahusha saw Sachi come, and said, "O sweet smiles, I am the lord of the three worlds. Take me for your lord as well."

That chaste Devi quivered in terror, like the slender stalk of a young plantain tree in the wind. She bowed her head to Brahma, then joined her hands and spoke to the truly fearsome Nahusha.

She said, "Devaraja, I need time. No one knows what became of Indra, or his whereabouts. I have sent my friends and servitors forth to look for him; if I get no news of him, I will come to you. I tell you this truthfully."

Nahusha was pleased, and said, "It shall be as you say. Come as soon as you discover what has happened. I hope you will keep your word."

The auspicious Sachi Devi went back to Brihaspati's home. There, she told Agni and the other Devas what had happened, and they began to deliberate on what they should do to best benefit Indra.

They went to the all-powerful Vishnu for refuge and said, "Indra has been overcome by the sin of killing a Brahmana. Devadeva, you are the Primeval One, the first creator, the ruler of the universe, and our refuge. You have assumed the form of Vishnu for the protection of all beings. When, by dint of your power, Indra slew Vritra he was guilty of the direst sin of killing a Brahmana, of Brahmahatya. How can he be absolved of his sin?"

Vishnu said, "Let him offer a yagna to me, and I will purify the Vajradharin. If he performs the Aswamedha yagna, the slayer of Paka will regain his position as king of the Devas. Nahusha's hubris and indulgences will destroy him. Be patient and bide your time, Devas, but remain vigilant."

Knowing that they are always true, Vishnu's words were like amrita to their ears. And the Devas, their Acharya and the Rishis went to where the troubled Indra waited in constant terror. And there, they performed a great horse-sacrifice, which could expiate the sin of killing a Brahmana, so that Indra would be purified.

O Yudhishtira, Mahavishnu divided Indra's sin among trees, rivers, mountains, the Earth and women; and Indra was rid of it. His fever of dread left him and he was himself once more.

From that place, Indra looked at Nahusha, before whom all living beings felt cowed, and who was unapproachable because of the boon that the Rishis had granted him. Sachi's lord made himself invisible and wandered the universe, biding his time.

When Indra disappeared, Sachi sank into a well of grief. In utter misery she cried, "O Indra! If I have ever given you a gift, if I have ever made an offering to the gods, if I have ever propitiated my gurus, if there is any truth in me, then I pray that my chastity remains inviolate. I bow to Nisha Devi, Goddess of Night, who is holy and pure, and who rules during uttarayana, the northern course of the Sun. I pray that she answers my plea!"

Saying this, she purified herself in body and soul and worshipped Nisha Devi, whom she was able to invoke because of her chastity and devotion to truth, and she said, "Show me where the king of the Devas is. Let truth reveal the truth.""'

CANTO 14

SENODYOGA PARVA CONTINUED

"Salya says, 'Devi Upasruti appeared before the virtuous and beautiful woman. Indra's queen gazed at this young and exquisite goddess and, with a glad heart, paid her worship. She said, "Who are you, lovely one?"

Upasruti said, "I am Upasruti. I have made myself visible to you because of your truthfulness, noble one. You are devoted to your husband, you are self-restrained, and you are devout in your worship; and so I will show you where Vritrasudana Indra is. Follow me quickly; and you shall see him."

Upasruti, with Sachi following her, crossed celestial groves and many mountains. She crossed the Himavat Mountain and, by its northern flank, arrived at the sea. Many yojanas over the ocean, she flew to a large island covered with marvellous trees and plants of all kinds.

And there the two devis came to an enchanting and heavenly lake, eight hundred yojanas long and wide, with flocks of birds all around and upon the shimmering water. Bhaarata, on its crystalline surface grew full-blown lotuses of five colours with thousands of bees humming above them. In the middle of the lake was a large and exquisite bank of these flowers, at the heart of which stood a singular white lotus upon a tall stem.

Upasruti infused herself and Sachi into the stem of this wondrous flower, and there Sachi saw her lord Indra in a miniature form. Sachi and Upasruti contracted themselves into tiny forms as well; and Indra's queen began to glorify her lord by reciting a litany of his celebrated deeds.

The divine Purandara said to Sachi, "Why have you come? How did you find me?"

Devi Sachi told him what Nahusha had done. She said, "O performer of a hundred sacrifices, he obtained the sovereignty of the three worlds and became powerful and haughty, and his soul became corrupt and vicious. He commanded me to serve him, and the wretch has even appointed a time by which I must go to him. If you do not save me, my lord, he will force me to give myself to him. That is why I have to come so desperately to you.

Mahabaho, kill the terrible Nahusha of the black soul. Reveal yourself, slayer of Daityas and Danavas. Assume your own power and rule Devaloka again.""

CANTO 15

SENODYOGA PARVA CONTINUED

"Salya says, 'The illustrious Indradeva said to Sachi, "This is no time for rashness. Nahusha is more powerful than I am, beautiful one. His power has been augmented by the benefits that the Rishis gain every time they make offerings to the Devas and the Pitrs. I have a judicious plan, which you will have to carry out. You must not disclose it to anyone, but do it secretly.

Go to Nahusha in private, address him as lord of the universe and invite him to visit you, riding on a palanquin borne by Rishis. Tell him that if he does this, you will gladly place yourself at his disposal."

Returning to Amaravati, the lotus-eyed Sachi went to Nahusha, who saw her and, smiling, said to her, "Welcome, devi of the rounded thighs and sweet smiles. What is your pleasure? Give yourself to me. I am devoted to you and I will do whatever pleases you. Do not be shy; trust me. I swear by truth that I will do whatever you ask."

Sachi said, "O Lord of the universe, I want the time that you granted me. After that, you will be my lord. And I do have a wish that you must fulfil before I become yours. I ask this indulgence, knowing your love for me. If you grant my wish, I will be yours to command.

Indra had horses to ride on, and elephants and chariots as well. I want you to have a unique vehicle, the like of which neither Vishnu nor Rudra, nor any of the Asuras and Rakshasas possess. Let a number of exalted Rishis carry you in such a palanquin. This is what I wish. You should not think of yourself as being merely equal to any Asuras or Devas. You absorb their strength as soon as they look at you and, thus, there is no one as great as you."

Nahusha was pleased, and he said to that perfect goddess, "Fairest one, you speak of a conveyance never heard of before. I am taken with your thought, Devi; ah, I am in your power! A man who has Rishis as his palanquin-bearers cannot be a feeble person. I have practised tapasya and am mighty. I am the lord of the past, the present and the future. The universe would cease to exist if I were to be moved to wrath, for all the universe is established in me.

Devas, Asuras, Gandharvas, Nagas and Rakshasas together cannot withstand me when I am angry. My very gaze divests the man it falls on of his energy, whoever he is. And I am pleased to grant your request. The Saptarishis and other lofty sages will carry me, and you will look upon our greatness and splendour, lovely one."

Saying this with arrogant confidence, Nahusha dismissed Sachi. He harnessed a number of Rishis, all devout tapasvins, to him. Contemptuous of Brahmanas, capricious and intoxicated with power and pride, Nahusha made those divine sages bear his palanquin.

Meanwhile, Sachi went to Brihaspati and said, "Just a brief time remains of the period of grace that Nahusha granted me. Out of compassion for one who reveres you so much, I beg you to find Indra quickly."

Brihaspati said to her, "Excellent one, there is no need for you to fear Nahusha. He will not keep his power for much longer. Indeed, the wretch has already fallen for having ignored dharma and making the Maharishis his palanquin-bearers. I will perform a yagna for his destruction, and I will find Indra. Have no fear; for now, farewell."

Brihaspati kindled a sacred fire, in accordance with the Shastras, and made the choicest offerings into it, in order to discover where Indra was. After making his offerings, he commanded Agni to search for Indra.

Agni Deva, the consumer of burnt offerings, assumed a wonderful feminine form and vanished from there. With the speed of the mind, he searched everywhere—on mountains and in forests, on Earth and in the sky—and came back to Brihaspati within the blink of an eye.

Agni said, "Brihaspati, nowhere can I find the king of the Devas. The only place I have yet to search is the waters, which I am loth to enter, O Brahmana. What would you have me do?"

The Acharya of the Devas said to Agni, "O Illustrious Deva, you must go into the water."

Agni said, "I cannot enter the water, for extinguishment awaits me there. I put myself into your hands, effulgent one; O may you be blessed. Fire originated in water; Kshatriyas rose from Brahmanas; iron was born in stone. All three, which can consume all other things, are powerless over the sources from which they spring.""'

CANTO 16

SENODYOGA PARVA CONTINUED

"Salya says, 'Brihaspati said, "O Agni, you are the mouth of all the gods. You are the conveyor of sacred offerings. You see into the inmost souls of all creatures. The poets call you single and three-fold at the same time. Consumer of burnt offerings, the Universe would cease to exist if you abandoned it.

By worshipping you, Brahmanas, their wives and sons win in Swarga the rewards of their good deeds. Agni, it is you who are the bearer of the havis offered at every homa and yagna. Why, you are yourself the finest offering. In the most sacred of yagnas, it is you who are worshipped with gifts and oblations.

You created the three worlds, and it is you who will unleash your power and consume them when the time comes. You are the mother of the Universe, and its destroyer, as well. Wise men say that you are the clouds and their lightning; your heat supports all life. All the waters are contained in you, as is this entire world. You purify all things. There is nothing in the Trilokas that you do not know. Every being looks kindly on its parent; enter the water without fear. I will imbue you with strength by chanting mantras from the Veda."

Agni was pleased at being glorified by Brihaspati and said, "I will reveal Indra to you. I say this truthfully."

Then Agni entered the waters, including seas and little ponds, and came to the lake where, as he searched among the flowers, he saw the king of the Devas lying among the fibres of a lotus stem. Quickly, he returned and told Brihaspati how Indra had made himself minuscule and taken refuge inside a lotus stalk. And Brihaspati, accompanied by the Devas, the Rishis and the Gandharvas, went to where Indra lay and eulogised him by reminding him of his great deeds.

He said, "O Indra, you killed the great Asura Namuchi, as well as the terrible Sambara and Bala. Now rouse yourself and vanquish your enemy. Rise, Indra, and see the Devas and Rishis who are gathered here.

You delivered the three worlds by killing the Danavas; with the foam of the sea, infused with Vishnu's fervour, you slew Vritra. You are the refuge of all creatures and worthy of worship. There is no one equal to you. You are the support of all creatures. And you made the Devas great. Now, regain your sway over the worlds and all living beings by reclaiming your might, O Mahatman."

Thus glorified, Indra became bigger, little by little, and finally assumed his own resplendent, magnificent form. His strength flaring, he said to Brihaspati, who stood before him, "What more needs to be done? I have annihilated the two terrible Asuras—Tvashtri's son and the gigantic Vritra who savaged the three worlds."

Brihaspati said, "The mortal king, Nahusha, who gained the throne of Devaloka through the power of the Devarishis, now persecutes us."

Indra said, "How did Nahusha gain the throne of heaven, which is well nigh impossible to have? What tapasya did he perform? How great is his power, O Brihaspati?"

Brihaspati said, "The Devas became insecure when you renounced the lordship of Devaloka, and they wished for a king to rule over them. The Devas, the Pitrs, the Rishis and the Gandharvas met together and asked Nahusha to be their king and protector of the universe. Nahusha claimed that he was feeble and asked them to infuse him with the power of their tapasya.

The Devas and Devarishis obliged him, O Indra, and Nahusha's strength grew and became terrible. That is how he became Trilokapati. And now the wretch has harnessed the Devarishis to his palanquin and travels, thus, over the three worlds.

May you never come within the dreadful Nahusha's vision, for he emits venom from his eyes and absorbs the strength of every being he looks at. All the Devas are in terror of him. They hide from Nahusha and do not dare even cast a glance at him."

While Brihaspati was speaking, there came to that place Kubera guardian of the worlds, Yama the son of Surya, the luminous Soma Deva and Varuna.

They said to Indra, "We are fortunate that you killed Tvashtri's first son and Vritrasura. How lucky we are to see you safe and well, with your enemies dead."

Indra received those Lokapalas and greeted them gladly and with proper ceremony. He said, "Nahusha is the king of the Devas, and is dreadful. You must help me overcome him."

They replied, "Nahusha is truly fearsome. His vision is poison, and we are afraid of him. If you overthrow Nahusha, we, too, should be entitled to a share of the punya.

Indra agreed, "So be it. You Devas—Varuna, Yama and Kubera—will be crowned alongside me. With the help of all the Devas, let us vanquish Nahusha of the venomous eyes."

Agni said to Indra, "Give me a share in sacrificial offerings, and I will help you, too."

Indra said to him, "O Agni, you will receive a large share in Mahayagnas; you and I will have an equal share each."

Accordingly, Indra conferred upon Kubera sovereignty over the Yakshas and the wealth of the worlds; upon Yama authority over the Pitrs; and upon Varuna dominion over the waters."

CANTO 17

SENODYOGA PARVA CONTINUED

"Salya says, 'While the brilliant Indra was with the Lokapalas and other Devas, deliberating the destruction of Nahusha, there appeared at that place the venerable Rishi Agastya.

Agastya paid his respects to the lord of the Devas and said, "How happy I am that you, who killed Vritra and his brother who assumed the form of the universe, are well and growing in strength. Purandara, we are fortunate that today Nahusha has been removed from the throne of Swarga and that you have slain all your enemies."

Indra said, "Have you had a pleasant journey here, Maharishi? I am glad to see you. Oblige me by accepting this padya to wash your face and feet, this arghya and this cow for your yagna."

After the Brahmanottama accepted these, and when he was seated, the happy Indra said to him, "Dvijottama, tell us how Nahusha was cast out of Swarga."

Agastya said, "Listen, Indra, to how the vicious Nahusha, intoxicated with the vanity of power, was cast down from Devaloka.

The chaste Brahmanas and Devarishis who were his palanquin-bearers, weary from carrying him, questioned the haughty one, asking if he believed that the hymns in the Vedas to be recited while sprinkling water over cows were authentic. Nahusha, whose mind had been overpowered by tamas, said that they were not. The Rishis then told him that in fact they were, and that the Maharishis had declared their sanctity. They accused him of having veered from dharma and of treading a sinful path.

At this, driven by evil, he touched me on my head with his foot. Immediately, he lost his power and majesty, and became agitated and frightened. I said to him, 'Because you have rejected the veracity of the Vedic hymns that the Brahmanas and Rishis validated, because you touched my head with your foot, and because, ignorant wretch, you have turned these exalted tapasvins who are like Brahma into your beasts of burden, I hereby divest you of your grandeur and cast you out of Devaloka.

You will fall straight down into Bhumi, for all your punya is exhausted. For ten thousand years, you will range the Earth in the form of an enormous snake. At the end of that time you may re-enter Swarga.'

O Parantapa, that is how black-souled Nahusha lost his throne. It is fortunate that our strength is waxing and that the thorn in the flesh of the Brahmanas has been removed. Go to Devaloka; subdue your senses, suppress your foes, protect the worlds and let the great Rishis glorify you."

The Devas and Rishis were joyful, as were the Pitrs, the Yakshas, the Nagas, the Rakshasas, the Gandharvas and all the Apsaras; and the lakes, rivers, mountains and seas, as well.

Together they came before Indra and said, "We are filled with gladness at your prosperity, O slayer of your enemies. How fortunate it is that Agastya cast the vicious Nahusha out of Amaravati and turned him into a snake on Earth!"' says Salya."

CANTO 18

SENODYOGA PARVA CONTINUED

"Salya says, 'With the adulation of the Gandharvas and Apsaras echoing all round, Indra mounted his Airavata, the king of elephants blessed with every auspicious mark. Accompanied by Agni, Maharishi Brihaspati, Yama, Varuna and Kubera, he went to Amaravati, surrounded by all the Devas, Gandharvas and Apsaras. There the performer of a hundred sacrifices was united with his queen and joyfully resumed his role as guardian of the three worlds.

The illustrious Devarishi Angiras came, too, to Indra's sabha and eulogised him with hymns from the Atharva Veda. Indra granted him a boon, saying, "Henceforth, your name will appear in the Atharva Veda as Rishi Atharvangiras, and from now on you will receive a share of all yagnas that are performed anywhere."

Maharajan, when Atharvangiras left after this honour was conferred on him, Indra honoured all the Devas and Rishis, rich with the wealth of tapasya and, in happy contentment, he ruled the Trilokas with dharma.

This is the story of the misery that Indra endured before being reunited with his wife; and, in order to slay his enemies, even he had to spend a time in hiding. Rajadhiraja, do not feel sorry for yourself because you, your brothers and Draupadi have suffered privations in the forest.

O joy of the Kurus, you will regain your kingdom in the same manner that Indra did after he killed Vritra. In the same way that Agastya cursed the arrogant Nahusha, bane of Brahmanas, reducing him to a snake for many long years, you will soon quell your enemies—Karna, Duryodhana and other evil ones. Then you and your brothers, with Draupadi, will enjoy dominion of the Earth, as far as the sea.

When his forces are arrayed in battle formations and ready to fight, the king who desires victory must listen to this story of Indra's triumph. That is why, Yudhishtira, I have narrated it to you, to ensure your victory. Exalted men attain prosperity when they are glorified. The destruction of countless noble Kshatriyas is imminent because of the crimes that Duryodhana has committed, and by virtue of the might of Bhima and Arjuna.

He who reads this story of Indra's victory, with faith in God, is cleansed of his sins. He attains a state of beatitude, both in this world and in the next. He will never need to fear his enemies; he will have sons; he will never encounter peril of any sort; and he will enjoy great longevity. Everywhere his victory will be proclaimed; and he will never face defeat,'" says Salya.

That best of virtuous men, Yudhishtira whom the Madra king Salya so exhorts, honours him with due ceremony and says to Salya, 'There is no doubt that you will be Karna's charioteer. You must dampen his spirits by praising Arjuna.'

Salya says, 'So it shall be. I will do as you ask, and whatever else is within my power to do for you.'

Then Salya bids farewell to the sons of Kunti and goes with his army to Duryodhana."

CANTO 19

SENODYOGA PARVA CONTINUED

Vaisampayana said, "Satyaki, that great hero of the Satvata vamsa, comes to Yudhishtira with a vast army of foot-soldiers, horses, chariots and elephants. His soldiers, all men of valour, hail from diverse lands. Carrying weapons of various kinds, and all of them fierce and doughty, they embellish the Pandava army.

Yuyudhana's army looks splendid, with battle-axes, missiles, spears and lances; with mallets, clubs and staves; with cords; with gleaming swords and daggers; and with a variety of sharp, tempered arrows. The splendid army, made more magnificent by these weapons, is the colour of a cloudy sky, like a mass of clouds flashing with lightning. It consists of an akshauhini of troops, yet when it merges with Yudhishtira's force it is subsumed like a small stream flowing into the sea.

Dhrishtaketu, the powerful king of the Chedis, brings his akshauhini of troops and comes to the sons of Pandu. The immensely powerful Jayatsena, king of Magadha, adds his akshauhini of warriors to Yudhishtira's army; and the Pandya king from his coastal kingdom does the same with his troops.

O king, when all these legions are massed, the army with its finely attired, mighty warriors is a joy to behold. Drupada comes, too, with his tremendous sons and heroic fighting men from different lands, and they further enhance the splendour of that army. Virata, king of Matsyas, accompanied by the king of the hill kingdoms, leads his legions to the sons of Pandu.

Seven akshauhinis augment the Pandava army, and a multitude of banners flutters in the air. Their eagerness to fight the Kurus gladdens the hearts of the Pandavas.

Raja Bhagadatta gives an akshauhini of his men to Dhritarashtra's son, pleasing him enormously. The unassailable mass of Duryodhana's army, filled with gold-clad Chins and Kiratas, sparkles in beauty, like a forest of Karnikara trees. To Duryodhana's aid come, also, the courageous Bhurisravas and Salya, each with one akshauhini. Kritavarman, the son of Hridika, comes with the Bhojas, Andhakas and Kukuras, with another akshauhini. All those terrific soldiers wear flower garlands and look as captivating as playful elephants ambling through a forest.

Other forces from the land of Sindhu and Sauvira, led by Jayadratha, come in such vast numbers that the mountains seem to tremble under their tread. One akshauhini they are, and as they move they look like clouds driven by the wind.

Rajan, more kings and their forces join the Kuru king. Sudakshina, the king of the Kambojas, along with the Yavanas and Sakas, comes with an akshauhini of troops that resembles a swarm of locusts. This force is absorbed by the Kuru army and blends seamlessly into it. King Nila comes from his capital Mahishmati with great warriors from the southern regions, who carry delicately wrought and lethal weapons. The two kings of Avanti come, each with a separate akshauhini of their men. Those tigers among men, the five princely brothers of Kekaya, hasten to Duryodhana with an akshauhini of warriors, adding to his elation. Illustrious kings from other parts of the land arrive with three divisions of fighting men.

Duryodhana now has an army of eleven akshauhinis, a sea of colour with countless flags, eager to do battle with the sons of Kunti. So crowded is Hastinapura that there is no space in it even for the commanders of Duryodhana's own army. This massive combined force fills the city of elephants and its surroundings.

The land of the five rivers, the entire region of Kurujangala, the wild forest of Rohitaka, Ahichatra and Kalakuta, the banks of the Ganga, Varana and Vatadhana, the hills bordering the Yamuna—the whole of this rich and extensive tract, abundant with corn, is entirely occupied by that Kaurava army. And the priest whom the king of the Panchalas has sent to the Kurus sees this."

CANTO 20

SANJAYA-YANA PARVA

Vaisampayana said, "Drupada's priest, the emissary of the Pandavas, comes to the Kaurava king Dhritarashtra who, with Bhishma and Vidura, greets him with ceremonial honour. The priest gives them news of the Pandavas and goes on to enquire about the welfare of the Kauravas. After this, he speaks in the presence of all the leaders of Duryodhana's army.

The wise and seasoned Brahmana says, 'You all know what the dharma of kings is. However, I will remind you of some things again before I begin what I have really come to say. Dhritarashtra and Pandu are sons of the same father. It is clear that they should inherit their father's wealth equally. How is it that the sons of Dhritarashtra possess ancestral wealth, but the sons of Pandu have none? Why did Pandu's sons not receive their share?

You are all aware that Pandu's sons did not receive their inherited share of their father's wealth because Dhritarashtra's sons usurped it. Dhritarashtra's sons attempted to remove them from their path to power even by trying to have the Pandavas murdered; but their destined time on Earth had not run out, and they could not send the Pandavas to Yama's halls. Then, when those noble princes had carved out a kingdom for themselves by dint of their own strength, the wretched sons of Dhritarashtra, helped by Subala's son, robbed them of it by low deceit. As was his wont, Dhritarashtra gave his approval, even to this.

For thirteen years the sons of Pandu were exiled, to live in the wilderness. Honourable though they were, in the sabha they and their wife were scorned, humiliated. Great was the suffering they had to endure in the forests; and unspeakable were the sorrows they had to bear, comparable only to the suffering that sinners undergo when they are reborn into inferior species.

O Kurusattama, the sons of Pandu are willing to overlook all past miseries and injustices; they want a peaceful settlement with the Kurus. Bearing in mind the exemplary conduct of the Pandavas, as well as Duryodhana's sinful ways, his friends should persuade Duryodhana to make peace. The heroic sons of Pandu are not eager for war with the Kurus. They want to reclaim their rightful inheritance without bringing the world to disaster and ruin. If Dhritarashtra's son finds an excuse for war, it can never be a just one.

The sons of Pandu are more powerful than him. Yudhishtira has gathered seven akshauhinis of troops, who are so eager to fight the Kurus that they just wait for his command. He has in his forces tigers among men, who are equal in strength to a thousand akshauhinis—Satyaki and Bhimasena, and the twins of untold prowess.

Yes, truly, these eleven oceanic divisions are arrayed on one side, but they are balanced on the other by the mighty-armed Dhananjaya of many forms. Arjuna's prowess is greater than that of all these legions put together. There is also Vasudeva's son of dazzling effulgence and tejas. Faced with Arjuna's awesome valour and Krishna's plumbless wisdom, who is there that can fight them? So, I ask you to give what ought to be given, in accordance with dharma and the agreement you made. Do not lose this opportunity to do the right thing, and save yourselves and other lives beyond count.'"

CANTO 21

SANJAYA-YANA PARVA CONTINUED

Vaisampayana said, "Bhishma hears what the Purohita says and, after paying his respects to him, speaks wise words, fitting to the occasion.

He says, 'I am glad that the Pandavas and Krishna are well. I am glad that they have found help and that they have set their hearts on a course of dharma. How fortunate that those sons of the Kuru vamsa want peace with their cousins. There is no doubt that you speak the truth; however, you speak bluntly. I presume that is because you are a Brahmana.

The sons of Pandu must indeed have been sorely afflicted, here and in the forest. By law, they are entitled to their father's kingdom. Arjuna is powerful, a master of all weapons and a Maharatha. Who can withstand Dhananjaya in battle? Even the wielder of the thunderbolt cannot, let alone mortal warriors. Arjuna is unmatched in the three worlds.'

Now, an angry Karna insolently interrupts Bhishma even while he is speaking. He directs his glance at Duryodhana, while saying to the priest, 'There is no one in the world, Brahmana, who is not aware of all this. What point is there in repeating them over and over again? Sakuni played the game of dice on Duryodhana's behalf, and won. Yudhishtira went into the forest according to the agreed stipulation, which was that if any of them was seen before thirteen years had passed they must spend another thirteen years in the vana. He now ignores that covenant and, confident of his alliance with the Matsyas and Panchalas, he wants his kingdom back.

Learned one, Duryodhana will not yield even a single foot of land if you try to threaten him; but if dharma required it, he would give up the whole Earth, even to an enemy. If the Pandavas want their ancestral throne back, they must pass another thirteen years in exile. Afterwards they can live as Duryodhana's liegemen, in safety and peace.

Let them not, out of stupidity, adopt a clearly sinful course. If they decide to abandon the path of dharma and go to war, they will, when they meet the unimpeachable Kurus, remember my words.'

Bhishma says, 'Of what use are your lofty, boastful speeches, Radheya? You would do better to remember the time when Arjuna single-handedly vanquished six Kuru Maharathas in battle. If we do not do what this Brahmana says, you can be sure that Arjuna will kill us all in battle.'

Dhritarashtra lauds Bhishma's words; then he rebukes the son of Radha, 'What Bhishma says is salutary—good for us, for the Pandavas and indeed for the whole world. I will deliberate over this and send Sanjaya to the sons of Pandu.

Brahmana, there is no need for you to wait; you can return today.'

The Kaurava king honours Drupada's priest and sends him back to the Pandavas. He then summons Sanjaya to the sabha and speaks to him."

CANTO 22

Sanjaya-yana Parva continued

"Dhritarashtra says, 'O Sanjaya, we hear that the Pandavas have arrived in Upaplavya. Go and enquire after them. You must greet Ajatasatru with these words: *It is fortunate that you have come out of the wilderness and arrived at a city such as this.* And to all of them you must say: *Are you well, after having endured the hardships of exile, which you did not deserve?* In no time they will think kindly of us, for, though we treated them treacherously, they are righteous and good.

Never have I known the Pandavas to be untruthful. It was their own efforts that won them their prosperity, yet they were always obedient to me. Despite the most severe scrutiny, I cannot find a single transgression for which I can blame them. They always conduct themselves with their status and with dharma in mind. They never yield to sensual temptations, to heat and cold, to hunger and thirst. They subdue sloth and apathy, joy, anger and thoughtlessness. The sons of Pritha are always conscious of dharma and are always pleasant and cordial.

When occasion demands, they give of their riches to their friends.

Friendship with them never cools with passing time, for they bestow justly deserved honours and wealth on everyone. No one amongst the Ajamidas has ever hated them, excepting this vile, capricious and foolish Duryodhana and the even more evil-minded Karna. These two always envy and goad those Mahatmans who have been divested of friends and happiness.

The spoilt and pampered Duryodhana, full of initial bluster, thinks he has done well for himself. He is foolish to think that he can rob the Pandavas of their rightful inheritance while they still live. Before war breaks out, he would be wise to yield what is due to Yudhishtira, who has the support of Arjuna, Krishna, Bhima, Satyaki, Madri's two sons and the warriors of Srinjaya. From his chariot, Savyasachi, the wielder of the Gandiva, can devastate the whole world on his own; and so can the ever-victorious and exalted Krishna, the invincible Lord of the three worlds.

What mortal could face him who is the worthiest man in all the world, whose countless arrows roar like clouds and fly like locust-swarms to cover all sides? Alone on his chariot, with his Gandiva in his hands, he conquered the northern realms, including the Kurus who live there, and took all their wealth. He made the Dravida soldiers part of his own army. It was Arjuna who defeated the Devas and Indra in the Khandava vana, he who made offerings to Agni and enhanced the honour and fame of the Pandavas.

Of all mace fighters there is none to equal Bhima, nor any as skilful riding an elephant. On his chariot, he yields not to even Arjuna. As for the power of his arms, he is equal to ten thousand elephants. Of boundless energy, he is bitterly hostile, and his anger would consume my sons, making short work of them. Quick-tempered and immensely strong as he is, even Indra cannot subdue him in battle.

Large-hearted, powerful and endowed with lightness of hand, the twin brothers, Madri's sons, have been meticulously trained by Arjuna. Like a pair of hawks preying on flocks of small birds, they will not leave a single enemy alive.

If truth be told, despite being so vast, our army will be as nothing when it encounters the sons of Pandu. On their side they have Dhrishtadyumna of the boundless tejas, whom the Pandavas consider one of themselves. They have the king of the Somakas, with his legions, who is devoted to their cause and ready to lay down his life for them. Who would be able to withstand Yudhishtira who has the jewel of the Vrishnis, Krishna, for his lord?

I have heard that, though old now, Virata, king of the Matsyas, with whom the Pandavas lived for a year and whose wishes they fulfilled, has espoused the Pandava cause and is loyal to them, as are his sons. The five great princes of Kekaya, who were deposed from their thrones and want to regain their kingdom, have become allies of the Pandavas; they wield mighty bows and are ready to fight.

All the bravest kings on Earth have come together on the side of Pandu's sons. All these, who have become allies of Dharmaraja Yudhishtira, are infused with great new courage, honour and devotion, by virtue of their love for him. Many warriors from the mountain kingdoms and other inaccessible fastnesses, many old and venerable ones and many Mlechcha tribes boasting weapons of myriad kinds have pledged themselves to the Pandava cause and gathered under the Pandava banner.

The Pandya king, who is as mighty as Indra, has come with innumerable warriors all eager for fight. Extraordinarily brave and of unparalleled might and energy, he is devoted to the Pandavas. Then there is Satyaki who, I have heard, was trained in the use of astras by Drona, Arjuna, Krishna, Kripa and Bhishma, and who is said to be equal to Krishna's son Pradyumna; and he, too, is faithful to the Pandavas.

Once, the kings of the Chedi and Karusha tribes assembled and combined their resources together. And there was one amongst them who blazed in beauty like the Sun, who was considered unassailable in battle and the best archer the Earth had known. Krishna killed him and, in an instant, robbed those Kshatriya kings of all their power. Kesava looked at that Sishupala, adulated by all the kings led by the king of Karusha, and beheaded him to enhance the glory of the Pandavas.

The other kings saw Krishna in his chariot drawn by Sugriva and his other horses, abandoned the king of the Chedis and fled like small animals at the sight of a lion. Left on his own and, from sheer audacity and folly, Sisupala faced Krishna in single combat. Krishna killed him, and he lay dead, looking like a karnikara tree uprooted by a storm.

O Sanjaya, the things I have heard about what Krishna has done for the sake of Pandu's sons, and what I know of his achievements, disturb me and drive away my peace of mind. No adversary can withstand those that have that lion of the Vrishnis for their lord. My heart trembles with fear when I hear that the two Krishnas will be together in one chariot.

If my dull-witted son abstains from fighting those two, he may yet do well. Otherwise, the two Krishnas will consume the very Kuru race, as Indra and Upendra did the Danavas. Arjuna is equal to Indra; and Krishna is Immortal Vishnu himself.

Pandu and Kunti's son Yudhishtira is virtuous and brave, and shuns any low deed. Duryodhana has wronged this man of awesome power. If not for his noble character, he would burn us all in a wink with his rage. Suta, I do not dread Arjuna, Bhima, Krishna or the twin brothers as much as I dread the wrath of Dharmaraja when his anger is kindled. He has practised austere tapasya and kept the vows of brahmacharya, and all his wishes will be fulfilled. When I think of his wrath and how justified it is, I am filled with alarm.

Go swiftly in a chariot, as my emissary, to the encampment of the Panchala forces. Ask Yudhishtira about his well-being and repeatedly address him in affectionate terms. Meet Krishna, bravest of all men, who is the most magnanimous soul. On my behalf, ask him, as well, about his well-being. And tell him that Dhritarashtra desires peace with Pandu's sons. There is nothing that Yudhishtira would not do at Krishna's bidding, for Kesava is as dear to the Pandavas as their life-breath. And wise beyond understanding or description, he is devoted to them. Declare yourself as my messenger and also enquire after the welfare of all the sons of Pandu, the Srinjayas, Satyaki and Virata, and the five sons of Draupadi.

In the midst of all those kings, Sanjaya, as the occasion arises, say whatever you deem appropriate and beneficial for the very race of Bharata, anything that is not distasteful or provocative.'"

CANTO 23

SANJAYA-YANA PARVA CONTINUED

Vaisampayana said, "Sanjaya goes to Upaplavya to see the mighty Pandavas. He goes to Yudhishtira and pays his respects to him before he speaks.

Sanjaya says to Ajatasatru, 'O king, I am so happy to see you in good health and surrounded by your friends, you who are as powerful as Indra. The aged and wise Dhritarashtra, the son of Ambika, enquires after your welfare. I hope Bhimasena is well, and Dhananjaya, and the two sons of Madri also. I hope Drupada's daughter, the princess Krishnaa, is well, too—she who never swerves from the path of truth, that devi of great tejas, that wife of heroes—as I hope are her sons, who are your joy, all that you hold dear, and whose welfare you constantly pray for.'

Yudhishtira says, 'O Sanjaya, have you had a safe journey here? We are pleased to see you. I hope that you are well. I am in good health and so are my brothers. It is after a long time that I hear news of that Bhaarata, the revered king of the Kurus. Seeing you makes me as happy as seeing the king himself. Is our grandsire Bhishma, who is blessed with boundless energy and the highest wisdom, and who is always devoted to

Kshatriya dharma, in good health? I trust he is as he ever was.

I hope the noble Dhritarashtra is well, and also his sons. I hope the great and learned king Bahlika, the son of Pratipa, is also in good health. I hope Somadatta is well, and Bhurisravas, and Satyasandha, and Sala, and Drona, and Drona's son, and Acharya Kripa. I hope all those mighty bowmen enjoy robust good health.

O Sanjaya, the greatest and best archers, all the most intelligent and deeply learned, and the best of warriors, have allied themselves with the Kurus. I hope they receive the honour that they deserve and that they are well. How happy the people are in whose kingdom that mighty and handsome archer, Aswatthama, the honourable son of Drona, lives.

I hope Yuyutsu, the brilliant son of Dhritarashtra by his Vaisya wife, is in good health. I hope Karna, whose counsel the dull-witted Suyodhana takes so to heart, is also well. I hope the elderly mothers of the Bhaaratas are well, and that the kitchen-maids, the servants, the daughters-in-law, the nieces and nephews, and the grandchildren of Dhritarashtra's house are all free from ill health.

I hope the king continues to provide a livelihood to good Brahmanas. I hope Dhritarashtra's son has not appropriated from the Brahmanas the gifts I gave them, and that Dhritarashtra and his sons treat any hauteur on their part with forbearance. I hope he never neglects to provide for them, for that is the only way to Swarga. This is the excellent and clear path that Brahma has revealed to all living beings. If the sons of the Kuru house foolishly abandon tolerance of Brahmanas' shortcomings, they will be ruined.

I hope king Dhritarashtra and his son look after the administrators of the kingdom. I hope they have no enemies who, disguised as friends, plot their downfall. I hope none of these Kurus talk of our having committed any crimes, and that Drona, his son and the heroic Kripa do not think we are guilty in any way.

I hope all Kurus look up to Dhritarashtra and his sons as their protectors. I hope that, when they see a band of criminals, they remember Arjuna's deeds as the greatest warrior of all. I hope they remember how swift, unerring arrows flew from his Gandiva, its bowstring pulled taut, and the thunderous sound his dexterous fingers made as he stretched and released the string again and again. I have yet to see an archer to equal Arjuna, who can shoot sixty-one sharp, feather-flighted arrows with a single fluid motion of his hand.

Do they remember the mighty Bhima, who, like an elephant with the juice of rut trickling from rent temples trampling through a forest of reeds, makes hostile armies arrayed for battle tremble with dread? Do they remember the powerful Sahadeva, who conquered the Kalingas in Dantakura by shooting arrows with both hands? Do they remember Nakula, whom you accompanied: how he subdued the Sibis and the Trigartas and brought all the western lands under my control?

Do they remember the disgrace they had to face when they came, ill-advised, to Dwaita vana on the pretext of inspecting their cattle? Those malevolent men were crushed in battle by the Gandharvas, and it was Bhimasena and Arjuna that rescued them. In the battle that ensued, Bhima protected Arjuna and Madri's sons from behind, and Arjuna emerged unscathed after savaging the enemy. Do they remember that?

O Sanjaya, a single deed cannot bring happiness now when, despite our many endeavours, we have not been able to win over Dhritarashtra's son.'"

CANTO 24

SANJAYA-YANA PARVA CONTINUED

"Sanjaya says, 'It is just as you say, noble son of Pandu! Those you ask about—the Kurus and the foremost among them—are in good health and spirits.

Dhritarashtra's son is surrounded by noble and righteous men, as well as by sinful, evil ones. He, who gives gifts even to his enemies, is not likely to withdraw the livelihood he provides to the Brahmanas. You Kshatriyas follow a dharma that makes you harm even those that bear you no ill will. Such dharma is fit only for butchers. If Dhritarashtra and his sons harbour ill will against you, who are righteous, they must be held guilty of treachery.

Dhritarashtra does not condone the injury done to you; he is sorry for it. The old man grieves, Yudhishtira, for he has learnt from wise Brahmanas that treachery is the greatest of all sins. O king of men, the Kurus remember your prowess on the battlefield, and that of Arjuna who leads your forces. They remember Bhima wielding his mace, and the sounds of his conch-shell and drum rising to a deafening, maddening pitch. They remember those fearless Maharathas, the sons of Madri, ranging in all directions on the battlefield, endlessly unleashing torrents of arrows at the enemy.

We cannot know what destiny has in store for anyone. See how you, Yudhishtira, who are endowed with every virtue, have had to suffer unendurable trials. I am certain that your wisdom will help you forget all that misfortune, and cleave to fortitude. The sons of Pandu are all equal to Indra and would never abandon dharma for the sake of pleasure. You in your wisdom will secure peace for the sons of Dhritarashtra and Pandu, for the Srinjayas and all the other kings assembled here. Listen to what your uncle Dhritarashtra said to me after consulting his ministers and sons. Lend your attention to his message.'"

CANTO 25

SANJAYA-YANA PARVA CONTINUED

"Yudhishtira says, 'O Suta, we are all gathered here—the Pandavas, the Srinjayas, Janardana, Yuyudhana and Virata. Tell us everything that Dhritarashtra asked you to say.'

Sanjaya says, 'I greet you all—Yudhishtira, Bhima, Arjuna and the two sons of Madri; Vasudeva, Chekitana, Virata, Satyaki, the venerable Drupada and his son Dhrishtadyumna. Hear what I say; I speak with a desire for the welfare of all the Kuru vamsa.

King Dhritarashtra welcomed the opportunity for peace and wasted no time in having the chariot prepared for my journey here. I hope Yudhishtira and his brothers, and his sons and kinsmen will accept the message I bring: Let there be peace.

The sons of Pritha are blessed with every virtue, with steadfastness, gentleness and candour. Born into a noble house, they are humane and generous, and eschew any shameful deed. They know dharma.

A base deed does not befit you, Yudhishtira, for you are noble, and the lord of a vast army. If you committed a sin, it would be a stain on your good name, like a smear of kohl on a white cloth. No one would ever knowingly acquire the guilt of an action that would result in universal slaughter; it is sinful and will lead to Naraka. Genocide is such an act, regardless of whether it results in victory or defeat.

The truly blessed are they who work for the success of their kinsmen's cause. The true son, relative or friend of the Kurus is he who would lay down his life, even at the risk of it being abused by evil, in order to ensure the welfare of the Kuru vamsa. If you, sons of Pritha, punish the Kurus by killing all your enemies, your life after that would be as death. Is life worth living after having killed your kinsmen?

Not even Indra himself, with all the gods on his side, can defeat you, who have Kesava, Chekitana and Satyaki by your side, and the protection of Dhrishtadyumna. On the other hand, who can defeat the Kurus who have Drona and Bhishma, Aswatthama, Salya, Kripa and Karna, and a host of Kshatriya kings supporting them? Who will be able to slay, without great loss of life on his side, the vast force that Dhritarashtra's son has assembled? I do not see any possible good ensuing from this war, either in victory or in defeat.

How can the sons of Pritha commit such a heinous crime, as if they were lowborn men who know nothing of dharma? I beg of you; I prostrate myself before Krishna and the venerable king of the Panchalas; I put myself under your protection, with folded hands, so that both the Kurus and the Srinjayas may prosper. Krishna and Arjuna are unlikely to ignore my words and spurn my plea. Both, if asked, would give up their lives for truth.

All this I say to ensure the success of my mission. The king and his mentor Bhishma both want to secure peace between you and the Kurus.'"

CANTO 26

SANJAYA-YANA PARVA CONTINUED

"Yudhishtira says, 'What have you heard me say, Sanjaya, that suggests that we wish for war, and which makes you apprehensive? Peace is always preferable to war, Sarathy; which man who had an alternative would choose to fight? If a man can have everything he wants without having to actually do anything, he would not make the smallest discomfiting effort in any direction, far less go to war. Why should a man ever go to war? Who is so cursed by the gods that he would choose this horrible option?

The sons of Pritha do desire happiness, but their conduct is always marked by dharma and promotes the welfare of the world. The only happiness they want is that which accrues from deeds of dharma. The man who, in order to avoid sorrow, allows his senses to lead him in his quest for happiness is lured into actions that are wretched and miserable. A man's hankering for pleasure results in suffering; he who is free of such craving knows no sorrow. Like a fire that blazes more fiercely when fuel is added to it, desire is never satiated with the acquisition of its object; rather, it flares up, like embers when ghee is poured on them, always wanting more.

Compare the abundance that the fortunate king Dhritarashtra enjoys with what we possess. Unfortunate is the man who is never victorious; who does not enjoy music; who does not take pleasure in the fragrance of garlands and perfumes, or in cool, scented salves; and who does not enjoy wearing fine clothes. If this were not so, we would not have been driven from our kingdom; and although all this is true, none of us brooded over our torments.

The king, in his troubled state, looks to the might of others for protection. This is not wise. Let their behaviour towards him reciprocate his own to them. The man who, at midday in spring, throws a burning log into the dense undergrowth in a forest has every reason to rue his lot as he tries to escape from the fire that is fanned into a blaze by the wind.

Sanjaya, why does Dhritarashtra complain even though his own prosperity is intact? It is because he followed the course of action espoused by his vicious and foolish son? Duryodhana disregarded Vidura, the best of his well-wishers, as if he were his enemy. Dhritarashtra, who wanted only to please his sons, knowingly chose a path of sin. Indeed, from his fondness for his son, he would not pay heed to Vidura who, of all the Kurus, is his wisest and most sincere friend, who is vastly learned, eloquent and virtuous in all that he does.

Dhritarashtra wants to please his son and, at the same time, have the respect of others. His son Duryodhana is full of envy and anger; he breaks the sacred laws laid down for the acquisition of dharma and artha. He has a foul tongue, allows anger to dictate his behaviour; and his soul is absorbed in indulging his senses and his vanity. He harbours hatred for so many; he obeys no law; his life is evil; he is obstinate and ruthless. For such a son as this, Dhritarashtra knowingly abandons dharma and true joy.

Even as long ago as the time when I was playing that game of dice, I suspected that the destruction of the Kurus loomed near, because Vidura's wise words received no praise from Dhritarashtra. It was when they ignored Vidura that the Kurus' downfall began. As long as they placed themselves under the guidance of his wisdom, their kingdom flourished.

Let me tell you, Sanjaya, who greedy Duryodhana's advisors are now: Dusasana, Subala's son Sakuni and the Sutaputra Karna. Look at his foolishness. However hard I think about it, I cannot see how the Kurus and the Srinjayas can prosper when Dhritarashtra has usurped the throne unlawfully and even once banished the far-sighted Vidura. Dhritarashtra and his sons now want undisputed sovereignty over the whole world. Peace is impossible. He thinks of what he has taken with deceit and treachery as being his own.

When Arjuna takes up his Gandiva, Karna believes that he can stand up to him. Why, then, was Karna not able to prevail in any of the battles that have already been fought? Karna, Drona, Pitamaha Bhishma, as well as many other Kurus know that there is no bowman to compare with Arjuna. All the kings know how Duryodhana became a king although Parantapa Arjuna was alive. He continues to convince himself that he can rob the sons of Pandu of what is theirs, despite knowing that it was Arjuna who once came to his rescue when he was helpless, with nothing but a bow, four cubits long, to fight an unearthly Gandharva host.

Dhritarashtra's sons are alive only because they have not yet heard the reverberation of the fully-stretched Gandiva. Duryodhana thinks that he has achieved his objective, because he has not yet seen Bhima's rage. Even Indra would not rob us of our rightful sovereignty as long as Bhima, Arjuna, heroic Nakula and patient Sahadeva live. The old king and his son fondly imagine that his sons will not be consumed on the battlefield by the fire of the Pandavas' anger.

Sanjaya, you know what misery they have made us suffer. Out of regard for you, I would forgive them all. You know what happened between the Kauravas and us, and how we conducted ourselves towards them; let things continue in the same way. I will take your advice and seek peace. Let me have Indraprastha for my kingdom; let Duryodhana give it to me.'"

CANTO 27

SANJAYA-YANA PARVA CONTINUED

"Sanjaya says, 'O Pandava, your unswerving dharma is known the world over. I also see it, Prithaputra. Considering that even a great life is transient, you must not kill the Kurus. Yudhishtira, if the Kurus will not give you your share peaceably, I think it is better for you to live on alms in the kingdom of the Andhakas and the Vrishnis than win your kingdom back through a bloody war.

Our mortal existence is short; blame easily attaches to us; we are subject to constant suffering; life is uncertain; and life can never be as important as a good name. Therefore, never sin. O king, desires cling to men and keep them from leading a virtuous life. A wise man, having extinguished all desire, acquires unblemished fame in the world. The thirst for wealth is a fetter; and the virtue of men who pursue it suffers. The wise man is one who seeks only dharma. Even as a man's worldly desires increase, their impermanence makes his miseries increase.

The man who places dharma before all else shines like the Sun at his most glorious. A man devoid of dharma, of sinful soul, is ruined, although he may gain the very Earth.

You have studied the Vedas and lived the austere life of brahmacharya; you have performed yagnas to satisfy the needs of Brahmanas and have given generously to them. With a view to achieving the loftiest state that a man can, you have devoted yourself, for years on end, to the pursuit of tapasya.

He who devotes himself excessively to mundane indulgences cannot concentrate his mind on yogabhyasa, spiritual discipline; and such a man is always miserable. These fleeting sensual pleasures forsake him after his wealth is gone, and his lusts continue to drive him, even in frustration. He who has never lived a spiritually disciplined life, and sins, abandoning the path of dharma, has no belief in the permanence of the soul. This fool is slated for torment after death.

In the next world, a man's actions, both good and evil, are not nullified. All his deeds precede a man as he journeys from the mortal world to the next, and he cannot but follow them. Your deeds in this life are celebrated as being exceptionally noble and pure. They are like the delicious sattvik food specially prepared to offer, along with gifts, to Brahmanas and officiating priests at religious ceremonies. All karma is performed only as long as the mortal body lives, Prithaputra. After death there is no karma to be done.

You have performed mighty deeds that righteous men admire, and they will benefit you in the world to come. Death brings entry into the next world and, with it, freedom from old age, fear, hunger and thirst, and from everything that is disagreeable to the mind. After death, there will be nothing to do except to delight; such will be the fruit of your actions.

So, do not allow desire for temporal happiness to spur what you do in this world. At the end of your life and deeds do not, Pandava, take a path that forsakes truth, sobriety, honesty and compassion. You may perform the Rajasuya and the Aswamedha yagnas, but do not even think about any action that is sinful in itself.

If, after such a long time, you sons of Pandu yield to hatred and commit such a horrific crime as this war, you will have endured all these years of suffering in the forests in vain. It will have been for nothing that you went into exile, parting with your army, which was then under your control; from your loyal friends Krishna and Satyaki, golden-charioted Virata of the Matsyas and his son at head of his warriors, and from all the other kings, whom you once vanquished, and who have now come to fight by your side.

With all these mighty resources, with this army, with being held in dread by all, and supported by Krishna and Arjuna, you could well have slain your worst foes in battle; you could have long ago crushed Duryodhana's pride. Why then have you allowed your enemies to grow so powerful and your friends so weak? What for have you lived in the wilderness for so many years? Why, having let slip the opportune moment, do you now want to fight?

A sinner of no wisdom may win apparent prosperity by fighting; a wise and righteous man can win enduring felicity by shedding his pride and, guided by his higher instincts, refraining from war. Yudhishtira, your instincts do not make you lean towards any adharma, and never have you committed any sin from anger. Why then do you now want to do this ghastly thing, against every dictate of dharma?

Wrath, mighty king, is a drug that cures no disease. Rather, indulging in it brings on a sickness of the mind; it robs a man of his justly earned fame, and leads him to sin. Good men quickly swallow and hold down anger, but not evil ones. I ask you to abjure your wrath and desist from war.

Who would indulge in anger which leads to mortal sin and perdition? Forbearance would be far better for you than the pleasures you would enjoy if your enemies—Bhishma, Drona and his son, Kripa, Somadatta's son, Vikarna, Vivimsati, Karna and Duryodhana—were killed. What happiness can you hope to enjoy after killing them? Tell me.

Even if you win all the sea-girdled Earth, you can never be free from decrepitude and death, pleasure and pain, bliss and misery. Knowing all this, do not go to war. If you want to take this savage course because it is what your advisors recommend, then abdicate everything to them and go away yourself. You must not leave the path that leads to Swarga.'"

CANTO 28

SANJAYA-YANA PARVA CONTINUED

"Yudhishtira says, 'Sanjaya, what you say is true; deeds of dharma are the best of all deeds. But, before you censure me, you should first determine whether my conduct has been in accord with dharma or not.

Sometimes, vice appears to be virtue and virtue to be vice; and sometimes, goodness is truly just that. The learned should use their discernment to distinguish one from the other. Then again, during times of distress, virtue and vice, which are indeed eternal and absolute, can appear to be the other.

A man should live according to the svadharma of his varna; however, one's dharma changes during a crisis. When his means of living are gone, the destitute man should certainly look for ways, other than those prescribed, by which he may fulfil his dharma. Not only such a man, but also one who is not destitute, must both be reproached if they act in contrariness to the condition of their lives at that moment.

The Creator decrees atonement for Brahmanas who, in their desire to avoid being destroyed, act in a manner opposed to their svadharma.

Surely, then, all men may, in times of dire distress, do what is contrary to the dharma of their varna. Sanjaya, you should regard as worthy those who live according to their dharma during normal times, as well as those who do not in a time of crisis. Equally, you should censure those who flout their dharma during normal times and those who live by it during a time of distress.

For men who wish to gain self-knowledge and bring their minds under control, the same practices that are ordained for Brahmanas are prescribed. However, for those who have no immediate desire for mukti, and who are not Brahmanas, the code that is prescribed for their particular varnas is the best. This is the path that our fathers, grandfathers and ancestors followed. As for those that want knowledge of the Atman and also to avoid all karma, they, too, hold the same view and consider themselves orthodox. There is no other way.

O Sanjaya, whatever wealth the Earth or the gods have; whatever is beyond reach—in the realm of Prajapati, in Devaloka or in Brahmaloka—I would not seek it by means that violate dharma.

Krishna is Dharmeswara—the lord of virtue; he has an all-lustrous mind and is a master of the artha shastra; he has waited upon Brahmanas; he is all-knowing; and he counsels many mighty kings. Let him say whether I shall be held to blame, whether I would be acting against my dharma by abandoning peace and pursuing war, for he is impartial and desires the welfare of both sides.

Satyaki, the Chedis, the Andhakas, the Vrishnis, the Bhojas, the Kukuras and the Srinjayas follow Krishna's advice and slay their enemies, to the delight of their friends.

The Vrishnis, the Andhakas and Ugrasena, led by Krishna, have become like Indra—high-spirited, devoted to truth, powerful and happy. Babhru of Kasi, having got Krishna, the fulfiller of wishes, as his brother, and upon whom Krishna showers all life's blessings, even as clouds shower the Earth's creatures with rain after the arid summer, has attained great prosperity. So great is Krishna.

Know that he is the authority on the propriety of all karma. Moreover, he is dear to us and our friend. I will never do anything against his advice.'"

CANTO 29

SANJAYA-YANA PARVA CONTINUED

"Krishna says, 'O Sanjaya, my wish is that the Pandavas live and prosper, and that their desires are fulfilled; and I wish the same for Dhritarashtra and his sons. I have always wanted to say to the Pandavas that peace is what king Dhritarashtra wants above all else; and I think it is best for them, too.

Yudhishtira has shown an extremely rare inclination to peace, but Dhritarashtra and his sons are so avaricious that I can understand why the Pandava's hostility has been aroused. You cannot claim to be more knowledgeable about dharma than Yudhishtira or me. Why then do you speak reproachfully of Yudhishtira's conduct? He has great tejas; he is devoted to his svadharma; he fulfils his familial duties thoughtfully and in keeping with justice.

Brahmanas have held various opinions on the matter we are discussing. Some say that success in the world to come depends upon karma; some declare that all action should be shunned and that salvation is attained by knowledge alone. Brahmanas say that although man knows there is food, his hunger is not appeased until he has actually eaten it. They say that only the knowledge that helps a man perform his duties bears fruit, for actions have visible results.

A thirsty man quenches his thirst by drinking water—effort produces results, and therein lies the efficacy of work. If anyone thinks that there is something more productive than effort, his work and his words are meaningless. In the other world, it is by virtue of work that the Devas flourish. It is by effort that the wind blows. It is by effort that sleepless Surya rises every day and causes day and night, and Soma passes through the months and fortnights and the constellations. Fire uses energy to kindle itself and burn, doing good to mankind. The sleepless Bhumi Devi sustains her great burden by dint of her ceaseless effort. The sleepless rivers carry their waters without rest to sustain all beings. The ever-wakeful Indra pours down rain, making his power resound through the heavens and the cardinal points.

Wanting to be the greatest of the Devas, Indra led an austere life of wakefulness, like a holy Brahmana. He renounced pleasure and the gratification of his senses. Scrupulously and diligently he devoted himself to virtue, truth and self-control, forbearance, impartiality and compassion. It was by no small effort of devoting himself to this way of life that he acquired kingship over the Devas.

Brihaspati, too, did the same. He lived the austere life of brahmacharya with his mind closed to everything else. He gave up pleasure and controlled his senses, and became the Acharya of the Devas. Similarly, the Navagrahas, the Rudras, the Adityas, the Vasus, Yama Deva, Kubera, the Gandharvas, the Yakshas and the Apsaras, all worked hard to attain their positions. In the other world the Rishis shine as a result of their life of study, austerity and work.

O Sanjaya, knowing that this is the way followed by the best of Brahmanas, by Kshatriyas and Vaisyas, you being one of the wisest men, why are you making this plea on behalf of the Kauravas? You must know that Yudhishtira is constantly engaged in the study of the Vedas; that he is inclined to performing the Aswamedha and Rajasuya yagnas. Also, he rides horses and elephants, has a chariot, is arrayed in armour, and bears a bow and all other weapons.

If the Pandavas could see a course of action that does not involve the slaughter of the Kurus, they would take it. Their virtue would be saved, and they would achieve an act of punya, even if meant forcing Bhima to restrain himself. On the other hand, they might, as destined, die whilst fighting. If so, in trying their utmost to fulfil their dharma, their deaths would be praiseworthy.

If you approve of peace, I would like to hear your answer to this question: Is the dharma of a king to fight or not to fight? You must, O Sanjaya, take into consideration the division of the four varnas and their respective callings. You must hear the course of action the Pandavas plan to take. Then you may allot praise or censure, as you wish.

A Brahmana's dharma is to study, offer sacrifices, do charity and go on pilgrimages to holy tirthas; he should teach, officiate as a priest in yagnas offered by those who merit his help, and accept gifts from persons he knows.

A Kshatriya protects the people lawfully; he should practise charity, offer sacrifices, study the Vedas, marry and lead the virtuous life of a grihasta. If his soul is noble, and if he lives by the scriptures, he will easily attain the realm of the Brahman.

A Vaisya's svadharma is to study, work hard to earn and accumulate wealth through commerce, agriculture and cattle-rearing. He should conduct himself in a way that pleases Brahmanas and Kshatriyas; he should be upright, do good works and be a householder.

From olden times, the Sudra has been ordained to serve Brahmanas and be obedient to them. A Sudra should not study or perform sacrifices; he should be conscientious and alert in performing his service.

The king protects all these with care and ensures that all the varnas perform their svadharma. The king should not be addicted to sensual indulgence; he should be impartial and treat all his subjects equally. The king should never give in to sinful desires. If there is, in his kingdom, a man who is more praiseworthy than himself, and who is well-known and gifted with all the virtues, the king should encourage his subjects to recognise that man. An unworthy king, however, would not understand this. He would increase his own strength and grow in inhumanity, and become a target for the wrath of destiny. He would cast a covetous eye on the riches of others.

Now we come to war, for which weapons, armour, bows and arrows came into being. Indra invented these for putting plunderers to death. Punya is acquired by doing away with thieves. Many horrible evils have manifested themselves because the Kurus have been unrighteous and neglected law and religion. This is not dharma, Sanjaya.

Dhritarashtra, with his sons, has taken what rightfully belongs to Pandu's sons. He does not care about the eternal dharma of kings. And all the Kurus follow him. The thief who steals wealth stealthily and the one who seizes it openly must both be condemned. What is the difference between them and Dhritarashtra's sons? His greed has convinced him that what he does out of anger springs from righteousness.

The share of the kingdom that the Pandavas are entitled to is clear. Why should that share be seized by that fool? This being the state of things, it would be great punya for us to be killed in battle. A kingdom gained as a birthright is preferable to a throne conferred by a stranger. Sanjaya, you must explain these time-honoured laws to the Kurus in the presence of the assembled kings—all those witless ones who have been brought together by Duryodhana and who are already marked by death.

Look once more at that vilest of all their deeds—what they did in the Kuru sabha on the day of the dice. It is shameful that the Kurus, with Bhishma at their head, did nothing while the beloved wife of the Pandavas, the chaste Draupadi of unblemished fame, was seized, even as she wept, by Dusasana, that monstrous slave of lust. All the Kurus, young and old, were there. If they had prevented the humiliation inflicted upon her that day, I would have been pleased with Dhritarashtra, and that would have boded well for his sons also.

Dusasana brutally dragged Krishnaa into the midst of the sabha, where her fathers-in-law sat. Expecting sympathy, she found none to take her part, except Vidura. None of the kings uttered a word of protest, because they were all fools. Vidura alone, from a sense of dharma, spoke just and righteous words; he alone opposed Duryodhana. Sanjaya, at that time you did not speak of law and morality, but now you come to instruct Yudhishtira about dharma.

Panchali, on the other hand, even though she was dragged shamefully into the sabha, set things right; and like a ship at sea, she rescued the Pandavas and herself from a tidal wave of misfortune.

As Krishnaa stood in that ancient hall, in the presence of her fathers-in-law, the Sutaputra said to her, "O daughter of Drupada, you have no refuge. Consider yourself a slave in Duryodhana's house. Your husbands are defeated and are no longer of any consequence. You have a loving heart, so choose someone else for your lord."

Karna's words were like arrows, cutting down all hope, piercing the very soul, so dreadfully. They buried themselves deep in Arjuna's heart.

When the sons of Pandu were about to put on garments made of black-deer skins, Dusasana said, scornfully, "These all are mean eunuchs, ruined, and damned for a long time to come."

And Sakuni, the prince of Gandhara, spoke slyly to Yudhishtira during the game of dice. He said, "I have won Nakula from you; now what else have you got? You had better stake your wife Draupadi."

Sanjaya, you know all the shameful things that were said at the dice-game. I want to go myself to the Kurus to settle this most difficult matter. If, without injury to the Pandava cause, I succeed in bringing about peace with the Kurus, not only will it fetch great punya, but the Kurus will be saved from certain death. I hope Duryodhana will take heed of what I say to the Kurus, which will be wise, founded in dharma, full of good sense and compassion. I hope that when I arrive, the Kurus will pay me proper respect, or else Dhritarashtra's vile sons, already branded by the evil of what they have done, will be consumed by Arjuna and Bhima, who are keened for battle. Of this you can be certain.

When Pandu's sons were beaten at dice Duryodhana spoke vile and searing words to them. You can be sure that Bhima will remind him of what he said, at the first opportune moment.

Duryodhana is a mighty tree of evil; Karna is its trunk, Sakuni its branches, Dusasana its blossoms and fruits, and the wise Dhritarashtra himself its roots. On the contrary, Yudhishtira is a great tree of truth, Arjuna its trunk and Bhima its branches. Madri's twin sons are its copious flowers and fruits; and I, dharma, and men of dharma are its roots.

Dhritarashtra and his sons are the forest, and the Pandavas are the tigers in it. Do not cut down the forest with its tigers in it, nor drive the tigers from it. The tiger makes easy prey when it is outside its home; and the forest without tigers is easily entered and destroyed. The tiger protects the forest, which shelters it. Dhritarashtra and his sons are creepers, while the Pandavas are Sala trees. Creepers cannot flourish unless they have trees to cling to.

Pritha's sons are as eager to wait on Dhritarashtra as his own sons are keen for war. Let King Dhritarashtra do the right thing. The virtuous sons of Pandu, though well prepared for war, still keep the peace. Learned one, tell Dhritarashtra everything as it truly is.'"

CANTO 30

SANJAYA-YANA PARVA CONTINUED

"Sanjaya says, 'Farewell, O divine one. Pandava, I will leave now; may you be prosperous. I hope I have not been carried away by my emotions and said anything to offend you. Farewell also to you Janardana, Bhima and Arjuna, sons of Madri, Satyaki and Chekitana; I take my leave of you. May peace and happiness be yours; and I pray that all the kings here will look upon me with affection.'

Yudhishtira says, 'You have our leave, Sanjaya; may peace be yours. Learned one, you harbour no ill will towards us. We all know that amongst those in the court of the Kurus, you are a pure-hearted soul. Besides, you are a faithful ambassador, loved by us, gifted with eloquence, of distinguished deportment and sympathetic to us. Your mind is never clouded and, even if spoken to harshly, you never retort in anger. You never speak harsh or slighting words, or false or bitter ones. We know that what you say is without malice, always full of truth, and serious. Amongst all dutas you are our favourite. Besides you, the other who is welcome here is Vidura. We used to see much of you, and you are as dear to us as Dhananjaya. Go with all speed, Sanjaya.

Go to those Brahmanas of pure tejas, who are devoted to learning and live as brahmacharis, who study the Vedas whilst living on alms; go to the ascetics who live in the forest, as well as to the aged ones of other varnas. Pay your respects to them and enquire about their welfare on my behalf. Go to Dhritarashtra's priest, his acharyas and his ritvijas; ask after their well-being, too.

There are those who, though not of high birth, are intelligent, righteous and are men of strong moral fibre; men remember us and speak of us; and who live to the extent they are able by their dharma—tell them I am well and ask after their health. Enquire about the welfare of the tradesmen in the kingdom and the officials.

In our name, salute our beloved Acharya Drona—our mentor, who is well versed in dharma; who took a vow of brahmacharya in order to master the Vedas; who has made the astra shastra full and complete and who is always gracious to us.

You should also greet Aswatthama from us and ask after his welfare. He is learned and devoted to Vedic study; by living as a brahmachari, he has acquired lustrous energy, even like a Gandharva youth; and he, too, has made the science of weapons full and complete. Sanjaya, you must go to the home of Saradvata's son Kripa, that Maharatha, that best of all realised souls. Repeatedly salute him and touch his feet in my name.

Convey news of my good health to Bhishma, the foremost of Kurus, who is always valiant and abstains from doing harm; in whom asceticism, wisdom and Vedic learning reside; that steadfast and most excellent of men.

Greet the wise and venerable king Dhritarashtra, the blind lord of the Kurus, who has vast gyana, and is respectful of the old.

Enquire, also, after Dhritarashtra's eldest son Duryodhana, that evil, ignorant, deceitful and vicious man, who now rules the world; and ask about the violent and vile Dusasana, hero and mighty bowman, who is like his elder brother, only more bestial.

Sanjaya, greet the wise chief of the Bahlikas, whose most cherished wish is for peace among the Bhaaratas. You must also pay our respects to Somadatta, who is endowed with the most noble qualities, who is wise and merciful, and whose affection for the Kurus makes him patient with them. The son of Somadatta is worthy of the greatest reverence among the Kurus. He is my friend and a brother to us. A mighty bowman and the foremost of rathikas, he is worthy in every way. Ask after his welfare, from me, as well that as of his friends and advisors.

Then there are the younger Kurus, our cousins. Ask about their health and prosperity and speak to each of them in ways that you deem appropriate. Enquire about the welfare of the kings who have been brought together by Duryodhana to fight the Pandavas—the Kekayas, the Vasatis, the Salvakas, the Amvashtas and the leading Trigartas; the brave warriors from the east, north, south and west; those who have come from the mountain kingdoms; and all among them who are not cruel and who lead pure lives. Let that mighty host of honourable men know that I am well and that I ask after them; let all the elephant warriors, the horsemen, the chariot warriors and the footsoldiers know that I am well. Ask kindly after the king's servants—the revenue officials, the guards, the leaders of his troops, the accountants and officials who monitor other aspects of the affairs of the kingdom.

Sanjaya, enquire about the welfare of Dhritarashtra's son by his Vaisya wife—that young man who is among the best of all the Kurus, Yuyutsu, who never errs, who has great wisdom, who is blessed with every virtue, and who abhors the idea of this war.

Ask about Chitrasena, who is unrivalled at the intricacies of dice, whose tricks others never detect, who plays with great skill, who is a master of the game, who is unbeatable at the dice-board but not in battle.

Enquire after the health of Sakuni, the king of the Gandharas, native of the mountainous country, who has no equal in cheating at dice, who boosts Duryodhana's pride, and whose cleverness leads him only to ruthless deceit.

Ask about the well-being of Vikartana's son Karna, that hero who, alone on his chariot and unassisted, is ready to vanquish all the Pandavas whom no one else dares challenge in battle; Karna, who is peerless at beguiling the already deluded.

Ask also after the welfare of Vidura, who alone is devoted to us, who is our true guru, who raised us, who is our father, mother and friend, whose understanding is clear and unclouded, whose knowledge is deep, and who is our sagest advisor.

Greet all the elder ladies, of great good qualities, who are like mothers to us. Say this first, *Mothers of living sons, I hope your sons treat you well, with kindness and compassion.* Then tell them that I and my sons are well.

Greet those ladies, Sanjaya, who are equal in rank to our wives, and say to them, "I hope you are well-protected. I hope your good names are unblemished. I hope your lives are blameless and thoughtfully lived. I hope you behave with your fathers-in-law in a kind, praiseworthy manner. I hope you conduct yourselves so that you win your husbands' approval."

Then there are the younger women who are like our daughters-in-law, who have come to us from noble families, who are mothers and who deserve praise. See them all and tell them that Yudhishtira sends his affectionate greetings.

Embrace the daughters of your own house, Sanjaya, and ask kindly after their health on my behalf. Say to them, "May your husbands be kind and loving to you; may you please your husbands; may you have fine, clean homes, ornaments, clothes and perfumes; may you be happy and have all the joys of life at your command; may your faces and forms be beautiful and your words sweet."

You must ask after the others in the Kuru household, and tell them I am in good health—the maid-servants and man-servants, the humpbacked and the lame. Say to them, "I hope Dhritarashtra's son continues to provide you with the same comforts as before."

You must also see the people that Dhritarashtra supports with food and clothing—the physically and mentally disabled, the dwarfs, the blind, the old, the lame and the legless. Tell them I am well and that I ask about their well-being. Say to them, "Have no fear; do not be dispirited by your unhappy lives that are full of pain. They are the consequence of your sins in past lives. When I have defeated my enemies and gratified my friends, I will give you food and clothes in plenty."

I ask that you also see the weak and unprotected, those who strive in vain to make a living, the ignorant and all who lead sorry lives, and anyone who you consider deserving of our concern. Ask on my behalf about their welfare and peace of mind. You should also enquire after any outsiders who have sought Dhritarashtra's protection, those who have come to the Kurus of their own accord or who have been invited, and the ambassadors from other countries. Tell them all that I am well.

As for the warriors that Duryodhana has amassed, there are none on Earth to equal them. Dharma, however, is eternal; dharma is my strength, with which I will destroy my enemies. Sanjaya, say to Duryodhana from me:

That desire which tortures your heart, the desire to rule all the Kurus without a rival, is unreasonable and unjust. We will never do anything that harms you. Most heroic of the Bhaaratas, give me back my own Indraprastha, or fight me.'"

CANTO 31

SANJAYA-YANA PARVA CONTINUED

"Yudhishtira says, 'O Sanjaya, the Creator controls everyone—the righteous and the sinners, the young and the old, the weak and the strong. It is that Supreme Being who imparts knowledge to the child and bestows innocence on the learned, at his will.

If Dhritarashtra asks you about our strength, tell him everything honestly, having first talked with all of us here and ascertained the truth. Go to the Kurus, greet the mighty Dhritarashtra, touch his feet and enquire about his welfare in our name. Then, when he is seated in the midst of his people, say to him,

"O king, the Pandavas live happily, because of your prowess. It was by your grace that those children got a kingdom. Having bestowed their kingdom on them, you should not neglect them now, for they would then be ruined."

Sanjaya, one person cannot rule over the entire kingdom. Say to him for us, "We wish to live united with you. Do not allow your enemies to divide us and vanquish you."

Sanjaya, with head bent, salute our grandfather Bhishma, the son of

Santanu. Say to him, "You revived Santanu's race when it was threatened with extinction. Pitamaha, do what you think is best to make sure that your grandsons live in friendship and unity."

Then address Vidura, and say, *Dear friend, for Yudhishtira's sake, counsel peace.*

Then address that brash Duryodhana, when he is amongst all the Kurus; plead with him on my behalf. Say to him:

"We will forget the insults you heaped on our innocent and helpless Draupadi in the midst of the sabha, only because we have no desire to see the Kurus killed. The Pandavas have silently borne all the other injuries too, both before and after that, although they have the power to avenge them. The Kauravas know all this. Dear cousin, you even sent us into exile wearing deer-skins. This also we have endured because we do not want to see all the Kurus slain.

Commanded by you, and ignoring Kunti, Dusasana dragged Krishnaa into the sabha. That too we will forgive. But, Parantapa, we must have our rightful share of the kingdom. Turn your covetous heart away from what belongs to others. Peace will then reign amongst us, and we wish for peace.

Give us each even a single province of the empire. Give us Kusasthala, Vrikasthala, Makandi and Varanavata, and any province of your choice for the fifth. This will end the enmity. Duryodhana, give your five brothers at least five villages."

Wise Sanjaya, let there be peace between our cousins and us. Tell him also, "Let brothers be loyal to each other; let fathers and sons unite; let the Panchalas and Kurus come together in joy, and let the two clans be one. This is my fervent wish. Bharatarishabha, with joy in our hearts, let us make peace."

O Sanjaya, I am as able to make war as I am to strike peace; I am as prepared to acquire wealth as to earn punya; I can be as harsh as I am soft,' says Yudhishtira," said Vaisampayana.

CANTO 32

SANJAYA-YANA PARVA CONTINUED

Vaisampayana said, "Given leave to go, and having listened to what Yudhishtira wants of him, Sanjaya sets out at once for Hastinapura. He enters the city and presents himself at the gate of the palace apartments.

He says to the gatekeeper, 'Dwarapala, inform Dhritarashtra that I have returned from meeting the Pandavas. Do this without delay, if the king is awake. I have important things to tell him.'

The gatekeeper goes to the king and says, 'Bhumipala, Sanjaya is at the palace gate and wants to see you. He comes with a message from the Pandavas. Command me, my lord; what shall I do?'

The king says, 'Tell Sanjaya that I am in good cheer and health. Bid him enter, and welcome him; I am always ready to receive him. Why does he, who is free to enter at any time, wait outside?'

Sanjaya enters the palace and, with folded hands, comes before Dhritarashtra who sits on his throne surrounded by his courtiers—the wise, the heroic and the noble.

Sanjaya says, 'Lord of the Earth, I, Sanjaya, bow to you. Rajan,

I went to the Pandavas from here. After paying his respects to you, Yudhishtira, the lustrous son of Pandu, enquired after your welfare. He enquired about your family and asked whether you are pleased with your sons and grandsons, friends and counsellors, and all your dependents.'

Dhritarashtra says, 'O child, my blessings upon Ajatasatru. Is Yudhishtira in good health, and are his sons, brothers and ministers all well?'

Sanjaya says, 'Pandu's son is well, as are those with him. He, who acquires wealth and virtue without doing anything dishonourable, who is intelligent, learned, far-sighted and good-natured, now desires what was once his. Yudhishtira regards ahimsa as being superior to dharma, and dharma as superior to artha. His mind always inclines toward tapasya and inward joy, and to deeds of dharma which are spiritually exalting.

In his worldly life, man is like a wooden puppet controlled by an outside force. Seeing how Yudhishtira has suffered, I realise that the power of destiny is stronger than the force of human endeavour. And seeing your adharma, which is not only sinful and shameful, but will also surely lead to misery, I am convinced that a man like you will enjoy praise only so long as your enemies bide their time.

Having renounced all wrong-doing, like a serpent sloughing its old skin, the heroic Yudhishtira shines resplendent in perfection; his sins are now transferred to you. Rajan, reflect on your actions, which are dishonourable and violate both dharma and artha, and which have earned you evil karma in this world and inevitable misery in the next.

You have followed your son's evil advice, in order to enjoy wealth that would, otherwise, have been hard to come by; and you hoped to keep your enemies at bay. The world has denounced this sin, which is so unworthy of you. Calamity befalls a man who lacks wisdom, or is low-born or cruel, who holds grudges for a long time, who is not steadfast in Kshatriya dharma, who has no tejas, or who is base and shameless.

It is fate that makes a man take birth into a good family, or become strong, or famous, or learned. It is fate that gives him life's comforts and fate that gives him the ability to subdue his senses and discriminate between virtue and vice. No man, who is waited upon by the best of advisors, who is intelligent and can tell right from wrong in times of distress, who performs the necessary rites and rituals, who has full use of all his faculties, would knowingly sin.

These, your loyal counsellors, are united in their determination that the Pandavas must not get back their share of the kingdom. Circumstances seem to move inexorably towards the destruction of the Kurus. Provoked by your crimes against him, if Yudhishtira wants to punish you, the very race of the Kurus will be prematurely extinguished. He will shift all his sins, such as they are, to you and you shall bear the blame and the burden for them. Nothing other than the will of the gods can prevent this, for Arjuna was honoured by them in Devaloka when he left this world and went there. In the face of fate, all individual effort is as nothing.

The advantages of a noble birth and courage depend on what a man does for their development; and seeing that prosperity and adversity, stability and instability hold equal sway over a man and his possessions, Mahabali the Great, in his quest for the roots of suffering, failed to discover where the chain of karma of a former life began. He thought that the eternal Essence is the cause of everything. The eye, the ear, the nose, the skin and the tongue are the portals of a man's knowledge; if he suppresses desire, he achieves spontaneous gratification through them. Therefore, one must control one's senses, happily and without misgiving.

Of course, there are those that do not agree. They believe that if a man behaves thoughtfully, his actions will produce the desired result, like a newborn child growing when nurtured with food and drink. Men in this world are subject to love and hate, pleasure and pain, praise and blame. The honest man deserves praise, but you I censure for being the root cause of the enmity between the Bhaaratas, which will result in the erasure of countless lives. If peace is not restored, it will be your fault that Arjuna burns the Kurus, as a blazing fire does a heap of dry grass.

Rajan, in this world you are singular in the way you have given in to your son, who is completely unrestrained; in the way you complacently wear the crown of success, having done nothing to prevent the shame that occurred during the game of dice. Now reap the fruit of your weakness. By rejecting the advice of faithful friends and accepting the counsel of treacherous men, undeserving of your confidence, and by acting like a servant to your evil son's whim, you have as good as lost your great and prosperous empire.

I am tired from my journey and ask your leave to retire to bed now, Purushavyaghra, for tomorrow morning the Kurus will assemble to hear Yudhishtira's message to you.'"

CANTO 33

PRAJAGARA PARVA

Vaisampayana said, "When Sanjaya leaves, Dhritarashtra says to an attendant, 'I want to see Vidura; have him come here at once.'

The messenger goes to Vidura and says, 'Wise one, our mighty king wishes to see you.'

Vidura comes immediately to the palace and tells the servant to inform the king of his arrival. The man goes to Dhritarashtra and says, 'Maharajan, Vidura is here as you commanded. He wants to worship your feet. What shall he do?'

Dhritarashtra says, 'Bid him of the great wisdom and foresight enter. I am never unwilling or unprepared to see Vidura.'

The attendant goes out and says to Vidura, 'Kshattri, the king bids you go into his inner apartment. He says he is always ready to see you.'

Vidura goes into Dhritarashtra's chamber and, with hands joined, says to his brother, who is sunk in dark thought, 'Wise one, here I am at your command, to do whatever you want.'

Dhritarashtra says, 'Vidura, Sanjaya has returned and has gone home after rebuking me. Tomorrow in the sabha he will deliver Yudhishtira's message. I could not get him to divulge what that is, and sleep evades my burning body. Tell me what is good for my feverish insomnia, my child, for you know dharma and artha well. Ever since Sanjaya came back from the Pandavas, my heart has known no peace; and filled with anxious thoughts about the message he will deliver, my senses are in turmoil.'

Vidura says, 'Sleeplessness is for a thief, a lustful man, one who has lost his wealth, one who has failed in his endeavour, or a weak man under attack by a strong one. I hope, my lord, that none of these has overtaken you, and that you do not grieve or covet another's wealth.'

Dhritarashtra says, 'I want to hear you speak wise words of dharma. In our race of Rajarishis it is only you that the Munis respect.'

Vidura replies, 'Yudhishtira is blessed with every virtue; he deserves to be the ruler of the three worlds. Despite his worthiness to rule beside you, you exiled him.

Your qualities, on the other hand, are the opposite of his. Neither your virtues nor your knowledge of dharma entitles you to a share of the kingdom, for you are blind. As a consequence of his mildness and compassion, his righteousness and love of truth, his strength, and his reverence for you, Yudhishtira patiently endures innumerable and grievous wrongs. How can you hope to have prosperity or peace of mind when you have handed over the reins of the kingdom to Duryodhana, Subala's son, Karna and Dusasana?

The wise man is one who uses Atmagyana, hard work, forbearance and adherence to dharma to earn punya. The wise man is one who is known by his dharma, his rejection of sin, and by his faith and reverence. The wise man is one who cannot be swerved from his dharma by anger, joy, pride, false modesty, a crisis or vanity.

The man who keeps what he intends to say and do from his enemies and whose deeds become known only after he has done them is wise. The man who does not allow heat, cold, fear born of attachment, prosperity or adversity to obstruct his plans is wise. The man whose judgment is detached from desire, who pays equal attention to dharma and artha, who disregards pleasure and chooses goals that will stand him in good stead in this world and in the next is wise.

He who exerts as much effort as he can and does his very best, dismissing nothing as insignificant is wise. He who has a quick understanding, who listens patiently, who pursues his goals with good sense and not from desire, and who does not waste his energy on talking, unasked, about other people's affairs is wise. He who does not yearn for the unattainable, who does not grieve for what is lost, whose mind is clear even in a crisis is wise. He who begins something and strives until it is completed, who never wastes his time, who has his soul under control is wise.

Bharatarishabha, wise men always delight in honest deeds; they do only what leads to their happiness and prosperity and never mock at what is good.

He who neither exults at being honoured nor grieves at being slighted, who remains serene like a lake on the Ganga is wise. He who knows the nature of all creatures—that no one and nothing is immortal—who is aware of the inter-connectedness of all things and all karma, and who knows the means that men may resort to for attaining their goals is wise. He who speaks confidently, who can converse on diverse subjects, who knows the art of debate, who has keen intelligence and who can interpret the meaning of what is written in sacred books is wise. He whose studies are regulated by reason, whose thinking follows the scriptures and who always pays homage to the good is wise.

On the other hand, he who is vain though ignorant of the Shastras, arrogant though poor, and who uses unfair means to reach his goals is a fool. He who ignores his own affairs and pries into those of others, and who deceives his friends is a fool. He who craves things he should not and pushes aside the things he can justly wish for and who maligns powerful men is a fool. He who thinks of his enemy as a friend and hates his friends and who commits evil is a fool.

Bharatarishabha, he who discloses his enterprises, who doubts everything and who dawdles over what can be done quickly is a fool. He who does not perform the sraddha for the Pitrs, who does not worship the Devas and who does not cultivate noble-minded friends is a fool.

He is a fool and the worst of men who enters a place uninvited, who talks a lot without being asked and who trusts the dishonourable. He is the most foolish of men who blames others for something he himself is guilty of and who, though powerless, gives vent to anger. He is a fool who does not know his own strengths, who ignores both dharma and artha and, without equipping himself adequately, yearns for something that is difficult to obtain.

O king, he who punishes the innocent, who pays homage to the undeserving and who keeps the company of misers is a man of little sense. But he who, having acquired great wealth and prosperity, as well as vast learning, is not haughty is wise.

Who is more heartless than the man who, though wealthy and who eats and dresses well, does not share his riches among his dependants? The sins of one person result in advantages for many; but eventually it is the sinner alone who suffers the consequences of the sin, while the others escape. When an archer shoots an arrow he may or may not succeed in killing anyone, but when an intelligent man applies his mind, he can raze a kingdom and destroy its king.

Discriminate between the two by means of the one. Control the three by means of the four. Conquer the five by knowing the six, abstain from the seven and be joyful. Poison kills only one person, as does a weapon; but one evil man can annihilate an entire kingdom, its king and all his subjects. One should not, on one's own, gorge on tasty food, think about material gains, go on a journey or be the only one awake amongst a group of sleeping people. Listen now to what these are.

O king, that Being who is the Supreme One without a second, whom you have not been able to comprehend, is truth manifest and, like a boat on the ocean, the Way to salvation.

There is only one defect in those who are forgiving by nature—they are considered weak. That defect, however, should be ignored, for forgiveness is a powerful quality—a virtue for the gentle, an ornament for the strong. Forgiveness conquers all; there is nothing that the power of forgiveness cannot achieve. What can an evil person do to one who holds the sword of forgiveness in his hand? Cinder falling on grassless ground extinguishes itself. An unforgiving man defiles himself with many atrocities. Righteousness is the highest virtue; forgiveness is the supreme peace; knowledge is the supreme contentment and benevolence the supreme happiness.

Just as a serpent swallows small animals living in burrows, the earth devours two kinds of people: a Kshatriya who is an inept warrior and a Brahmana who does not undertake pilgrimages to holy tirthas. A man may attain fame in this world by doing two things: refraining from harsh speech and ignoring those that are evil.

Naravyaghra, there are two kinds of people who have no will of their own: women who desire men only because other women want them, and persons who worship another just because others do. Two things are like sharp thorns tormenting the body: the desires of a poor man and the anger of the impotent. There are two people who never shine because of their contrary conduct: a householder who makes no effort and a beggar who plots intrigues.

There are two kinds of persons, Rajan, who live in a more blissful place than Swarga: a powerful man who is graced with the quality of forgiveness and a poor man who is charitable. There are two ways of misusing that which is honestly gained: by making gifts to the unworthy and by turning away the worthy.

Two kinds of men should be cast into deep water with weights tied to their necks: a wealthy man who does not give and a poor man who is proud. Two other kinds of men shine more splendidly than the Sun: a mendicant accomplished in yoga and a warrior who dies in battle.

Vedic scholars say that a man's means may be great, average or poor. A man's ability may be good, middling or bad. Every man should, therefore, be employed in work for which he is fit.

There are three kinds of persons who cannot have wealth of their own: the wife, the slave and the son; whatever they earn becomes the property of the man to whom they belong. There are three kinds of crimes which inspire great fear: the theft of another's property, the outrage of another's wife and the fight with a friend. There are three qualities which, besides being self-destructive, also lead to hell: lust, anger and greed; everyone should renounce them. There are three kinds of persons whom one should never abandon, even in the face of grave danger: a follower, the person who puts himself under one's protection and a guest in one's house. There are three actions that bring as much merit as rescuing an enemy from distress: conferring a boon, acquiring a kingdom and having a son.

Learned men have declared that a king, however powerful, should never consult with these four kinds of men: the dull-witted one, the procrastinator, the indolent one and the flatterer. Rajan, crowned with prosperity and leading the life of a grihasta, let these four kinds of persons live with you: elderly relatives, noblemen who have fallen on hard times, impoverished friends and childless sisters.

When Indra asked him, Brihaspati declared that there are four things that can come to fruition in a single day: the resolve of the gods, the understanding of intelligent people, the humility of learned men and the destruction of the sinful. These four, which are intended to remove fear, fetch fear when they are improperly performed: the agnihotra, the vow of silence, study and sacrifice.

A man should worship these five fires: the father, the mother, the sacred fire, the soul and the guru. Men attain great fame in this world by serving these five: the Devas, the Pitrs, other men, beggars and guests. These five follow a man wherever he goes: his friends, his enemies, those that are indifferent to him, his dependents and those that are entitled to his maintenance. If one of man's five senses develops a flaw, then from that single egress all his intelligence leaks out, like water out of a perforated water bag.

These are the six evil habits that a man who wants to attain prosperity must avoid: sleep, heedlessness, fear, anger, sloth and procrastination. These six should be abandoned like a broken ship at sea: a teacher who cannot explain the Shastras, a priest who is illiterate, a king who gives no protection, a wife who speaks unpleasantly, a cowherd who does not want to go out to the pasture and a barber who wants to leave the village to live in the forest.

Man must never forsake these six virtues: truth, charity, diligence, benevolence, forgiveness and patience. These six things are instantly destroyed if neglected: cattle, service, agriculture, a wife, learning and a Sudra's wealth.

These six forget those who have done them favours: educated disciples forget their gurus; married men forget their mothers; men forget the woman once she has gratified their sexual desires; they who have achieved success forget those who helped them; they who have crossed a river forget the boat that carried them over; and patients who have been cured forget their physicians.

These six, O king, promote happiness: good health, freedom from debt, living at home, the companionship of good men, certainty of one's livelihood and living without fear. These six kinds of persons are always miserable: the envious, the malicious, the discontented, the bad-tempered, the suspicious and those depending upon the wealth of others. These six make up the happiness of men: acquisition of wealth, continuous good health, a loving and sweet spoken wife, an obedient son and knowledge that is lucrative.

There are six desires that are ever present in the human heart; and the man who gains mastery over them by controlling his senses never sins or suffers any calamity. There are six kinds of persons who subsist on six other kinds: thieves upon those who are careless; physicians upon the ailing; women upon the lustful; priests on those that want to perform sacrifices; a king upon men who quarrel; and men of learning upon those that do not have it.

A king should renounce these seven faults that lead to disaster; they can bring even firmly established monarchs to ruin: women, dice, hunting, drinking, harsh speech, inhuman punishment and the misuse of wealth.

These eight conditions indicate a man's imminent downfall: hating Brahmanas, disputes with Brahmanas, appropriation of a Brahmana's possessions, taking the life of Brahmana, taking pleasure in abusing Brahmanas, an aversion to praising Brahmanas, forgetting Brahmanas on ceremonial occasions and giving vent to spite when Brahmanas ask for something. A wise man should understand and avoid them.

Bhaarata, only these eight conditions can produce sublime happiness: meeting with friends, accession of immense wealth, embracing a son, sexual union during intercourse, conversation with friends at proper times, the advancement of those one is allied to, the acquisition of what has been anticipated and being respected in society.

Eight qualities glorify a man: wisdom, noble birth, self-restraint, learning, prowess, moderation in speech, charity according to one's capacity to give and gratitude.

This house has nine doors, three pillars and five witnesses; and it is presided over by the soul. The learned man who realises this is truly wise.

Dhritarashtra, these ten do not know what virtue is: the intoxicated man, the inattentive one, the raving man, the exhausted one, the angry, the starving, the hasty, the covetous, the frightened and the lustful one. The wise man must avoid their company. In this connection there is an old story about what happened between the Asura lord and Duryodhana, for the sake of the Asura's son.

The king who renounces lust and anger; who gives wealth to deserving people; who is discerning, learned and active is a lord of men. The king who knows how to inspire confidence in others, who punishes the guilty with just punishment and knows when to show clemency enjoys great prosperity.

The wise man does not ignore even a weak enemy and is intelligently cautious about the foe who waits for an opportunity; he does not invite hostilities with people who are stronger than himself; and he shows his strength only when he needs to. He is the most noble-minded of men, who does not grieve once a calamity has struck him, but deals with the crisis sensibly, and who patiently endures adversity; this man will defeat all his enemies.

Always happy is the man who does not live away from home without good reason, who does not make friends with sinners, who never molests another man's wife, who is never arrogant, who never steals, who is never ungrateful and who does not drink.

He is wise, who never boastfully pursues dharma, artha and kama; who always tells the truth when asked; who does not argue even for the sake of a friend; and who never gets angry even if insulted.

Everyone praises the man who has no malice towards others but is kind to all; who, being weak, avoids disputes; who does not speak arrogantly; and who forgives a wrong done to him.

Everyone loves the man who is never haughty, who never speaks ill of others while praising himself, and who never forgets himself and speaks harshly. Sages consider him a good man who does not rake up old quarrels, who is neither arrogant nor obsequious and who never violates dharma even when in distress.

The man who neither exults in his own happiness nor delights in another's misery, and who has no regrets after giving a gift is a good man. The man who is eager to learn about the customs of other countries and the languages and dharma of different varnas knows everything—important and insignificant; and wherever he goes, he gains authority over others, even the great. The intelligent man, who renounces pride, folly, insolence, sinful deeds, treasonous actions, dishonesty, enmity and arguments with men who are drunk, mad or evil is the best of men.

The gods bestow prosperity on the man who makes a daily habit of self-restraint, self-purification, performing sacred rites, worshipping the gods and conducting rituals of penance. The learned man, whose actions are well thought out and properly executed, arranges a marriage with someone of equal status to his own; he looks up to people who are better than him; he talks, mixes and forms friendships with persons of his own status.

The man who eats frugally after dividing the food amongst his dependents, who sleeps little after working hard, and who, when asked, gives even to his enemies is a man with his soul under control. Disaster stays away from such a man.

The man who keeps his own counsel with plans and executes them without others knowing much about these, and whose actions, consequentially, never injure others, succeeds in achieving even the most trifling goal. The man who is intent upon abstaining from doing injury to all creatures, who is truthful, gentle, charitable and pure-minded shines among his kinsmen like a precious gem of the purest quality from the best mine.

The man who is ashamed of his faults, even though only he knows of them, is the most honourable of men. With his pure heart and boundless energy, with his mind turned inwards, he blazes in energy like the Sun.

King Pandu, suffering under a Brahmana's curse, had five sons born to him in the forest; they are like five Indras. You brought up those children and taught them everything; they are obedient to you. Give them back their fair share of the kingdom, and you and your sons will be happy; and then, Rajan, you will regain the trust and confidence of both gods and men.'"

CANTO 34

PRAJAGARA PARVA CONTINUED

"Dhritarashtra says, 'Tell me how a man copes with sleeplessness and burning anxiety. Only you know dharma and artha. Give me the benefit of your wisdom, generous Vidura; tell me what you think is good for both Yudhishtira and the Kurus. I think of my guilt, and I fear the dreadful things that may be in store for me. It is with terrible apprehension that I ask you this: what is Yudhishtira thinking?'

Vidura says, 'Even if one is not asked, one should be truthful in what one says—be it good or bad, pleasing or hateful—to the man whose downfall one does not wish. I will tell you what is for the good of the Kurus, which is both beneficial and dharma. Listen, Rajan.

Do not set your heart on unjust, sinful ways to achieve your ends. An intelligent man must not grieve if he does not succeed, despite using fair and righteous means. Before he embarks on a course of action, a man must take three things into consideration that all actions depend on: the competence of the person executing the plan, the nature of the deed itself and its purpose. He should think carefully about these and not act on impulse. The wise man must decide either to do something or not, after considering his ability, the act, and the consequences of failure and success.

The king who does not know the true extent of his kingdom, his profits and losses, his treasury, his population and the nature of the danda neeti—the law of punishment, cannot hope to keep his kingdom for long. On the other hand, the king who is aware of all these, as prescribed in the ancient treatises, and who is learned in dharma and artha will retain his kingdom.

Just as the planets affect the stars, the senses affect this world, regardless of whether they are directed or uncontrolled in their journey to their respective goals. Like the Moon waxing during the bright fortnight, calamities pile up for the man who allows his senses to control him and direct his actions. The man who tries to control his counsellors before controlling himself, or to subdue his adversaries before controlling his counsellors, ultimately succumbs in weakness. Hence, the man who first achieves mastery over himself, thinking of the ego as an enemy, always succeeds in subduing his counsellors and adversaries.

Great prosperity is his who has subdued his senses, controlled his soul and is able to punish all offenders; who acts with discernment and is blessed with patience. A man's body is his ratha; the inner soul is the sarathy; the senses are the horses. When this chariot is drawn by well-trained steeds, the wise man journeys pleasantly through life and finds ultimate peace. Horses that are unbroken and wild always lead an unskilful charioteer to doom during the course of his journey; so, too, do one's senses, if they are not subdued.

The inexperienced man, who is driven by his rampaging senses, thinks he can extract evil from good and good from evil, and he confuses sorrow with happiness. He who forsakes dharma and artha, and follows his senses, soon loses prosperity, wealth, his wife and his life. He who is the master of riches but not of his senses loses his riches. One should strive to know one's self by using the Self, by controlling one's mind, intellect and senses; for the self is as much an ally as an enemy. The man who has conquered his self through the Self, has his self for a friend—the self can be either friend or foe.

Desire and anger tear at wisdom, just as large fish rip apart a flimsy net. The man who strives for success, paying heed to dharma and artha, wins happiness and all that he aspires for. He who wants to vanquish his outward adversaries without first conquering his inner enemies—his five senses—is overpowered by them. Many evil kings, because of their lack of mastery over their senses, are ruined by their own actions, which are directed by their unending lust for more territory and possessions.

Just as wet fuel burns along with the dry, so, too, is an innocent man punished by association with evil men. Friendship with sinful men must be avoided. The ignorant man who fails to control his five greedy enemies, each of which has its own selfish goals, is overwhelmed by disaster.

Evil men never have these attributes: guilelessness, simplicity, innocence, contentment, sweetness of speech, self-restraint, truth and steadiness. Inferior men do not have Atmagyana; they are never stable, patient or devoted to dharma, and neither trustworthy nor charitable.

Fools try to injure the wise with false accusations and harsh words. In consequence, they acquire the sins of the wise who, freed from guilt, gain forgiveness. Malice is the strength of evil-minded men; protection of the weak and of women is the strength of kings; forgiveness is the strength of the virtuous.

To control speech is said to be most difficult. It is not easy to hold a long conversation full of meaningful words that also delight the ear. Well-spoken words produce many benefits, but harsh ones are the cause of all evils. A forest destroyed by arrows or cut down by hatchets may grow again, but a heart wounded by cruel words never recovers. Weapons such as arrows, spears and bearded darts can be removed from the body, but a dagger of words plunged into the heart cannot. The mouth shoots word-arrows that strike deep and cause anguish through day and night. A learned man should never discharge such arrows; they pierce the very soul.

The man whom the gods have destined for defeat loses his good sense and debases himself by dishonourable conduct. When one's intellect becomes clouded and one's destruction is imminent, one is convinced that wrong is right. Bharatarishabha, you do not see that your sons are in the grip of their deluded minds because of their hostility toward the Pandavas. Neither do you see that Yudhishtira, blessed with every auspicious mark and worthy of ruling the three worlds, is obedient to you.

Dhritarashtra, exclude all your sons and make Yudhishtira Dharmaraja your heir. Intelligent and wise, steeped in dharma and artha, he has suffered untold misery out of kindness and sympathy for you and in order to preserve your good name.'"

CANTO 35

PRAJAGARA PARVA CONTINUED

"Dhritarashtra says, 'Effulgent one, tell me more about dharma and artha. My thirst for them remains unquenched, and your words delight my ears and my heart.'

Vidura says, 'Ritual bathing in all the tirthas and compassion towards all creatures have equal merit, with kindness having the edge. Rajan, be kind to all your sons; by that you will win great fame in this world, and heaven thereafter. A man is glorified in Swarga for as long as his good deeds are spoken of in this world. Listen to an ancient story about the conversation between Virochana and Sudhanwan, both suitors for Kesini's hand.

Once, long ago, there was a maiden named Kesini, whose beauty was unrivalled. Wanting a good husband, she decided to choose one through a swayamvara. Wanting her for himself, one of Diti's sons, Virochana, went to her swayamvara.

Kesini noticed this Daitya lord and said to him, "O Virochana, tell me, who are superior—Brahmanas or the sons of Diti? Why is Sudhanwan not sitting on the grander seat?"

Virochana said, "O Kesini, because we are the firstborn of Prajapati, we are superior to all creatures. The world is ours. Who are the Devas, and what are the Brahmanas before us?"

Kesini said, "We will remain in this pavilion, Virochana. Sudhanwan will come here tomorrow, and I want to see both of you sitting together."

Virochana said, "Sweet and timid one, I will do as you say. Tomorrow morning, you will see Sudhanwan and me together."

When the night passed and the Sun rose Sudhanwan came there and saw Virochana waiting with Kesini. Kesini got up; she offered him her seat, padya to wash his feet and arghya.

When Virochana invited him to share his seat, Sudhanwan said, "O Son of Prahlada, I will touch your beautiful golden seat, but since you are not my equal, I cannot sit on it with you."

Virochana said, "You have the right to sit only on a wooden plank, an animal skin or a mat of grass or straw. You do not deserve to sit on the same seat as me."

Sudhanwan said, "Only father and son, Brahmanas of the same age and equal learning, two Kshatriyas, two Vaisyas or two Sudras can sit together on the same seat; no others may sit together. Your father used to pay his respects to me and take a seat lower than mine. You are young, brought up in every luxury at home, and you understand nothing."

Virochana said, "I will wager all the gold, cattle, horses and every other kind of wealth that we have among the Asuras to the one who is able to answer this question that has arisen."

Sudhanwan said, "Leave aside your gold, your cattle and your horses, Virochana. Let us stake our lives and ask this question of those who can answer."

Virochana said, "Who shall we go to when we wager our lives? I will not go before any of the Devas and never before any man."

Sudhanwan said, "With our lives as wager, we will approach your father. Prahlada will never tell a lie, not even for his son's sake."

So, they made a wager, and Virochana and Sudhanwan, both roused, went to Prahlada.

Seeing them together, Prahlada said, "These two, who have never been companions, have come here like two angry snakes that have travelled by the same road.

He said, "Have you two become friends now, who never were before?"

Virochana said, "There is no friendship between Sudhanwan and me. Rather, we have both wagered our lives. O Lord of Asuras, I will ask you a question, which you must answer truthfully."

Prahlada said, "Bring water, honey and curds for Sudhanwan. You deserve our worship, Brahmana. A plump white cow is ready for you."

Sudhanwan said, "Water, honey and curds have already been given me on my way here. I will ask you a question, Prahlada; answer it truly. Are Brahmanas superior, or is Virochana?"

Prahlada said, "O Brahmana, here you both are in person—my only son and you, a Brahmana. How can I answer this question over which you two have fallen out?"

Sudhanwan said, "Keep your cattle and your other precious wealth, but you must declare the truth to settle our dispute."

Prahlada said, "What will a person who misuses his tongue, to answer falsely rather than truly, suffer?"

Sudhanwan said, "The person who uses his tongue to lie suffers like a deserted wife who pines at night, with visions of her husband in the arms of another woman. He suffers like a man who loses at dice, or like one who is weighed down with an unbearable load of anxieties. He suffers like a man who is denied entry into a city and sits outside its gates, starving, and he is always faced with his enemies.

He who tells a lie for the sake of an animal will have five of his forefathers cast down from heaven. He who tells a lie for the sake of a cow will have ten of his Pitrs cast down from Swarga; a lie for the sake of a horse causes the downfall of a hundred; and a lie for the sake of a human being results in the fall of a thousand of one's manes. An untruth for the sake of gold ruins the members of one's race both born and unborn, while an untruth for the sake of land ruins everything. So never lie about land."

Prahlada said, "Angiras is superior to me, and Sudhanwan is superior to you, Virochana; and Sudhanwan's mother is superior to yours. You have been defeated by Sudhanwan; and he is now in command of your life.

Sudhanwan, I ask that you grant Virochana his life."

Sudhanwan said, "O Prahlada, you have chosen dharma and not been tempted to lie. So, I grant the life of your son, who is so dear to you, and restore Virochana to you. He shall, however, have to wash my feet in Kesini's presence."

This is why, Rajan, you must never utter the slightest falsehood about the kingdom. Do not hasten your death and the deaths of your children and close associates by lying for your son. The gods do not protect men by taking up wooden clubs as herdsmen would; however, they grant intelligence to those they wish to protect.

There is no doubt that the degree of a man's success is in direct proportion to the attention he pays to dharma. The Vedas never save a man who lives by falsehood from the guilt of sin. They forsake him while he is on his deathbed, like fledglings flying from their nests.

Drinking, quarrels, enmity with many, marital disputes, severance of marital relationships between husband and wife, internal dissent and treason are all sins that must be shunned. A palmist, a thief turned merchant, a fowler, a physician, an enemy, a friend and a minstrel are not acceptable witnesses. Performed from motives of pride, an Agnihotra, abstention from speech, study and sacrifice become harmful, although they are intrinsically innocent.

A man who sets fire to a house, one who gives poison, a pander, a vendor of alcohol, a fletcher, an astrologer, one who injures his friends, an adulterer, one who performs abortions, one who violates the wife of an elder, a Brahmana addicted to alcohol, one who is harsh-tongued, one who opens old wounds, an atheist, one who insults the Vedas, a taker of bribes, one whose upanayanam has been delayed beyond the appropriate time, one who secretly kills cattle, one who kills the man that comes to him for protection: all these are as lacking in dharma as a man who kills a Brahmana.

Gold is tested for purity by fire, a high-born man by the way he carries himself and an honest man by what he does. A man's courage is tested in a crisis, a man's self-control in times of poverty and the strength of a man's friendship or enmity in times of danger. Old age destroys beauty; ambition destroys patience; death ends life; envy removes righteousness; anger ruins prosperity; companionship with base persons destroys good conduct; lust sheds modesty; and pride takes away everything. Prosperity is born of good deeds; it grows by dint of work; its roots penetrate deep from well honed skill; it becomes stable from self-control.

Wisdom, good lineage, restraint, knowing the scriptures, prowess, not being garrulous, giving gifts as one is able, and gratitude are the eight qualities that glorify a man. But there is one factor which, on its own, can make all these attributes coalesce: royal favour can make all these qualities cover the favoured person with their lustre. These eight are celestial qualities in this world of men.

Of the eight, four are inherent in good people, and the other four they always practise. The four that are integral to good men are sacrifice, charity, study and asceticism; and the other four that good men always practise are self-restraint, truth, simplicity and abstention from causing injury.

Sacrifice, study, charity, asceticism, truth, forgiveness, mercy and contentment constitute the eight paths of dharma. The first four of these may be practised from motives of pride, but the last four can exist only in those that are truly noble.

No gathering of people can truly be a satsanga unless there are venerable men in it; and no one can be considered worthy of veneration unless he can say what dharma is. It is not dharma if it can be separated from truth; and it is not truth if it is tinged with deceit.

Truth, beauty, knowledge of the scriptures, learning, noble birth, good conduct, strength, wealth, courage and the ability to speak on a variety of subjects are ten qualities of divine origin.

A man who sins is overwhelmed by evil consequences; a man who is virtuous reaps great happiness. So, a man must be firm in his resolve to abstain from sin. Repeated sinning destroys intelligence, and the man who loses intelligence repeatedly sins. Being constantly virtuous enhances intelligence, and the man whose intelligence increases is constantly virtuous. The virtuous man attains bliss. Thus, a man should be firm in his resolve to be virtuous.

The man who is envious, he who is hurtful, the man who is cruel, the man who is quarrelsome and one who is deceitful come to grief. The wise man who is not envious always does what is dharma and never suffers sorrow; instead, he shines. The man who acquires wisdom from wise men is himself learned and wise. He who is wise pays attention to dharma and artha, and achieves joy.

Behave during the day in a way that will ensure an untroubled night; conduct yourself during eight months of the year in a way that will ensures happiness during the monsoon; spend your youth in a way that ensures a comfortable old age; and conduct your whole life on Earth in a manner that ensures bliss in the hereafter.

The wise man thinks highly of food that is easily digested, of the wife who is young no more, of the hero who is victorious and of the sannyasin whose efforts have been rewarded with success. The empty space that a man tries to fill with wrongfully acquired wealth will never be filled; rather, new voids appear in other places.

The Guru controls those who have restrained their souls; the king controls the black-souled one; Yama controls those who sin in secret. The greatness of Rishis, of rivers, of river-banks, of mahatmans cannot be determined, like a woman's immorality.

O king, the man who is devoted to the worship of Brahmanas, he who is generous, he who is charitable to his relatives, and the Kshatriya who conducts himself honourably rule the Earth for ever. The man who is brave, learned and who knows how to protect others can always gather flowers of gold from the Earth.

Of all works, those performed by using the intellect are the best; next come those performed with the use of one's arms; those for which the legs are used are worse; and those performed by carrying loads are the lowest.

How can you expect to prosper when you have entrusted your kingdom to Duryodhana, Sakuni, the witless Dusasana and Karna? The Pandavas, who are blessed with every virtue, look up to you as a father. You must rely on them as your true sons.'"

CANTO 36

Prajagara Parva continued

"Vidura says, 'I know an ancient tale that is told in this connection: of the discussion between Atri's son and the Sadhyas.

Long ago, the deities known as Sadhyas approached the son of Atri, the wise Maharishi of the stern tapasya, while he wandered the world in the guise of a mendicant, and said to him, "O Maharishi, we are deities known as Sadhyas. We cannot tell who you are. You seem highly intelligent and a man of rigid self-control, which comes from a deep knowledge of the Shastras. Share your knowledge with us."

The mendicant Rishi answered, "Immortal ones, I have heard that by untying the knots in one's heart by means of tranquillity, by mastering one's passions and by following true dharma, one must learn to look on all beings—likeable or hateful—as if on oneself. One should not retaliate to slander or accusations, because when one bears pain silently it consumes the slanderer, and one also acquires the merit of his good deeds.

Do not indulge in slander or accusations; do not humiliate or insult others; do not quarrel with friends; do not seek the companionship of the vile and the base; do not be arrogant or dishonourable. Avoid speaking sharp or angry words, because they burn deep—into the heart and bones, and into prana itself. That is why the virtuous man never speaks harshly or in anger. He that does is the very worst of men. With hell on his tongue, he sears the inmost parts of a man with his piercing words, and always causes misery.

The wise man, when wounded by another's wordy arrows that scorch like fire or the Sun, endures them silently, remembering that the slanderer's blessings become his. The man who serves a good man or an evil one, a saintly man or a thief, absorbs the characteristics of his companion, like a cloth soaked in dye.

The gods like to be with the man who, when stung with criticism, neither criticises nor makes others do so in retaliation; who, when struck, neither strikes back nor makes someone else do so for him; and who does not wish even the slightest injury on the one who hurt him.

Silence is better than speech; if you must speak, then it is better to speak the truth; if the truth is to be spoken, it is better to say what is pleasing; and if what is pleasing is to be said, then it is best to say what is dharma.

A man becomes like the person he lives with, or like the one he sees regularly, or like the one he wants emulate. A man is liberated from those things from which he abstains; and if he abstains from everything, he will not suffer even the least sorrow. Such a man neither vanquishes others, nor is vanquished by any. He is never hurtful or antagonistic to anyone. He is unmoved by praise or reproach. He neither grieves nor exalts.

The best human being is one who wants the prosperity of all and never gloats over the sorrows of others; he is truthful and humble; and he has his senses under control. The mediocre man is one who never consoles another with false platitudes; he gives what he has promised; and he is mindful of others' weaknesses. The despicable man is one who is difficult to control; he is easily affected by the prospect of danger; he is short-tempered; he is ungrateful; he cannot make friends; and he has an evil heart. The worst among men is one who is unappreciative of any good that comes to him from others; he is suspicious by nature; and he drives away all his true friends.

He who wants to prosper should keep the company of good men, perhaps occasionally those that are mediocre, but never those that are bad. The sinful man does, indeed, earn wealth by working hard, by his intelligence and by his strength; but he can never win fame, nor can he acquire the virtues and ways of noble families, even if he is born into one.'

Dhritarashtra says, 'The gods, those who respect dharma and artha and do not swerve from either, and those who have great learning have an affinity to noble families. Tell me, Vidura, what families are truly noble?'

Vidura says, 'The family whose life is characterised by simplicity, self-restraint, Vedic knowledge, sacrifice, proper marriages and gifts of food is considered noble. Such vamsas never deviate from dharma; their ancestors are never pained by having to see their progeny's wrong-doings; they cheerfully practise all the virtues; they aspire to enhance the fame of their line; and they avoid every kind of falsehood.

Noble families fall and debase themselves because they neglect to perform sacrifices, make impure marriages, abandon the Vedas and insult Brahmanas. They are degraded because their members ignore or speak ill of Brahmanas, or because they misappropriate what others have entrusted to them.

Even if a family is extensive and owns much wealth and cattle, you cannot think of it as a cohesive family if its members lack good manners and deportment; whereas a family that lacks wealth, but is distinguished by good conduct, is noble indeed, and earns a great reputation. So, families must pay attention to good demeanour, for material wealth comes and goes. The man who is wanting in wealth is not really wanting, but the man who is wanting in decorum is really in want. Families that are rich in cattle and agricultural produce do not deserve fame if they lack good conduct.

Let none in our dynasty provoke quarrels, serve another king as minister, take what is not his, stir dissent, be deceitful or false, or eat before serving the Rishis, Devas and Sadasyas. Any of our vamsa who kills a Brahmana or feels antipathy towards them, or who obstructs farming, does not deserve to mix with us.

A seat of straw, a piece of ground to sit on, water to wash one's face and feet, and sweet words are never wanting in the house of a good man. Virtuous men devoted to dharma have these things ready to reverently offer to any guest who might come to his home. Just as the sandalwood tree is able to support weights that larger trees cannot, so too are those from noble families able to shoulder great cares which ordinary men cannot.

A man whose anger inspires fear, or whom people serve in fear is not a friend; but the man who is trusted like a father is. All other friendships are in name only. The man who acts as a friend, though not related by blood, is one's true friend, refuge and protector. The man of wavering affections who does not care for the elderly or one who is restless can never make friends. Like swans abandoning a tank whose waters have dried up, success forsakes a man whose heart is unsteady, a man who cannot control his mind and a man who is a slave to his senses.

Weak-minded men give in to anger and are gratified too easily; they are as changeable as clouds. Even birds of carrion will not touch the dead bodies of men who are ungrateful to friends who have helped them. Whether you are poor or rich, you must honour your friends. The sincerity of a friend is tested only when you ask for his help.

Sorrow kills beauty; it debilitates; it destroys knowledge; and it makes the body vulnerable to disease. Rather than helping a man achieve his goals, grief dries up his body, to the delight of his enemies. Do not yield to grief. Men repeatedly die and are reborn; repeatedly they wither away and grow; repeatedly they ask others for help, and they themselves are asked for help; repeatedly they lament and are lamented.

Everyone experiences happiness and misery, plenty and want, gain and loss, life and death, at one time or other. The man who is self-controlled should neither exult in joy nor wilt in sorrow at these twinned opposites.

The six senses are always restless. One's understanding leaks out through the sense that is heightened, in direct proportion to the level of its dominance, like water from a pot with holes, big and small.'

Dhritarashtra says, 'I have deceived Yudhishtira, who is like a flame. He will surely kill all my sons in battle. I see danger everywhere and my heart churns within me. Wise one, soothe my anxiety.'

Vidura says, 'Anagha, I see good only in knowledge and tapasya, in restraining the senses and in giving up greed. Atmagyana dispels fear; tapasya brings rich rewards; serving one's superiors gives learning; and self-restraint results in peace. Those who want moksha without first earning blessings by giving charity and practicing Vedic rituals go through life bound by anger and hatred. The happiness gained by a judicious course of study, by a battle fought virtuously or by stern tapasya always increases at the end.

Those who quarrel with their relatives get no sleep, even if they lie on the most comfortable beds; nor do they derive any pleasure from women or from hearing bards sing hymns and eulogies in their praise. Such men can never practise dharma; they can never be happy; they can never have honour. Peace holds no charm for them. They never appreciate good advice; they never get what they want or keep what they have. O king, such men can expect to meet with ruin.

As natural as milk is to cows, so is asceticism to Brahmanas, inconstancy to women and distrust to one's own kin. Many thin threads of equal length can, when stranded together, stand the strain of the shuttle passing constantly over them, because of their numbers. It is the same with family members who are bound by ties of dharma. Burning twigs produce only smoke, singly; but together they burst into flame. It is the same with kinsmen, Dhritarashtra.

Men who want to assert their authority over Brahmanas, women, relatives and cattle soon fall off their pedestals, like ripe fruits from their stems. The trunk of the tree that grows alone, though massive, strong and deep-rooted, is smashed and twisted by a strong wind. However, trees that grow close together in stands can resist violent gales by leaning on each other. In the same way, his enemies see the man who is alone, though blessed with all the good qualities, as being easy to bring down, like a lone tree by the wind. In contrast, relatives who are united grow in strength, like lotus-stalks in a lake.

These must never be killed: Brahmanas, cows, relatives, children, women, hosts whose food one has eaten and persons who surrender and ask for one's protection.

Rajan, without health a man's good qualities do not manifest themselves. If you are healthy, you can do much good; but if you have bad health, you might as well be dead.

Rajan, anger is a bitter, pungent, acrid and scalding drink, painful in its consequences; it is a dark draught not born of any physical illness; and those that lack wisdom can never digest it. Swallow your anger, Rajan, and be at peace. Men who are wracked by disease derive no joy from pleasures or from wealth; they are so full of sorrow that they do not know what happiness is nor enjoy wealth.

When I saw Draupadi won as a wager at dice, I told you that men of dharma never use deceit at gambling and urged you to stop Duryodhana. You paid no heed to me then. True strength is not opposed to softness; rather, the combination of both is the best and most effective course. Prosperity which is dependent on deceit is destined to be short lived; but that which depends on strength and softness is passed down to sons and grandsons intact.

Your sons and the Pandavas must love each other. Let them have the same friends and enemies and live together in happiness and prosperity. Rajan, you are the refuge of the sons of Kuru. Indeed, the entire Ajamida vamsa depends on you. Preserve your good name by cherishing the sons of Pandu, especially for the great suffering they have endured in exile. O Kaurava, make peace with the Pandavas; do not let your enemies find a chink in your armour. The Pandavas are devoted to dharma. Draw Duryodhana away from his evil ways.'"

CANTO 37

Prajagara Parva continued

"Vidura says, 'Manu, the son of the Svayambhuva, the Self-Created One, spoke of the seventeen kinds of men who vainly strike air with their fists, who seek to bend Indra's heavenly bow of vapour—the Indradhanush, or want to catch the intangible rays of the Sun.

These foolish ones are the man who wants to control another who cannot be controlled; the man who is content with small gains; the man who humbly pays court to enemies; the man who seeks to control women; the man who solicits gifts from one who should not be asked for gifts; the man who boasts without having done anything; the high-born man who acts basely; the weak man who enters into hostilities with one that is powerful; the man who talks to one who listens with disdain; the man who desires the unattainable; the father-in-law who flirts with his daughter-in-law; the man who boasts about his fears being allayed by his daughter-in-law; the man who sows his seeds in another man's field; the man who speaks ill of his wife; the man who does not acknowledge having received something from another; the man who, in a holy tirtha, commits to give something away and then makes excuses when asked to make good his words; and the man who tries to prove the truth of what is false. Yama's dutas, with nooses in hand, drag these people away to hell.

A man should behave towards others in the same manner as others behave towards him, for this is good policy. One may behave deceitfully with the deceitful, but must be honest with those who are honest. Old age withers beauty; patience takes away hope; death ends life; the practice of virtue denudes worldly enjoyments; lust abandons modesty; companionship with evil men destroys good character and deportment; anger ruins prosperity; and pride destroys everything.'

Dhritarashtra says, 'According to the Vedas, man's life-span on Earth is one hundred years. Why is it, then, that not all men attain the allotted span?'

Vidura says, 'Too much pride, excessive speech, overindulgence in food, giving in to anger, yearning for pleasure and inner discord are the six swords that cut short man's life on Earth. It is these six, not death, which kill men. Know this and be blessed.

Bhaarata, these acquire the guilt of killing a Brahmana: one who steals the wife of a friend who trusts him; one who violates the bed of his Guru; a Brahmana who marries a Sudra woman or drinks alcohol; a man who wields authority over Brahmanas, becomes their master or confiscates lands that support them; and one who kills those who give themselves up into his protection. The Vedas declare that contact with these kinds of people requires penance to purify oneself.

These persons attain Swarga: one who accepts the teachings of the wise; one who knows dharma; one who is generous; one who eats only after offering his food to the Devas and Pitrs; one who has no envy; one who is incapable of doing anything injurious; and one who is grateful, truthful, humble and learned.

O king, many are those who always say pleasing things; but rare is the man whose words are not always pleasant but yet medicinal, and the man who listens to him. The man who, without worrying about whether his words will please his master or not, tells him things that may seem unpalatable but are wise and in keeping with dharma, is an asset to the king.

For the sake of the family one of its members may be sacrificed; for the sake of the village, a family may be sacrificed; for the sake of a kingdom a village may be sacrificed; and for the sake of one's soul, the whole world may be sacrificed. A man should conserve his wealth, in case calamity strikes; he should use his wealth to protect his wives; and with his wealth and his wives he should safeguard himself.

From time immemorial it has been obvious that gambling causes disputes. The wise man should never gamble, even light-heartedly. At the time of that game of dice I told you it was sinful and dangerous. To you, however, my words were as unpleasant as bitter medicine to a sick man. O king, you want to vanquish the sons of Pandu, who compare with your sons as peacocks to crows. You forsake lions in favour of jackals. The time will come when you will regret this.

The master who does not vent his displeasure against devoted servants that want only his welfare, gains their confidence. They stand by him even in times of distress. A man must never seek to save wealth by confiscating grants or not paying his employees; for, deprived of their means of livelihood and prosperity, even those who are fond of him will turn against him and abandon him in his time of need.

A king should first consider all his future plans, then fixing his servants' wages with his own income and expenditure in mind, he should make suitable contracts, for there is nothing that cannot be accomplished by just and strategic alliances. The officer who, with a complete understanding of his king's intentions, discharges his duties promptly and enthusiastically, who is respectable and devoted to his master, always tells him what is best for him. The king should regard the officer who is well aware of the strength of his own and the enemy's forces as a second self. However, the king should immediately rid himself of the servant who is so proud of his own intelligence that he disregards his master's instructions, refuses to obey him and argues with him.

Learned men say that a good servant possesses these eight qualities: he is not arrogant; he does not procrastinate; he is able, kind, clean and incorruptible; he is from a family free of disease; and he weighs his words before he speaks.

A man must never enter an enemy's house confidently after dusk, even with notice; he must never lurk in the yard of another's house at night; and he must never seek to be with a woman whom the king might enjoy.

One must never disagree with the decision arrived at by a man who keeps company with sinners and who is in the habit of consulting all and sundry. Never tell him you disagree with him; instead dismiss him on some pretext.

One must never borrow from, or lend to, these: a king who is inordinately soft-hearted, a woman of bad character, the servant of a king, one's son, one's brother, a widow with a child, one serving in the military and one who has suffered a great loss of wealth.

Eight qualities bestow lustre on a man. They are wisdom, noble lineage, knowledge of the scriptures, self-restraint, prowess, moderation in speech, the giving of gifts such as one can afford and gratitude. These qualities, sire, are mustered and held close by the wise.

The man who performs ritual ablutions acquires strength, beauty, a clear voice, the ability to clearly enunciate all the alphabet, delicacy of touch, a fine sense of smell, cleanliness, grace, delicacy of limbs and beautiful women. The man who eats sparingly wins good health, long life, ease, healthy children and freedom from sloth and accusations of gluttony.

A man should not shelter the following in his house: one who is ill-behaved, one who eats too much, one whom everyone dislikes, one who is deceitful, one who is cruel, one who does not know the correctness of time and place and one who dresses immodestly. A person, even in dire distress, should never ask a favour of a miser, of one who speaks badly of others, of one who has no knowledge of the Shastras, of a forest dweller, of one who is cunning, of one who does not respect those who are worthy of reverence, of one who is cruel, of one who is quarrelsome or ungrateful.

One should never serve these six worst types of men: an enemy, one who always errs, a habitual liar, one who wavers in his devotion to God, a cold-hearted man and one who is overconfident of his own abilities.

One's objectives depend on the means for their success; and means depend on the nature of the objective to be achieved through them. They are intimately intertwined, and success depends on both. A man must have sons, make them independent by providing for them, give daughters in marriage to suitable men and then retire to the life of a Vanaprastha. To receive the grace of the Supreme Being a man must always work for universal good as well as for his own happiness; and this is the root of success of all man's endeavours. A man who has intelligence, energy, prowess, strength, promptness and perseverance need have no anxieties about his livelihood.

Look at the evils that a quarrel with the Pandavas will bring, which would sadden Indra and all the Devas. Firstly, enmity with those who are like sons to you; secondly, a life of constant anxiety; thirdly, the ruin of the fame of the Kurus; and lastly, the joy of your enemies. O you who are as splendid as Indra, the wrath of Bhishma, Drona and Yudhishtira will consume the whole world, like a massive comet blasting through the Earth.

Your hundred sons, Karna and the sons of Pandu can together rule this vast Earth with its girdle of oceans. Rajan, your sons are the forest, and the Pandavas are its tigers. O, do not destroy the forest and its tigers. O, do not let the tigers be driven away from the forest. Without tigers there can be no forest and without a forest there can be no tigers. The forest shelters the tigers and tigers guard the forest.

Those who are sinful look more for the faults than for the good qualities of others. He who desires total success in his material ventures should be virtuous from the very beginning, for true artha is impossible to obtain without dharma, like amrita without swarga. He whose soul has been cleansed of sin and firmly fixed on dharma has understood all things, whether natural or artificial. He who pursues dharma, artha and kama at the appropriate times gains all three, in this world and the next. He who restrains the force of both anger and joy, and never loses his composure in a crisis, wins prosperity.

Listen to me, O great king. Men are said to have five different kinds of strength. Of these, the strength of arms is regarded as the least. The acquisition of good advisors is seen as the second most important. The wise have said that the acquisition of wealth is the third; the strength of one's lineage is considered the fourth. However, Bhaarata, the one by which all these are won, and which is the best and most important of all kinds of strength is the strength of the intellect.

After provoking the hostility of a man who is capable of doing great injury to others, one should not reassure oneself with the thought that one lives far away from him. A wise man does not repose his trust in women, kings, serpents, his own master, enemies, enjoyments or his longevity.

There are no physicians or physics for a man who has been struck by the arrow of wisdom; neither the mantras of homa nor auspicious ceremonies, neither the mantras of the Atharva Veda nor any of the antidotes for poison are of any use.

A man should not ignore snakes, fire, lions and blood relatives; all these are powerful. Fire is a thing of great energy in this world. It hides itself in wood but does not consume it until it is ignited by an outside agent. That same latent fire, when sparked by friction, consumes not only the wood in which it hides, but also an entire forest. Men of noble lineage are just like fire in their energy. Of a forgiving nature, they do not betray outward symptoms of wrath, and lie quiet like fire in wood.

O king, you and your sons are like creepers and the Pandavas are like Sala trees. A creeper cannot grow unless there is a large tree for it to twine round. Your sons are like a forest and the sons of Pandu are its lions. Without its lions the forest is doomed to destruction, and lions, too, are doomed without the forest to shelter them.'"

CANTO 38

Prajagara Parva continued

"Vidura says, 'The heart of a young man soars in joy when an older and venerable person comes to his house as a guest. His heart comes down to earth again when he goes forward and greets him. One who has self-control must first offer his guest a seat, then have his feet washed in clean water, after which he must make the usual enquiries of welcome, then give his own news and offer him food.

Wise men say that the man cannot be considered to be truly alive, in whose home a Brahmana conversant with mantras does not accept water, honey, curds or cattle from fear of either being unsure of whether he can take the gifts away, or from the miserliness and unwillingness with which the gifts are made. A householder must look on a newly arrived guest as being very dear, regardless of the fact that he may not be worthy of being offered water to wash his feet, be the guest a physician, a fletcher, a lapsed Brahmachari, a thief, a Brahmana who drinks, an abortionist, a soldier or a seller of the Vedas.

A Brahmana should never sell salt, cooked food, curds, milk, honey, oil, ghee, sesame, meat, fruits, roots, potherbs, dyed clothes, perfumes and sweets. The man who never gives way to anger, the one who is beyond grief, the one to whom friendship and quarrels are meaningless, he who disregards praise and blame and he who is detached from both the pleasant and unpleasant is completely withdrawn from the world, and is a real Yogin of the Bhikshu order.

The virtuous sannyasin who lives on wild rice, roots or herbs, who has his soul under control, who carefully maintains his sacred fire for worship, who lives in the forest and is always mindful of guests is indeed the best of ascetics.

If a man wrongs an intelligent person, he should never become complacent in that he lives a great distance away from the one he has wronged. Far is the reach of an intelligent man, by which he can avenge the wrongs done to him. One should never trust an untrustworthy man, nor indeed repose too much trust on a reliable man, for both these make one most vulnerable.

Men should renounce envy, protect their wives, give everyone their due and speak pleasantly. A man should always speak sweetly to his wife but must never be enslaved by her. It has been said that wives who are blessed and virtuous, who are worthy of worship and who are the ornaments of their homes are embodiments of domestic prosperity, of the Grihalakshmi. They should be protected.

A man should delegate the supervision of his inner apartments to his father; of the kitchen to his mother; of his cattle to somebody he looks upon as his own self; but he must himself tend to his farming. A man should assign his servants to care for guests who are Vaisyas and give his sons the responsibility of looking after Brahmanas.

Fire has its origin in water, Kshatriyas in Brahmanas and iron in stone. Their energy can affect all things but is neutralised as soon as these things come in contact with their progenitors. Fire lies hidden in wood without showing itself. Good men of a forgiving nature and fiery tejas do not betray outwardly what is within them. The king whose plans are unknown to outsiders as well as to those around him, but who knows what others are planning, through his spies, enjoys long prosperity.

One should never talk about what one intends to do. Let anything you do, with regard to dharma, artha or kama, remain unknown until it is done. Reflect over and settle on your plans secretly, climbing to the top of a mountain or the terrace of a palace or going to a deserted wilderness devoid of trees and plants to do so. O Bhaarata, neither an ignorant friend nor a learned one who has no self-restraint should be trusted with secrets.

Rajan, never make a man your minister without examining him well, for your finances and inmost thoughts are in his hands. Fortunate is the king whose ministers know what he does, with respect to dharma, artha and kama, only after he has acted. The king whose counsels are kept close, and with complete faith, has success.

He who commits reprehensible deeds from ignorance loses his life because of unexpected consequences of those actions. Commendable deeds are always followed by peace of mind, and their omission leads to repentance.

Just as a Brahmana who has no Vedic learning is not fit to officiate at a Sraddha, so too, the king who is ignorant of the six ways of protecting his kingdom is not fit to engage in politics. The king who monitors the increase, decrease and surplus to his revenue, who is familiar with the six ways of protecting his kingdom, who has self-knowledge and whose conduct is always praised brings the whole world under his rule. The king whose anger and joy always produce results, who personally oversees all activity in his kingdom and who keeps his treasury under his own control brings the very earth under subjection.

A king should be content with the name he wins and the royal parasol that is held over his head. He should divide the wealth of the kingdom among those that serve him and not keep everything for himself.

A Brahmana knows a Brahmana, a husband understands the wife, a king knows his minister, and monarchs know monarchs. An enemy who deserves death should never be set free once he is subdued. If a man is weak and he deserves death, he should pay court to his enemies who are stronger than him. However, one must kill such an enemy as soon as one is powerful enough, for otherwise the enemy will become dangerous.

A man should make an effort to control his anger against gods, kings, Brahmanas, old men, children and the helpless. The wise man should avoid unprofitable quarrels, in which only fools get involved. Thus one wins great fame in this world and avoids suffering and sorrow.

The people never want for their master a man whose grace is without favour and whose anger is ineffective, just as a woman never wants a eunuch for a husband. Intelligence does not result in the acquisition of wealth nor idleness in adversity.

Only the wise man knows what causes conditions on Earth to be so diverse. The fool, Bhaarata, always ignores his elders, those eminent in their conduct, the learned, the intelligent, the wealthy and the noble. Calamities befall those that are wicked, ignorant, filled with envy, sinful, foul-tongued and prone to anger. On the contrary, absence of deceitfulness, generosity, the observance of decorum, and controlled speech give a man domination over all creatures.

The man who is straightforward, active, grateful, intelligent and guileless wins friends, advisors and servants, even if his coffers are empty. Intelligence, tranquillity of mind, self-control, purity, refraining from harsh speech and the unwillingness to do anything unpleasant to friends are qualities that fan the flame of prosperity.

A man must avoid the wretched fellow who does not give others their due, who has an evil soul and is ungrateful and shameless. The guilty man who provokes suspicion about an innocent one cannot sleep peacefully at night, like a man in a room with a snake in it. A man must propitiate, as he would the gods, those who, when angry, put one's possessions and means of acquiring them in jeopardy. Success is doubtful for goals that depend upon women, careless persons, men who do not follow the dharma of their varna and those who are evil.

Like a stone raft has no choice but to sink, so do men who let a woman, a deceitful person or a child guide them. Those who are experts at something look down on men who are generally competent but have no particular skill. A man whom swindlers, actors and women of bad character speak highly of might as well be dead.

Bhaarata, you have forsaken the sons of Pandu, those Kshatriyas of immeasurable energy, and entrusted care of this mighty empire to Duryodhana. You will soon see your burgeoning prosperity falling away, as Bali did from Swarga.'"

CANTO 39

PRAJAGARA PARVA CONTINUED

"Dhritarashtra says, 'Man has no control over his own prosperity or adversity. He is like a wooden string-puppet, and God subjects him to destiny. Go on speaking; I am listening attentively to everything you say.'

Vidura says, 'Bhaarata, words spoken at the inappropriate time, even by Brihaspati, are considered ignorant and reprehensible. There are three ways for a man to become popular—giving gifts, speaking sweet words and using spells and narcotics. However, the man who is naturally likeable is always so.

In the eyes of one who hates him, a man is always dishonest, stupid and foolish. A man attributes everything good to him whom he loves and everything bad to him that he hates.

O king, I told you on Duryodhana's birth that you should do away with this one son, for, by that, you would ensure the prosperity of the rest of the hundred of them; and that by keeping him, you would doom them all. One should never give importance to a gain that leads to loss. One must, instead, place great store by a loss that will eventually bring gain. It is no loss which results in gain; only the loss that begets greater losses is a real loss.

Some gain eminence because of their good qualities, others because they are wealthy. Dhritarashtra, keep away from the wealthy man who lacks dharma.'

Dhritarashtra says, 'You speak wisely and for my good, but I dare not abandon my son. Let us reassure ourselves with the conviction that victory and dharma go hand in hand.'

Vidura says, 'Those who are humble and graced with every virtue are always sensitive to the least suffering of living beings; but those who spend their time speaking ill of others always look for opportunities to quarrel with them and to inflict pain. It is wrong to accept gifts from, or to give to, those whose very presence is inauspicious and whose companionship is fraught with danger.

Those who are contentious, covetous, shameless and deceitful are without dharma, and one should avoid being with them. One should also avoid those who have other serious flaws in their character. When the circumstances which created the friendship end, one must end friendly relations with those of bad character; the good that comes from that connection, and the happiness, come to an end. Such men will then speak ill of the man who was their friend and try to make him suffer losses and be unhappy if the loss is small. Lacking control over themselves, they cannot find peace. The learned man will carefully and objectively analyse everything and shun the friendship of such evil-minded ones.

The man who helps his poor and helpless relatives will have children and animals, and will enjoy unending prosperity. Those who want their own good should always help their relatives. Therefore, Rajan, work for the glory of your great vamsa in any way you can. You will prosper if you treat all your kinsmen well and protect even those who are destitute of virtue.

Bharatarishabha, think about how much more they, who are blessed with goodness and humbly await your favour, deserve your protection. Grace the heroic sons of Pandu with your favour and give them some part of the kingdom for their livelihood. This will bring you fame in this world. You are old. You should control your sons; that alone will benefit you.

Know that I am your well-wisher. The man who wants his own good must never have enmity with his kin. Happiness must always be shared and enjoyed with one's family, and not without them. Relatives should always eat together, talk with one another and love each other; they must never fall out. It is kinsmen who come to your rescue, and kinsmen who ruin you. The righteous ones are the ones who come to your help, while the sinful ones let you down.

O, you who are the giver of honours, use dharma in your dealings with the sons of Pandu. Surrounded by them, you will be invincible.

If a man shrinks in the presence of a prosperous kinsman, like a deer at the sight of a hunter armed with arrows, then the prosperous relative will absorb the sins of the other. Purushottama, you will regret your present course, of doing nothing to prevent a war, when you hear of the deaths of the Pandavas or your sons.

O, think of this: when life itself is uncertain, one should from the start avoid any awful deed that will plunge one into a world of fear and grief and give cause for irremediable regret later. It is true that anyone, other than Bhargava who authored the Dharmashastra, is likely, at one time or other, to sin. Intelligent men understand the justness of the consequences of their crimes.

As an elder of the Kuruvamsa, it is your duty to undo all the wrongs that Duryodhana inflicted on the Pandavas. By reinstating them to their rightful position you will be cleansed of all your sins in this world and be worshipped even by enlightened souls. The man who acts after carefully reflecting on what wise men say about the inexorable fruit of karma never loses renown.

Wisdom imparted by knowledgeable men is imperfect if misunderstood, or if understood but not put into practice. The learned man who never does anything that will result in sin and sorrow always grows in prosperity. The heedless, evil man, who stubbornly pursues the sinful course he has embarked on, falls into a deep mire.

The wise man must always be aware of these six ways by which his plans become known, and if he wants success and a lasting dynasty, he will be on his guard against them. They are intoxication, sleep, heedlessness of spies, one's own demeanour which reflects one's thoughts and confidence placed in evil-hearted advisors and inept representatives. The man who knows of these six doors through which secrets can slip out, who keeps them shut while conducting his life in dharma, artha and kama, succeeds in outwitting his enemies.

Even Brihaspati cannot win dharma or artha if he has no knowledge of the Shastras and if he does not serve the elderly. As anything cast into the sea is lost are words spoken into the ears of one who does not listen. The Shastras are lost on one who does not have his emotions under control. An offering of ghee is wasted if poured over the ashes of an extinguished fire.

The man who is blessed with intelligence forges friendships with the wise, having first used his intelligence to examine, his understanding to investigate and his ears to hear what others who have known and seen the man say about him, and then by relying on his own discernment. Humility prevents humiliation; prowess ends adversity; forgiveness conquers anger; and dharma neutralises evil omens.

Rajan, a man's lineage is judged by the things he enjoys, his place of birth, his home, his demeanour, his food and dress. Even a man who has attained spiritual freedom is tempted to indulge in pleasure, let alone the man who is still a slave to his desires. A king should treasure a minister who reveres the wise; who is blessed with knowledge and virtue; who has a pleasant appearance, good friends, sweet speech and a good heart.

Whether he is of low or high birth, the man who does not break the rules of polite conversation, who is conscious of dharma and who is humble and modest is superior to a hundred men of noble lineage. The friendship of men, whose hearts, private lives, pleasures and acquisitions are in complete accord with one's own, never cools.

The intelligent man should avoid an ignorant and evil man even like a deep pit covered by grass, for friendship with such a man is short-lived and dangerous. The wise man should never make a friend of one who is proud, ignorant, fierce or reckless and who has strayed from the path of dharma. One should want for a friend the man who is grateful, virtuous, truthful, large-hearted and devoted, and one who has his senses under control, who preserves his dignity and never forsakes a friend.

While the detachment of the senses from their objects is like death, excessive indulgence of the senses would ruin even the gods. Learned men say that humility, love of all creatures, forgiveness and respect for friends lengthen one's life. The wise say that the man who, with determination, uses means of dharma to accomplish goals that have been thwarted possesses real manhood. The man who knows of all the remedies that may be applied in the future, who is firmly resolved in the present time and who can predict at the start the result of his actions attains all his goals.

That which a man follows in thought, word and action wins him for itself; therefore, a man should always seek what is truly good for him. After achieving this, many other factors make a man prosper: effort, timely action in the right place, the means to do so, knowledge of the Shastras, diligent work, honesty and frequent contact with the good.

Perseverance is the key to prosperity, achievement and all that is beneficial. The man who pursues his goal with perseverance, without giving up in impatience, is great; and he will enjoy everlasting happiness. Then, O king, there is the quality of mercy; nothing promotes happiness, nothing is more appropriate for a powerful man than forgiveness, anywhere and always. The weak man must be forgiving under all circumstances; the mighty should show forgiveness, keeping dharma in mind; but forgiveness comes naturally to the man who is detached from the success or failure of his endeavours.

One must pursue, to the fullest extent, pleasure that does not go against dharma and artha. However, one should not be a fool and indulge one's senses indiscriminately. Prosperity never attaches itself to a man who tortures himself with grief; nor to one who is addicted to evil, who is an atheist or idle; nor to one whose senses are uncontrolled; nor to one who makes no effort. The humble man's modesty is mistaken for weakness, and the deluded persecute him.

Prosperity fearfully avoids the man who is too honest, who gives without limit, who is too brave or who is vain about his wisdom. She stays neither with the man who is highly accomplished nor with one who is not in the least so. She does not prefer a conjunction of all the virtues, nor is she pleased with their complete absence. At random, like a mad cow that cannot be steered, prosperity blindly finds her home.

The result of studying the Vedas is the performance of the homa; the fruits of knowing the Shastras are good manners and good conduct; the fruits of women are the pleasures of intercourse and children; and the consequence of wealth is the pleasure of doing charity.

He that performs rituals, with ill-gotten wealth, for his good in the next world does not enjoy the usual fruits of such rites because of the means by which the wealth used for this purpose was acquired. The man who has strength of mind knows no fear, not in the midst of the desert, in forests or other inaccessible fastnesses; not amidst dangers, crises or in the face of deadly weapons raised against him. Prosperity is born out of effort, self-control, skill, meticulousness, steadiness, a good memory and mature deliberation before any action.

Tapasya is the strength of tapasvins; the Vedas are the strength of scholars; envy is the strength of evil men; and in forgiveness lies the strength of the virtuous. Eight things could never negate a vow: water, roots, fruit, milk, ghee, obliging a Brahmana's request, obeying a guru's command and good medicine.

One should never do to others anything that is against one's own self-interest. This is virtue. There are other kinds of virtue, but these issue from caprice. Anger must be conquered by forgiveness, evil by dharma, the miser by generosity, and falsehood by truth.

One must not trust a woman, a swindler, an idler, a coward, a vicious man, one who boasts of his own power, a thief, an ingrate and an atheist. The man who is respectful of his elders and serves the elderly will always see the growth of his achievements, longevity, fame and power.

Do not set your heart on things that can be acquired only through painful exertion, at the cost of dharma or by bowing down to an enemy. A man without knowledge is pitiable, as is intercourse that does not bear fruit, and also the people of a kingdom who have no food and a kingdom without a king. These cause pain and debility in the living. Rain erodes hills and mountains; the absence of enjoyment gives women anguish; and sharp words wound the heart like arrows.

The worst thing for the Vedas is not to study them, and for Brahmanas it is not to observe vratas; the worst beings on Earth are the Bahlikas; the worst characteristic in a man is falsehood and in the chaste woman, curiosity; and the worst condition for a woman is to be away from her home. The worst part of gold is silver; of silver, tin; of tin, lead; and of lead, grit. One cannot conquer sleep by lying down, women by desire, fire by fuel and wine by drinking. The crown of success rests on the man who has won over his friends by gifts, his foes by battle and his wife with food and drink.

Those who have a hundred possessions are just as alive as those who have a thousand. O Dhritarashtra, renounce your greed for excessive possessions. There is no one who cannot live within the considerable means you own. All the paddy, wheat, gold, animals and women on Earth cannot satiate even one man. A wise man reflects on this and does not grieve for want of owning everything. Rajan, I say to you again, treat your children equally—your sons and Pandu's.'"

CANTO 40

Prajagara Parva continued

"Vidura says, 'The good man will win fame by abandoning pride and pursuing his goals. He must take care not to overstep the limits of his power because honourable men can make the man who pleases them happy.

The man who voluntarily gives up something, even if it is magnificent, because it is charged with adharma lives happily and shakes off his enemies, like a snake shedding its skin. A victory won by a lie, by treachery towards the king and by insincerity towards one's elders is equal to the sin of killing a Brahmana.

Envy, death and boastfulness destroy prosperity. Carelessness in serving one's elders, undue haste and vanity are the three enemies of knowledge. Idleness, inattention, mental turmoil, restlessness, passing time idly with friends, hauteur, pride and jealousy are particular shortcomings of students. How can they that seek pleasure gain knowledge? Students cannot pursue learning and, at the same time, indulge themselves. Devotees of pleasure must give up knowledge, and those who seek knowledge must first abjure pleasure.

Fire can never have enough fuel; the mighty ocean can never receive enough water from the rivers that feed it; Death cannot be satiated even by devouring all living creatures; and a beautiful woman can never have too many men around her.

Hope kills patience; Yama kills growth; anger kills prosperity; miserliness kills fame; neglect kills cattle; and the anger of just one Brahmana destroys an entire kingdom. Ensure the presence of goats, brass, silver, honey, antidotes to poison, birds, Brahmanas versed in the Vedas, aged kinsmen and impoverished noblemen in your house.

Bhaarata, Manu has said that for the worship of the gods one must always have these in one's house: goats, bulls, sandalwood, flutes, mirrors, honey, ghee, iron, copper, conch-shells, salagramas and gorochana, Brahmanas and guests. All these are auspicious.

I will tell you of another sacred lesson, more exalted than these, one which will bear great fruit: virtue should never be forsaken from desire, fear or temptation, and not for life itself. Dharma is everlasting; pleasure and pain are transitory; indeed life itself is everlasting but transitory in each phase. Abandon the transitory and devote yourself to the permanent; and contentment, that best of all blessings, will be yours.

See how illustrious and mighty kings, having ruled lands abounding in wealth and corn, have fallen to Yama, leaving behind their kingdoms and vast fonts of enjoyment. When the child who is nurtured with loving care dies, weeping and wild-haired men carry his body in grief to the smasana and throw it onto the pyre, where it burns as if it were just another log of wood. Others enjoy a dead man's wealth, while birds and fire feast on his body. Only two things accompany him into the next world: his punya and his paapa. After discarding his body his kinsmen go home, even as birds abandon a tree that has no flowers or fruit.

The one cast into the funeral pyre takes with him only his own deeds. Therefore, men should carefully and purposefully earn punya for themselves. In the worlds above and below ours are regions of terrible darkness, O king, where men's senses suffer great torture. Do not allow yourself to go to there.

If you listen attentively to me and act accordingly, great fame will be yours in this mortal world, and you will never have fear now or hereafter. The soul is like a river; deeds of punya are its sacred tirthas; truth, its water; self-control, its banks; and kindness, its waves. The righteous man purifies himself by bathing in it, for the soul is scared, and the absence of desire is the highest merit. Life is a river whose waters are the five senses, and whose crocodiles and sharks are desire and anger. Make self-control the raft by which you cross its eddies, which are your repeated births.

The man who worships and pleases friends, who are wise, virtuous, knowledgeable and mature in years, is never misguided by the advice they give him. A man must restrain lust and hunger with patience, his hands and feet with his eyes, his eyes and ears with his mind and his mind and speech with his conduct.

The Brahmana who unfailingly performs his ritual ablutions, who always wears his sacred thread, who never neglects his Vedic studies, who avoids unclean food, who always tells the truth and who honours his guru by his actions never falls from Brahmaloka. The Kshatriya who studies the Vedas, who makes offerings to Agni, who performs yagnas, who protects his subjects, who has purified his soul by arming himself with weapons in order to safeguard Brahmanas and his cattle and who dies on the field of battle attains Swarga. The Vaisya who distributes his wealth among Brahmanas, Kshatriyas and his own dependants at the appropriate time, and who breathes the sanctified smoke of the three kinds of fires gains joy in the other world. The Sudra who worships Brahmanas, Kshatriyas and Vaisyas as is their due; who has washed away his sins by gratifying them; and who peacefully casts off his mortal body enjoys celestial bliss.

This is the dharma of the four varnas. Now listen to the reason I have told you all this. Yudhishtira has been unable to fulfil his Kshatriya dharma. You must place him in a position that he may discharge his kingly duties, Rajan.'

Dhritarashtra says, 'What you teach me is always right, and I, too, am inclined to do as you say. Although, in keeping with your advice, my heart moves towards the Pandavas, it veers in a different direction as soon as I see Duryodhana. No one can avert fate, which will always take its course; and I think individual effort is futile.'"

CANTO 41

SANAT SUJATA PARVA

"Dhritarashtra says, 'O Vidura, if there is anything you have not told me, tell me now, for I am eager to listen. Your words delight my heart.'

Vidura says, 'Dhritarashtra, the ancient and immortal Rishi Sanat Sujata, who was a celibate all his life, said that there is no death. That most brilliant of all men will clear every doubt you have.'

Dhritarashtra says, 'Do you not know what the deathless Rishi would say to me? You can advise me as well as he would; you have as much wisdom.'

Vidura says, 'I am a Sudra by birth and cannot say more than I have already said. The wisdom and knowledge of that Brahmarishi is infinite. A man who is born a Brahmana does not incur the disapproval of the gods, even when he expounds the most profound mysteries. This is why I will speak no more to you on this matter.'

Dhritarashtra says, 'Tell me, Vidura, how I, in my mortal body, can meet this immortal and ancient one.'

Vidura meditates on that Rishi of stern vratas and, knowing that he was thought of, the sage appears. Vidura receives him reverently with the ordained rites and when, after a brief rest, Sanat Sujata is seated at his ease, Vidura says to him, 'O illustrious one, Dhritarashtra has doubts which I am not able to clear. I beg you to do what I cannot. He might then overcome his sorrow, which stems from being confused about gain and loss, what is agreeable and disagreeable, old age and death, fear and jealousy, hunger and thirst, pride and prosperity, dislike, sleep, lust, wrath, decrease and increase.'"

CANTO 42

SANAT SUJATA PARVA CONTINUED

"Vaisampayana said, 'Dhritarashtra applauds what Vidura says and, eager to obtain the highest knowledge, puts his questions to Sanat Sujata without speaking.

In his mind the king asks the Rishi, 'O Sanat Sujata, I hear that you believe there is no death. On the other hand, it is said that Devas and Asuras practise austere tapasya in order to avoid death. Which of these two is true?'

Sanat Sujata says, 'Some say that death can be averted by specific karma; others are of the opinion that there is no death. You have asked me which of these is true. Listen to me, O king, while I tell you about this, so that your doubts are removed.

Kshatriya, both of these are true. The learned are of opinion that death results from ignorance. I say that ignorance is death. Thus, knowledge is immortality.

It is from ignorance that the Asuras became subject to defeat and death, and it is from the absence of ignorance that the Devas attained Brahman. Death does not devour, as a tiger does; its form cannot be known.

Some imagine Yama to be Death, deluded as they are by their weak minds. Immortality lies in the search for self-knowledge, the eternal Brahman. That imaginary Deva, Yama, rules over the realm of the Pitrs; he is the source of joy to the virtuous and a scourge to sinners. It is at his command that death walks among men, in the form of wrath, ignorance and covetousness.

Swayed by pride, men walk the ways of dharma, and none amongst such men attains Atmagyana. With darkened minds and led by their passions, when they cast off their mortal bodies they fall into Naraka, over and over, and their unruly senses follow them always. That is why ignorance goes by the name of death. So, death also attaches to men who want the fruit of their actions. When the time for enjoying these fruit comes, they cannot avoid death. They leave their mortal bodies and go to Swargaloka. Men who do not desire to see the fruit of their deeds also go to Swarga when they leave their bodies; but for them there is no death.

Creatures with physical bodies are caught in a cycle of birth and re-birth in varying states because of their inability to attain Brahman and due to their attachment to worldly enjoyment. Man has a natural inclination towards pursuits that seek illusory goals, and this is the single cause of his senses being led astray. The soul that is led towards illusions remembers only that with which it is constantly occupied and, so, worships only the mundane pleasures that surround it. The desire for pleasure is the first cause of death for man; lust and anger come next. It is these three—craving for pleasure, lust and anger—that lead foolish men to death.

Those who have conquered their souls by self-restraint escape death. The man who has restrained his soul without falling prey to his ambitious desires subdues them; self-knowledge reveals their worthlessness to him. Ignorance, in the form of Yama, cannot overcome the learned man who controls his passions.

The man who follows his desires is destroyed along with his desires. However, the man who can renounce desire can keep grief away, whatever form it may take. Desire is ignorance; it is darkness and hell for all creatures, for, swayed by it they lose control of their senses. Just as drunken men walking along a street reel towards ruts and holes, so too, men intoxicated by desire and lured by illusory joys stagger headlong towards their downfall.

What can death do to a man whose soul has not been led by desire? For him death holds no terrors; it is like a straw tiger. Kshatriya, if you want to destroy desire, which is ignorance, you must not dwell on or pursue even the smallest wish.

Your soul, which is in your body, enmeshed as it is in wrath and covetousness, is filled with ignorance, which is death. Realising that death comes in this way, the man who relies on knowledge need have no fear of it. Indeed, as surely as death destroys the body, knowledge destroys death.'

Dhritarashtra says, 'The Vedas say that the sacred and eternal realms that Dvijas can attain through prayer and sacrifice offer emancipation. Why then should a learned man not perform such karma?'

Sanat Sujata says, 'It is true that the man who has no knowledge can take the path you mention, and what the Vedas say about bliss and moksha being there is also true. The man who has given up all material wants attains Brahman at once; but even the man who confuses the physical body with the Atman attains Brahman, if he is able to renounce desire. If, however, one seeks mukti without destroying desire, one has to go step by step along the prescribed path, leaving every step he takes irrevocably behind oneself and being careful not to have to retrace one's way.'

Dhritarashtra says, 'Who is it that stimulates the Unborn and Ancient One into action? If He is this universe because he is present in everything, what form do action and happiness take for him who is without desire? Tejasvin Rishi, speak to me of this.'

Sanat Sujata says, 'You should not think of two essentially different things as being one. Creatures come into being by the union of the Purusha with Prakriti, both of which have no beginning, like time.

This in no way lessens the supremacy and importance of the unborn and all-pervading Brahman. Men, too, have their origin in the same Supreme Being. All that appears to you is nothing but that everlasting Paramatman. Indeed, the universe is created by the transformations that the Supreme Soul goes through.

The Vedas say that the Paramatman has the power to transform Himself, and by that, causes transformations in this world.'

Dhritarashtra says, 'Some practise dharma; some do not, but renounce all action and take sannyasa. Does virtue destroy vice, or is it destroyed by vice?'

Sanat Sujata says, 'The fruits of virtue and of perfect stillness, or inaction, can both be used to attain moksha. The wise man succeeds by gyana, knowledge; the worldly man acquires punya through karma, action, but in the process he also acquires paapa, sin.

After earning the transitory fruits of both virtue and vice and existing for a limited time in Swarga or Naraka the man of karma is involuntarily drawn to a life of action because of his previous karma. The wiser amongst such men exorcises his sins by his acts of dharma; dharma is powerful and is the path to moksha.'

Dhritarashtra says, 'Tell me about those eternal realms, in the order of their importance, that Dvijas attain as a result of following their svadharma. Tell me about other, similar realms. Learned one, I do not wish to hear of man's nature, sinful and condemnable as it is.'

Sanat Sujata says, 'The Dvijas who have good reason to be proud of their skills at Yoga, as strong men are of their physique, shine in Brahmaloka when they leave this world. Those Dvijas who can take pride in their knowledge and the pure performance of yagnas and Vedic rites attain Devaloka when they are freed from their mortal lives. There are Vedic scholars who believe that the performance of yagnas will lead to moksha. They, too, seek Atmagyana but place undue emphasis on rituals. They are not worthy of the highest respect.

The Yogi should seek his sustenance in a place where sattvik food and drink is abundant, like grass during the rainy season, rather than being a burden on a householder of scanty means. By no means, however, should he suffer from hunger or thirst.

In a situation where revealing one's superiority is fraught with uncertainties, the man who does not do so is more praiseworthy than the one who does. Wise men approve of the food offered by a man who is not offended by one who makes his superiority known and who never eats without first having offered a proper share to Brahmanas and Sadasyas. Just as a dog sickens because it eats its own vomit, so, too, do Yogins who get their sustenance by making their superiority obvious.

Wise men recognise as a Brahmana the man who practices his religion discreetly, so that even his family, in whose midst he lives, is unaware of it. Only such a Brahmana is worthy of realising Brahman, who is formless, unchangeable, singular and without duality. By similar conduct a Kshatriya, too, can realise Brahman as being within himself. He who takes his Soul to be his doing, feeling self sins by robbing the Atman of its true attributes.

A Brahmana should never try too hard or accept gifts; he should earn the respect of men of dharma; he should be quiet and modest about his Vedic knowledge. Only then will he gain Atmagyana and attain the Brahman. He who is poor in material wealth but rich in punya and sacrifices, becomes unconquerable and fearless; and he is Brahman embodied.

The man who performs yagnas and succeeds in invoking the Devas and having them grant his wishes is a lesser man than one who knows that Brahman is the real performer of his yagnas; the former realises Brahman by effort, whereas the latter attains Him with ease. The man whom the Devas respect, though he does nothing for it, is truly honoured; the respect bestowed by men is not true honour. The lack of the honour of men is no cause for grief.

People generally act unthinkingly according to their natures, as involuntarily as they blink their eyes. It is only the learned who respect other men, and the man who receives respect should be aware of this. Men who are foolish, inclined towards sin and deceitful, never respect those who are worthy; in fact they go out of their way to be disrespectful.

The esteem of the world and the ascetic vow of silence, mowna vrata, can never go together. This world is enjoyed by men who want esteem, while the other world is for those who keep the vow of silence. In this world, Kshatriya, happiness rests in worldly prosperity, which is actually an obstacle to moksha, eternal bliss. Heavenly prosperity cannot be had by one who is not truly wise.

Wise men say that there are several closely guarded gates that are portals to moksha. They are truth, integrity, humility, self-control, purity of mind and conduct, and Vedic knowledge. These six portals destroy vanity and ignorance as one passes through them.'"

CANTO 43

SANAT SUJATA PARVA CONTINUED

"Dhritarashtra says, 'What is the purpose of the mowna vrata? Which of its two kinds do you approve of—not speaking or dhyana? Learned one, tell me about true mowna. Can a learned man attain a state of stillness and freedom by practising it? Muni, how should it be practised?'

Sanat Sujata says, 'Veda gyana, even if acquired with concentration and discipline, cannot reach the Paramatman; therefore Brahman itself is known as mowna. It is from mowna that the Vedic sound AUM and other ordinary sounds have been born; it is the Supreme Word, O king.'

Dhritarashtra says, 'Is the man who knows the Rig, Yajur and Sama Vedas tainted by any sins he may commit?'

Sanat Sujata says, 'A man who has not controlled his senses cannot escape from his sins by virtue of his knowledge of the Rig, Yajur or Sama Vedas. The Vedas never rescue a false man who lives by deceit; on the other hand, they forsake him at his end, like fledglings leaving their nests.'

Dhritarashtra says, 'O you who have restrained your senses, if, as you say, the Vedas cannot save a man from the consequence of his sins, then why do Brahmanas labour under the delusion that the Vedas destroy sin?'

Sanat Sujata says, 'Although this universe has been born from the Brahman uniting with the gunas—attributes such as name and form, the Vedas stress that it is distinct from them. Mowna and yagnas are prescribed for the attainment of Brahman, and they are the means by which a learned man acquires dharma. Sin is destroyed by virtue and the soul is enlightened by knowledge.

It is with the help of knowledge that a learned man realises Brahman. The man of little wisdom covets the four material goals and takes the fruits of these with him into the next world. There he dwells and enjoys these fruits for a limited time and, because they are only short-lived, he comes back into this world of karma. The worldly fruits of mowna are enjoyed by those who have not restrained their souls; but those who have, enjoy fruits of the other worlds as well.'

Dhritarashtra says, 'Muni, how can the same ascetic austerities be sometimes successful and sometimes not? Tell us how this is so.'

Sanat Sujata says, 'Mowna that is not corrupted by desire or other failings is successful and results in moksha; the aspirant succeeds. The answers to all your questions touch the very roots of tapasya. It is with gyana and mowna that learned men realise Brahman and live forever.'

Dhritarashtra said, 'I now know the eternal mystery, with the understanding you have given me about the mowna that is untainted by defects. Tell me now, Sanat Sujata, about mowna that is marred by faults.'

Sanat Sujata says, 'Twelve human vices mar the effectiveness of mowna: anger, lust, avarice, ignorance of right and wrong, discontentment, cruelty, jealousy, vanity, grief, love of pleasure, envy, and speaking ill of others. Manavarishabha, a man should take care to avoid these twelve, for any one of them by itself can destroy him. Indeed, every one of these vices waits for its opportunity, like a hunter in ambush for a deer.

There are six forms of evil that sinful men practise, which make them arrogantly fearless of dangers in this world and the next: boasting about one's own superiority, enjoying the wives of other men, humiliating others, anger, fickleness and refusing to maintain those who deserve it.

These seven kinds of men—the man who makes the gratification of lust his main aim in life, one who is haughty, one who regrets the gifts he gives, the man who is miserly, one who oppresses his people with excessive taxes, one who delights in the humiliation of others and the man who hates his own wives—are also evil.

Twelve are the true attributes of a Brahmana's way of life: righteousness, non-violence, truthfulness of speech, self-restraint, asceticism, joy in the happiness of others, modesty, forbearance, love of others, sacrifices, gifts, perseverance and knowledge of the Shastras. The man who acquires these twelve earns the power to control the Earth. A man who has three, or two, or even one of these can consider that he has reached his goal. Moksha lies in self-restraint, renunciation and Atmagyana. Wise Brahmanas say that these attributes are founded in truth.

There are eighteen defects that, if avoided, pave the way for a man to achieve self-control: non-performance of the prescribed rituals from laziness, falsehood, malice, lust, wealth, love of sensual pleasure, anger, grief, thirst, avarice, deceit, joy in the misery of others, envy, injuring others, regret, aversion to piety, forgetfulness of duty, speaking ill of others and vanity. These eighteen faults constitute mada, pride.

Renunciation is of six kinds, and the opposite of these six are also definitions of mada, making the total number twenty-four. All six kinds of renunciation are good; only the third is difficult to practise, but by it a man overcomes all sorrow. In fact, the man who is accomplished in this form of renunciation transcends the pairs of opposites, like joy and sorrow, pleasure and pain.

O king, the first kind of renunciation is not feeling joy on gaining prosperity; the second is giving up non-performance of yagnas and prayers; the third is the abandonment of desire, or withdrawing from the world. As a result of this third kind, one renounces the objects of enjoyment without having enjoyed them, not after knowing them; nor does one relinquish an acquisition after acquiring it and having no appetite for it.

The fourth kind of renunciation is not to allow oneself to grieve at the failure of one's efforts even those made using dharma and artha, wealth. It is to feel no pain when something unpleasant happens. The fifth kind of renunciation is to not ask for anything from anyone, even sons, wives and other dear ones. The sixth kind is to give to a deserving person who asks, which always brings punya. These five enable Atmagyana or Self-knowledge.

The last kind of renunciation has eight characteristics: truth, meditation, the ability to distinguish subject from object, the capacity to draw inferences, withdrawal from the world, never taking what belongs to another, adherence to brahmacharya—the vow of celibacy, and not accepting charity.

In the same way as renunciation has characteristics, so, too, are defects characteristic of mada, which is the opposite of dama—self-restraint—that the Shastras elucidate. These faults should be avoided. I have told you about renunciation and self-knowledge. Just as self-knowledge has eight virtues, the want of it has eight faults. Those should also be avoided.

Bhaarata, the man who is liberated from his five senses, the intellect, the past and the future becomes happy. Let your soul be devoted to truth; all the worlds are established in truth. Truth is also the first attribute of self-control, renunciation and self-knowledge. Avoid these faults and practise mowna. Brahman has ordained that truth alone should be the vow of the righteous. Mowna that is dissociated from these faults and endowed with the virtues becomes the source of great prosperity.

I have now told you in brief about the sin-destroying and sacred subject which liberates a man from the cycle of birth, old age and death.'

Dhritarashtra says, 'The fifth Veda, the Akhyana, says that the Supreme Soul is the universe. Others recognise four Vedas, while some recognise three, some two and some only one. Then there are those who acknowledge Brahman alone as the one thing that exists, everything else having its existence in Him. Tell me, which of these has true knowledge of Brahman?'

Sanat Sujata says, 'There is but one Brahman, who is Truth. It is from ignorance of that One that men have conceived several Vedas. But who is there, O king, who has attained Brahman, that Absolute Truth?

Without knowing that One object of knowledge that they ought to, men think they have gained wisdom. From the hope of gaining happiness they engage in study and practice daana and perform yagnas. The purposes of such men, who have strayed from Truth, match their condition; they rely on the Vedic texts as the Truth and so emptily perform their yagna and daana.

Some perform and attain the object of sacrifices by dhyana, meditation; some by chanting prayers, japa; some by the completion of the yatishtoma and other costly rites. However, the man who seeks Brahman through Truth gets what he wants, in his very home.

When a man's objectives are aborted by lack of Atmagyana he must adopt vows such as mowna vrata and diksha vrata. In fact, the word diksha is its own root, and it means observance of vratas. For those who have attained Atmagyana, Truth is the highest object of their pursuit.

The fruits of gyana are visible; the fruits of mowna are only enjoyed in the hereafter. A Brahmana who, without gyana and mowna, has read much should only be regarded as a great reader; never assume that a man can be a Brahmagyani—one who knows Brahman—merely by reading the Shastras. Know, on the other hand, that the true Brahmana is one who never deviates from the Truth.

O Kshatriya, the verses that were recited in olden times by Atharvan to a conclave of Maharishis are also called the Chhandas. Those who have read the Vedas but do not have knowledge of the One Being, that should follow, must not be considered as having acquired true Vedic knowledge. The Chhandas are the independent means of attaining Brahman without the need for doing anything else. Those who are only acquainted with the modes of sacrifice prescribed in the Vedas cannot be regarded as knowing the Vedas. On the other hand, those who have served men with true Vedic knowledge have as good as attained knowledge of the One Being that Veda gyana leads to.

There is no one quality of the intellect that can help a man acquire the true meaning of the Vedas, nor can all the qualities of the intellect; yet there may be some few men who have grasped it. Whatever might happen, the man who has only read them does not gain knowledge of the One Being that can be known through knowing the Vedas; it is the man who is firmly established in the Truth who knows Him.

There are no qualities, which delude men to perceive the physical body as the Self, that can lead to Atmagyana. A man's intellect alone cannot help him distinguish the Self from the not-Self. He who knows the Self also knows what is not-Self; but he who knows only what is not-Self does not know Truth.

He who knows the proofs knows that which he seeks to prove, but neither Vedic knowledge nor the Vedas themselves can perceive its true nature. But Brahmanas who have true knowledge of the Vedas succeed in knowing the One Being that a study of the Vedas can lead to.

Just as the twig of a particular tree is sometimes used for indicating the day of the new moon, the Vedas are used for indicating the highest attributes of the Paramatman. In my opinion, a Brahmana, or one who knows Brahman, is one who explains men's doubts, having first cleared his own; he is one who has true knowledge of his Self, Atmagyana.

You cannot find the Atman by searching in the East, South, West, North or in subsidiary cardinal directions, or even laterally. Very rarely can the man who thinks his body is the Self find Atman. Beyond the conception of even the Vedas, the man of Yoga dhyana can behold the Supreme Being. Completely restrain all your senses and your mind and seek Brahman who resides in your own soul.

A man is no Muni who practises dhyana in silence, nor is he one who retires from the world and lives in the forest; a Muni is the man who knows his true nature.

A man is said to be a Vaiyakarana, or grammarian, who can trace every word to its root and explain it—Vyakarana. Every word has its root in Brahman. The man who sees all the Lokas before his eyes knows everything; the man who is established in Truth and knows Brahman is a real Brahmana; and a Brahmana possesses universal knowledge.

A Kshatriya who practises Brahmana dharma also beholds Brahman. He can also attain to that supreme state by going step by step in accordance to the teachings of the Vedas. I know all this for certain; and that is why I tell it to you.'"

CANTO 44

SANAT SUJATA PARVA CONTINUED

"Dhritarashtra says, 'O Sanat Sujata, what you say of Brahman and the origin of the universe is illuminating indeed and lightens my heart. Tell me more of such things that are not to do with worldly pursuits and, so, not common among men.'

Sanat Sujata says, 'Brahman, about which you ask me so joyfully, cannot be attained in a hurry. After you have restrained your senses, when conscious thought is merged in pure intellect, the state that succeeds is one of utter absence of worldly thought. That condition is true knowledge and leads to the realisation of Brahman. It can be attained only by practising brahmacharya.'

Dhritarashtra says, 'You say that the mind is where knowledge of Brahman naturally resides, being discovered only through brahmacharya; that, dwelling in the mind, it needs no effort to manifest itself; and that this happens whilst one seeks it through brahmacharya. How then is immortality associated with the attainment of Brahman?'

Sanat Sujata says, 'Though dwelling in and inherent to the mind, the knowledge of Brahman is still unmanifest. Pure intellect and brahmacharya are needed to make it emerge into consciousness. Then, having attained that knowledge, Yogis forsake this world naturally. True gyana is found among great gurus. I will tell you now about this knowledge.'

Dhritarashtra says, 'What should be the nature of brahmacharya by which the knowledge of Brahman might be attained without too much difficulty? Dvijottama, tell me this.'

Sanat Sujata says, 'Those who live in the asramas of their gurus, who win their goodwill and friendship and who practise austere celibacy become earthly embodiments of Brahman. They cast off their bodies and become one with the Paramatman. Those who seek to attain the state of Brahman subdue all desires and, living in dharma, they succeed in dissociating their souls from their bodies, like a blade of grass standing upright on a flat heath.

The mother and father create the human body, but the birth that occurs as a result of obeying the guru is sacred and free from old age and death. The guru who discourses on Brahman, while granting immortality, wraps all his disciples in the mantle of Truth. The sishya should think of him as father and mother; and remembering the good he does, never do him injury.

A sishya must always greet his guru with respect; with a pure mind and body, he must direct his attention to his studies. He must not consider any service too humble to perform for him and must never feel anger. This is the first step of brahmacharya. The disciple who learns about his own duties by observing the duties of other disciples also takes the first step on the path of brahmacharya.

A sishya should do whatever pleases his guru in thought, word and deed, even at the expense of his own life and all his possessions. This is the second step of brahmacharya. Also a second step is for the disciple to behave towards his guru's wife and son in the same way that he does to his guru.

The sishya must appreciate all that his guru has done for him and, understanding the goals, think with joy, *He has taught me and made me great*. This is the third step of brahmacharya. The good disciple should not leave his guru's home without first getting his leave and without paying gurudakshina, while disassociating himself from being the giver of it. This is the fourth step of brahmacharya.

He achieves the first step towards knowledge of Brahman, which is the object of brahmacharya, in due course; the second step is through the guru's teachings; the third is by his own intellect; and finally, the fourth is by satsanga and discussion.

Learned men have said that Brahmacharya consists of twelve virtues; the Yoga practices are called its Angas, and perseverance in Yoga dhyana is its nutrient. The man who has achieved mastery in Yoga, with his guru's help and with true understanding of the Vedas, becomes a successful Yogi.

A man must give whatever wealth he may earn, whilst he is a disciple, to his guru. It is in this way that the guru makes his livelihood by his svadharma. The sishya should do the same for his guru's son. Living in this manner as a Brahmachari, the disciple thrives and is blessed with progeny and renown. Men from all over the world shower him with wealth, and many come to his home to practice brahmacharya. It is through brahmacharya of this kind that the Devas obtained their divinity, and blessed sages of great wisdom attained Brahmaloka. This is how the Gandharvas and the Apsaras acquired physical beauty, and it is through brahmacharya that Surya rises to make the day.

In the same way that seekers of the stone that turns base metals into gold derive joy when they find what they are looking for, the Devas and others obtain great happiness on completion of their brahmacharya, for then they can have whatever they wish.

Rajan, the man who is devoted to tapasya takes up brahmacharya in its entirety and thus purifies himself. This man is wise for, by this, he becomes like an innocent child, free from dark passions; and he triumphs over death. Through karma, men can only obtain worldly wealth, which is perishable; but the man who is blessed with true gyana uses it to attain Brahman, which is everlasting. There is no path other than gyana and the attainment of Brahman that can lead to Moksha.'

Dhritarashtra says, 'You say that a wise man sees Brahman in his own soul. Is Brahman white, red, black, blue or purple? Tell me what is the true form and colour of the omnipresent and eternal Being?'

Sanat Sujata says, 'Brahman may be seen as white, red, black, brown or fulvid. But neither on Earth nor in the sky, nor in the waters of the ocean is there anything like It. You will not see the like in stars, in lightning or in clouds. It cannot be compared with anything one may see in the air, in the Moon, in the Sun or in the celestial bodies.

Neither the Rig nor the Yajur, neither the Atharvan nor the pure Saman has anything that is comparable. It is not to be found in Rathantara, Varhadratha or in great yagnas. It cannot be measured and it lies beyond the limited reach of the intellect. Even the universal Destroyer loses himself in It after the Pralaya.

One cannot see It, for It is as subtle as a razor's edge and also more immense than a great mountain. It is the basis upon which everything is founded; It is unchangeable; It is this visible universe; It is omnipresent, vast and delightful. All creatures have sprung from It and will return to It. It is free from duality; It is manifest as the universe; and It is all-pervading. Learned men say that It is changeless, except in the language that is used to describe It.

Those that know this Entity in which everything is established are emancipated.'"

CANTO 45

SANAT SUJATA PARVA CONTINUED

"Sanat Sujata says, 'Sorrow, anger, avarice, lust, ignorance, sloth, malice, self-importance, love of profit, affection, jealousy and evil speech are grave and destructive flaws in character. Each of these waits for an opportunity to capture a man, who then yields his good sense up to them, and helplessly sins.

A man who is covetous, one who is fierce, one who speaks harshly, a man who is garrulous, one who fosters anger and a man who is boastful are evil-minded and, once they acquire wealth, treat others discourteously. A man whose life's objective is sensual gratification, one who is vain, a man who boasts about the gift he gives, a miser, a man who is feeble-minded, one who admires himself and a man who hates his own wife are seven that one must consider sinful.

The twelve characteristics of a Brahmana are righteousness, truthfulness, asceticism, self-restraint, contentment, humility, self-sacrifice, selflessness, generosity, knowledge of the Shastras, patience and forgiveness. The man who adheres to these has the power to rule the world. The man who is invested with three, two or even one of these qualities never claims exclusive ownership of anything. Moksha lies in self-restraint, renunciation and knowledge. These are the attributes of wise Brahmanas who regard Brahman as the highest of all goals. Be it true or false, it is not proper for Brahmanas to speak ill of others; those who do will surely find Naraka.

I have not yet spoken to you of the eighteen defects that mada has. They are ill-will towards others, obstruction of dharma, defaming others, dishonesty, lust, anger, excessive reliance on other people, slander, casting blame, wasting money, disputatiousness, insolence, cruelty to living creatures, malice, ignorance, disrespect of those that are worthy of deference, not recognising right and wrong, and hurtfulness. A wise man should never give in to mada, for its attributes are condemnable.

Friendship is indicated in six ways. Firstly, a true friend delights in the prosperity of his friends. Secondly, he is distressed by their adversity. Thirdly, if his friend asks him for something he values, even that which ought not to be asked for, he gives it unreservedly. Fourthly, a true friend would give away all his wealth, his beloved sons and even his own wife for the sake of his friend. Fifthly, a friend would rather enjoy only what he can earn than live in the home of his friend to whom he may have given everything. Sixthly, a friend would think nothing of sacrificing his own good for his friend.

The affluent man who wants to acquire these qualities, and who becomes charitable and keeps dharma, can do so by restraining his five senses. Such restraint is asceticism. When it grows it can take a man to realms of bliss in the hereafter. Gyana, however, can lead a man to moksha even in this world.

Men who, from impatience, are unable to acquire wisdom, can still gain such asceticism through the power of their goal of attaining moksha. As a consequence of his ability to grasp that Truth, which is Brahman, the source of all yagna, a Yogi can perform sacrifices with the power of his mind; others perform yagnas by sacred chanting, japa; and some by work, karma. Brahman resides in him who knows Brahman as being saguna, vested with attributes, but is established more firmly in him who knows Brahman as being nirguna, without any attribute.

Listen now to something else. All seekers should know this great and exalted philosophy; all other systems of belief are just so many words. The universe is established in this faith; those who know it never die. O king, one cannot attain Brahman merely by virtue of karma, regardless of how well one accomplishes one's work. The man who is destitute of knowledge can never achieve moksha through karma, even if he conducts countless homas and yagnas. He does not experience lasting joy at their end. A man must restrain all the outward senses and on his own seek Brahman. He should give up all karma and still his mind. By this, he should neither feel elation on being praised nor anger on being censured.

O Kshatriya, by conducting himself in this way, step by step as prescribed in the Vedas, a man can attain Brahman in this very world. Of this I assure you.'"

CANTO 46

SANAT SUJATA PARVA CONTINUED

"Sanat Sujata says, 'The Seed from which the universe originated is called Mahayasas. It is pure knowledge, devoid of extrinsic attributes, and It blazes with lustre. It leads the senses; It is what makes Surya shine. Yogis see the Eternal One with their inner eye.

The Seed, which is bliss itself, gives Brahma the ability to create and to grow. It is this Bija that gives heat and light to luminous bodies; It generates its own light and heat and is an object of terror to all heat- and light-giving bodies. Yogis see the Eternal One with their inner eye.

From Brahman arise the five subtle elements, the mahabhutas, from which are born the five gross elements, the bhutas, which constitute the human body. The heart contains both the living soul, Atman, as well as the divine soul, Iswara, or Paramatman. Respectively, these two lose consciousness during sleep and at the time of Pralaya. Brahman, on the other hand, is ever awake. He is the Sun's Sun and holds up Bhumi and Swarga. Yogis see the Eternal One with their inner eye.

The Seed supports Atman and Paramatman, Bhumi and Swarga, the cardinal directions and the whole universe. The points of the compass and the rivers spring from the Seed; It is the point of origin of the vast seas. Yogis see the Eternal One with their inner eye.

The body is a chariot set on a course of destruction; its deeds, however, are undying. The wheels of that chariot are the deeds of past lives; the horses that pull it are the senses that draw a man of true knowledge through the realms of the unconscious to the Immortal Being. Yogis see the Eternal One with their inner eye.

The form of the Supreme One cannot be described by comparison with any other. No one ever sees Him with the body's eye; the man of wisdom who sees Him with his mind and heart has no death. Yogis see the Eternal One with their inner eye.

The river of illusion is fearful; it is guarded by the gods and it bears twelve fruits. As they swim along, men drink its waters and see many desirable things in its midst. This river has its source in the Seed. Yogis see the Eternal One with their inner eye.

The Atman is destined to journey to and fro, from life to afterlife, enjoying only half the fruits of earthly actions in the other world. Iswara, however, is all pervading and the ordainer of all sacrifices. Yogis see the Eternal One with their inner eye.

The Soul is originally naked. Resorting to Avidya, which is like a tree with golden leaves, it clothes itself in attributes and takes birth again and again in different castes according to its current dominant guna. Thus does the Paramatman take forms that house the Atman. Yogis see the Eternal One, in whom all souls reside, with their inner eye.

External attributes come into contact with Brahman, giving him many forms. From the One has the universe sprung, and from the One have also sprung outward attributes that are in themselves whole. When a man succeeds in dispelling everything extrinsic, what remains is Brahman who is the intrinsic whole. Yogis see the Eternal One with their inner eye.

It is from the Seed that the five elements have arisen, and the Seed is the seat of power that controls them. It is from the Seed that both the one who consumes and the consumed—Agni and Soma—have sprung;

it is in the Bija that all life rests. Everything originates from It. In the Vedas the Seed is named Tat, and it is beyond description. Yogis see the Eternal One with their inner eye.

The vital air called apana is absorbed by the air called prana; prana is swallowed by the mind; the mind dissolves in the intellect; and intellect is consumed by Brahman. Yogis see the Eternal One with their inner eye.

The Supreme Soul, when embodied, is like a man with four legs, each leg a state of being—waking, dream, deep sleep and turiya. In the last, he is like a swan wading out from the deep waters of samsara, hiding one leg deep in its wing. For the man who sees this hidden state of turiya as the means by which the other three are guided, death and moksha are the same. Yogis see the Eternal One with their inner eye.

Only as large as a man's thumb, this eternal organism, the Seed, the Bija, is ever full. When It becomes part of a human body—with its prana, mind, intellect and ten senses—It is set in motion. That Supreme Sovereign, worthy of reverential hymns, capable of everything when vested extrinsically, the prime cause of everything, is manifest as Gyana in the human Atman. Only a fool does not see him. Yogis see the Eternal One with their inner eye.

There are those who have gained mastery of their minds and those who have not. Yet the Supreme Soul is equally present in all men—in the emancipated and in the bound; the difference being that nectar flows in a thick stream into the emancipated Yogis, who see the Eternal One with their inner eye.

If, on his life's journey, a man attains knowledge of self and not-self, it matters little whether he performs Agnihotra or not. O king, do not let words like *I am your servant* fall from the lips of such a man. Brahman has another name, Pure Knowledge. Only those who have restrained their minds know Him. Yogis see the Eternal One with their inner eye.

He is illustrious and complete; all living creatures are merged into Him. The man who knows this embodiment of Oneness achieves moksha whilst alive in this world. Yogis see the Eternal One with their inner eye.

Everything, even that which flies away, stretching thousands of wings and with the speed of the mind, must come back to the central spirit within the body, in which the most distant things reside. Yogis see the Eternal One with their inner eye.

The eye cannot perceive his form; only the pure of heart can behold him. He is pure-hearted who seeks universal good, succeeds in controlling his mind and does not allow his heart to be touched by grief. Such a man can abandon the world and all its cares and become immortal. Yogis see the Eternal One with their inner eye.

Like serpents lying coiled and hidden in a pit, there are those who despite their learning follow their own instincts; but they keep their vices hidden. They deceive only those who have little sense. They deceive people by an outward show of dharma and lead them to hell. Know that Brahman may well be attained by companionship with unlikely men. Yogis see the Eternal One with their inner eye.

The man who is freed knows that his impermanent body cannot give him grief or joy, or indeed any other attributes that attach to it. For him there can be no death or birth. Since he realises that Brahman, which has no dualities and which is constant everywhere and all the time, is where reality and illusion both reside, he can be emancipated. He knows that Brahman alone is the beginning and end, all causes and effects. Existing in the form of I, or Self, the divine, Eternal One is beheld by Yogis with their inner eye.

The man who knows Brahman is equal to Brahman. He is neither glorified by good deeds nor defiled by evil ones. It is only in ordinary men that good and bad karma produce different results. The man who has seen Brahman is immortal, Amrita; he is in the singular state called Kaivalya, unaffected by virtue or vice. In this way a man receives the essence of sweetness that is Brahman. Yogis see the Eternal One with their inner eye.

The heart of such a man is not distressed by slander, or by not having studied the Vedas, or by not having performed the Agnihotra. The knowledge of Brahman imparts to him the wisdom that only they who have restrained their minds have access to. Yogis see the Eternal

One, the Brahman which frees the soul from grief and ignorance, with their inner eye.

The man who sees himself in everything no longer grieves, for grief is the lot of those who are occupied with worldly pursuits. Just as one's thirst may as easily be quenched in a well as in a vast reservoir, a man's knowledge of Brahman will quench his thirst for knowledge as easily as does knowledge of the entire Veda. Dwelling in the heart, and only as big as a thumb, that illustrious embodiment of wholeness cannot be seen. He is unborn, yet moves in wakefulness, day and night. The man who knows him becomes learned and is filled with ineffable joy.

I am the mother and father. I am the son. I am the soul of all that ever was and of all that shall ever be. I am the venerable grandfather; I am the father; I am the son. You live within my soul; but you are not mine nor am I yours. The Soul is the cause of my birth and procreation. I am the warp and weft of the universe. The foundation upon which I rest is indestructible. Unborn, yet awake, I move day and night. To know me is to be learned and full of joy.

Thus is the Brahman.

Subtler than the subtle, capable of looking into the past and the future, Brahman is awake in every creature. Those who know Him know that the Universal Father dwells in the heart of everything in creation.'"

CANTO 47

YANASANDHI PARVA

Vaisampayana said, "Dhritarashtra passes the night in conversation with Sanat Sujata and Vidura.

In the morning, all the kings and princes come to the sabha, full of joy on hearing that the Suta has returned and looking forward to seeing him. Both anxious and eager, they go to the beautiful hall with Dhritarashtra at their head to hear Yudhishtira's message that is charged with dharma and artha. The capacious sabha is spotlessly clean and adorned with a golden floor. It is as bright as the Moon and sprinkled with fragrant sandalwood water; luxurious seats made of gold, wood, marble and ivory, covered with exquisite fabric, fill that majestic court.

In one body do these kings and powerful others enter the Kuru sabha, with Dhritarashtra leading them: Bhishma, Drona, Kripa, Salya, Kritavarman, Jayadratha, Aswatthama, Vikarna, Somadatta, Bahlika, the immensely wise Vidura and Maharatha Yuyutsu. With the regal and choleric Duryodhana at their head, Dusasana, Chitrasena, Subala's son Sakuni, Durmukha, Dussaha, Karna, Uluka and Vivimsati enter the sabha, looking like Indra with his entourage of Devas. The hall, filled with these heroic men, their arms like iron maces, is like a mountain cave filled with lions. Those mighty and fiery archers blaze like the Sun as they enter and sit down on wonderful thrones.

Once all the kings are seated, the door keeper announces the arrival of the Sutaputra Sanjaya, saying, 'Here comes the chariot that was despatched to the Pandavas. Borne by the fleet Sindhu steeds, our duta has returned swiftly.'

Approaching with speed, Sanjaya, adorned with golden kundalas, alights from the ratha and strides into sabha filled with noble kings.

The Suta says, 'O Kauravas, I have returned from seeing the sons of Pandu. The Pandavas salute all the Kurus, each according to his age. They pay their homage to the elderly and send greetings and blessings to their contemporaries and the younger men. Listen, O Kshatriyas, to what I said to the Pandavas, as I was instructed by Dhritarashtra when I went from here, and hear what they said in reply.'"

CANTO 48

YANASANDHI PARVA CONTINUED

"Dhritarashtra says, 'O Sanjaya, I ask you in the presence of my son and all these kings, what did the illustrious and mighty Dhananjaya, that first among warriors, the scourge of evil men, say?'

Sanjaya says, 'Let Duryodhana hear the words that noble Arjuna, who is eager to fight, said in Krishna's hearing and with Yudhishtira's approval. Fearless in battle, aware of the might of his arms and eager to fight, the heroic Kiriti spoke to me in Krishna's presence.

He said, "O Suta, say these words to Dhritarashtra's son, in the presence of all the Kurus, also in the hearing of that foul-tongued, black-souled, dull-witted Karna, whose days are numbered and who spoils for battle with me, and in the hearing of all the kings who have gathered to go to war against the Pandavas. Make sure that the king and his ministers mark my words well."

O king, as attentively as the Devas listen to Indra did the Pandavas and Srinjayas listen to Arjuna's grave words.

The wielder of the Gandiva, his eyes as red as lotuses and eager for war, said, "If Duryodhana does not give Yudhishtira of the Ajamida vamsa his kingdom, it is plain that the sons of Dhritarashtra must have committed some heinous sin whose consequences they have not yet reaped, for there can be no other reason why they should want to go to war against Bhimasena, Arjuna and the twins, against Vasudeva, Sini's son, the infallible marksmen Dhrishtadyumna and Sikhandin, and against Yudhishtira, who is a second Indra and who can consume heaven and earth by merely wishing them ill. If Dhritarashtra's son wants war with these men, then the goals of the Pandavas will be accomplished. Therefore, do not propose peace to the sons of Pandu, but let us have war if you like.

Yudhishtira lay on a bed of sorrows in the forest when he lived in exile; O, let a more painful bed than that, on bare earth, be Duryodhana's now, and let him lie down on it at his end, deprived of life. Win Duryodhana's men over to Yudhishtira's side, for my brother is blessed with modesty and wisdom, asceticism and self-restraint, courage and the might of dharma. Our king is also humble, righteous and ever truthful, and though he was deceived and betrayed in so many ways, he has forgiven it all and patiently borne great injustice.

When this eldest son of Pandu, of the controlled soul, directs the terrible anger that has accumulated for years at the Kurus, Duryodhana will repent. In the same way that a blazing fire burns dry grass in summer, so will Yudhishtira's flaming wrath consume Dhritarashtra's army, why, with a mere glance of his eye.

When Duryodhana sees the great and furious Bhimasena standing in his chariot with his mace in hand and vomiting the venom of his wrath, he will repent. When he sees the mail clad Bhima, who always fights in the front, on whom even his own followers can scarcely bear to look, felling hostile heroes and devastating the enemy's ranks, as if he was Yama himself, then vain Duryodhana will remember my words.

When he sees Bhima strike down elephants like mountain peaks, and sees blood flowing from their shattered heads like water from broken casks, Duryodhana will repent. When the fierce Bhima of fearful form falls upon Dhritarashtra's sons, mace in hand, and slaughters them, like a great lion attacking a herd of cattle, Duryodhana will repent. When the heroic Bhima, undaunted even by great danger and skilled in the use of all weapons, that crusher of enemy hosts, mounted on his chariot, grinds into the dust innumerable and better chariots, as well as entire divisions of footsoldiers, seizing enemy elephants with his iron-hard noose and mowing down Dhritarashtra's forces, like a sturdy woodsman a forest with his axe, Duryodhana will repent.

When he sees Dhritarashtra's armies consumed like a village of straw huts by fire, or like a field of ripe corn by lightning; when he sees his vast army scattered, its leaders slain and the terrified men turning to flee, and all the warriors, humbled to the dust, scorched by fire of Bhimasena's weapons, Duryodhana will repent.

When Nakula, Kshatriya of wonderful feats, foremost of rathikas, shoots endless streams of deadly arrows and mangles Duryodhana's chariot-warriors, Duryodhana will repent. When Nakula, who is accustomed to comforts and luxuries, thinks back on that bed of anguish on which he slept for years in the vana and spews his wrath in a venomous jet, like an angry snake, Duryodhana will repent.

When Duryodhana sees our allied kings, who are ready to lay down their lives for Dharmaraja Yudhishtira, urged into battle by him, furiously advance in their resplendent chariots against the enemy, the son of Dhritarashtra will certainly repent. When the Kuru prince sees the five heroic sons of Draupadi, tender in years but not in deeds, and all masters of arms, storm fearlessly at the Kaurava legions, Duryodhana will repent.

When Sahadeva, bent on carnage, and mounted on his chariot of silent wheels and inexorable course, set with golden stars and drawn by superb horses, makes the heads of kings roll on the field with his volleys of arrows; when Duryodhana sees that masterly warrior, riding his ratha in the frightful havoc of bloody war, attack the enemy in all directions, Duryodhana will repent. Indeed, when the modest but mighty Sahadeva, skilled in battle, truthful, devoted to dharma and of boundless vigour, attacks the son of Gandhari in fierce encounter and routs all his followers,

Duryodhana will repent.

When he sees Draupadi's sons, all great archers, all heroes and masters of weapons and fighting from chariots, dart at the foe like vicious, poisonous snakes, then will the son of Dhritarashtra repent for this war. When Parantapa Abhimanyu, as expert in arms as Krishna, overpowers the Kaurava legions with dark gales of arrows, Duryodhana will repent.

When he sees Subhadra's son, a child in years but not in prowess, as skilled with weapons as Indra himself, attack the enemy ranks like Yama, Duryodhana will repent. When young Prabhadraka of leonine vitality, experienced in battle, is among Dhritarashtra's sons and their troops, Duryodhana will repent.

When those veteran Maharathas, Virata and Drupada, attack Dhritarashtra's sons as they stand at the head of their legions, Duryodhana will repent. When the master of astras, Drupada, seated in his chariot and eager to take the heads off your young warriors, decapitates them with inexorable arrows, Duryodhana will repent. When Parantapa Virata and his cool-headed Matsya warriors penetrate the ranks of the enemy, felling them all around as they advance, Duryodhana will repent. When he sees the eldest son of the Matsya king fighting from the van of the Pandava army, sitting in his chariot, calm and courageous, and clad in shining mail, Duryodhana will repent.

When that greatest of all Kaurava heroes, the virtuous son of Santanu, is slain in battle by Sikhandin, then all our enemies will die. This I know beyond doubt. When Sikhandin advances on his armoured ratha towards Bhishma, shattering multitudes of enemy rathas on the way, Duryodhana will repent. When Duryodhana sees Dhrishtadyumna, who has learnt all the secrets of the astra shastra from Drona, standing in splendour in the van of the Srinjaya force, he will repent.

When the Senapati of the Pandava host, of immeasurable prowess, who can withstand the charge of any army, flies at Drona, on his way razing Dhritarashtra's warriors with his arrows, Duryodhana will repent. What enemy can withstand him, who has for his lord that lion of the Vrishni race, the chief of the Somakas, who is modest and intelligent, mighty and invested with untold urjas and blessed with every noble quality?

Say this also to Duryodhana: Do not covet the kingdom. We have with us the dauntless Maharatha Satyaki, the grandson of Sini, who is an unsurpassed master of weapons on this Earth. Broad-chested and long-armed, that Parantapa, unrivalled in battle and a master of the greatest astras, wields a bow four cubits long. When that bane of his foes, the chief of the Sinis, lashes the enemy with his arrow storms, at my urging, overwhelming their leaders, Duryodhana will repent.

When that shining warrior of the long arms and firm grasp is resolved to fight, then, like cattle that scent lions on the wind, enemy forces flee, even before battle begins. This Kshatriya can split mountains and consume the universe in revelational flames. Blessed with awesome lightness of hand, he shines on the field of war like the Sun in the sky.

That lion of the Vrishnis, scion of Yadu's line, whose tutelage has been meticulous, commands supernal weapons; Satyaki commands all the greatest astras. When he sees Satyaki's golden chariot on the field, drawn by four white steeds, Duryodhana of the uncontrolled passions will repent.

When he sees my own chariot, glittering like gold and with bright gemstones inlaid, drawn by white Gandharva steeds, flying the banner of Hanuman, and driven by Krishna himself, that wretch of uncontrolled passions will repent. When, in the midst of the great war, he hears the incessant thrumming of my leather-gloved hands pulling the bowstrings of the Gandiva, loud as rolling thunder, Duryodhana will repent.

When he sees his troops abandoning him and running like deer from the field, overwhelmed by the darkness that I create with my arrow banks; when he sees countless winged arrows, which excoriate a man's bowels, flash from the Gandiva like lightning from storm clouds, and raze enemies by the thousands and devour horses and armour-clad elephants, Duryodhana will indeed repent.

When he sees me turn enemy arrows back on their courses, or shred them with my own shafts, foolish Duryodhana will repent. When my broad-headed arrows pluck the heads of young warriors from their bodies, like birds picking fruit from the treetops, Duryodhana will repent. When he sees his peerless warriors fall from their chariots, and elephants and horses roll lifeless on the field, slain by my arrows, Duryodhana will repent. When he sees his brothers fall all around him, dying even before they come within range of his enemy's weapons, and without having raised a weapon in battle, Duryodhana will repent.

I will loose an endless river of blazing arrows and, like Yama with mouth agape, swallow multitudes of chariots and foot-soldiers, and then that dog Duryodhana will repent. When he sees his own troops, covered with the dust whipped up by my chariot as it wheels swiftly in all directions, torn to shreds by shafts from the Gandiva, and the living deranged by fear, the wretched Duryodhana will repent.

When he sees his entire army flee in terror, their arms and legs mangled, and their minds unhinged; when he sees his horses, elephants and his best warriors slain, and his dry-mouthed and panic-stricken troops dead or wailing aloud as they lie dying beside their exhausted animals; when he sees hair, bones and skulls lying in mounds, like half-finished works of the Creator, that vile prince will repent.

When he sees on my chariot Krishna with his Panchajanya, and me with my pair of inexhaustible quivers, my Gandiva, my Devadatta and my white horses, Duryodhana will repent. When I consume the Kauravas, as Agni consumes all the evil souls that throng together at the beginning of a new yuga, Dhritarashtra and all his sons will repent.

When the evil and wrathful son of Dhritarashtra is deprived of his prosperity, along with his brothers, his army and his followers, that fool, stripped of pride and trembling, will repent.

One morning, when I had finished my ritual bath and prayers, a Brahmana said to me, *Partha, you will have a difficult task to perform; you will have to fight your enemies. Either Indra will ride before you on his superb mount and with his Vajra in hand, razing your foes in battle, or Vasudeva's son Krishna will protect you from behind, in his chariot drawn by horses with Sugriva at their head.*

With complete faith in what he said, I have passed over Indra the wielder of the thunderbolt, preferring to have Krishna on my side. I have chosen Krishna to help me annihilate these evil ones. I see the hand of God in all this. The man, whose success Krishna merely wishes for, is sure to prevail over his enemies without Krishna needing to take up arms on his behalf. This is so, even if the adversaries are the Devas with Indra leading them, let alone mere mortals.

The man who wants to vanquish that first among all heroes, Krishna of the mighty urjas, in battle, may as well try to cross the ocean by swimming across it. Such a fool is like a man who tries to split open the Kailasa mountain by striking it with his palm; he does not cause the mountain the slightest damage, while his hand might break and his nails tear. He may as well be able to put out a raging forest fire with his bare hands, or stop the Sun and Moon from moving, or steal amrita from the Devas.

This is the same Krishna who mowed down all the Bhoja warriors and carried off Rukmini in his chariot, to make her his wife; and their son is the noble Pradyumna. Krishna is the darling of the Devas; he devastated the Gandharas and defeated all Nagnajita's sons to rescue the mighty king Sudarshana from confinement. It was Krishna who killed King Pandya by striking him with his chest; and he who destroyed the Kalingas in battle. It is he who burnt the city of Varanasi, which remained kingless for many years because there was no one to succeed its prince Sudakshina.

Ekalavya, the king of the Nishadas, always challenged him to battle; but Krishna slew him and he lay dead on a hillside like the Asura Jambha of old. Krishna, with Baladeva at his side, slew Ugrasena's evil son Kansa, while he sat in the midst of the Vrishnis and the Andhakas, and then gave Ugrasena the kingdom. It was Krishna who, fearless with his fathomless powers, fought Salya, lord of Saubha, the city that floats in the skies; and Krishna caught the Satagni of a hundred fires in his hand, when Salya hurled it at him at the gates of Saubha. No mortal can face Krishna's might.

The Asuras had a city called Pragjyotisha, formidable and inaccessible. There, Narakasura, the son of Bhumi Devi, kept the jewelled ear-rings of Aditi that he had taken by force. The Devas, who do not fear death, with Sakra at their head, could not subdue Naraka. The Devas saw Krishna's prowess; they saw his irresistible Chakra; they knew the purpose of his birth, and they begged him to quell Naraka and his fell Asuras; and blithely Krishna agreed. In the city of Nirmochana he slew six thousand Asuras; he shredded their arrows and killed Mura and hosts of other Rakshasas; then he entered the city.

There, a stupendous duel erupted between the dreadful Naraka and Vishnu's Avatara; until, slain by Krishna, Naraka lay lifeless, like a karnikara tree uprooted by the wind. Having killed the Earth's son and Mura, and having recovered the incomparable ear-rings, Krishna of unearthly prowess came back, alight with divine lustre and crowned with undying fame. The Devas, who witnessed his ineffable feats, blessed him, saying, *You will never tire in a fight; neither earth nor water will obstruct you; weapons shall never pierce your body.* And Krishna regarded this blessing as ample reward. This is Krishna, who is beyond all compare.

Dhritarashtra's son aspires to vanquish this same Vishnu, of infinite tejas; and the evil one often thinks of imprisoning him. Krishna bears all this for our sake. And vile Duryodhana wants to create a rift between Krishna and me. He will see for himself, when he is on the battlefield, how far he will be able to take Krishna's love away from the Pandavas!

I will bow to Bhishma, to Drona and his son, and to the peerless son of Saradwat, our acharya Kripa; but then I will begin the battle to regain our kingdom. Dharmadeva will bring righteous destruction down on our sinful cousin who is so eager to fight us.

Deceitfully beaten at dice by those base men, we, of royal birth, spent twelve agonising years in the forest and one long year in hiding. While we, the Pandavas, are still alive, how can the sons of Dhritarashtra rejoice in their affluence or power?

If they defeat us in battle, with the help of Indra and the Devas, it will mean that vice is superior to virtue, and the very concept of dharma would cease to exist. If indeed a man's actions do bear fruit and if we are better men than Duryodhana, I believe that, with Krishna at my side, I will kill Duryodhana and all his kinsmen. Lord of men, if robbing us of our kingdom is evil, if our own good deeds are not in vain, Duryodhana's is doomed.

O Kauravas, you will see with your own eyes that, if they come to war, the sons of Dhritarashtra will surely die. If they desist from fighting, they might live; but if there is a battle, none of them will be left alive. I will kill all Dhritarashtra's sons and Karna, and take the entire kingdom. Do whatever you think is best and, meanwhile, enjoy the time you have with your wives and other sweet things of life.

There are many venerable Brahmanas with us, who are knowers of the Shastras, of pure conduct, of noble birth, witnesses to all the events that have transpired. They, who can understand and interpret the astrological significance of the movements of the planets and their relative positions to the stars; who can explain the mysteries of destiny and predict the future; and who know the signs of the zodiac and what is happening every hour, prophesy a great defeat for the Kurus and the Srinjayas, and final victory for the Pandavas.

Because of this, Yudhishtira, who never made an enemy, considers that he has already achieved his goal, of vanquishing his enemies. Krishna, who sees the invisible future, sees all this; and I, too, with the clear and unerring foresight that I acquired years ago, the chaksushi I had from the Gandharva Angaraparna, see into the future. If they fight, the sons of Dhritarashtra will not live. My Gandiva stretches without my touching it; the bow-string trembles without being drawn; and arrows stand up in my quiver, impatient to fly out. My gleaming sword slides out of its scabbard by itself, like a moulting snake from its old skin; and terrible voices scream from atop my flag-staff, saying, *When will you yoke your chariot, Arjuna?* Hordes of jackals howl hideously at night; Rakshasas land from the sky in dense swarms; deer and jackals, peacocks and crows, vultures, cranes and wolves, and golden-plumed birds follow my chariot when I yoke my white horses to it.

Single-handedly, with torrents of arrows, I will despatch all these warrior kings to Yamaloka. Just as a blazing conflagration consumes a forest in summer, I will consume my enemies with the astras I invoke. I will loose the Sthuna, Karna, Pasupata, Brahma and the other inexorable missiles that Indra gave me; and with my heart set on the death of those kings, I will obliterate all who enter the battlefield. Only after this, will I rest; this is my resolve.

Tell them all this, Sanjaya.

Look at Duryodhana's foolishness. He is planning to go to war against men who are invincible, even to Indra with the Devas. So let the wish of Santanu's aged son Bhishma, Kripa, Drona and his son, and the unfathomably wise Vidura—*May the Kauravas have long lives*, be proven true!" said Arjuna,' says Sanjaya."

CANTO 49

YANASANDHI PARVA CONTINUED

Vaisampayana said, "O Bhaarata, in the midst of all the assembled kings, Santanu's son Bhishma says to Duryodhana, 'Once long ago, Brihaspati and Indra went to Brahma, accompanied by the Maruts, the Vasus and Agni, the Adityas, the Sadhyas, the seven Devarishis, the Gandharvas, Viswavasu and the Apsaras. Reverentially the Swargavasis bowed to the Lord of the universe and sat surrounding him. Then, the two ancient deities, the Rishis Nara and Narayana, drew into themselves the vital energies of all present there, and left the place.

On seeing this, Brihaspati asked Brahma, "Who are these two that leave without worshipping you? Pitamaha, who are they?"

Brahma replied, "These two, endowed with great tapasya, blaze in lustrous beauty, illuminating both Bhumi and Swarga. They, who are mighty, all-pervading and unequalled, are Nara and Narayana, who have come from the other world to live in Brahmaloka. Of incomparable glory, they shine with their tapasya and, by everything they do, enhance the joy of the world. The Devas and Gandharvas worship them, and their purpose is to destroy the Asuras."

Indra and the Devas, with Brihaspati at their head, went to the place where Nara and Narayana sat in tapasya. At that time, the Devas were in turmoil from a war that raged between them and the Asuras, and Indra asked the exalted pair to grant him a boon. They told him to name his wish, and Indra asked for their help, promising that the Devas would do as Nara and Narayana wished. It was with their help that Indra vanquished the Daityas and Danavas. Parantapa Nara slew hundreds of thousands of Indra's foes—the Paulomas and the Kalakhanjas.

It was Nara, as Arjuna, who, from his whirling chariot that was broken during their duel, cut off Jambhasura's head with a broad-headed arrow just as the demon was about to swallow him. It was he who stormed Hiranyapura, the Daitya city across the ocean, and vanquished sixty-thousand Nivatakavachas. It was this conqueror, Mahabaho Arjuna, who gratified Agni by vanquishing the Devas led by Indra. Narayana, also, has slain countless other Daityas and Danavas. Such is their inexhaustible tejas and urjas; and you now see them together, their purpose one.

The two Maharathas you face, Krishna and Arjuna, are the same timeless and divine Narayana and Nara. Of all who live on this Earth, they alone cannot be vanquished by the Asuras or, indeed, by the Devas with Indra at their head. Narayana is Krishna and Nara is Phalguna.

They are one soul born as two. Their karma gives them the enjoyment of many eternal and inexhaustible realms; and they are born again and again into the world when cataclysmic wars become necessary to cleanse Bhumi Devi. Their mission is to fight and make a great sacrifice of human blood. This is what Narada, who is an authority on the Vedas, told the Vrishnis.

O Duryodhana, when you see Kesava, with his conch-shell, discus and mace in hand, together with the awesome bowman Arjuna armed with various astras; when you behold those eternal and irradiant ones, the two Krishnas, riding the same chariot, then you will remember what I have just said. Child, danger threatens the Kurus because dharma and artha have deserted your mind. If you pay no heed to what I say, you will hear of an unimaginable, revelational carnage, for all the Kauravas follow your lead.

All the Kurus listen to me but, Bull of the Bhaaratas, you put your faith in the opinions of just three men: Karna, a low-born Suta's son cursed by Parasurama; Sakuni, the son of Subala; and your vile and sinful brother Dusasana.'

Karna says, 'Bhishma, it is not right for you to still mock me as a Sutaputra, for I have adopted Kshatriya dharma without abandoning those who are my own. Besides, what evil is there in me? None among Dhritarashtra's people will accuse me of having committed any wrong; never have I done any injury to Dhritarashtra's son. And I will kill all the Pandavas in battle. How can wise men make peace again with those who were once their sworn enemies? It is my duty to do whatever I can to please king Dhritarashtra, and especially Duryodhana, for the kingdom is his.'

Bhishma hears Karna and says to Dhritarashtra, 'Although this man often boasts about his intentions to kill them, he is not equal to even a sixteenth part of the noble Pandavas. The great calamity that is about to overtake your evil sons is the work of this Sutaputra. Relying on him, foolish Duryodhana insulted his cousins, those Kshatriyas of divine descent. Over the years, what feat has Karna achieved to equal any that each of the Pandavas has?

What did this man do when he saw mighty Dhananjaya kill his beloved brother? Why was he absent when Dhananjaya charged the assembled Kurus outside Virata's city, routed them in battle and stripped them of their clothes? Where was this son of a Suta, who roars like a bull now, when the Gandharvas captured your son during the Goshayatra? It was Bhima, the illustrious Partha and the twins who challenged the Gandharvas and vanquished them.

Heedless of dharma and artha, what Karna does best is boast. O may you be blessed, Bharatarishabha.'

Bharadwaja's high-souled son Drona listens to Bhishma and, after paying homage to the gathered kings, says to Dhritarashtra, 'O king, do what Bhishma says. It is not wise for you to follow the counsel of covetous men. Making peace with the Pandavas, before war breaks out, is the most judicious course open to you. Arjuna will do everything he has said, which Sanjaya has repeated here, for there is no bowman to equal him in all the three worlds.'

The king takes no notice of what Drona and Bhishma have said and, without responding to them, asks Sanjaya again about the Pandavas. It is at this moment, when the king does not offer any response to Bhishma and Drona, that the Kauravas lose all hope of living."'

CANTO 50

YANASANDHI PARVA CONTINUED

"Dhritarashtra says, 'What did Dharmaputra Yudhishtira say, Sanjaya, when he heard that a great force has assembled here in our support? What is he doing, in view of the war to come? Which of his brothers and sons look to him, waiting for his command? Who amongst his advisors tries to dissuade that honourable and virtuous king from war, and persuades him to make peace instead, knowing that my son's evil, deceitful deeds have provoked him?'

Sanjaya says, 'May you be blessed! All Pandu's sons, as well as the Panchalas, wait eagerly for his command, but he restrains them. Multitudes of battle-ready war chariots belonging to the Pandavas and the Panchalas have come in separate divisions, making Yudhishtira glad. Just as the sky brightens at sunrise, so have the Panchalas' hearts at being reunited with Kunti's resplendent son, who floods the world with his lustre.

All the Panchalas, Kekayas and Matsyas, even their cowherds and shepherds rejoice with an equally happy Yudhishtira. Bevies of Brahmana, Kshatriya and Vaisya girls have come to catch a glimpse of Arjuna in his coat of mail.'

Dhritarashtra says, 'Sanjaya, tell us about the armies that Dhrishtadyumna, the Somakas and others have brought, using which the Pandavas will fight us.'

With this barrage of questions put to him in the great sabha, Sanjaya falls into dark thought and heaves long, deep sighs. Suddenly, he collapses onto the floor.

Vidura cries to his blind brother, 'Rajan, Sanjaya has fallen to the floor, unconscious and unable to speak.'

Dhritarashtra says, 'I am sure it is from anxiety after seeing those Purushavyaghras, those Maharathas.'

Sanjaya recovers consciousness and is comforted. Then in the presence of all the Kurus in the sabha, he says to Dhritarashtra, 'O Rajarajan, I did indeed see those great warriors, the sons of Kunti. They are lean and trim from the austerities they observed while they lived in the Matsya kingdom. Listen, Rajan, to which kings and princes have joined them to fight you.

The noble Dhrishtadyumna will fight against you. He is a virtuous soul, who never forsakes virtue, not from anger, fear or temptation; not for the sake of wealth or because of an argument. He is an authority on dharma; and he is the best of righteous men. He has never made an enemy, but he will fight on the side of the Pandavas, against you.

Then there is the man who has no equal in the strength of his arms, who with his bow subjugated all the kings of this Earth, who long ago vanquished the kings of Kasi, Anga, Magadha and Kalinga. This man, Bhimasena, will fight for the Pandavas, against you. It is by his strength that his four brothers survived after he rescued them from the burning house of lac. This same Vrikodara saved them from the cannibal Hidimba; it is he who rescued Yagnaseni when Jayadratha abducted her; and it is he who saved the Pandavas from the forest fire at Varanavata. This formidable Bhima will fight for his brothers against you.

Then there is the warrior who slew the Krodhavasas to please Draupadi, successfully crossing the rugged and fearsome mountains of Gandhamadana. His arms have the strength of ten thousand elephants;

and with him for their ally the Pandavas will fight against you. Long ago, and with only Krishna's help, this Kshatriya vanquished Purandara in order to please Agni; and he also gratified, with his prowess, the God of gods, Uma's trident-bearing lord Mahadeva, who dwells in his mountain fastness. This Arjuna, the greatest warrior, subjugated all the kings of the Earth, and with him the Pandavas will face you in war.

There is also that wonderful warrior Nakula, who vanquished all of the western world, the Mlechcha lands. He, too, this handsome son of Madri's, this unrivalled archer, will fight against you, O Kaurava.

Then there is the Kshatriya who defeated the warriors of Kasi, Anga and Kalinga. With Sahadeva on their side, the Pandavas will meet you in battle. There are only four men on Earth to equal him in sheer vitality—Aswatthama, Dhrishtaketu, Rukmi and Pradyumna. And against this youngest of the Pandavas, the terrible Sahadeva Manavottama, source of Madri's joy, you must do battle.

There is also Sikhandin, who was once born on Earth as the king of Kasi's daughter, during which life she practised the most severe tapasya, praying to become the instrument of Bhishma's death in another birth. She passed through death and was born as the Panchala king's daughter; but by divine chance, she has become a man. Sikhandin knows the strengths and weaknesses of both sexes; this invincible prince of Panchala, who fought the Kalingas, who is skilled in all the astras, will now fight on the side of the Pandavas, against you. With this woman who was turned into a man, and a formidable bowman whose destiny it is to bring Bhishma down, the Pandavas will fight against you.

There are others. The mighty archers, the five Kekaya princes clad in wondrous mail, will fight beside the Pandavas against you. You must face Yuyudhana, Satyaki the warrior of the long arms, who is a master of astras, intelligent and of indefatigable prowess, that lion of the Vrishnis. You will encounter Virata, who has been the refuge of the Pandavas for some time.

The lord of Kasi, that Maharatha who rules in Varanasi, has become an ally of the Pandavas, and with him in their army they will fight you.

The noble sons of Draupadi, tender in years but invincible in battle, as unapproachable as serpents, will fight beside the Pandavas against you.

Do not forget Abhimanyu, whose tejas is as lustrous as Krishna's and whose self-restraint is as stern as Yudhishtira's; with him on their side the Pandavas will fight you.

Sisupala's warlike son Dhrishtaketu, of great fame and incomparable energy, is inexorable when roused. With this king of the Chedis, who has come to their side with an akshauhini of troops, the Pandavas will fight you.

Krishna is the refuge of the Pandavas, as Indra is of the Devas; and with him on their side they will fight you. Sarabha, brother of the king of the Chedis, has come with Karakarsa; and with both these in their army, the Pandavas will fight you.

Jarasandha's son Sahadeva, and Jayatsena, both unrivalled in battle, have also pledged themselves to the Pandava cause; and with them the Pandavas will fight you. And the mighty and fearless Drupada, with a vast force, is resolved to fight on the Pandava side against you.

O Bharatarishabha, with the support of these and hundreds of other kings from the east and north, Yudhishtira Dharmaraja prepares for war.'"

CANTO 51

YANASANDHI PARVA CONTINUED

"Dhritarashtra says, 'All the men you mention are, indeed, great and valiant, but Bhima is equal to all of them together. I am as afraid of Bhima's anger as a plump deer of a hunting tiger. I pass my nights in fearful sleeplessness, heaving feverish sighs, yes, like a small animal terrified of a lion.

He is mighty-armed and as powerful as Indra, and I do not see in our whole army even one man who can withstand him in battle. Wrathful and unwavering in his hatred, this son of Kunti and Pandu does not smile even in jest; mad with rage, he looks askance at all and speaks in a thunderous voice. Impetuous and with no knowledge of fear, long-armed and dreadfully strong, he will not leave even one of my foolish sons alive.

Vrikodara, that bull among the Kurus, whirling his mace in battle like Yama, will kill all my sons, who have set themselves on this calamitous course. Even as I speak, I see that terrible mace of his—six-sided, made of iron and adorned with gold—raised in fury: like a Brahmana's curse. Bhima will wreak havoc among my troops like a lion amongst a herd of deer. He is the only one of the brothers who will seek the death of all my sons.

Since his childhood, he has a voracious appetite and was endowed with fiery energy; and also since then he has been hostile towards my sons. Even now my heart trembles at the memory of how Bhima crushed Duryodhana and my other princes during their childhood fights. With his superior strength, he always dominated and bullied my sons, and it is Bhima of the terrible prowess who is the cause, the root, of this enmity.

I see Bhima, mad with rage, and fighting from the very van of their legions, devour my entire force of men, elephants and horses. He is also Drona and Arjuna's equal in his skill with other weapons; he is as swift as the wind, and in wrath like Maheswara himself. Who is there, Sanjaya, who can kill that dreadful Kshatriya in battle? I deem it a blessing that my sons have not already been killed by that awful Parantapa. How can any man withstand the prowess of this absolute warrior who has single-handedly savaged so many great Yakshas and Rakshasas? I was never able to control him even when he was a child. How will I do so now, especially since my dishonourable sons have wounded his great heart?

He is bitter and full of anger; he will not relent. Frowning and ever looking askance, as he does now, he cannot be persuaded away from horrible vengeance. He is heroic and has no equal in might or handsomeness. Fair-skinned and tall as a palmyra, taller than Arjuna by the span of the thumb, this second son of Pandu is swifter than a horse and stronger than an elephant. His voice is soft, deep and dangerous, and his eyes are the colour of honey.

Vyasa told me long ago of his remarkable physique and strength even when he was a child. Swinging his iron mace he will shatter chariots, elephants, men and horses. My child, for his disobedience to me I have, in the past, insulted this best of Kshatriyas, whose rage is so quickly sparked. How will my sons resist the power of his beautiful iron mace, which can kill a hundred men in moments, and which, when hurled at an enemy, makes the most fearful sound?

O, my foolish sons want to cross the vast, shoreless ocean that is Bhima, fathomless, swirling with vicious, tempestuous currents that are as deadly as whistling storms of arrows. My sons believe themselves wise and ignore my piteous appeals for caution. They see only the imagined honey of victory, not their impending doom. My sons, who will not hesitate to do battle with Yama, are doomed to death by the Supreme Ordainer; they are like little creatures already in a great lion's jaws.

Bhima's six-sided mace is four cubits long, and always lethal. When he hurls it at them how will my sons defy it? Bhima will whirl his mace around and smash the heads of our elephants; wetting the corners of his mouth with his tongue, he will draw deep breaths and rush, roaring, against our tuskers, matching the angry beasts roar for roar. He will erupt into the tight knot of our chariots and with unerring aim kill the greatest of our warriors who dare face him. When this happens, will even one of my men escape this conflagration of a man? Bhima Mahabaho will crush my forces, scythe a passage through them and, dancing with his mace in his hand, reveal the spectacle of the pralaya at the end of this yuga.

Like a maddened elephant which brings flowering trees crashing down, Vrikodara in rage will mow down the ranks of my sons. Sanjaya, he will divest my warriors of their chariots, sarathies, horses and flagstaffs; wildly, he will be among our elephant warriors; and, like the tempestuous Ganga in spate uproots trees on her banks, that Purushavyaghra will devastate my sons' troops in battle. Terrified of Bhimasena, my sons, their followers and the kings allied to them will fly in all directions.

It was Bhima who, long ago with Vasudeva's help, entered the inmost apartments of Jarasandha, the invincible king of Magadha, and killed him, thereby enabling the Pandavas to subjugate Bhumi Devi herself and perform the Rajasuya yagna. That he did not conquer the Kauravas, who were protected by Bhishma's prowess, and the Andhakas and the Vrishnis with their brilliant diplomacy, is only because fortune smiled on these. Ah, Bhima went to Jarasandha, who had no equal, and with bare hands, tore his massive body in two. What could be more astounding than that?

O Sanjaya, like a serpent who has stored his poison for years, Bhima will spew all the venom of his wrath at my sons in battle. As Indra incinerated the Danavas with his thunderbolt, Bhimasena, mace in hand, will blast all my sons to their deaths. Oh, he is irresistible, and in my mind's eye, I see him even now, his coppery eyes ablaze, slaughtering my princes. Even without his mace or bow, chariot or armour, there is no man on Earth who can withstand Bhima.

Bhishma, Dronacharya, and Saradwat's son Kripa know as well as I do, Bhima's intelligence and strength. These bulls among men, who are deep knowers of Kshatriya dharma, and for whom death in battle is desirable, will take their stand in the van of our forces. Destiny is inexorable, especially for men; so, even though I see victory for the Pandavas, I will no more try to restrain my sons. These mighty bowmen of mine, keen to take the time-honoured path to Swarga, will lay down their lives in battle, but without betraying their fame on Earth.

Child, my sons and the Pandavas are equals; all of them are grandsons of Bhishma and disciples of Drona and Kripa.

These three venerable ones are men of honour and will repay the small services that we have done them. For a Kshatriya who has taken up arms and wants to observe his dharma, death in battle is the highest good and brings punya. I weep, however, for all those that will fight the Pandavas. The danger that Vidura foresaw is near.

On the one hand, Sanjaya, wisdom cannot overcome sorrow but, on the other, grief seems to make wisdom evaporate. When even Rishis who are free from worldly concerns and who view the affairs of the universe with detachment are all affected by adversity and prosperity, it is small wonder that I, who am attached to a thousand things, my sons, my kingdom, my wives, my grandsons and my kinsmen, grieve. What good can there possibly be in store for me in the face of this terrible danger? Considering all things, I am convinced that the end of the Kurus is at hand.

That game of dice was the cause of the terrible fate which overtakes us each moment. Foolish Duryodhana committed that sin out of greed, and ever-fleeting, all-knowing Time, who controls all things, made him do it. I am bound helpless to the wheel of Time and cannot escape it. Tell me, Sanjaya, where shall I go? What shall I do? How shall I do it?

My foolish Kauravas will all die, for their time has come. Helplessly I will have to hear their women wailing when my hundred sons are killed. Ah, how will death come to me?

As a summer fire, fanned by the wind, consumes dry grass, Bhima, mace in hand and with Arjuna beside him, will raze all who fight for me.'"

CANTO 52

YANASANDHI PARVA CONTINUED

"Dhritarashtra says, 'He whom we have never heard uttering a falsehood, he who has Dhananjaya to fight on his side, will attain sovereignty over the three worlds.

I cannot think of anyone who can face the wielder of the Gandiva in battle. When he shoots winged arrows, nalikas and other shafts that pierce men's mail and breasts, he has no rival. Perhaps, if those bulls among men, Drona and Karna, stand united against him the outcome could be uncertain; but I am sure that final victory will not be mine.

Karna is compassionate and, at the same time, rash; the Acharya is elderly and most fond of his favourite pupil, Arjuna of the firm grasp of the bow, Arjuna who is brilliant and mighty. The encounter between them will be ferocious and will not result in any one's clear defeat. All these are heroic, masters of weapons, and have earned great fame. They might give up sovereignty over the gods if it is offered them, but not the chance to prove themselves in the coming war.

Peace will certainly result if either Drona or Karna or Phalguna falls. However, if truth be faced squarely, there is no one who can kill

Arjuna. O, how can we pacify his anger against my foolish sons? There are others who are masters of weapons, who conquer and are conquered, but Arjuna always prevails.

Thirty years have passed since Arjuna gratified Agni Deva in the Khandava vana by vanquishing all the Devas. We have never heard of him being defeated anywhere, my child. Like Indra, victory is always Arjuna's; he has Krishna for his charioteer, who is also never conquered. We hear that the two Krishnas riding in the same chariot and the Gandiva are united as a single ineluctable force. As for us, we do not have a bow of that calibre, or a warrior like Arjuna or a charioteer like Krishna. Duryodhana's foolish followers do not think of this.

O Sanjaya, even a thunderbolt that falls on one's head leaves something undestroyed, but Arjuna's arrows leave nothing. Even now I see him unleashing his arrows in hurricanes, wreaking devastation all round, unerringly plucking heads from bodies. Even now I see flaming arrows flare from the Gandiva, burning all around and consuming the armies of my sons. Even now I see my vast army with its diverse forces struck with panic at the rumble of Savyasachi's chariot, and fleeing in all directions.

Just as a great conflagration, its flames fanned by the wind and spreading wild in all directions, consumes dry leaves and grass, so will the flames that are Arjuna's astras consume my troops. He will loose arrows beyond count each moment; ah, he will be irresistible, like Yama Deva himself.

When I hear that all kinds of evil omens manifest in the homes of the Kurus, on the battlefield and all around them, I am certain that annihilation will overtake our Bharata vamsa.'"

CANTO 53

YANASANDHI PARVA CONTINUED

"Dhritarashtra says, 'The followers of the Pandavas are as strong and eager for victory as the Pandavas themselves are, and determined to sacrifice their lives for it.

My son, you have told me who my enemies are—the mighty kings of Panchala, Kekaya, Matsya and Magadha. Not only them, but Krishna, that Creator of the universe, that all-mighty one who can conquer the three worlds with Indra at their head, is on the side of the Pandavas and bent on giving them victory. Then there is Satyaki, who acquired the entire astra shastra from Arjuna in a moment. That scion of the Sini vamsa will stand on the battlefield, shooting arrows as effortlessly as a farmer sows seeds. The prince of Panchala, Dhrishtadyumna, awesome and ruthless Maharatha, a master of all the astras, will also fight my forces.

Great is my fear of Yudhishtira's anger, of Arjuna's prowess, and of the twins and Bhimasena. I am afraid that when those lords of men spread their mesh of unearthly arrows over them, my troops will not extricate themselves. That is why I weep, Sanjaya.

Pandunandana Yudhishtira is majestically handsome, endowed with great tejas, blessed with the power of Brahma, intelligent beyond common ken, wise and virtuous. He has the best allies and advisors and is surrounded by men who are ready for battle. His brothers and father-in-law are Maharathas. That Purushavyaghra, the son of Pandu, is also blessed with profound patience; he keeps his own counsel, is compassionate and modest; his might is unassailable; he is deeply learned, has his passions under control and his senses subdued, and is dedicated to serving the elderly. Possessed of every virtue, he is like an unquenchable fire.

What man is fool enough to fly moth-like into that blazing Pandava fire! Alas, I have deceived him and, like a long-tongued inferno, he will burn my foolish sons in battle, leaving none alive. I have come to the conclusion that it is better not to fight against him.

O Kauravas, let your minds be in accord with mine. Without doubt, all the Kuru vamsa will perish if there is war. I am blind, but this I see so clearly. If we do as my better lights urge, my heart might still find peace. If you agree that war is not the best option, we will do our utmost to bring about peace. Yudhishtira will not be unmoved when he sees us in distress; he is angry with me only because he blames me for this unjust war.'"

CANTO 54

YANASANDHI PARVA CONTINUED

"Sanjaya says, 'Great King, you speak truly. In the event of war, the annihilation of the Kshatriyas by the Gandiva is certain. I cannot understand how you, who are wise and well aware of Arjuna's power, still follow your son's lead.

You have wronged the sons of Pritha from the very beginning and repeatedly sinned against them; this is no time for remorse. A father is his children's best friend and, if he is always watchful and selfless in his affection, should swiftly seek their welfare. The man who wrongs them, instead, cannot be called a father.

When you heard of the defeat of the Pandavas at dice, you laughed foolishly like a child and said, *This is won, this is ours!* When cruel words were spoken to the sons of Pritha you did not intervene, for you were pleased at the prospect of your sons gaining the entire kingdom. At that time you did not foresee their inevitable downfall.

The Kuru kingdom, the lands called Jangala, is your paternal inheritance, but you have gained the whole Earth thanks to the might of the Pandava heroes, who made over their empire and all their vast conquests to you. You cannot imagine that you acquired all of it yourself. When the king of the Gandharvas seized your sons and when they were about to sink in a shoreless sea without a boat to save them it was Partha, O king, who rescued them.

In foolish glee you laughed at the Pandavas when they were beaten at dice, and again as they went into exile. When Arjuna looses a shower of his astras the very oceans will dry up and be no more, let alone men of flesh and blood. He is the best of all archers; the Gandiva is the best of all bows; Kesava is the best of all beings; the Sudarsana is the best of all weapons; and his chariot, with the Vanara emblazoned on its banner, is the best of all rathas. That chariot of his, flying that flag and drawn by white steeds, will consume us all in battle like the whirling wheel of Kaala.

Bull of the Bhaaratas, that best of kings who has Bhima and Arjuna fighting for him already owns the world. The Kauravas led by Duryodhana will see their forces fall, terror-struck and in despair; and when Bhima strikes they will all be razed. Paralysed by their fear of Bhima and Arjuna, your sons and their followers will find yawning defeat, and death.

The Matsyas, the Panchalas, the Salvas and the Surasenas have all withdrawn their homage and disregard you. Knowing the tejas of that wise king, they have all joined the son of Pritha and, loyal to him, will oppose your sons. He who has committed evil and wronged the sons of Pandu, who are all wedded to dharma and deserve neither punishment nor death; he who hates them even now, your sinful son Duryodhana, with all his followers, must be restrained by all the means you command.

It is not fitting that you grieve like this. The wise Vidura and I said as much even during the game of dice. Lamenting for the Pandavas as if you had no part to play in what resulted in their present condition is only hypocrisy, and will prove futile, O my king.'"

CANTO 55

YANASANDHI PARVA CONTINUED

"Duryodhana says, 'Fear not, O king; do not grieve for us. We are more than able to vanquish our enemy in battle. When the Pandavas were living in exile in the forest many Maharathas came to them: Krishna came with a huge army, in battle array and able to crush entire kingdoms; the Kekayas, Dhrishtaketu and Pritha's kinsman Dhrishtadyumna came with numerous other kings. And, assembling in a place not far from Indraprastha, those great warriors denounced you and all the Kurus. Bhaarata, those Maharathas, led by Krishna, paid homage to Yudhishtira, who sat amongst them, wearing deerskin.

The kings urged Yudhishtira to take back his kingdom and expressed their fervent wish to kill you and all your adherents. When I heard this I was struck with fear at the danger that threatened our people and spoke to Bhishma, Drona and Kripa.

I said to them, "I do not think the Pandavas will keep the pact they made. Krishna wants to kill us all. With the exception of Vidura, all of you will be killed; Dhritarashtra, who knows dharma, will also be spared.

Krishna wants to bestow the entire kingdom of the Kurus on Yudhishtira.

What should we do? Shall we surrender, or flee? Or shall we fight the enemy, even if it means giving up all hope of life? If we fight them, our defeat is certain, for Yudhishtira still commands all the kings of the Earth. The people of the realm are disgruntled and our friends are also irate with us. All the kings, especially our friends and relatives, speak ill of us.

There can be no shame in our surrendering, for from time immemorial the weaker side has chosen to make peace. However, I grieve for that Purushottama, my blind father, who will be overcome by sorrow and endless misery. You already know, Rajan, that all your other sons opposed the enemy only to please me. The mighty sons of Pandu will avenge the wrongs done to them by butchering all Dhritarashtra's race along with all our ministers and royal counsellors."

Drona, Bhishma, Kripa and Aswatthama saw how I was wracked with anxiety and said to me, "Have no fear, Parantapa. If the enemy declares war against us, they will not vanquish us in battle. Each of us, singly, can quell all the kings of the Earth. Let them come. Our arrows will curb their pride.

Long ago, inflamed with anger on the death of his father, Bhishma humbled all the kings single-handedly from his chariot. Countless Kshatriyas that furious Kurusattama killed, and in terror those that lived surrendered themselves into his protection. This Bhishma is on our side, and even now can crush all our enemies in battle. Therefore, Bhaarata, you quell your fear."

The Pandavas of great prowess have now resolved to fight us. Once they ruled all the world, but now our enemies without allies and their old power, and cannot possibly defeat us. Bharatarishabha, I am now Sovereign of the Earth, and all these kings assembled here are loyal to me in prosperity and adversity. They will enter fire or water for my sake.

They laugh to see you lament like an ignorant child and so full of fear to hear the Pandavas being praised. Every one of these kings can withstand the Pandavas. Indeed, Rajan, every one of them thinks he is all-powerful. Indra himself cannot subdue my vast host. Brahma himself cannot destroy it, though he may wish to.

Yudhishtira has given up hope of getting a city and asks for just five villages because he is afraid of the army I have assembled and of my power. Your belief in Vrikodara's strength is baseless. You do not know how strong I am. There is no one on Earth who can match me in a duel with maces. No man has ever beaten me in a gada yuddha, nor ever will.

I suffered many privations out of my devotion to learning when I lived in the home of my Acharya. I have mastered all the knowledge and skills he had to impart. I am not afraid of Bhima or the others. Blessed one, waiting humbly upon my guru Sankarshana as I did, he was sure that I, Duryodhana, have no equal in battle. In battle I am Balarama's equal, and in strength there is no one on Earth superior to me.

Bhima will not bear even a single blow of my mace. One wrathful stroke will send him to Yama. Rajan, I am eager to see Vrikodara with his mace in hand; long have I wished for this. I will strike him like thunder and my detested cousin will die, all his limbs shattered. Why, one blow of my mace will split the mountains of Himavat into thousands of pieces. Vrikodara knows the truth of this, as do Krishna and Arjuna: that there is no one equal to Duryodhana at the mace.

Dispel the fear that Bhima invokes in you, for have no doubt that I will kill him in savage battle. My lord, do not be dejected. After I have slain Bhima, my numberless chariot warriors, all as mighty as me, will quickly bring Arjuna down. Bhishma, Drona, Kripa, Drona's son, Karna, Bhurisravas, Salya, the king of Pragjyotisha and Jayadratha king of the Sindhus can each kill the Pandavas on his own. United, they will send Arjuna to Yama in an instant.

There is no reason why the combined armies of all the kings, fighting as one, cannot vanquish Dhananjaya. Bhishma, Drona, Drona's son and Kripa will cover him in a hundred shrouds of arrows and, broken, Arjuna will vanish into death's catacombs.

Our Pitamaha Bhishma, born of Devi Ganga, is superior to Santanu. He was born amongst men, but he is a holy being, whom even the Devas cannot face. There is no man on Earth who can kill Bhishma. Pleased with the sacrifice Bhishma made for his sake, his father gave him an exceptional boon: *You shall not die except by your own wish.*

Drona was born of Bharadwaja Muni in a water-pot, with complete knowledge of the astra shastra at his very birth. Kripa, the best of Acharyas, whose father is Rishi Gautama, was born in a bank of river reeds and he, too, cannot be killed.

Aswatthama's father, mother and uncle were not born from a woman's womb. That hero, too, is on my side. All these Maharathas are veritable gods and can confound Indra himself in battle. Arjuna cannot even look upon any one of these. When united, these tigers among men will bring him down like a pride of lions does a deer.

Karna is equal to Bhishma, Drona and Kripa. Parasurama, too, declared him his equal. Karna was born with kundalas of dazzling beauty; and to please Sachi Devi, Indra begged him for them in exchange for an infallible shakti. How will Arjuna escape Karna when Radheya has that astra?

I am sure of victory; it is a fruit I hold in my hand. The rout of my enemies is already being talked about everywhere.

Bhaarata, in war Bhishma kills ten thousand soldiers in a day. As powerful as him are the master bowmen Drona, Drona's son and Kripa. In addition, the Samsaptaka warriors are resolved to fight Arjuna to the death. There are other kings, too, who regard themselves as being superior to Savyasachi, and who are determined to kill him.

Why then are you so fearful of the Pandavas? Once Bhimasena is killed who amongst them will continue to fight? Seven warriors—the five Pandava brothers, Dhrishtadyumna and Satyaki—are the backbone of the Pandava forces. We have Bhishma, Drona, Kripa and Drona's son; Karna, Somadatta and Bahlika; Salya of Pragjyotisha, Vinda and Anuvinda of Avanti, and Jayadratha. We have your sons Dusasana, Durmukha and Dussaha, and the others; we have Srutayu, Chitrasena, Purumitra and Vivimsati; Sala, Bhurisravas and Vikarna. And I have assembled eleven akshauhinis. The enemy's army is far smaller than mine, with only seven.

How will they defeat me?

Brihaspati has said that a king should fight an army which is less than his by a third. My army is bigger by more than that, my king. Besides, I know that the enemy has many shortcomings, while my forces are endowed with as many strengths. Knowing all this, and that my force is superior and that of Pandavas inferior, you must not to lose heart and good sense.'

Saying this, Duryodhana questions Sanjaya again, anxious to know more about the Pandavas' thoughts."

CANTO 56

YANASANDHI PARVA CONTINUED

"Duryodhana says, 'Sanjaya, I have gathered an army of seven akshauhinis; what have Yudhishtira and the kings who support him done to prepare for war?'

Sanjaya says, 'Yudhishtira is eager for war and full of assurance. Bhimasena, Arjuna and the twins are also confident and fearless. Arjuna yoked his horses to his chariot and took it out to test the astras he has acquired, lighting up the world in all directions. Clad in mail, he looked like a mass of clouds charged with lightning.

He was thoughtful for a while and then he said to me, "Sanjaya, look at the omens, they all predict our victory," and indeed what he said was true.'

Duryodhana says, 'You are happy to praise these sons of Pritha whom we routed at dice. Tell me, what sort of horses has Arjuna yoked to his chariot, and what banners has he raised?'

Sanjaya says, 'The divine architect Tvashtri has, with Indra and Dhatri's help, created all kinds of wonderful and beautiful forms for Arjuna's chariot. Using maya, he adorned Partha's banner with celestial spirits of diverse forms and sizes. At Bhimasena's plea, Vayuputra Hanuman will also enliven Arjuna's pennant with his own splendid and fearsome form. Tvashtri's genius is so powerful that the flag covers one Yojana, both in width and length, and even great trees cannot obstruct it.

Tvashtri's creation is like Indra's evanescent and colourful bow that appears in the sky; nobody knows what it is made of and its form changes constantly. This banner rears its head like a column of fire and smoke rising up into the sky, filling it with dazzling colours and beautiful shapes, weightless, yet finding no impediment anywhere.

Yoked to the chariot are one hundred celestial white horses endowed with the speed of the mind; they are the gift of the Gandharva king Chitrasena. Nothing can stand in their way, nothing can arrest their careen, not on Earth, in the sky, or in heaven. A boon ensures that their number will always be a hundred, regardless of how often or how many are killed.

Yudhishtira's chariot is drawn by great ivory-coloured horses of equal strength. The horses that pull Bhima's chariot are as fleet as the wind and as splendid as the Saptarishis. Sable-hued horses with backs streaked like the wings of the tittiri bird are yoked to Sahadeva's chariot; they are Arjuna's gift to him, and superior to Dhananjaya's own. And Madri's son Nakula, of the Ajamida vamsa, is borne, like Indra, by exalted steeds given by Indra himself, all mighty and quick as the mind.

Superb horses, gifts of the Devas, large and equal to those of the Pandava brothers in experience and strength, swift and handsome, bear Subhadra's and Draupadi's sons into war.'"

CANTO 57

YANASANDHI PARVA CONTINUED

"Dhritarashtra says, 'Sanjaya, whom have you seen come to the Pandava camp out of love for them? Who will fight for them against my son's forces?'

Sanjaya says, 'Krishna, chief of the Andhakas and the Vrishnis, has arrived. I have also seen Chekitana and Satyaki, also called Yuyudhana, both Maharathas, proud of their strength and renowned the world over; and they have each brought an akshauhini of troops. Drupada, the king of the Panchalas, has come, accompanied by his ten heroic sons—Satyajit and the others, led by Dhrishtadyumna, the fire-born.

Sikhandin has come in Drupada's support to honour Yudhishtira, with a full akshauhini of soldiers whom he has equipped well with everything they need. That lord of Earth Virata, and his two sons, Sankha and Uttara; Suryadatta and others headed by Madiraksha, with one akshauhini of troops and the support of his brothers and sons, have joined the son of Pritha.

Jarasandha's son, the king of Magadha, and Dhrishtaketu, the king of the Chedis, have arrived separately, each accompanied by an akshauhini.

The five Kekaya brothers, flying purple flags, have joined the Pandavas with their akshauhini of warriors. All these valiant men, whom I have seen assembled there, will fight on the Pandava side against Duryodhana's armies. Maharathika Dhrishtadyumna, who knows all the vyuhas of Manavas, Devas and Gandharvas, leads the Pandava host as its Senapati.

O Rajan, Sikhandin is appointed to meet Santanu's son Bhishma in battle, with Virata and his Matsya warriors to support him. Yudhishtira will face the king of the Madras, though some feel that the two are not evenly matched. Bhimasena will fight Duryodhana, his sons and his ninety-nine brothers, as well as the eastern and southern kings. Arjuna will meet Vikartana's son Karna and Jayadratha, king of the Sindhus, those irresistible Kshatriyas so proud of their strength.

The five mighty bowmen, the Kekaya brothers, will fight the Kekaya soldiers who are with Dhritarashtra. Also in their lot are the Malavas and the Salvakas, and the two famed Trigarta warriors who have sworn to conquer or die. Subhadra's son has been assigned to kill all the sons of Duryodhana and Dusasana, and also king Brihadbala. And those great archers, the sons of Draupadi, with gold embroidered banners on their chariots, and led by Dhrishtadyumna, will do battle against Drona.

Chekitana wants to meet Somadatta in his chariot, in single combat; Satyaki is anxious to do battle against the Bhoja lord Kritavarman; Madri's heroic son Sahadeva, who roars so dreadfully in battle, means to kill your brother-in-law, Sakuni son of Subala; and Madri's other son Nakula will meet the deceitful Uluka and the Saraswatas. The Pandavas have placed all the other kings under the leadership of one or other of their allies. Thus has the Pandava host been divided. You and your sons must do as you think best, and without delay.'

Dhritarashtra says, 'Alas, my foolish sons, who cheated at dice, are already as good as dead, for it is Bhima they have chosen to meet in battle. Like moths to the flame, all the other kings will rush inexorably towards the Gandiva, as if consecrated for a yagna by Yama himself. In my mind's eye I see my host routed and killed by those illustrious Kshatriyas whom I have grievously wronged. Who will follow my warriors, when the sons of Pandu break their ranks?

The Pandavas are Maharathas of awesome accomplishments, with the energy of the fiery Sun and ever victorious. Indra himself cannot wrest the Earth from them, who have Yudhishtira for their king, Krishna for their protector, the heroic Savyasachi and Vrikodara for their warriors, and Nakula, Sahadeva and Dhrishtadyumna also fighting for them.

Indra cannot prevail against them, who have with them the son of Prishata, Satyaki, Drupada and Dhrishtaketu with his son, Uttamaujas, the unconquerable Yudhamanyu of the Panchalas, Sikhandin, Kshattradeva, Virata's son Uttara, the Kasayas, the Chedis, the Matsyas, the Srinjayas, Babhru, the sons of Virata, the Panchalas, and the Prabhadrakas. These heroes are calm and steadfast on the battlefield; they can cleave the very mountains; they are endowed with every virtue and blessed with superhuman strength; and it is against them that my foolish son wants to pit himself, ignoring all my pleas.'

Duryodhana says, 'The Pandavas and we are of the same vamsa; we tread upon the same earth. Why do you think that victory will be theirs? Bhishma, Drona, Kripa, the unconquerable Karna, Jayadratha, Somadatta and Aswatthama are all mighty bowmen and endowed with great powers. When even Indra and the Devas cannot subdue them, what can the Pandavas do against them, O my father?

All these noble and heroic kings of the Earth, bearing weapons on my behalf, will easily contain and quell the Pandavas; the sons of Pandu cannot dare look at my troops, let alone face them in war. Why, by myself I can crush the Pandavas and their sons in battle. Bhaarata, all these sovereigns of the Earth, who are anxious to serve my cause, will even capture the Pandavas as they would net a herd of young deer. Rest assured, O Dhritarashtra, that, with our numberless chariots and tempests of arrows, we will annihilate the Panchalas and the Pandavas.'

Dhritarashtra says, 'Sanjaya, my son speaks like a madman; he cannot prevail over Dharmaraja Yudhishtira. Bhishma knows the true might of the Pandavas and their sons, which is why he does not want war with them.

Tell me again, Sanjaya, of their movements. Tell me, who incites those bowmen of the wonderful tejas like priests feeding the homa fire with libations of ghee?'

Sanjaya says, 'Dhrishtadyumna urges the Pandavas to war, saying, "Fight, Bharatottamas! Have no fear whatever. All those rulers of the Earth, whom Dhritarashtra's son woos, will be no more than easy targets for your astras in war. I by myself can devour all the angry kings assembled, together with their kinsmen, like a whale swallowing swarms of little fish. Bhishma, Drona, Kripa, Karna, Drona's son, Salya and Duryodhana—I will contain them all, as the shore does the swelling sea."

Yudhishtira said in reply, "The Panchalas and the Pandavas depend on your prowess and fortitude to see us safely through the war. I know, Mahabaho, that you are devoted to Kshatriya dharma. Indeed, you can kill the Kauravas on your own. Parantapa, when they face us, eager for war, whatever strategy you decide on will be the best for us, of that I am sure.

Those who know the Shastras say that the Kshatriya who manifests his strength, and then helps those who flee the battlefield after the rout he has made and ask for his protection, is worth a thousand men. Purusharishabha, you are such a man—peerless. I have no doubt that you will be the refuge of those who are taken by fear on the field of war."

When Dharmatma Yudhishtira said this, Dhrishtadyumna said to me, "Go, Suta, without delay and say to all those that have come to fight for Duryodhana—the Kurus of the Pratipa vamsa, the Bahlikas, the son of Saradwata, Karna and Drona, Drona's son and Jayadratha, Dusasana, Vikarna and to Raja Duryodhana and Bhishma: *Do not offer yourselves up to be slain by Arjuna, whom the Devas protect. Before that happens, let some good man approach Yudhishtira with all repair and entreat that son of Pandu, that Purushottama, to accept the kingdom that they surrender to him, without delay.*

There is no warrior on the Earth like Arjuna, of the pure and unquenchable prowess. The Devas protect the wielder of the Gandiva's celestial ratha, and he cannot be vanquished by a human. Therefore, steer your minds away from war."''

CANTO 58

YANASANDHI PARVA CONTINUED

"Dhritarashtra says, 'Yudhishtira has the power of a Kshatriya by birth and since his youth led a life of brahmacharya. Sadly, my foolish sons ignore me and want to fight this noblest man, which is why I weep.

I beg you, Duryodhana, to turn away from this enmity. War is never commended under any circumstances. Half the Earth is quite enough for you and all your followers. Give back their rightful share of the kingdom to the Pandavas. All the Kauravas consider this course of action—to make peace with the sons of Pandu—to be in keeping both with nyaya and dharma.

Think carefully, my son, and you will realise that your own army will become the instrument of your death. Your folly prevents you from understanding this. I myself do not want war and neither do Bahlika, Bhishma, Drona and Aswatthama; nor do Somadatta, Salya and Kripa; nor Satyavrata, Purumitra and Bhurisravas. If truth be told, none of these kings wants war. The warriors upon whom the Kauravas depend disapprove of the war. My child, accept this. In your own heart, you do not wish for war, but sadly, Karna and the vile-minded Dusasana and Sakuni lead you to it.'

Duryodhana says, 'I challenge the Pandavas to battle without depending on you, Drona, Aswatthama or Sanjaya, on Vikarna, Kamboja, Kripa or Bahlika, on Satyavrata, Purumitra or Bhurisravas, or on any of the others in our force. Purusharishabha, Karna and I, by ourselves, are prepared to celebrate the Yuddha yagna—the sacrifice of war—with all the needful rites and make Yudhishtira the yagnapasu, the sacrificial animal.

At that yagna my chariot will be the altar; my sword will be the small ladle and my mace the large one for pouring libations; my coat of mail will be the witness; my four steeds will be the officiating priests; my arrows will be the blades of kusa grass; and fame will be the ghrita, the clarified butter. Rajan, by performing such a sacrifice with war in honour of Yama, and by providing the ingredients for it ourselves, we will return crowned with victory and covered in glory after slaying our enemies.

The three of us—I, Karna and my brother Dusasana—will kill the Pandavas in battle. Either I will slay them and rule the Earth or, having killed me, they will. My king, O you of unfading glory, I am ready to sacrifice my life, my kingdom, my wealth and everything else, but I cannot live at peace with the Pandavas. *I will not surrender to the Pandavas even such land as may be covered by the point of a needle!*

Dhritarashtra says, 'Ah, I now cast Duryodhana off forever; however, I grieve for all you kings who will follow this fool into Yamaloka. Like tigers let loose amongst a herd of deer, the sons of Pandu will devour all of you, who are so agog for battle.

I think of the Bhaarata host as a helpless woman who will be brutalised, then slain and cast into the distance by Yuyudhana of the long arms. Augmenting the strength of Yudhishtira's army, which was already powerful enough, Sini's son will take his stand on the field of battle and scatter his arrows like seeds on a ploughed field. And each one will take a life.

Bhimasena will assume his position at the very front of the Pandava forces with his soldiers arrayed fearlessly behind him, as behind a rampart.

O Duryodhana, when you see elephants as big as hills fallen on the ground with their tusks broken, their heads crushed and their bodies dyed with their own blood; when you see them lying on the field of battle like splintered mountains; then, terrified of Bhima, you will remember my words. When you see your forces of chariots, horses and elephants devastated by Bhimasena, and looking like the ruined, smoking wake of a great conflagration, you will remember my words.

If you do not make peace with the Pandavas, inexorable doom will find you. You will meet your end by the hand of Bhimasena with his gada, and rest finally in peace. When you see the Kuru host levelled to the ground by Bhima, like a vast forest of trees torn up by their roots, then you will remember my words.'

Having spoken thus to all those rulers of the Earth gathered there, the king addresses Sanjaya once more."

CANTO 59

YANASANDHI PARVA CONTINUED

"Dhritarashtra says, 'Wise one, tell me what Krishna and Dhananjaya said. I am eager to hear that.'

Sanjaya says, 'Listen, O king, and I will tell you how Krishna and Arjuna are, and what those heroes said. With my eyes turned down, my hands joined in reverence and with my senses under control, I entered the antahpura to confer with those gods among men. Not Abhimanyu or the twins have free access to the apartments that Arjuna and Krishna share with Draupadi and Satyabhama. There I saw those Parantapas, anointed with sandalwood paste, and cheerful from having drunk sweet wine. They wore grand clothes and celestial ornaments and sat on a golden dais decked with gems and covered with closely woven, many-hued carpets.

Krishna's feet rested on Arjuna's lap, while Arjuna's lay on Draupadi's and Satyabhama's. Arjuna pointed to a golden foot-stool for me to sit on; I touched it in ritual salutation and sat on the ground. And when he drew his feet away from the foot-stool, I saw auspicious marks on both his soles—two dark lines ran from heel to toe.

Seeing the two Krishnas—both of them tall, dark and straight like the trunks of sala trees—sitting on the same seat, a great foreboding gripped me. They looked like Indra and Vishnu seated together. Relying on Drona and Bhishma, and on Karna's vain boasts, the deluded Duryodhana does not realise that Yudhishtira, with these two obeying his every command, will have all his wishes fulfilled. My lord, of that I am entirely convinced.

They entertained me with food and drink and honoured me with other courtesies, too; then, raising my folded hands over my head in reverence, I conveyed your message to them. Arjuna, with his cicatrised hand, removed Krishna's auspicious foot from his lap and urged him to speak. Sitting up erect as Indra's banner, adorned with every ornament, and splendid in tejas as Indra himself, Krishna addressed me. His words were sweet, charming and mild, but full of doom for Duryodhana. Krishna spoke directly, clearly and meaningfully, but what he said at the end rent my very heart.

He said to me, "O Sanjaya, after greeting the elders and enquiring about the welfare of the younger ones there, say this to the wise Dhritarashtra, in the hearing of Kurusattama Bhishma and Drona:

'We hope that you have been performing yagnas, giving gifts to Brahmanas, and enjoying your sons and wives, for dire peril is imminent. We hope you have been giving wealth to the deserving, helping your near and dear ones and that you have been blessed with good sons, for Yudhishtira is eager for victory. My old vow to Draupadi remains unfulfilled. You have provoked Arjuna, whose bow is the fiery and invincible Gandiva, and who has me by his side. Even if he were Indra, is there any man who would challenge Arjuna, who has me to help him, unless that man's time on Earth has ended? Only the man who can lift the Earth in his arms, consume all creation in anger and who can cast the Devas out of Swarga, can hope to vanquish Arjuna. I do not see even one among the Devas, Asuras, Manavas, Yakshas, Gandharvas and Nagas who can face Dhanajaya in war.

That wonderful battle in Virata's kingdom is proof of this: when one man faced countless Maharathas and quelled them. That you all fled, routed single-handedly by this Pandava, is proof enough. No one has the might, prowess, energy, speed, lightness of hand, boundless stamina and patience that Partha does.'"

Krishna cheered Arjuna with these words and, also, with roars of exultation, like thunder in the sky, that would frighten even Indra. When he heard what Krishna said, Arjuna, too, spoke in similar vein to me, and his words made the hairs on my body stand on end.'"

CANTO 60

YANASANDHI PARVA CONTINUED

Vaisampayana said, "The wise Dhritarashtra weighs Sanjaya's words, their merits and flaws. Once he has done this as best he can and has gauged the strengths and weaknesses of both sides, the Kuru king compares the might of each side, always keeping his sons' interest at heart. He comes to the conclusion that the Pandavas, endowed with both human and divine ancestry and prowess, are more powerful.

He says to Duryodhana, 'My child, I cannot shake off the anxiety that grips me. It clings to me so that I can almost see it, like some demon. My dark forebodings cannot be explained away by your reasoning; and it is natural, for you are my son. All beings love their progeny; they do everything in their power to please them, and work for their advantage. It is the same with benefactors—good men always want to reciprocate the good done to them and do what pleases their patrons.

Agni will remember what Arjuna did for him in the Khandava vana and will certainly help Arjuna in this unthinkable war. From paternal affection, Dharma, Indra, Vayu and the Aswins will come together to help the Pandavas; other Devas will join them. To protect them from

Bhishma, Drona and Kripa, the wrath of the Devas will manifest itself like the very Brahmastra. Those Purushavyaghras, the sons of Pritha, are blessed with immense strength and are masters of all the godly and fell astras. When they are as one with the Devas, our warriors—mere mortals, all—will not be able to even look at them.

He whose bow is the divine Gandiva; he who has a pair of inexhaustible celestial quivers from Varuna; he whose banner, which flies as freely as smoke in the air, has the Vanara upon it; he whose chariot has no equal on the Earth bound by the four seas, its rumble like clouds roaring, and which, like the crash of thunder, terrifies his enemies; he whose superhuman tejas the whole world knows; he whom all the kings of the Earth know to be the conqueror of the Devas; he who takes up five hundred arrows at a time and in the twinkling of an eye shoots them in a blur into far distances; this son of Pritha, Parantapa, tiger among Maharathas, whom Bhishma, Drona, Kripa, Drona's son, Salya the king of the Madras and indeed all impartial men of thought consider invincible even by kings possessing phenomenal prowess; he who shoots five hundred arrows at each stretch of his bow and whose arms are as powerful as Kartavirya's—I see this great bowman Arjuna, who is equal to Indra or Upendra, this Kshatriya himself without equal, wreaking unimagined havoc in this war.

O Bhaarata, this thought preys on my mind night and day, and I am miserable and sleepless because of my fear for my sons and for all the Kurus. Savage and bloody carnage is about to overtake them unless this war is averted by striking peace. With all my heart, I am for making peace with the Pandavas and not for war. My son, I have always considered them greater than the Kurus.'"

CANTO 61

YANASANDHI PARVA CONTINUED

Vaisampayana said, "At his father's words, Dhritarashtra's volatile son is inflamed with rage and in a voice heavy with envy says, 'You assume that the sons of Pritha are invincible because they have the Devas on their side. Best of kings, dispel your fear. The Devas achieved divinity by virtue of the absence of desire, covetousness, hatred and of detachment from worldly affairs.

Bharatarishabha, once, Dwaipayana-Vyasa, Maharishi Narada and Jamadagni's son Parasurama told us that, unlike human beings, the motive for what the Devas do is never desire, anger, covetousness or envy. Indeed, if Agni, Vayu, Dharma, Indra or the Aswins had actively taken their side, the sons of Pritha would never have fallen into this pit of distress. Do not be anxious, for the Devas always act dispassionately, in accord with principles worthy of their divinity. If envy and lust are incentives, the laws that rule the Devas will nullify them.

Besides, even if he flares into an all-consuming blaze, I will charm Agni into extinguishment. The tejas of the gods is great, but mine is greater. If the Earth herself cleaves in two, or mountain peaks split, I can reunite them with my mantras, Rajan. If a violent tempest or a roaring deluge threatens the universe of animate and inanimate, moving and immobile creatures, I can, from compassion for life, stop them. I have the power to freeze all the great waters of the Earth, so chariots and fighting men can pass over them.

It is I who set in motion all the affairs of the Devas and Asuras. My horses take me anywhere at my will, wherever I go with my akshauhinis, on whatever mission. Within my dominions there are no fearful nagas and, protected by my mantras, innocent creatures within my kingdom never fall prey to others. The clouds bring rain at the appointed time and in the quantity wished for by my people. All my subjects are devout, and natural calamities never visit them.

The Aswins, Vayu, Agni, Dharma and Indra with the Maruts will not dare protect my enemies. Had they been able to, would the sons of Kunti have suffered for thirteen years? Know that neither Devas nor Gandharvas, neither Asuras nor Rakshasas can save him who has incurred my wrath. I have never before had any doubt about the aptness of reward or punishment to friend or foe. Parantapa, whenever I say something it is always just so. The people know me as a speaker of truth.

Everyone can bear witness to my greatness, whose fame has spread all around. I say this, Rajan, for your information and not from vanity. I have never praised myself before; to sing one's own praises is petty. And I say to you, my father, you will soon hear of my victory over the Pandavas, the Matsyas, the Panchalas, the Kekayas, Satyaki and Krishna.

Just as rivers cease to be when they enter the ocean, so will the Pandavas and all their followers when they encounter me. My intelligence is sharper, my energy is greater, my prowess is mightier, my knowledge is deeper and my resources are superior, by far, to theirs. The knowledge of weapons that our Pitamaha, Drona, Kripa, Salya and Sala have, I have it all.'

Saying this, Parantapa Duryodhana questions Sanjaya once more about Yudhishtira's preparations for the war.

CANTO 62

YANASANDHI PARVA CONTINUED

Vaisampayana said, "Ignoring Dhritarashtra, who was about to ask about Arjuna, Karna addresses Duryodhana with words to cheer the spirit of the assembled Kurus.

He says, 'When Parasurama discovered the false pretence by which I obtained the Brahmastra from him, he cursed me that I would forget the mantra for that astra at the end of my days. Even for so great an offence, that Rishi, my guru, cursed me lightly; that Maharishi of the fierce tejas can consume the very Earth with her seas. By my diligence and bravery, I appeased him. I have that weapon with me still, and my end has not yet come. I am confident of victory. Let the charge of winning the war be mine.

Through my guru's favour, I will, in the twinkling of an eye, wipe out the Panchalas, the Karushas, the Matsyas, as well as the sons of Pritha, their sons and grandsons. I will win the war and bestow many realms upon you. Let the Pitamaha, Drona and all the kings remain here with you. I will go forth with the best of my warriors and kill Kunti's sons. Let that task be mine.'

Bhishma says to him, 'What are you saying, Karna? The approach of your end has dimmed your intellect. Do you not know that when our chieftains are killed, all the sons of Dhritarashtra will die? Considering that you know how Arjuna burnt down the Khandava vana, with only Krishna helping him, you ought to restrain yourself and your friends and relatives.

You will see the shakti that Indra gave you burnt to ashes when Krishna strikes it with his chakra. Your other astra, with the serpent's head, that shines in your quiver and which you worship with offerings of flowers, will be consumed and you with it, when Arjuna's arrows flare at you. Karna, remember that it is Krishna, who killed Bana and Bhumi's son Naraka in fervid battle, and who has slain many others much greater than you, who protects Arjuna.'

Karna says, 'There is no doubt that Krishna is all that you say, and I believe he is even greater. Pitamaha, you are invariably harsh to me, and this is my response to you today: I hereby lay down my weapons! From now, you will see me only in the sabha and not on the battlefield. When death stills your voice, Bhishma, and only then, will the rulers of the Earth see my prowess,' and with these words, the great archer, Mahadhanushman Karna, leaves the Kuru sabha and goes home.

Bhishma laughs mockingly and says to Duryodhana in the midst of the Kurus, 'How truly the Sutaputra keeps his word. When Bhimasena arrays his forces and brings havoc by decimating our legions, scattering hundreds of thousands of heads, how does Karna intend to keep his pledge to kill the kings of Avanti and Kalinga with Jayadratha, Chedidhvaja and Bahlika looking on?

When he presented himself as a Brahmana before the holy Parasurama, he did indeed obtain the Brahmastra, but he lost his dharma and punya.'

When Bhishma says this after Karna lays down his weapons and leaves, Vichitravirya's foolish grandson Duryodhana testily addresses Bhishma."

CANTO 63

YANASANDHI PARVA CONTINUED

"Duryodhana says, 'Pritha's sons are men like any others, mortals like other men. Why then are you so sure victory will be theirs? Both we and they are equal in energy, in prowess, in age, in intelligence, in our knowledge of the Shastras, in our mastery over astras, in the art of war, in lightness of hand and every other skill. We are all human by birth. How then, Pitamaha, do you know that victory will be theirs?

I do not seek to accomplish my goals by relying on you, Drona, Kripa, Bahlika, or on any of the other kings. Vikartana's son Karna, my brother Dusasana and I will slay the five sons of Pandu in battle. Having done this, we will gratify Brahmanas by performing great yagnas of all kinds, with abundant dakshina and gifts of cattle, horses and wealth.

When my warriors haul the Pandavas' legions across the field, like hunters a herd of deer caught in a net, or like whirlpools do a crewless boat, Pandu's sons will see the might of our vast host of soldiers, chariots and elephants, and not only they, but Krishna as well, will surrender their pride.'

Hearing this, Vidura says, 'Venerable men of infallible knowledge say that self-restraint is the best of all virtues; and for a Brahmana it is his eternal dharma. He whose self-control follows the path of daana, tapasya, gyana and Veda dhyana, always wins success, forgiveness and the punya of his charity. Self-restraint enhances a man's tejas and is a most holy attribute. By absolving a man of his sin and increasing his vitality, it even leads him to Brahman.

People always fear those who have no self-restraint, as if they are Rakshasas; and it is to curb Rakshasas that Brahma created Kshatriyas. Indeed, self-restraint is an excellent vow for all the four varnas to keep.

And these are the qualities of a man with self-restraint: forgiveness, firmness of mind, non-violence, respect for all things, truthfulness, simplicity, control over the senses, patience, gentle speech, modesty, steadiness, liberality, mildness, contentment and faith. He who is self-controlled sheds lust, avarice, pride, anger, sloth, vanity, malice and sorrow. Purity and straightforwardness are the hallmarks of a self-restrained man.

He who is not covetous, who is content with a little, who is indifferent to all things provocative or seductive, and who is as deep as the ocean, is a man of self-restraint. He who is virtuous, always pleasant and contented, who has Atmagyana and wisdom wins great respect in this world and bliss in the hereafter. The man who is wise and mature, who has no fear of other creatures and whom other creatures do not fear is the foremost of men.

Such a man, who seeks the good of all, is a universal friend and makes one and all happy. Blessed with depth of character, like the ocean, and happily content by virtue of his wisdom, this man is always serene and light-hearted. A man who has self-control and serenity, regulates his life by the example of men of dharma of the past and the present, and lives in joy. Alternatively, such a man, whose gyana has endowed him with contentment, abandons karma and, with his senses firmly restrained, wanders over the Earth, impatient for death and absorption into Brahman.

The path of the man who enjoys the contentment that his gyana brings is as invisible as the paths of birds in the sky. He who abandons the world and takes to sannyasa in pursuit of Moksha can look forward to the bright and eternal realms that are reserved for him in Swarga.'"

CANTO 64

YANASANDHI PARVA CONTINUED

"Vidura says, 'O king, there is a tale told by men of old of the fowler who spread his net on the ground to snare birds. Two birds that lived together were trapped in the net at the same time, but they took the net up and soared up into the air. Seeing them fly into the sky, the fowler, without giving way to despair, began to follow them on the ground. Just then, a hermit living in a nearby asrama, who had finished his morning prayers, saw the fowler running to catch the birds.

The Muni said to the man, "Fowler, I find it strange and wonderful that you, who walk on solid ground are pursuing a pair of winged creatures of the air."

The fowler said, "These two, united now, are taking away my snare. Once they fall out I will indeed catch them."

Sure enough the two doomed birds soon began to quarrel, and they fell to the ground. Still caught in the net and facing death, they argued angrily with each other. The fowler came up stealthily and seized them both.

Kinsmen who fall out with one another over wealth fall into the hands of their enemies, like the quarrelling birds. The duty of kinsmen is to eat together and talk with one another, and not argue under any circumstances. Family members who lovingly wait on the elderly become unconquerable, like a forest guarded by lions; but those who are mean, although wealthy, always contribute to the prosperity of their enemies. Dhritarashtra, cousins are like charcoal, blazing when united but only smoking when divided.

I will tell you of something else I once saw on a mountainside. Listen to this, O Kaurava, and then do what you think best. Once, we went to the northern mountain, Gandhamadana, accompanied by some hunters and a number of Brahmanas who liked talking about magical charms and medicinal plants.

Gandhamadana was a great sylvan tapovana, its slopes covered with trees and luminous herbs, and Siddhas and Gandharvas lived there. There we saw a jar of bright golden honey perched on an inaccessible precipice. That honey, which was Kubera's favourite drink, was guarded by poisonous snakes. To the one who drank it, it had the power to grant immortality to the mortal, sight to the blind and youth to the old. It was this honey, too, that those Brahmanas had spoken of. The hunters saw that honey and, in their frantic attempt to secure it, they all died either falling from that snake ridden cliff or being stung by the vicious serpents.

In much the same way, your son lusts for unrivalled ownership of the Earth. He sees the prize but, foolishly, not the terrible fall. Duryodhana wants to do battle with Savyasachi, but I do not see in him enough prowess or vigour to give him success.

On a single chariot Arjuna conquered all the Earth. Bhishma, Drona and others, with huge armies behind them, were terrified of Arjuna, who routed them outside Virata's city. Keep in mind what happened there. Arjuna still forgives you and looks to you in hope, waiting for your decision. When roused, Dhananjaya, Drupada and the king of Matsyas will leave no remnant of your army; they will be like apocalyptic flames fanned by the winds of yuganta.

O Dhritarashtra, embrace Yudhishtira. If you go to war, neither side can win without dreadful losses to themselves, not under any circumstances.'"

CANTO 65

YANASANDHI PARVA CONTINUED

"Dhritarashtra says, 'O my son Duryodhana, think carefully about what I tell you. Like an ignorant wayfarer, you mistake the wrong path for the right one.

The five sons of Pandu, whose tejas you are so eager to extinguish, are like the Panchabhutas, the five elements that support the very universe. You cannot vanquish Yudhishtira without sacrificing your life in the effort; this son of Kunti is the most virtuous man in the world. Like a weak tree against a howling storm, you dare defy Bhimasena, whose strength is unrivalled on Earth, and who is like Yama himself in battle. And what man of any sense would choose to face the wielder of Gandiva, greatest of all Kshatriyas, who is a man among men as Meru is among mountains?

There is no man whom Dhrishtadyumna cannot vanquish, the prince of Panchala who looses astras at his enemies even like Indra hurling his Vajra. The noble, irresistible Satyaki, whom the Andhakas and the Vrishnis honour, is always with the Pandavas. He, too, will slaughter your forces.

No man in his right senses would face the lotus-eyed Krishna, whose tejas and might surpass any in the three worlds. This same Krishna puts his wives, relatives, his own soul and the entire Earth on one side of a scale, and considers Arjuna on the other side to be equal to them all. Krishna, on whom Arjuna relies, is invincible; and the army with which he allies himself also becomes irresistible.

Listen, my son, to your well-wishers; they advise you for your own good. Accept your Pitamaha Bhishma as your mentor and guide. Listen to what I say and to what these other true friends of the Kurus—Drona, Kripa, Vikarna and Raja Bahlika—say. They feel for you as I do, and you would do well to regard them as you do me. Bhaarata, they all know dharma and love you as much as I do.

The rout by one man, and the ensuing panic of your troops, which you and your brothers saw outside Virata's city, is proof enough of the truth of what I am saying. When Arjuna could single-handedly do that, what can the Pandavas not achieve when united? Take them by their hands as your brothers and cherish them with a share of the kingdom.'"

CANTO 66

YANASANDHI PARVA CONTINUED

Vaisampayana said, "Having said this to Duryodhana, the wise Dhritarashtra asks Sanjaya, 'Now, Sanjaya, tell me what you have not yet told me—what Arjuna said after Krishna spoke. I am eager to hear it.'

Sanjaya says, 'Having heard what Krishna said, the irresistible Dhananjaya spoke to me in Krishna's presence.

He said, "O Sanjaya, all the kings and the others who have assembled here to fight for the Kauravas are about to die—our Pitamaha, Dhritarashtra, Drona and Kripa; Karna and king Bahlika; Drona's son, Somadatta and Subala's son Sakuni; Dusasana, Sala, Purumitra and Vivimsati; Vikarna, Chitrasena and Jayatsena; Vinda and Anuvinda; the two lords of Avanti; Bhurisravas, Bhagadatta and Jarasandha and the other rulers of the Earth. Dhritarashtra's son has brought them together to serve as a libation in the Pandava fire.

In my name, Sanjaya, enquire after the welfare of those kings according to their status, making sure that you accord them proper respect. In their presence, address Duryodhana, that worst of evil men, who is wrathful, of sinful soul, and covetous. Make sure that fool and his advisors hear my message."

Saying this first, Pritha's son, Dhananjaya of the large eyes with red corners glanced at Krishna and then spoke words of dharma and artha.

He said to me, "You have heard the measured words of the high-souled lord of the Madhus. Tell the assembled kings that they are mine as well.

Say this for me to those kings, *Make peace with us so that you will not be poured as offerings into the arrow fire of the great yagna of war, in which the rumble of chariot wheels are the mantras and the annihilating bow is the sruva, the ladle which will pour blood into death's great fire. If you do not give his rightful share of the kingdom to Yudhishtira, I will send all of you, with your footsoldiers, horsemen and elephants, into the dark regions of departed spirits."*

I bowed before Dhananjaya and Hari of four arms and took leave of them, and here I am, come speedily to convey their grave message to you who are as effulgent as the Devas themselves.'"

CANTO 67

YANASANDHI PARVA CONTINUED

Vaisampayana said, "Duryodhana shows scant regard for Sanjaya's words; the other kings mutely rise to leave the sabha. As they go, Dhritarashtra, who, out of blind love, always does whatever his son wants, wishes all those kings success and secretly asks Sanjaya what the Kurus plan, and what the hostile Pandavas.

Dhritarashtra says, 'Tell me truly, Gavalgana putra, what are the strengths and weaknesses of our forces? You are minutely acquainted with the affairs of the Pandavas, so tell me where their superiority and inferiority lie. You are aware of the strength of both sides; you know everything; and you are versed in all matters pertaining to dharma and artha. I ask you, Sanjaya, which side will lose in the war?'

Sanjaya says, 'I will not say anything to you in secret, Rajan, for then you might bear ill-will towards me. Have your father Vyasa of the stern vratas and your queen Gandhari come here. Being knowledgeable about dharma, perceptive and able to discern the truth, they will remove any ill-feelings that you might have. In their presence, I will tell you what Arjuna and Krishna intend.'

Dhritarashtra sends for Gandhari and Vyasa, and Vidura ushers them in. Vyasa Dwaipayana, the wise, says, 'Sanjaya, tell Dhritarashtra everything he wants to know. Tell him honestly all that you know about Krishna and Arjuna.'"

CANTO 68

YANASANDHI PARVA CONTINUED

"Sanjaya says, 'Those wonderful archers Arjuna and Krishna, who are equally godlike, have been born of their own divine will. Krishna's chakra, of the boundless energy, is five krosas wide. At will, and empowered by maya, he can cast it at any adversary, great or small. It blazes in refulgence but will be invisible to the Kurus. Krishna's Sudarshana chakra is what determines the strength or weakness of the Pandavas.

With it that mighty scion of the Madhus effortlessly, almost playfully, vanquished the formidable Naraka, Sambara, Kamsa and the Chedi king Sisupala. Krishna is the most exalted of all men; he is divine and a Paramatman; and he can bring Bhumi, Akasa and Swarga under his sway, just by willing it. Again and again you ask me about the strengths and weaknesses of the Pandavas. Listen and I will tell you of these, simply.

If the whole universe is placed on one side of a balance and Krishna on the other, Krishna will be heavier. He can, at his pleasure, reduce the universe to ashes, but if all the forces in the universe combine, they cannot do the same to him. Wherever there is truth, righteousness, modesty and compassion, there is Krishna; and where he is, victory must be.

Janardana is the soul of all creatures; he is the highest of all Purushas; and he guides, as if in sport, the earth, the sky and heaven. Beguiling the world, he uses the Pandavas as his instruments to destroy your evil sons, who are great sinners. The divine Kesava keeps the wheel of time, the wheel of the universe and the wheel of the yuga in constant motion.

Know that this glorious One is the lord of time, of death and of this brahmanda of mobile and immobile things; and this Mahayogi Hari, though the Lord of the universe, still performs his dharma, even like a humble labourer who tills the fields.

Indeed, Krishna beguiles the world with his maya; only those who have attained Him are not deceived.'"

CANTO 69

YANASANDHI PARVA CONTINUED

"Dhritarashtra says, 'How have you come to know Krishna as the Lord of the universe, and I have not? Tell me this, Sanjaya.'

Sanjaya says, 'Listen, Rajan. You have lost your gyana, while the gyana I have acquired has not diminished. The man who has no gyana is wrapped in the dark cloak of ignorance and does not know Krishna. Through my gyana I know that in Madhusudana the three states—the gross, the subtle and the causal—come together. He is the Creator of all but is, himself, uncreated. He is divine; from him everything arises and into him everything returns.'

Dhritarashtra says, 'What is the nature of your faith in Krishna, which makes you know him to be the union of the kartaram, the akrutam and Devam?'

Sanjaya says, 'Rajan, worldly pleasures, which are really maya, hold no importance for me. I never perform empty rituals, like keeping vratas without a pure heart or faith in Krishna. With faith I have purified my soul and then realised Krishna through the shastras.'

Dhritarashtra says, 'O Duryodhana, turn to Krishna for protection. My child, Sanjaya is one of our truest friends. Seek refuge with Krishna.'

Duryodhana says, 'Even if the divine son of Devaki, united with Arjuna, were to destroy all mankind, I will not surrender to him.'

Dhritarashtra says, 'Gandhari, this evil son of yours is determined to plunge us all into hell. Envious, black-souled and vain, he disregards the wisdom of his elders.'

Gandhari says to Duryodhana, 'O covetous child who ignores the commands of your elders, you abandon your father and me; you give up prosperity and life; you enhance the joy of your enemies; and I am deeply distressed. When Bhimasena strikes you down and you die, you will, foolish boy, remember what your father said to you.'

Vyasa says, 'Listen to me, Dhritarashtra. Krishna bears you love. Sanjaya, as your envoy, will do what is good for you. He knows Krishna, the ancient and exalted One. If you pay heed to him, he will certainly save you from the great danger that threatens you.

Son of Vichitravirya, men trap themselves because they are victims of krodha and kama. Those who are not content with what they have are like the blind leading the blind, into deep pits; deprived of their senses by avarice and desire, their actions lead them to a never-ending cycle of births and deaths. The path that the wise take is the only one that leads to Brahman. Those who are superior overcome death by keeping that path in view and reach their goal by it.'

Dhritarashtra says, 'Sanjaya, tell me of that path without terrors, by which I can realise Hrishikesa and attain mukti.'

Sanjaya says, 'A man of uncontrolled mind cannot know Krishna Janardana, who has perfect and absolute control over his soul. The performance of yagnas with uncontrolled senses is not the means to that end. Renunciation of the objects of our turbulent senses comes from true gyana. Spiritual enlightenment and abstention from injury arise from true wisdom. Therefore, O king, subdue your senses with all possible effort; let your mind not deviate from true knowledge; and detach your heart from the worldly temptations that surround you. Learned Brahmanas say that this subjugation of the senses is true wisdom; and this wisdom is the path by which learned men strive for their goal.

Rajan, Krishna cannot be realised by men who have not subdued their senses. He who has subdued his senses is gratified by spiritual knowledge that he gains from knowing the shastras and from the joy of absorption in Yoga, communion.'"

CANTO 70

YANASANDHI PARVA CONTINUED

"Dhritarashtra says, 'Sanjaya, tell me again about the lotus-eyed Krishna, so that, by knowing the significance of his names, I may attain that Purushottama.'

Sanjaya says, 'I have heard many of Krishna's auspicious names, and I will tell you of those that I know. They all describe him as immeasurable and beyond description.

He is called Vasudeva because he wraps all creatures with the cloak of maya, because of his glorious splendour and because he is the foundation and resting-place of the Devas. He is called Vishnu because he is all-pervading. He is called Madhava because he is an ascetic whose energy is always focused on the truth and absorbed in Yoga.

He is called Madhusudana because he killed the Asura Madhu and because he is the substance of the twenty-four objects of knowledge. He is called Krishna because he is of the Sattvata vamsa, because he is the embodiment of the unity of the words Krishi, *that which exists*, and Na, *eternal peace.*

His name Pundarikaksha comes from Pundarika, *the high and eternal abode*, and Aksha, *indestructible*.

He is called Janardana because he strikes fear into the hearts of all evil beings. He is called Sattvata because the sattva guna is embodied in him. He is called Vrishabhakshana because he is the union of Vrishabha—the Vedas—and ikshana—eye: the Vedas are the eyes through which he can be seen. He is called Aja because he is Unborn; he has not taken birth in the usual way.

That Supreme Soul is called Damodara because, unlike the Devas, his effulgence is not acquired but emanates from him and because he has self-control and great splendour. He is called Hrishikesa because he is the union of joy and divinity—Hrishika, *eternal happiness* and Isa, *the six divine attributes*. He is called Mahabahu because of his mighty arms with which he supports the Earth and the sky.

He is called Adhokshaja because he never falls or deteriorates in any way. He is called Narayana because he is the refuge of all human beings. He is called Purushottama because he is the one who creates, preserves and destroys the universe—Puru means creator, preserver and destroyer. He is called Sarva because he knows and is all things. He is called Satya because he is the truth of Truth—Krishna exists in Truth and Truth in him. He is called Vishnu because of his prowess and Jishnu because of his success. He is called Ananta because he is eternal and Govinda because he knows all languages.

He makes the unreal appear real and beguiles all creatures. With these his attributes, being ever devoted to dharma, and divine, the slayer of Madhu, that mighty-armed one who does not decay, will come here to try and prevent the slaughter of the Kurus.'"

CANTO 71

YANASANDHI PARVA CONTINUED

"Dhritarashtra says, 'O Sanjaya, I envy those who are gifted with sight, who will see Krishna, his beauty and radiance illuminating all the cardinal points of Earth and sky; Krishna, whose words the Bhaaratas listen to with reverence, which the Srinjayas consider sacred and auspicious, which those who seek prosperity regard as faultless and that the doomed find unpalatable; Krishna, who is full of exalted resolve, who is eternal and incomparably heroic, who is the bull of the Yadavas and their lord; Krishna who inspires awe in his enemies, who slays them and destroys their fame.

The assembled Kauravas will behold that high-souled and adorable One, that Parantapa, the lord of the Vrishnis, speaking words of kindness and enthralling my people. I surrender to the refuge of that Eternal One, whom Rishis blessed with Atmagyana, that ocean of eloquence, that Being whom ascetics realise, that bird called Arishta of the beautiful wings, that destroyer of creatures, that refuge of the universe, that thousand-headed one, that Creator and Destroyer of all things, that Ancient One without beginning, middle or end, of the infinite achievements, that cause of the primeval Seed, that Un-born one, that embodiment of Eternity, that highest of the high, that Creator of the three worlds and of Devas, Asuras, Nagas and Rakshasas, that foremost of all the learned and rulers of men, that younger brother of Indra.'"

CANTO 72

BHAGAVAD-YANA PARVA

Janamejaya said, "When Sanjaya left the Pandava encampment and went back to the Kurus, what did my grandfathers, the sons of Pandu, do? Brahmanottama, I want to hear all this; I beg you, tell me."

Vaisampayana said, "After Sanjaya has gone, Yudhishtira addresses Krishna, scion of Dasarha vamsa and lord of the Sattvatas.

He says, 'O you who are faithful to your friends, the time has come to show your friendship. There is no one but you who can save us from our distress. We put our faith in you and fearlessly demanded our share of the kingdom from Duryodhana, who is swollen with bottomless pride, and from his counsellors.

Parantapa, you protect the Vrishnis during all their times of misfortune; do the same for us Pandavas, who are in grave danger, for we deserve your protection.'

Krishna says, 'Here I am, Mahabaho. Tell me what you want and I will do it.'

Yudhishtira says, 'You have heard about Dhritarashtra's intentions; all that Sanjaya has said to me has Dhritarashtra's approval. Sanjaya, whom we must think of as Dhritarashtra's soul, has spoken the king's mind. A duta says what he is instructed to, for otherwise he deserves to die.

With a mind not inclined to look impartially upon all that is his, and impelled by avarice and a sinful heart, Dhritarashtra wants to make peace with us without giving us back our kingdom. It was at Dhritarashtra's command, and believing that he would honour the pledge we made with him, that we spent twelve years in the forests and one more year in hiding. The Brahmanas who were with us will bear out the fact that we did not deviate from our given word.

Now the covetous Dhritarashtra does not want to keep Kshatriya dharma. Out of his love for his son, he listens to the counsel of evil men. Prompted by greed and selfishness, he takes Duryodhana's advice and treats us deceitfully.

What can be more sorrowful, Janardana, than my being unable to look after my mother and my friends? Even with the Kasis, the Panchalas, the Chedis and the Matsyas for my allies, and with you, Madhusudana, as my protector, I asked for only five villages—Avisthala, Vrikasthala, Makandi, Varanavata, and any one more of their choice.

Grant us five villages or towns, we said, *where we five may live together; we do not want to see Bharata vamsa destroyed.*

However, the evil-minded son of Dhritarashtra thinks he is the sole master of the whole world, and he did not agree. What can be more sorrowful than this?

When a man, born and raised in a noble family, covets the possessions of others his avarice destroys his intelligence. Once intelligence is lost, he feels no shame; the lack of shame leads to an erosion of dharma; and the loss of dharma leads to the withering of prosperity. The destruction of prosperity, in its turn, ruins a man, for poverty is like death. Kinsmen, friends and Brahmanas shun a poor man, just as birds avoid a tree that has neither flowers nor fruit. Krishna, to me my relatives shunning me feels like death; I feel as if my prana is leaving my body.

Sambara said that nothing is more distressful than being wracked with anxiety about where one's next meal will come from and the uncertain future. It is said that wealth is the highest dharma and that everything depends on it. Those who have it are considered alive, whereas those who have none might as well be dead. A man who forcibly robs another of his wealth not only kills his victim but ruins his dharma, artha and kama.

When poverty overtakes them, some men choose death; others leave their cities and retire to villages; many retire to the forest; while some become sadhus and beggars in a bid to destroy themselves. For the sake of wealth, some drive themselves to madness; others live as subjects of their enemies; and many go into the service of others. Poverty is more distressful to a man than death, for prosperity is the sole cause of a man's dharma as well as his kama. Actual death is not as painful, for it is inevitable and none can overcome it.

Krishna, a man who is poor from birth does not suffer as much as the man who, born into wealth and used to living in luxury, loses his prosperity. He may lose his wealth through his own fault, but he blames the gods and Indra, rarely himself. Even knowledge of the shastras fails to mitigate his pain.

Sometimes he gets angry with his servants and harbours malicious envy towards his friends. In his anger, he loses the clarity of his mind and, because his intellect is clouded, he commits evil. His sinfulness makes him careless about maintaining caste divisions. Varnasankarshana, the mixing of castes, leads to Naraka and is the worst sin of all. If a man is not made aware soon, he goes straight to hell. Wisdom is the only thing that can awaken him, and if he regains the eye of wisdom, he is saved. When wisdom returns the man turns to the shastras, which enhance his virtue. Shame becomes a treasured ornament.

The man who feels shame has an aversion to sin; his prosperity increases; and he is truly a man. He who is devoted to dharma, who has his mind under control and who always acts after careful deliberation, is never inclined towards adharma, nor does he sin.

He who feels no shame and has lost good sense is neither man nor woman. He cannot earn punya and is like a Sudra. He who feels shame pleases the Devas, the Pitrs and his own self, and thus attains moksha, the highest aim of all men of dharma.

Madhusudana, in me you have seen the truth of all that I say. You know how we have lived these years in exile, deprived of our kingdom. It is against our dharma to abandon what is rightfully ours. Our first efforts will be towards ensuring that both ourselves and the Kauravas enjoy prosperity and be united in peace. Otherwise, we will kill the Kauravas and regain the kingdom that is ours by right, although success won through bloodshed, even by killing the most hateful enemy, and in this case our close kin, is the very worst of violent deeds.

We have many kinsmen, and many of our elders have ranged themselves against us. To slaughter these is a grievous sin indeed. What good can come of war? Sadly, war is the dharma of a Kshatriya; and we are born into that wretched varna. Sinful or virtuous, any other way of life would be wrong for us. A Sudra serves; a Vaisya lives by trade; the Brahmana has the wooden begging bowl to sustain himself; we have to live by war! A Kshatriya kills a Kshatriya; fish live on fish; a dog eats a dog. See how they all live according their inherent dharma.

O Krishna, Kali, wrath, is always present in battlefields; lives are lost; and despite the strict laws that govern warfare, success and defeat cannot be foretold. None of Earth's creatures control their own lives; and neither prosperity nor adversity come until their time is ripe.

Sometimes one man kills many; sometimes many together kill one; a coward may slay a renowned and celebrated hero. In war both sides cannot win, and both cannot lose, even though both sides may suffer equal losses. If a Kshatriya flees a battle, he loses honour and glory. Ah, under any circumstances war is a sin.

Who in striking another is not himself struck? For the one attacked, victory and defeat are the same, O Hrishikesa. Defeat is almost as bad as death, but the victor's losses are no less. Even if the victor is himself not killed, one or more of his dear ones may die and, stricken by the loss of his kin, he becomes indifferent to his own life.

Those who are quiet, modest, virtuous and compassionate are

generally killed in battle, while evil ones escape unscathed. After killing his enemies a man is gripped by remorse. Moreover, the vanquished survivor will muster another army, to challenge the victor. In the hope of ending a dispute with finality, one often tries to annihilate the enemy, at times without success; and victory creates hatred, for the vanquished lives on in sorrow.

The man who wants peace sleeps happily, giving up all thoughts of victory and defeat, while the man who provokes hostilities sleeps in misery and anxiety, as if he shares the room with a serpent. The man who kills seldom wins renown; in fact he gains eternal and universal infamy. A war waged over a long period of time never ends, because even if there is one family member left alive, there is no dearth of those who will remind him of past enmities.

Krishna, enmity is never converted to peace by further enmity; it feeds on itself like a fire on ghee. There can be no peace without the complete obliteration of one side, because otherwise there will always be chances for a survivor to take revenge on the victor, a vice to which opportunists are addicted.

Confidence in one's own prowess is an incurable disease that can bring heartache. The only way to know peace is by renouncing war, or by death. Madhusudana, although it is true that we can achieve the goal by ridding oneself of an enemy by tearing him up by the very root, that is savage and cruel. The peace that one may achieve by giving up kingdom is almost like death, which comes if one loses one's kingdom and is utterly ruined by the enemy. We do not wish to give up our kingdom, nor do we wish to see the extinction of our vamsa. Considering all this, it is better to make peace by giving in to the Kauravas.

The time to show one's might is when those who desire peace and not war fail at conciliation and war becomes inevitable. Horrible results follow the failure of peacemakers. Learned men have seen this in fights even between dogs. First, the dogs wag their tails, then they bark, then they circle each other and bare their teeth, then growl and, finally, attack each other. The dog that is stronger prevails and takes his meat. It is the same with men; there is no difference whatever. Those who are powerful should avoid disputes with the weak, who will yield, for they must.

The father, the king and the elder always deserve respect and, so, Dhritarashtra deserves regard and reverence from us. But Dhritarashtra's love for his son is great; he will be obedient to his son and reject what we propose. What do you, O Krishna, think is best at this juncture? How can we preserve both our interest and our virtue? Whom else, besides you, Madhusudana, shall we consult in this most difficult matter? What other friend do we have, who is as dear to us as you are, who wants our welfare, who knows the consequences of all karma, and who knows the truth?'

Krishna says to Yudhishtira, 'I will go to the sabha of the Kurus, for both your sakes. If I can make peace without sacrificing your interests, I will have performed an act of great punya, which will bear immortal fruit. I will also have saved the angry Kurus and Pandavas, as well as Dhritarashtra's sons and this sacred Bhumi herself from the snare of death, and perdition worse than death.'

Yudhishtira says, 'I am not in favour of you going to the Kurus; Duryodhana will never do as you ask, even if you use the best advice to persuade him. All the Kshatriyas of the world are assembled there, obedient to his command. I do not like the thought of you going into their midst. If any harm comes to you, nothing, not the promise of godhood, not sovereignty over all the Devas, let alone mere mundane success, will please us.'

The Divine One says, 'Rajan, I know how base and vicious the son of Dhritarashtra is; but by going there we will escape the censure of the kings of the Earth. Just like other animals before the lion, all the kings of the Earth united cannot stand before me when I am roused. If by some chance they try to do me harm, I will consume the Kurus. My going there will not be fruitless, for if our object is not fulfilled, we shall at least escape blame. And this is my intention.'

Yudhishtira says, 'Krishna, do whatever pleases you. May your plan be blessed. Go to the Kurus. I hope to see you return successful and in joy.

Go and make such a peace that all the sons of Bharata may live together happily and in contentment. You are our brother and friend, as dear to me as to Arjuna. So close are we to you that we are not in the least concerned that you might neglect our welfare. Go there for our good.

You know us and you know our enemies; you know what our intentions are and what to say. Whatever you say to Duryodhana will be for our good. By whatever means peace is achieved, Kesava, keep our welfare at heart.'"

CANTO 73

BHAGAVAD-YANA PARVA CONTINUED

"Krishna says, 'I have heard what Sanjaya said and now I have heard you. I know Dhritarashtra's intentions as well as yours. Your wishes are based on dharma, while theirs stem from malice. You greatly value what you might obtain without war.

Yet, a long life of brahmacharya is not the way of a Kshatriya, O lord of the Earth. Men of all four varnas say that a Kshatriya should never live on alms. Brahma has ordained that either victory or death in battle is the eternal dharma of a Kshatriya; humiliating yourself by surrender is not for you. Yudhishtira Mahabaho, you cannot live by humbly giving in. Display your prowess and vanquish your enemies, Parantapa.

Through his long association with many kings, and because of their affection and friendship, Dhritarashtra's son has become powerful indeed. There is no hope that he will make peace with you. The Kurus think they are strong because they have Bhishma, Drona, Kripa and others with them. As long as you behave mildly towards them, they will not give up your kingdom. Dhritarashtra's sons will not accede to your wishes from compassion or mildness or from a sense of righteousness.

There is, Pandava, more evidence that they will not make peace with you. They felt no remorse despite having made you suffer terrible deprivation and hardship and making you wear a kaupina for your attire. The ruthless Duryodhana cheated to beat you at dice, in the sight of Pitamaha Bhishma, Drona, the wise Vidura, many holy Brahmanas, the king, the citizens and all the important Kauravas; he deceived you, who are charitable, gentle, self-controlled, virtuous and of stern vratas; and he was not ashamed of his vile deed. Do not show the wretches any compassion. These men, who are so deserving of death at anyone's hands, are that much more deserving of it at yours, O Bhaarata.

With what ugly words Duryodhana, with his brothers, gladly and boastfully, tormented you and your brothers. He said, "The Pandavas now own nothing in this wide world. Their names and lineage are already extinct. In time, which is eternal, they have already died. I have all their punya, and they will now be scattered into the five elements."

While the game of dice was being played, the brutal Dusasana seized the weeping Draupadi by her hair and dragged her to the sabha, as if she had no protectors. In the presence of Bhishma, Drona and others he repeatedly called her "cow". Restrained by you and bound by dharma, your mighty brothers did nothing to avenge her. After you were exiled to the forests, Duryodhana spoke savage words and boasted to his kinsmen, who knew you were innocent and sat mute in the sabha and wept silently.

The assembled kings and the Brahmanas did not applaud him for this deed. Indeed, all in the court censured him. To a man of noble descent, Parantapa, censure is equal to death. Death is many times better than a life of blame. That was when he already died; but he felt no shame although all the kings of the Earth disapproved of what he did.

He whose character is utterly despicable is destroyed as easily as a tree supported by a single weak root. Duryodhana deserves death by any hand, like a snake. Kill him, Parantapa, without the slightest hesitation or remorse.

It is incumbent upon you, and I approve of it, that you should pay homage to your uncle Dhritarashtra and to Pitamaha Bhishma. I will go there and remove the uncertainty of all men who are still in any doubt of Duryodhana's evil nature and ways. There, in the presence of all the kings, I will tell of your shining virtues and Duryodhana's vices. The rulers of kingdoms, who hear my words full of dharma and artha, will recognise that you are virtuous and truthful while Duryodhana is moved only by his greed.

I will speak of Duryodhana's vices before the citizens of Hastinapura and the other people of the kingdom, before the young and the old, of all the four varnas, who will be gathered there. Because you ask for peace no one will consider you sinful, while all the lords of the Earth will castigate the Kurus and Dhritarashtra. When Duryodhana dies the death of dishonour and of being forsaken by all men, my work will be complete. After that, do what needs to be done.

Mindful of your noble intentions but never sacrificing your interest, I will go to the Kurus and try to make peace. I will observe their preparations for war and return to make you victorious, Bhaarata.

I fear that war is certain; all the omens I see point to it. Birds and animals screech and howl at dusk; the best elephants and horses assume dreadful shapes; fires flame in many sinister hues. Such signs appear only when the pralaya is imminent.

Let your warriors ready their weapons, their machines of war, armour, chariots, elephants and horses, and prepare for battle. Collect everything you need for the war that looms. As long as he lives Duryodhana will never give back your magnificent kingdom, which he stole from you at a game of dice.'"

CANTO 74

BHAGAVAD-YANA PARVA CONTINUED

"Bhima says, 'Madhusudana, speak in such a way that there may be peace with the Kurus. Do not threaten them with war. Do not speak harshly to Duryodhana, who is always quick to anger, resentful, flouts his own best interest and is arrogant. Treat him gently. His heart, like a criminal's, is naturally inclined to sin; he is intoxicated with pride in his own prosperity, and he is hostile towards the Pandavas. He has no foresight, is cruel and always blames others for his own sins; his strength is vicious; his wrath is not easily or quickly subdued. He does not learn from the mistakes of others or his own; his very soul is evil and he is full of deceit and treachery. He would rather give up his life than his opinion. Peace with such a man, Krishna, is difficult.

Duryodhana disregards the advice of his well-wishers; he is without virtue and loves falsehood; his actions violate the advice of his best counsellors, which wounds their hearts. Like a snake hiding in the reeds, he is a slave to his evil nature and his anger, and he sins again and again. You know well the strength of Duryodhana's army, his ways, his character and his prowess. Until now the Kauravas and their sons passed their days happily, and we, too, with our friends and Indra, as if we were Indra's younger brothers. But now, sadly, Duryodhana's wrath will consume all the Bhaaratas, as fire does forests at the end of winter.

O Krishna, you know about the eighteen kings who killed their friends and relatives. When Dharma's time came to an end, Kali[1] was born among the Asuras, who blossomed in prosperity and blazed with energy; Udavarta was born among the Haihayas; Janamejaya was born among the Nipas; Bahula among the Talajghanas; proud Vasu among the Krimis; Ajabindu among the Suviras; Rushardhika among the Surashtras; Arkaja among the Balihas; Dhautamulaka among the Chinas; Hayagriva among the Videhas; Varayu among the Mahaujasas; Bahu among the Sundaras; Pururavas among the Diptakshas; Sahaja among the Chedis and Matsyas; Vrishadhvaja among the Praviras; Dharana among the Chandravatsas; Vigahana among the Mukutas and Sama among the Nandivegas.

Vile and powerful souls, Krishna, take birth at the end of each yuga, in their respective races, for the destruction of their kinsmen. So has Duryodhana, the embodiment of sin, and the disgrace of his vamsa, been born at the end of the yuga into our clan, of the Kurus. Therefore, mighty one, you should speak gently to him in sweet, not bitter words, imbued with dharma and artha, and in depth on his favourite subjects, so you please him. All of us would rather submit humbly to Duryodhana than let the Bhaaratas be annihilated.

Krishna, conduct yourself in such a way that we may rather live as strangers to the Kurus than incur the sin of destroying the whole vamsa. Encourage our Pitamaha and other elders and counsellors to foster feelings of kinship amongst us cousins and to pacify the son of Dhritarashtra.

I say this and Yudhishtira approves. Arjuna, too, is opposed to war, for he is deeply compassionate.'"

---

[1] Kali refers to the demon Kali, not the Goddess Kaali.

CANTO 75

BHAGAVAD-YANA PARVA CONTINUED

Vaisampayana said, "Hearing Bhima speak with such uncharacteristic mildness, as unexpected as hills without their bulk, or fire without heat, Krishna throws back his head and laughs aloud. And as if to provoke Bhima, like the wind fanning a fire, he speaks to him who was at that moment seized by an impulse of kindness.

Krishna says, 'O Bhimasena, you usually applaud war in your longing to slaughter Dhritarashtra's vile sons who delight in every bestiality, in destroying the lives of others. Parantapa, you stay awake the whole night, sitting with your head bent down. Frequently, you utter frightful exclamations of anger that express the storm that rages in your heart. Inflamed by the fire of your fury, you sigh in restlessness, like a smoking flame. You go off by yourself and lie down, your fevered breaths labouring, like a weak man weighed down by a heavy burden. Those who do not know the reason for all this think that you are mad.

Just as an elephant trumpets in rage while it tramples uprooted trees to pulp, you run wildly here and there, heaving sighs and making the Earth tremble under your tread. You take no delight in company and pass your time in solitude. Night or day, nothing pleases you so much as seclusion. Sitting by yourself, you suddenly laugh out loud; at times, you put your head between your knees and stay like that interminably, with your eyes shut; at other times, you frown and bite your lips and stare fiercely, fixedly ahead of you, your eyes seeing nothing. These are all symptoms of anger.

Once, in the midst of your brothers, you seized your mace and cried, "As surely as the Sun rises in the east and displays his radiance, and as truly as he sets in the west by journeying around Meru, so do I swear that I will kill Duryodhana with this gada of mine. And this I, Bhima, solemnly vow."

How does this same heart of yours now advocate peace, Parantapa? When fear enters even your heart, Bhima, all those who want war are dismayed as war draws nearer. Asleep or awake, you see inauspicious omens. Perhaps that is why you want peace. You seem to have lost your manliness, even like a eunuch. Panic grips you, which is why you are distraught. Your heart trembles; your mind is taken by despair; your thighs quiver in weakness, and all this makes you want peace. The hearts of mortal men, O son of Pritha, are as inconstant as the pods of a salmali seed in the wind.

At this moment, your words are as soft and mild as the language of cows; and your brothers' hearts sink into a sea of despair to listen to you, like swimmers in the sea without a raft. That you of all men should speak such tame and cowardly words is as strange as a mountain moving. Remember your strength, your achievements, and the race into which are born; and do not give in to grief. Be strong, Bhima. This weakness is not worthy of you; a Kshatriya never enjoys anything he has not acquired through his own prowess.'"

CANTO 76

BHAGAVAD-YANA PARVA CONTINUED

Vaisampayana said, "The choleric Bhima, who can never tolerate a slight, is stung to the quick, and responds like a mettlesome thoroughbred to a whip.

He cries, 'Krishna, you wrong me! What I want is one thing and one thing alone: war. We have known each other a long time and you well know that I delight in war and that my prowess is irresistible. Or, perhaps you don't know me at all, like a swimmer unaware of the depth of the lake he swims in. That is why you speak to me like this. No one else, knowing Bhimasena, could say what you have to me.

And so let me tell you, O joy of the Vrishnis, about my unrivalled might. I know that to boast is vulgar, but you have wounded me, and I will tell you about myself and what I am.

Krishna, Sky and Earth are immovable, immense and infinite; they shelter the countless beings that are born into them. If, through anger, they suddenly come to collide like two mountains, I can keep them apart with my arms. Look at my mace-like arms; no man alive can extricate himself from their grasp. Indeed, the mountain Himavat, the

Ocean and the mighty wielder of the thunderbolt—the slayer of Bala himself—cannot free the one that I seize in my great arms.

I will grind under my feet all the Kshatriyas who come to fight against the Pandavas. You do not know, Krishna, the prowess with which I vanquished the kings of the Earth and subjugated them. If you really do not know my strength, which is as fierce as the midday Sun, you will see soon it in battle. You wound me deep with your cruel words; I feel the pain as of a foetid tumour being lanced. Ah, know that my strength is greater than I have described!

On the very day that the havoc of war breaks out you will see me fell elephants, warriors on chariots, elephants and horseback; and, my long withheld fury unleashed, you will see me butcher countless brave Kshatriyas. You and the others will see me do all this, and mow down the greatest Maharathas. The marrow in my bones has not yet dried, nor does my heart tremble. Even if the whole world rush at me in wrath, I will feel no fear.

Madhusudana, it is only from compassion that I advocate showing goodwill to the enemy. I quietly bear all our injuries, lest our Bharatavamsa become extinct.'"

CANTO 77

BHAGAVAD-YANA PARVA CONTINUED

"The Divine One says, 'I said what I did in affection and from a desire to know your true mind; it was not in reproach, from pride of knowledge, in anger, nor from any desire to hold forth. I know the magnanimity of your soul, your strength and your accomplishments. That is not why I was critical of you.

O Bhima, the benefit that the Pandava cause will gain from you is a thousand times greater than you give yourself credit for. You, Vrikodara, with your kinsmen and friends, are exactly the man that should be born into a noble house such as yours, which is honoured by all the kings of the Earth. However, those who have doubts about the consequences of dharma and adharma, and strength and weakness, can never arrive at the truth. Indeed, the very thing that is responsible for a man's success also causes his downfall. The consequences of human actions can never be certain.

Learned men, who can gauge the evil in any deed, declare how worthy or not any action is; yet, action can have the opposite and unforeseen results, even like the wind suddenly changing direction. Even those deeds of men, performed after great deliberation and with well directed policy, and consistent with dharma, are baffled by providence. Then, again, providential circumstances, such as heat, cold, rain, hunger and thirst, which do not depend on human endeavour, can be overcome by man's efforts. Also, apart from the course that a man is destined to follow as a result of his past lives, he can be rid of all other karma if he so pleases; the Smritis and the Srutis testify to this.

Pandava, one cannot move through life on Earth by doing nothing. One should act in the knowledge that one's goals will be achieved by a combination of destiny and effort. The man who does with this belief is never pained by failure, nor delighted by success. To explain this, Bhimasena, was what I intended, not to proclaim that war would ensure victory for you.

When a man's mind is upset he should not lose his cheer or succumb to lassitude or dejection. This is why I spoke to you as I did: to put heart into you. Tomorrow I will go before Dhritarashtra; and I will strive to make peace without compromising your interests.

If the Kauravas make peace, everlasting fame will be mine; your goals will be achieved, and they, too, will reap great benefits. However, if the Kauravas disregard my advice and are obdurate with their opinion, there will surely be war. Bhimasena, the burden of fighting this war rests on you and Arjuna, and you two will have to lead all the others. In case of war, I will drive Arjuna's chariot; that is his wish, not that I want to fight.

I was fearful of the weakness your words conveyed. I only re-ignited your wrath, Mahabaho.'"

CANTO 78

BHAGAVAD-YANA PARVA CONTINUED

"Arjuna says, 'O Janardana, Yudhishtira has already said whatever needed to be said. But after hearing you, it appears that you think that Dhritarashtra's greed and our relative weakness will make peace difficult to attain. Also, you think that human prowess alone is fruitless, that without showing our might our goals cannot be achieved. What you say may be true but, also, perhaps not always so. Nothing should be regarded as impossible. It is true that peace does seem to be unattainable, given our present condition, yet if peace is properly proposed, they might agree.

O Krishna, strive to strike peace with our enemies. You are the truest friend of both the Pandavas and the Kurus, even as Prajapati is of the Devas and the Asuras. Accomplish what is in the best interests of both sides. Bringing about our welfare is not difficult for you to achieve; if you try, you will surely succeed. Why, as soon as you go to Hastinapura, it will be done. Even if you decide to deal with Duryodhana in any other way, you must do as you wish. Whether you want peace or war with the enemy, Krishna, we will honour your decision.

Does the vile Duryodhana, with his sons and kinsmen, not deserve death when, unable to bear the sight of Yudhishtira's prosperity and finding no other honest course to assuage his own burning envy, he took our kingdom by cheating at dice? When invited to combat, what Kshatriya turns away from the fight, even if death is certain for him? When Duryodhana defeated us with the lowest treachery and banished us to the forest, I thought that he deserved death at my hands. What you want to do for your loved ones is not strange; what is mysterious, though, is how you will achieve your objective, by mildness, or other means. If you think that for you to kill them all immediately is best, do it now; we need no further debate.

Surely, you know how Duryodhana shamed Draupadi in the Kuru sabha, and how we bore it with profound fortitude. I cannot believe that the same Duryodhana will now behave with dharma towards the Pandavas. Wise counsel will be lost on him, like seeds sown in barren soil.

So, Krishna, do what you think is right, and beneficial for the Pandavas, and also decide what should be done next.'"

CANTO 79

BHAGAVAD-YANA PARVA CONTINUED

"The Divine One says, 'I will do as you say, Mahabaho, and do my best to bring about an outcome that will benefit both the Pandavas and the Kauravas.

Arjuna, of the two options, war and peace, only peace lies somewhat within my power. A farmer may, through his effort, water and weed his field, but without rain it will not yield crops. Some do say that his effort will result in success if he irrigates his field artificially; but even that is uncertain because a drought sent by fate may still make it dry. In view of all this, the Rishis of old have said that human endeavour will only succeed when providence collaborates. I will do all that can humanly be done, but I cannot prevail over providence.

Duryodhana goes in defiance of dharma and the world, and he feels no remorse. Moreover, his appetite for sin is fed by Sakuni and Karna, and by his brother Dusasana. Duryodhana will never make peace by giving back your kingdom, even if his obstinacy entails a bloody death for himself and his kinsmen at our hands. Yudhishtira does not wish to meekly give up his kingdom; neither will Duryodhana surrender it at any price. I think I need to deliver Yudhishtira's message to him, though Duryodhana will not agree to Yudhishtira's conditions. If he refuses, he deserves to die. Bhaarata, he deserves death at my hands because he is the one who always tormented all of you, ever since you were children, and later after cheating you of your kingdom when he could not restrain his overweening envy of Yudhishtira's prosperity.

Many times he has tried to draw me away from you, but I never paid him any heed. You know what dreams Duryodhana dreams, and you also know that I want Yudhishtira's welfare. Knowing Duryodhana's heart and my own wishes, why do you doubt me, as if you knew nothing?

You know that an apocalyptic, revelational war has been ordained by the gods; how then, can we make peace with the enemy? I will say and do as much as I can, but do not expect peace. When Duryodhana made off with Virata's cattle, did Bhishma not try to persuade Duryodhana to make peace for the good of all?

I say to you today: as soon as you decided to fight them, their death was a foregone conclusion. Inexorably, and not surprisingly, Duryodhana has refused to part with even a very small part of the kingdom, for even a short time. As for me, I am always obedient to Yudhishtira's commands, and I must ponder again the sins of the wretched Duryodhana.'"

CANTO 80

BHAGAVAD-YANA PARVA CONTINUED

"Nakula says, 'O Krishna, the benevolent Yudhishtira, who knows about dharma, has spoken at length; Bhimasena has heard him and has weighed his own strength against the desire for peace on the scales of dharma; you have heard what Arjuna said, too; and I have repeatedly expressed my own opinion, as well.

Set all this aside; concentrate now on what the enemy has in mind and do what you think is best, given the circumstances. Kesava, each situation warrants a different decision, but a man wins success if he does the apt thing for the particular situation in which he finds himself. A decision that suits one situation becomes the opposite in another. One cannot hold the same opinion all the time.

While we were in the forest, we adopted a particular way of life; things were different during the ajnatavasa. Now, when we need no longer hide, what we want has changed again. While we wandered in the vana, we were not as eager to have back our kingdom as we are now. Now our exile has ended and we have returned; and we hear that an army of seven akshauhinis has gathered to help us, by your grace, Janardana.

Seeing these tigers among men, of immeasurable force, armed and ready for battle, what enemy of ours will not be terrified? Go to the Kurus; speak mildly first, then employ threats, so that the vile Duryodhana is filled with fear and anxiety.

What man of flesh and blood can stand up to Yudhishtira and Bhimasena, to the invincible Arjuna and Sahadeva, to Satyaki of the scintillating tejas, to me, to you or Balarama in battle, Kesava? Who can face Virata and his sons, Drupada and his allies, Dhrishtadyumna and the powerful king of Kasi, and Dhrishtaketu, lord of the Chedis?

Mahabaho, Yudhishtira Dharmaraja's objective will be accomplished immediately as you arrive there. Vidura, Bhishma, Drona and Bahlika will understand the wisdom of what you say. They will advise Dhritarashtra and the sinner Duryodhana to do as you say. When you, Krishna, are the speaker and Vidura is the listener, what is there in any of the worlds that cannot be communicated easily and effectively?'"

CANTO 81

BHAGAVAD-YANA PARVA CONTINUED

"Sahadeva says, 'What the king says is Sanatana Dharma, but you, Parantapa, must ensure, by what you do and say in Hastinapura, that there is war. Even if the Kauravas express a desire for peace with the Pandavas, you must provoke war with them. Krishna, you know how Panchali was dragged into the sabha and shamed. How can my anger be appeased without killing Duryodhana? Even if Bhima, Arjuna and Yudhishtira chose to be virtuous and peaceful, I will abandon dharma and meet Duryodhana in battle.'

Satyaki says, 'Mahabaho, noble Sahadeva speaks the truth. The anger I feel towards Duryodhana can be appeased only by his death. Do you not remember how enraged you were when you saw the distressed Pandavas in the forest, wearing rags and deer-skin? Purushottama, all the kings and warriors gathered here support what this fierce Kshatriya, Madri's heroic son, says.'

Hearing this, all the Kshatriyas set up a huge roar. They applaud Satyaki with shouts of *Excellent! Well said!* and, eager to fight, they are exhilarated.'"

CANTO 82

BHAGAVAD-YANA PARVA CONTINUED

"Vaisampayana said, 'Grief-struck Krishnaa of the long black tresses applauds Sahadeva and the great warrior Satyaki, whose words for her are resonant with dharma. Overwhelmed with sorrow to hear Bhimasena speak for peace, she turns to Krishna.

Her eyes are bathed in tears as she says, 'Madhusudana, you know how deceitfully Dhritarashtra's son, with his counsellors, robbed the Pandavas of their every happiness. You also know what message Yudhishtira sent through Sanjaya.

Effulgent one, he said, "Give us just five villages—Avisthala, Vrikasthala, Makandi, Varanavata, and for the fifth, any other of your choice." Krishna, this was the message sent to Duryodhana and his counsellors. Duryodhana heard what the humble Yudhishtira wants, and despite knowing that he is anxious to make peace, has done nothing towards it. If Duryodhana wants peace only without returning our kingdom, there is no need for you to go to Hastinapura.

The Pandavas, with the Srinjayas, can easily withstand the Dhartarashtra forces. When they are not amenable to conciliation, it is not right for you to show them mercy. To safeguard himself, a man must be severe with enemies with whom he cannot make peace either by conciliation or gifts. Krishna, the punishment you mete out, with the help of the Pandavas and Srinjayas, must be immediate and harsh. This is the best course for the sons of Pritha and will, if accomplished, add to your glory and that of the entire Kshatriya race.

The man who is covetous, be he a Kshatriya or of any other varna, other than even the most sinful Brahmana, must surely be killed by a Kshatriya, true to his dharma. The exception in the case of a Brahmana is because a Brahmana is the teacher of all the other varnas, and he is the first to get a share in everything. Those who know the shastras declare that sin is incurred only by killing one who does not deserve killing. It is just as sinful not to kill one who does deserve it. With the Pandava and Srinjaya forces behind you, you must act in a manner that will not taint you with sin. I keep repeating what has already been said because I have faith in you.

Krishna, what other woman is there on Earth like me? I am the daughter of King Drupada, born from the fire of yagna. I am your beloved friend Dhrishtadyumna's sister. By marriage I have become a queen of the Ajamida vamsa, the daughter-in-law of the illustrious Pandu. I am the queen of Pandu's sons, who are each like Indra in splendour. To these five heroic Kshatriyas I have borne five sons, all mighty warriors, who are as close to you as Abhimanyu is.

I, this same woman, was dragged by my hair into the Kuru sabha and humiliated in the very sight of the sons of Pandu, and even while you live. Krishna, the Pandavas, the Panchalas and the Vrishnis all lived to see me treated like a slave by those sinners. And while the Pandavas sat silent without giving way to their anger, I called out to you in my heart, saying, "Save me, Krishna, save me!"

Then the illustrious Dhritarashtra, my father-in-law, said to me, "Ask for any boon, O princess of Panchala. You deserve that and honour from me."

I said, "Let the Pandavas be free men with their chariots and weapons."

The Pandavas were freed, only to be exiled into the forest. Janardana, you know all these sorrows of mine. Save me, lotus-eyed One, with my husbands, kinsmen and relatives, from that grief. By dharma I am a daughter-in-law to Bhishma and Dhritarashtra. Yet, I was forcibly enslaved before them. O, shame on Arjuna's skill as an archer; shame on Bhimasena's might, for letting Duryodhana live for even a moment after what he did. If I deserve any favour from you, if you have any affection for me, Krishna, direct your wrath at the sons of Dhritarashtra.'

The bewitching Panchali, her black eyes, large like lotus leaves, bathed in tears, walks with the lovely gait of a she-elephant and comes up to Krishna. Taking in her hands her lustrous tresses with wavy ends, so dark, almost deep-blue, scented with myriad perfumes, of every auspicious sign and, though braided, soft and glossy like some mighty serpent, she addresses him.

She says, 'O Lotus-eyed, who are anxious for peace with the enemy, remember in all that you do, these tresses of mine that Dusasana seized in his coarse hands. If Bhima and Arjuna have stooped so low as to long for peace, my old father will avenge me, with battle. My five sons, too, of the mighty tejas, with Abhimanyu at their head, will fight the Kauravas. What peace can my heart know unless I see Dusasana's dark arm severed from his body and cut into pieces?

Thirteen long years have I passed in expectation of better times, hiding my anger in my heart like a smouldering fire. Now, pierced by Bhima's words like arrows loosed by dharma, my heart is about to break.'

The doe-eyed Draupadi is convulsed with sobs, tears pouring down her cheeks and over the lovely princess's breasts like liquid fire.

The mighty-armed Kesava speaks comfortingly to her, 'Krishnaa, you will soon see the women of Bharata vamsa weep as you do. Timid one, they will cry for their relatives and friends who have been slain. They, with whom you are angry, have already lost their warriors and their power. For, at Yudhishtira's command, and with Bhima, Arjuna and the twins, I will accomplish what is ordained by destiny.

Their hour has come. If they do not listen to me, the sons of Dhritarashtra will lie on the earth and become food for dogs and jackals. Himavat might shift from his place; Bhumi might shatter into a hundred fragments; the sky with its countless stars might fall down; but what I say can never be in vain.

Stem your tears, Panchali; I swear that soon you will see your husbands crowned with prosperity, and their enemies slain.'"

CANTO 83

BHAGAVAD-YANA PARVA CONTINUED

"Arjuna says, 'O Kesava, you are the truest friend of all the Kurus. You are related to both sides and a dear friend to both. You must bring peace between the Pandavas and the sons of Dhritarashtra, for only you can. Lotus-eyed Parantapa, go now with that intention and say what needs to be said to our irascible cousin. If the foolish Duryodhana does not accept your good advice, in keeping with dharma and artha, he will surely fall prey to what fate has destined for him.'

The Divine One says, 'Yes, I will go to Dhritarashtra. I want to achieve dharma, and weal for both ourselves and the Kurus.'

The night has passed and the Sun risen brightly in the east. The hour called Maitra has begun, and the rays of the Sun are still mild. The month is Kaumuda Kartika, the nakshatra Revati. It is the season of dew, for autumn has departed; and the Earth is verdant with lush crops.

This is how the world's stage is set that day, when Krishna, that mightiest of men, hears the auspicious and sacred sound of Brahmanas chanting the sweet mantras of prayer, like Indra hearing the adorations of the Devarishis. He performs his morning rituals, purifies himself with a bath, puts on his pitambara robes, adorns himself with ornaments and rubs himself with unguents, and worships Surya and Agni. He touches the tail of a bull and reverently bows to the Brahmanas; then he walks around the sacred fire and looks at the auspicious offerings laid out.

He remembers Yudhishtira's words and says to Satyaki, who sits nearby, 'Have my chariot prepared. Have my conch-shell, discus and mace, my quivers and arrows, and all my other astras placed in my ratha. Duryodhana, Karna and Subala's son are evil men and, yet, they must not be taken lightly.'

Krishna's attendants immediately begin to yoke his chariot, which is as effulgent as the fire that rages at the Pralaya, and which has no comparison in speed. Its two wheels are like the Sun and the Moon in lustre; it is emblazoned with crescent and full moons, fish, animals and birds; and it is adorned all over with garlands of flowers and with pearls and other gemstones of various kinds. It is grand and beautiful, and as splendid as the Sun. Besides its gold and jewelled decorations, it bears a wonderful flag-staff flying the finest pennants. Equipped with everything needed for battle, it is irresistible. Covered with tiger-skins, it can strip every enemy of his fame and enhance the joy of the Yadavas.

Yoked to this ratha are the superlative horses, Saibya, Sugriva, Meghapushpa and Balahaka, all of which have been bathed and exquisitely caparisoned. And adding to Krishna's glory is Garuda, the Lord of birds, who is perched on the flagstaff of that awesome chariot.

Krishna ascends his ratha as lofty as Meru's summit, the deep rumble of its wheels like massed clouds, which, like the pushpaka vimana, takes its rider where he wills it. Taking Satyaki with him, Krishna sets out, filling the earth and the sky with the thunder of his chariot-wheels.

The sky becomes cloudless; cool, fragrant winds blow in the pure, clear air. Auspicious animals and birds, whirling always to their right, fly around the ratha; cranes, peacocks and swans follow the slayer of Madhu, uttering cries of good omen. The fire, fed with libations to the accompaniment of mantras, blazes up, smokeless, also sending its flames towards the auspicious right.

Vasishta, Vamadeva, Bhuridyumna, Gaya, Kratha, Sukra, Kusika, Bhrigu and other Brahmarishis and Devarishis stand to the right of Krishna, the joy of the Yadavas and Indra's younger brother. Worshipped by these and other illustrious Rishis and Munis, Krishna sets out for the city of the Kurus, being seen off by Yudhishtira, Bhima, Arjuna and the twin sons of Madri; as well as by the heroic Chekitana, Dhrishtaketu of the Chedis, Drupada and the king of Kasi, that great warrior Sikhandin, Dhrishtadyumna, Virata with his sons and the princes of Kekaya. All these Kshatriyas ride a respectful distance behind that bull of the Kshatriya race to honour him.

Yudhishtira Dharmaraja follows Krishna for some distance and then speaks to him in the presence of the other kings. The son of Kunti embraces that Purushottama, who has never sinned, not from desire, anger, fear or any wish for profit; whose mind is steady; who knows no greed; who is dharma embodied, and endowed with fathomless intelligence and wisdom; who knows the hearts of all creatures; who is the Lord of all and the God of gods; who is eternal; who has every virtue and bears the auspicious Srivatsa on his chest. The king embraces Krishna and tells him what he must do.

Yudhishtira says, 'We should ask after the welfare of our mother, who always keeps dharma, performing tapasya and propitiatory rituals; who is devout in her worship of Devas and Atithis; who always waits upon her superiors; who loves her sons with a boundless affection; and whom we love dearly. She rescued us from Duryodhana's many snares, like a boat saving shipwrecked sailors from the terrors of the sea. Krishna, though undeserving of woe, she has suffered untold misery because of us. We should pay homage to her. Embrace and comfort her repeatedly by telling her about the Pandavas.

Ever since her marriage she has been the victim of pain and grief because of the way her father-in-law behaved; suffering has been her lot. Krishna, will I ever see the day when my afflictions end and I can make my grieving mother happy? On the eve of our exile she ran after us, crying in anguish, but we left her behind and went into the forest. Sorrow does not always kill; she might still be alive and, though grieving constantly for her sons, being looked after in Hastinapura.

Glorious one, salute her for me, and salute Dhritarashtra also, as well as all the kings who are older than us. Greet Bhishma, Drona, Kripa, Bahlika, Aswatthama, Somadatta and everyone of the Bharata vamsa. Salute the wise Vidura, counsellor of the Kurus, of the profound intellect and knowledge of dharma. Madhusudana, embrace everyone on our behalf.'

Having said this to Krishna in the presence of the kings, Yudhishtira circles him in pradakshina and asks his leave to return. Arjuna walks ahead a few steps and says quietly to his friend Krishna, the Avatara, 'Illustrious Govinda, all the kings know that we have decided to ask for our kingdom back. If, without insulting us and by honouring you, they give us what we demand, I will be pleased and they will escape mortal danger. If, however, Dhritarashtra's son, who is always deceitful, does otherwise, I will obliterate the very race of Kshatriyas.'

Bhima is delighted when Arjuna says this. That Pandava, who constantly quivers with rage he can scarcely contain, now lets out a dreadful roar of joy. Hearing him, all the bowmen tremble, and horses and elephants helplessly urinate and excrete in terror.

Having declared his resolve to Krishna, Arjuna takes his leave and turns back after embracing his divine cousin. Once all the other kings are persuaded to turn back, as well, Krishna sets out with a cheerful heart, on his chariot drawn by Saibya, Sugriva and the other horses. Urged by his sarathy Daruka, those steeds fly, devouring road and sky as they go.

On his way, Krishna Mahabaho meets some Rishis who shine with Brahmatejas, standing on both sides of the road. He gets down and greets them reverently and worships them.

He says, 'Is there peace in the world? Is dharma being practised? Are the other three varnas obedient to Brahmanas? Where have you met with success? Where are you going and why? What can I do for you? What brings you illustrious ones to Earth?'

Jamadagni's son, Brahma's friend, that lord of Devas and Asuras, comes forward and embraces Krishna. Parasurama Bhargava says, 'O Dasarha, Devarishis of pious deeds, Brahmanas of deep knowledge of the Shastras, Rajarishis and venerable Munis, who are witnesses to the feats that the Devas and Asuras have achieved, want to see all the Kshatriyas of the Earth gathered together from everywhere, the counsellors sitting in the ancient Kuru sabha, the kings, and, amongst them, you who are the Truth incarnate, O Janardana.

We are going to Hastinapura to witness that awesome sight. We are also anxious to hear what you will say to the Kurus in the presence of all those kings, words full of dharma and artha. Bhishma, Drona and others, as well as the illustrious Vidura and you, Yadavapumgava, will adorn that ancient sabha. We want to hear what you say there—divine words of wisdom.

You now know our purpose, Mahabaho. We will meet you again; go safely. We hope to see you in the midst of that sabha, seated on a noble throne, radiating lustre and might.'"

CANTO 84

BHAGAVAD-YANA PARVA CONTINUED

Vaisampayana said, "O Parantapa, when Devaki's mighty-armed son sets out for Hastinapura, ten powerful, fully armed and battle-ready Maharathas follow in his train. A thousand foot-soldiers, a thousand horsemen and hundreds of attendants carrying plentiful provisions also go with him."

Janamejaya said, "How does the illustrious Krishna of Dasarha vamsa, the slayer of Madhu, leave on his journey? What omens appear when he sets out?"

Vaisampayana said, "I will tell you about the earthly and heavenly omens that appear on Krishna's departure for Hastinapura. At first, the sky is clear and cloudless, yet thunder rolls and lightning flashes above. Later, light, fleecy clouds appear and pour down rain behind him, in his wake, as if in tribute. The seven great rivers, including the Sindhu, change their eastward courses and flow west instead. The cardinal directions seem to be reversed and all things seem in dizzy thrall. Fires blaze up everywhere, Rajan, and the Earth trembles.

In hundreds of wells and earthen pots water gushes up spontaneously and overflows. The whole universe is enveloped in darkness. Akasa is filled with dust that obscures the cardinal and subsidiary points of the horizon. Loud roars sound in the sky, but no creature is seen to make them. This wonderful phenomenon is seen all across the land. A southwesterly wind, roaring, uproots trees by the thousands and crashes them down upon the city of Hastinapura.

However, in those places through which Krishna passes delicious breezes blow and everything becomes auspicious. Lotuses and fragrant flowers fall in showers from above. The road becomes smooth and miraculously free from prickly grasses and thorns. Wherever Krishna stays, thousands of Brahmanas glorify that munificent One and worship him with offerings of curds, ghee, honey and rich gifts. Women come out onto the road and fling redolent wildflowers over him who is devoted to the welfare of all creatures.

Bharatarishabha, Krishna comes to wonderful Salibhavana abundant with every crop, an enchanting and sacred realm. He sees, with delight, villages crowded with animals; he passes through many cities and kingdoms. He passes through Upaplavya where its happy, good natured citizens, who have the protection of the Bhaaratas and, so, free from fear of invasion, and unknowing of danger or calamities of any kind, come out of their town and stand together on the way, eager to set eyes on holy Krishna. They see that illustrious one like a fire, and they worship him as they would an honoured and welcome guest.

When at last Krishna comes to Vrikasthala, the Sun is reddening the sky with his last rays of light. Alighting from his chariot, the Avatara performs the customary rites of purification, orders the horses unharnessed and sits down to his sandhya vandana. Daruka unyokes the horses, tends to them and lets them loose to graze and drink.

Krishna says, 'We must spend the night here, for the success of Yudhishtira's mission.'

His attendants quickly set up camp and serve fine food and drink.

Rajan, amongst the Brahmanas who live in that village, those who are of noble descent, and humble and obedient to the injunctions of the

Vedas in their ways, approach Krishna and honour him with blessings and worship. They place their rich homes at his disposal.

Krishna joyfully accepts their hospitality and pays homage to each of them as befits their status. He visits their homes, then returns with his own people to his ample tent. Having eaten his meal with them and fed all the Brahmanas with sweet-meats, Krishna passes the night happily in Vrikasthala.'"

CANTO 85

BHAGAVAD-YANA PARVA CONTINUED

Vaisampayana said, "Dhritarashtra, in the meantime, has discovered through his spies that Krishna is on his way. His hair stands on end as he reverently faces the mighty-armed Bhishma, Drona, Sanjaya and the illustrious Vidura, and Duryodhana and his confederates.

He says, 'O son of Kuru vamsa, we hear strange and wonderful news. Old men, women and children are talking of it in their homes; most speak of it in awe; others gather in groups outside and talk of it; wherever men congregate, in homes or open spaces, they are discussing just one thing. They all say that Krishna, the great scion of Dasarha vamsa, is one his way here on behalf of the Pandavas. He is worthy of every honour we can do him and our worship. He is the Lord of all creatures; everything in the universe depends upon him; intelligence, strength, wisdom and energy are centred in him.

This Narasreshta deserves the reverence of good men, for He is eternal virtue—Sanatana Dharma incarnate. He will bestow felicity and happiness if worshipped, and misery if not. If we please him with our offerings, we might have all our wishes fulfilled by his grace, in the presence of these kings.

Parantapa, waste no time; make arrangements to receive him worshipfully; have pavilions built on the road and furnish them with every luxury, so that Krishna is pleased with you. What does Bhishma think?'

Bhishma and the others warmly laud what Dhritarashtra says. Duryodhana immediately orders pavilions to be erected at regular intervals, at the most charming sites, and adorned with myriad jewels. The king has them furnished with luxurious beds and seats; he sends beautiful maidens, perfumes, ornaments, fine clothes, a variety of the best food and drink and fragrant garlands of many kinds. Especially for Krishna's reception and use, the king has a splendid, gem-studded pavilion built at Vrikasthala. Once these arrangements, made by superhuman or even divine effort, are complete, Duryodhana informs Dhritarashtra of them.

Krishna arrives at the Kuru encampment, but casts not even a glance at these opulent pavilions.'"

CANTO 86

BHAGAVAD-YANA PARVA CONTINUED

"Dhritarashtra says, 'Vidura, Krishna has left Upaplavya. He is in Vrikasthala now and will be here tomorrow. He is the lord of the Ahukas; he is the foremost of the Sattvatas; he is a Mahatman endowed with great lustre and might. He is the guardian and protector of the prosperous kingdom of the Vrishnis; he is the Pitamaha of the three worlds. The vastly intelligent Vrishnis and Andhakas worship Krishna's wisdom, just as the Adityas, the Vasus and the Rudras do Brihaspati's. Virtuous one, I will, in your presence, offer our worship to this noble son of the Dasarha vamsa. Let me tell you what I plan to do.

I will give him sixteen rathas made of gold, each drawn by four superb, well-adorned, identically coloured Bahlika horses. I will give him eight elephants with the juice of musth running down their temples, with tusks as big as plough shares, which can smite down hostile ranks, and eight mahouts for each one. I will give him a hundred lovely maid-servants with golden skins, all virgins, and a hundred man-servants as well.

I will give him eighteen-thousand soft woollen blankets that the mountain dwellers gave us. I will give him a thousand deer-skins from Cheena, and everything else that one like him deserves. I will give him this great and serene gemstone of the purest rays that shines day and night, for only Krishna is worthy of it. I will give him my own chariot, which can traverse fourteen yojanas in a day. I will set food and drink before him, eight times more than what the animals and attendants in his entourage need.

All my sons, except Duryodhana, will go out to welcome him on their chariots. Thousands of graceful dancing girls, decked in ornaments and unveiled, will receive Krishna. Let all the citizens with their wives and children feast their prayerful eyes on the illustrious Madhusudana with as much devotion as they look at the rising Sun. Let pennants and banners be raised and the road by which Krishna comes be well-watered to settle the dust.

Let Dusasana's palace, which is better than Duryodhana's, be cleaned and decorated for Krishna to stay in. With its many beautiful mansions, and its abundant riches, it is enchanting indeed. All my wealth, as well as Duryodhana's, is kept there. Give Krishna all that befits one as great as him.'"

CANTO 87

BHAGAVAD-YANA PARVA CONTINUED

"Vidura says, 'O Rajan, you have the respect and love of everyone in all the three worlds, and you are considered the best of men. You are venerable and your mind is so serene that whatever you say will be in accord with the shastras and the dictates of reason. Your subjects are confident that dharma is as integral to you as writing etched on stone, as rays to the Sun or waves to the ocean. Your virtues make your subjects love you. Take care to preserve your noble traits. Be straightforward in all that you do. Do not, out of foolishness, be the cause of a slaughter of your sons, grandsons, friends, kinsmen and all your dear ones.

You plan to give much to Krishna as your guest; he deserves all that and more, indeed he deserves the Earth. However, your generosity does not stem from motives of dharma or a desire to please him, but from selfish reasons. It reeks of insincerity, falseness and deception. I clearly see the hidden intentions behind what you plan to do.

The Pandavas want only five villages, but you do not want to give them even that for the sake of peace. Instead, you are trying to win

Krishna over with gifts and to alienate him from the Pandavas. You will not succeed in separating Krishna and Arjuna, neither with wealth, nor worship, nor with all your cunning stratagems. I know Krishna's magnanimity; I know how unshakeable Arjuna's devotion to him is; I know that Arjuna is as Krishna's life and he will never forsake him.

Krishna will not accept any hospitality from you other than water to wash his feet and to drink; the only courtesy he will offer is to enquire after the well-being of those he sees with you, nothing else. Rajan, offer him the honour of a welcome that he will accept. He is worthy of every reverence and deserves no less. Give Krishna what he comes for, which he desires for the good of both the Kurus and the Pandavas. He wants peace between you and Duryodhana, on one side, and the Pandavas on the other.

Do as he says, Rajan; you are like a father to the Pandavas; you are old and they are children to you by age. Behave as a father would towards them, for they look upon you as one.'"

CANTO 88

BHAGAVAD-YANA PARVA CONTINUED

"Duryodhana says, 'All that Vidura has said about Krishna is true. Krishna is devoted to the Pandavas and inseparable from them. The gifts that you plan to give him are inappropriate. Kesava is indeed worthy of it all, but this is neither the time nor the place for it. He will think that we are honouring him out of fear. An intelligent Kshatriya must never do anything that may be considered cowardly or shameful.

I am well aware that Krishna of the large eyes is worthy of the worship of the three worlds, but given the circumstances we should not give him anything. The war that we have set our minds on should not be set aside or delayed out of considerations of hospitality.'

Listening to Duryodhana, the Kuru Pitamaha Bhishma says, 'Krishna will not be pleased or angry whether he is honoured or not; nor will he be insulted, for he is above such things. No one, however powerful he may be or however hard he may try, can obstruct his purpose. Do not hesitate to do as Krishna says, and use him to make peace with the Pandavas. He is righteous and his advice will be in keeping with dharma and artha. What is fitting is that you gratify him by doing what he asks.'

Duryodhana says, 'Pitamaha, I cannot live if I have to share my fortune with the Pandavas. I have made my own decision: when he arrives here in the morning, I will imprison Krishna, who is the refuge of the Pandavas. With him confined, the Vrishnis and the Pandavas, indeed the whole world, will submit to me. Tell me how I should do this, so that Krishna does not guess what I intend, and so that we are not endangered.'

Dhritarashtra and his advisors are shocked to hear Duryodhana's abysmal plan.

Dhritarashtra says to Duryodhana, 'Never speak of this again, it is sinful! Hrishikesa comes as an ambassador. Besides, he is related to us and we love him. He has done us no wrong; how can you even think of imprisoning him?'

Bhishma says, 'Your sinful son faces his end by choosing evil over dharma despite his well-wishers' pleas; and you follow the lead of this wretch, who ignores all wise counsel and treads the path to doom. This vile prince of yours, with all his counsellors, will die the instant they lay hands on the pure Krishna. I dare not tarry to listen to this sinner anymore.'

And the inflamed Bhishma of the awesome might gets up and leaves the Kuru sabha."

CANTO 89

BHAGAVAD-YANA PARVA CONTINUED

Vaisampayana said, "Krishna rises at dawn and, having performed his morning ablutions and rituals and taken leave of those who rode with him, sets out for Hastinapura. The citizens of Vrikasthala bid farewell to the mighty-armed one and return to their homes.

Other than Duryodhana, all the grandly attired sons of Dhritarashtra, along with Bhishma, Drona, Kripa and others, go out to meet Krishna. Thousands of people come out to look at him—on chariots and on foot. He meets Bhishma of the immaculate deeds, Drona and Dhritarashtra's sons on his way; and they escort him into the city of elephants.

In honour of Krishna's visit, Hastinapura is vividly adorned and the main streets are bedecked with gold and gemstones of all kinds. Rajan, not a single man, woman or child remains indoors, so eager are the citizens to see Krishna. They come out and line the streets, and bow their heads in worship while they sing in his praise as he passes. Noble women crowd the balconies and terraces of great mansions to look at Krishna as he passes by; filling them until it seems they might collapse under their combined weight. And although swift, Krishna's horses move slowly through the thronging streets.

The lotus-eyed Parantapa enters the compounds of Dhritarashtra's ash-coloured stone palace with its numerous edifices. He passes through the first three chambers of the palace and then he meets Dhritarashtra. The blind king stands to honour Krishna in welcome, and Drona, Bhishma, Kripa, Somadatta and king Bahlika rise with him. The Vrishni hero comes forwards and pays his respects first to the illustrious Dhritarashtra and Bhishma; he then greets the other kings one by one, in proper order. Finally, after Krishna has greeted Drona and his son, Bahlika, Kripa and Somadatta, Dhritarashtra shows him to a throne of wondrous artistry, made of gold and inlaid with resonant jewels.

When Krishna is seated, Dhritarashtra's priests make a ritual offering to him of a cow, honey, curds and water. Krishna stays awhile, surrounded by the Kurus, exchanging pleasantries with each one as befits their relationship with him. In due course, having accepted the honours of welcome accorded to him and having greeted all the Kurus in their sabha, he takes Dhritarashtra's leave and goes to Vidura's fine home. Vidura comes out to welcome Krishna of the Dasarha vamsa with all kinds of auspicious and loving offerings.

Tears in his eyes, Vidura says, 'O Lotus-eyed Lord, I cannot begin to describe the joy I feel to see you, for you are the inner soul of all the living, the antaratman.'

Vidura, who knows dharma, asks after the Pandavas. Krishna, for whom the past and future are merged into the present, who knows that the Pandavas love Vidura and he them, that he is learned, constant in dharma, ever truthful and wise, and that he bears no anger against the sons of Pandu, tells him in detail about what the sons of Pandu have been doing.'"

CANTO 90

BHAGAVAD-YANA PARVA CONTINUED

Vaisampayana said, "After noon, after visiting Vidura, Krishna, chastiser of his enemies, goes to see his aunt Kunti. When she sees him, his face glowing with the radiance of the Sun, she embraces him and begins to pour out her sorrow for her sons. At the long denied sight of Krishna, who is her sons' very prana, her tears flow. When Krishna has received her ritual welcome she speaks to him, her face careworn, her voice choked with tears.

Kunti says, 'O Kesava, from their childhood my sons have served their elders and superiors with reverence. They were always devoted to each other. They were cheated of their kingdom and sent into exile, when they ought to have lived in the midst of their friends and kin. They have mastered anger and joy; they are devoted to Brahmanas and always truthful. These children of mine, the noble sons of Pandu, tore my heart out when, abandoning kingdom and pleasures, and leaving me behind, they went into the forest. How did my sons live in the vana full of lions, tigers and wild elephants?

They have suffered untold misery. Deprived of their father in their infancy, I raised them all so tenderly. How did they live in the forest without seeing their mother? From their infancy the music of conches, drums and flutes woke them from their sleep. While at home, they slept in palatial apartments on soft sheets and skins of the runku deer; and were woken in the morning by the trumpeting of elephants, the neighing of horses, the clatter of chariot-wheels, and the music of flutes and veenas, the sounds of conches and cymbals. They would worship at dawn while listening to sacred hymns chanted by Brahmanas; they worshipped the eldest of those Brahmanas with grand gifts of clothes, jewels and ornaments. And those illustrious Dvijas blessed them in return.

I cannot imagine how they slept in the deep forest where only the feral cries of predators ring. O how unjustified was their torment. They who were roused from their beds by music of cymbals, drums, conches and flutes, by the sweet voices of singers and by their praises being sung, how could they bear to be awoken in the forest by the roars of panthers and tigers?

My eldest son is modest and devoted to truth; he has his senses under control, and compassion for all creatures; he has conquered lust and malice; he always walks the path of dharma; he was able to bear the heavy burden of the ancient Rajarishis—Ambarisha, Mandhatri, Yayati, Nahusha, Bharata, Dilipa and Usinara's son Sibi; his character is taintless and his disposition immaculate; he is deeply versed in dharma; his prowess is irresistible; his accomplishments make him fit to rule the three worlds; his profound learning and devotion to dharma make him rightfully the foremost of the Kurus; he is handsome and mighty-armed; and he has no enemies. How is my Yudhishtira, O Krishna?

My pure-souled and golden-skinned second son is as strong as ten thousand elephants and as swift as the wind; he is the mightiest of the Pandavas and the most quick-tempered; he is devoted to his brothers and is beloved of them all. It is he who killed Kichaka and his brothers; he who slew the Krodhavasas, Hidimba and Baka. In prowess he is Indra's equal, in might Vayu Deva's; his anger is terrifying and like Rudra's; he is the foremost of all warriors. This Parantapa, this wrathful son of

Pandu, restrains his anger, might and impatience, and he controls his soul in implicit obedience to his elder brother. Tell me, Krishna, how is my Bhimasena of immeasurable valour, whose terrifying appearance suits his name Vrikodara?

Krishna, what of my Arjuna, who with only his two arms is more powerful than his thousand-armed namesake of long ago, my son who shoots five hundred arrows with one draw of his bow? He is Kartavirya's equal with the astras; Surya Deva's equal in blinding energy; a Maharishi's equal in self-restraint; Bhumi Devi's equal in forgiveness. It is by his strength that the Kuru kings have acquired their vast empire that blazes in splendour; and the Pandavas greatly value his prowess. This son of Pandu is the foremost of all Maharathas; his might is true and irresistible; no enemy has ever escaped him with his life; he is the conqueror of all, and invincible; he is the refuge of the Pandavas, as Indra is of the Devas. Krishna, how is your brother and friend, my Dhananjaya?

Ah, tell me about my tender-hearted son, who is kind to all creatures and blessed with modesty, who is a master of powerful astras, who is delicate and virtuous, who is my most beloved child. The mighty archer Sahadeva is the hero and ornament of all sabhas; he is young and devoted to the service of his brothers; he knows artha and dharma; his brothers always praise his noble character and manner. Madri and Pandu's son, the heroic Sahadeva, is the best of warriors; he waits submissively on his older brothers and reverentially on me; he is tender in years and of a gentle disposition; he is brave and handsome. He is loved by all and most dearly by his brothers, whose very life he is, though he inhabits his own body.

And tell me about my Nakula, who is a master of the various vyuhas of war; who is strong and a mighty archer also. My precious child was raised in luxury; is he well in body and mind? Mahabaho, shall I ever see my Nakula again? That Maharatha is still a stripling to me; he does not deserve this grief. O, how could I, who knew no peace if Nakula was out of my sight for even the blink of an eye, be still alive today?

Dearer to me than all my sons is Draupadi. She is nobly born and completely beautiful; she is endowed with every accomplishment; she always speaks the truth. She chose to accompany her husbands rather than stay with her sons and, leaving her children behind, followed the Pandavas. Once, a retinue of servants waited on her; her husbands, who love her, gratified her every little wish. She bears all the auspicious marks on her person and is accomplished in every way. Krishna, how is Draupadi?

Although she has five heroic husbands, all slayers of foes and all peerless bowmen who are each equal to Agni in urjas, she has suffered great torment. I have not seen my daughter-in-law Panchali for fourteen years; she herself has not seen her sons for as long, and must have endured constant anxiety for them. That Draupadi does not enjoy the happiness that should be hers for her wonderful character convinces me that happiness is not the result of one's deeds or nature.

Whenever I remember how she was forcibly dragged into the Kuru sabha, I stop loving Yudhishtira, Arjuna, Bhima, Nakula and Sahadeva. Never before have I borne a heavier burden of grief as when the villainous Dusasana, driven by rage and lust, hauled Draupadi, who was in her menstrual period and wore only a single length of cloth, into the sabha where her father-in-law sat; and exposed her to the gaze of all the Kurus. Everyone knows that Dhritarashtra, Bahlika, Kripa, Somadatta and all the others were struck by sadness at this; but of all who were present in that sabha, it is only Vidura who spoke out for her, only him that I worship.

One does not become worthy of homage by learning or wealth. It is one's character alone that makes a man deserve honour. Krishna, the illustrious Vidura, with his great intellect and deep wisdom, is an ornament that adorns the world.'

Pritha is filled at once with joy at Krishna's presence and sorrow for her sons; and she vents all her grief. She says, 'O Parantapa, dissolute kings of ancient times occupied themselves with gambling and hunting deer. Can this be a happy way of life for the Pandavas? I am consumed by dark thoughts and images, Krishna—of Draupadi being violently dragged into the presence of the Kurus in their sabha by Dhritarashtra's sons, and abuse worse than death being heaped on her; of my sons being banished from their city; of them wandering in the wilderness. These and other sorrows fairly crush me.

Nothing could have been more painful to me or my sons than to have lived a year in wretched hiding, in a stranger's house. Fourteen years have passed since Duryodhana exiled my sons. If suffering destroys the karma of paapa, and if happiness depends on punya, then considering the torment we have been through, we might yet enjoy happiness again. I never treated Dhritarashtra's sons differently from mine. By virtue of that, O Krishna, surely I will see you emerge safely from this war, and with the Pandavas, their enemies slain and their kingdom restored to them. My sons have kept the oath they swore and lived so faithfully by dharma that their enemies cannot hope to vanquish them.

As for my sorrows, I blame neither myself nor Duryodhana, but my father alone. Like a wealthy man making a gift of money, my father gave me away. When I was still a girl, playing with toys, or with a ball in my hands, your grandfather gave me away to his friend, the illustrious Kuntibhoja. Abandoned then by my father and now by my father-in-law, and suffering unbearably as I do, what point is there in my being alive?

On the night of Arjuna's birth, a disembodied voice said to me, "This son of yours will conquer the whole world and his fame will reach the heavens. Your son will destroy the Kurus in a great war and recover the lost kingdom, and with his brothers he will perform three mahayagnas."

I do not doubt the truth of that marvellous announcement. I bow to dharma that upholds creation. If dharma is real, you will surely make good all that the asariri said. Neither the death of my husband, nor the loss of wealth, nor our conflict with the Kurus inflicted such eviscerating pain on me as the separation from my children. What peace can my heart know when I do not see Dhananjaya, wielder of Gandiva and best of all Kshatriyas? I have not seen Yudhishtira, Arjuna and Bhima for fourteen years, Krishna. Men perform sraddha, last rites, for those who have gone missing for a long time, assuming that they are dead. Practically, my children are dead to me and I to them.

Tell Yudhishtira Dharmaraja that his dharma diminishes with each passing day. Tell him to stop this with a Kshatriya's rough deeds. Cursed are they, Krishna, who live as dependents at another's mercy. Death is better than a livelihood gained by such meanness.

You must tell Dhananjaya and Vrikodara that the time has come for them to fulfil the purpose for which a Kshatriya woman bears a son; that if they let time slip by without achieving anything, then, although they are still universally respected, they will become objects of contempt; and that if men's disdain taints them, I will abandon them for ever. Tell those Purushottamas that when the time comes even life, which is precious, should be laid down.

Tell Madri's sons, who are more devoted to Kshatriya dharma than to life itself, that they must strive to win comfort and wealth back through their prowess, for only objects gained like that can please the heart of a man who wants to live by Kshatriya dharma.

Go now, Mahabaho, and tell Arjuna, foremost of all Kshatriyas, to walk the path that Draupadi shows him. You know well, Krishna, that when inflamed Bhima and Arjuna are each like Yama and can vanquish even the Devas. Their wife Krishnaa being dragged into the sabha and spoken to as she was by the beasts Dusasana and Karna was a searing insult to them. Duryodhana, too, insulted the mighty Bhima in the presence of the Kuru kings. I am certain he will pay for that, for Vrikodara knows no peace when an enemy provokes him. Indeed, once provoked, Bhima remembers the slight until he has killed his foes and their allies.

The loss of kingdom did not crush me; the defeat at dice did not sadden me; but the illustrious and beautiful princess of Panchala being dragged into the sabha, wearing only a single cloth, and there forced to hear the vilest taunts and abuse, grieved me more than anything I have known. Krishna, what could be a greater sorrow for me? Alas, that incomparable Kshatriya princess, so devoted to her dharma, had to suffer such savagery while in her delicate period and, though she had powerful protectors, was as helpless as if she had none.

O Madhusudana, I find it strange that I have had to bear such a burden of grief in spite of you, and that mightiest of men Balarama and that Maharatha Pradyumna being protectors of my children and myself; and despite my sons, the invincible Bhima, and Arjuna who never turns his back on the enemy, being alive.'

Krishna comforts his aunt so grief-stricken by the plight of her sons. He says, 'There is no other woman in the world like you, Matuli. You are the daughter of King Surasena, and by marriage you are of the Ajamida vamsa. The families of your birth and marriage are both noble; you are like a lotus transplanted from one great lake into another. You were blessed with prosperity and adored by your husband. You are the wife of a hero and have given birth to heroic sons. You possess every virtue and are endowed with great wisdom. It is fitting that you should bear joy and sorrow with equanimity and patience.

Your children have overcome sleep and sloth, anger and joy, hunger and thirst, cold and heat and enjoy happiness in the true Kshatriya way. They are endowed with great light and strength and, abandoning the sensual pleasures which the low-minded are addicted to, pursue the noble felicity which Kshatriyas should. Nor are they content with a little. Wise men enjoy the limits of joy or unhappiness from objects that give these. Ordinary men choose mediocre pleasures and are content with lethargy. Those that are superior desire either the most acute human suffering or the highest bliss that man can have. The wise delight in extremes; they find no pleasure in mediocrity. They hold the extremes with true happiness and see the in-betweens as real sorrow.

The Pandavas and Draupadi greet you through me. They send the message that they are well and ask after your welfare. You will soon see them become the lords of the whole world, with their enemy slain and themselves reinstated to power and prosperity.'

Consoled by Krishna, the sorrowing Kunti shakes off the gloom in which temporary ignorance has enveloped her and says to Krishna, 'Mahabaho, let us do whatever you think is proper, without abandoning dharma, and without deceit. I know the power of your truth and of your birth. I know also what wisdom and strength you will employ to accomplish what is best for your beloved cousins. In our vamsa you are dharma personified; you are truth; you are the embodiment of tapasya; you are Brahman. Everything is founded in you; and what you say must always be true.'

The mighty-armed Krishna bids her farewell, and after walking around her in pradakshina, leaves for Duryodhana's palace.'"

CANTO 91

BHAGAVAD-YANA PARVA CONTINUED

Vaisampayana said, "Having taken leave of Kunti and walked round her in pradakshina, Krishna goes to Duryodhana's opulent palace. It is richly adorned, with beautiful furniture, and as grand as Indra's abode. Krishna walks unobstructed through three large courtyards and enters the palace, which is as imposing as a mass of clouds, as tall as a hill, magnificent and resplendent.

There he sees Dhritarashtra's son of the mighty arms seated on his throne in the midst of a thousand kings and surrounded by all the Kurus. There he also sees Dusasana, Karna and Subala's son Sakuni, who sit next to Duryodhana. When Krishna enters the sabha, Dhritarashtra's illustrious son and his counsellors rise to honour him. Krishna greets Duryodhana and his counsellors, as well as all the kings present, according to their status, and then sits on a beautifully wrought golden throne spread over with a rich gold-embroidered cover.

The Kuru king makes the ritual offering to Krishna of a cow, honey, curds and water; and he places at his service all his palaces and other mansions, and the whole kingdom. In the presence of all the kings, the

Kauravas worship Krishna, who is like the Sun in all his glory. Once the ritual of worship is completed, Duryodhana invites Krishna to eat with him in his palace. Krishna declines.

Duryodhana glances at Karna and, in a deceptively mild voice underlaid with malice, says to Krishna, 'O Janardana, why will you not accept the feast of food and drink, and the garments and beds that I have arranged for you? You are helping both sides in this dispute; you want the good of both. You are the greatest of Dhritarashtra's relatives and he loves you dearly. You also know dharma and artha, fully and in detail. Krishna, I want to hear the reason for your refusing my hospitality.'

Krishna raises his mighty right arm and, in a voice as deep as rumbling clouds, says to Duryodhana, 'Rajan, envoys accept food and worship only after the success of their missions. So, Bhaarata, when my mission succeeds, you may entertain me and my attendants.'

Duryodhana says, 'Krishna, it is not fitting that you behave in this manner. We are trying to please you because of your kinship to us, regardless of the success or failure of your mission. Our efforts seem to be futile; and we see no reason why you reject our worship, which we offer out of love and friendship. We have no quarrel or war with you; and on reflection, it seems what you say and do is not becoming.'

Krishna looks at Duryodhana and all his counsellors and says, 'I could never forsake dharma, not from desire, from wrath or malice; not for gain or for the sake of argument and not from temptation. One accepts food from another when one is in distress. You have not inspired love in me by anything you have done, nor am I in distress. Without any reason, you hated your gentle cousins the Pandavas, who have every virtue, from the moment they were born. The unreasonable hatred you bear the sons of Kunti does not become you.

The sons of Pandu are all devoted to dharma. Who would hurt them in the least? He who hates them, hates me; he who loves them, loves me. Know that the Pandavas and I have one soul. He who is driven by lust, anger and by the darkness of his heart, who hates and seeks to injure one who owns every good quality is the worst of men, even if he possesses every noble quality himself.

That wrathful villain of uncontrolled soul, who, from ignorance and greed, hates his godlike kinsmen, will never enjoy his prosperity for long. On the other hand, the one who, through good judgement, wins over virtuous men, even if he has an aversion to them in his heart, enjoys undying felicity and fame. The food you offer me is defiled by your vileness, and I cannot eat it. The only food I will eat here is what Vidura offers me.'

Saying this to the wilful Duryodhana, who cannot bear to hear anything contrary to his wishes, Krishna leaves the glittering palace and sets out for Vidura's home. While he is there, Drona, Kripa, Bhishma, Bahlika and many of the Kauravas come to see him.

The Kauravas who have come place their palaces with all the wealth in them at Krishna's disposal. Krishna thanks them for the honour they have done him and gives them leave to go.

After the party of Kurus has left, Vidura entertains Krishna, the unvanquished, with lavish hospitality, providing him with everything he could want; and Kunti places sattvik, delicious food in abundance before him. Krishna first gratifies the Brahmanas who know the Vedas; he gives them food and gold. Only then he and his attendants, like Indra with the Maruts, dine on what remains of the feast that Vidura has prepared.'"

CANTO 92

BHAGAVAD-YANA PARVA CONTINUED

Vaisampayana said, "In the night, when Krishna has dined and is refreshed, Vidura says to him, 'O Krishna, your coming has not been a well judged one. Dhritarashtra's son violates dharma and artha; he is evil and wrathful; he insults anyone he pleases, while he himself craves honour; and he disobeys the elders. He ignores the shastras; he is foolish and vile; he has set himself on a fateful, inexorable path to perdition; and he is malevolent towards those who are concerned for his welfare.

His soul is overcome by desire and lust, and he foolishly believes he is wise. He is the enemy of all his true friends. He is always suspicious, has no control over himself, is ungrateful and, having abandoned dharma, is infatuated by every sin. He is vain and immature, a slave to his senses, driven by bottomless greed, and indecisive.

And these are not his only faults. Even if you point out what is good for him, his arrogance makes him ignore such counsel. He has great faith in the prowess of Bhishma, Drona, Kripa, Karna, Drona's son and Jayadratha and, so, he spurns peace. Dhritarashtra's sons and

Karna firmly believe that the Pandavas cannot even face Bhishma, Drona and the other Kshatriyas, let alone fight against them. Duryodhana has assembled an immense army and thinks that victory is already his. The fool believes that Karna can single-handedly vanquish the enemy, and so Duryodhana will never make peace.

Krishna, you want peace and brotherhood between the Kauravas and the Pandavas; but know that Dhritarashtra's sons have decided not to give the Pandavas what is rightfully theirs. Whatever you say to these men will be in vain, for they their minds are already made up. A wise man would not waste his breath when his words, good or bad, will surely prove ineffectual, even like singing to the deaf. Just as a Brahmana's discourse is wasted on Chandalas, your words will be utterly disregarded by these ignorant and evil men, who have no reverence for anything that is worthy of it.

Duryodhana is fatuous and, as long as he has strength, he will never heed your advice; everything you say to him will be futile. I do not think it is apt for you to go into the midst of these sinners, and speak out against them, who are black-souled, and many. Because they have no respect for age, are blinded by wealth and vanity, are full of the arrogance of youth and impatient, they will never accept your wise counsel.

Duryodhana has mustered a strong force and does not trust you. He will never do as you say. Dhritarashtra's sons are inspired by the conviction that Indra himself, with all the Devas, cannot defeat them in battle. Your words, always profound, will not move men of such dark beliefs, men driven by lust, greed and anger.

Secure amidst his vast army of elephants, chariots and soldiers, Duryodhana is fearless and thinks he has already conquered the Earth. He wants his empire without rivals. Peace with him is not possible, for he assumes that what he owns is unalterably his. Sadly, the end of the world as we know it is at hand because of Duryodhana, for kings of the world and all their Kshatriya warriors have gathered here to fight for him against the Pandavas.

Krishna, in the past, you have made all these kings, who are now arrayed against you, suffer grievous losses. Prompted by fear of you, these Kshatriyas have joined Karna and made an alliance with Dhritarashtra's sons. Reckless, and even prepared to die, they have joined Duryodhana for the pleasure of fighting against the Pandavas and you. I do not think it wise for you to go to them. How will you manage, surrounded by so many treacherous enemies all seated together? I am aware that you cannot be vanquished by the Devas themselves; I know how powerful and intelligent you are.

Krishna, I love you as much as I love the sons of Pandu, and what I say is from affection, respect and friendship for you. Need I tell you how delighted I am to see you, Lotus-eyed One? You are the inner soul of all the living.'"

CANTO 93

BHAGAVAD-YANA PARVA CONTINUED

"The Divine One says, 'Vidura, all that a wise man should say; all that a far-sighted man would say; all that a man could to say to me as a friend; all that is truly worthy of you, in keeping with dharma and artha: all this you have said to me, as if I am your child. What you have told me is true, praiseworthy and sensible. Now, Vidura, listen to my reason for being here.

I am well aware of Duryodhana's evil nature and of the hostility of the Kshatriyas who support him; yet I have come to the Kurus. The Earth is in the grip of an enormous danger, and the man who saves her, with her elephants, chariots and horses, from imminent death will earn great punya. If this man does not succeed despite his best efforts to do what is dharma, he is anyway certain to merit the punya attached to that achievement, even though he fails. Similarly, as men who are versed in religion and the shastras know, if a man does not actually commit a sin, even if he intended to, he will not accrue the punishment attached to that sin.

I will try with all sincerity to bring about peace between the Kurus and the Srinjayas, who are about to be slaughtered in battle. Doom hangs over them because of the Kurus, fetched by the crimes of Duryodhana and Karna, while the other Kshatriyas only follow their lead.

Learned men condemn the man who does not persuade a friend who is about to plunge into death's maw to save himself. A man must do his utmost, even seizing his friend by the hair, to turn him away from a grave sin. Such a man will win praise, not blame. Duryodhana would do well to accept my good advice, which is in keeping with dharma and artha, and which can avert the unimaginable war that looms. I will sincerely try to secure the welfare both of Dhritarashtra's sons and Pandu's, as well of all Kshatriya kind. If Duryodhana disregards me, I shall at least have the satisfaction of having followed my conscience, for a true friend is one who mediates when hostility breaks out between kinsmen.

I have come here so that no one can later say that, although he could have done so, Krishna made no attempt to stop the Kauravas and the Pandavas from slaughtering one another. I have come here to serve both sides and not all the gathered kings can reproach me.

If, after listening to my well-meant advice, Duryodhana does not accept what I say, he will only invite a horrific destiny to take millions of lives. If I can bring about peace among the Kurus without sacrificing the interests of the Pandavas, what I accomplish will be worthy indeed, and the Kauravas will be freed from death's clutches. If the sons of Dhritarashtra reflect calmly on what I say, then my objective will be achieved and the Kauravas will worship me as the one who brought peace to them.

If, instead, they try to injure me, I tell you now that all the kings of the Earth together are no match for me. They will be as a herd of deer before an angry lion.'

Saying this to Vidura, that bull of the Vrishnis and joy of the Yadavas lies down on his soft bed to rest."

CANTO 94

BHAGAVAD-YANA PARVA CONTINUED

Vaisampayana said, "The starlit night is spent in conversation between these two illustrious tejasvins. The night passes too quickly for Vidura, who listens and talks to Krishna about so many things, both of them speaking words filled with dharma and artha and delight.

At dawn, a choir of singers awaken Krishna with melodious voices, accompanied by the sweet sounds of cymbals and conches. Krishna rises and performs his morning rituals; he bathes, recites the sacred mantras and pours ghee onto the sacrificial fire. He dresses himself and worships the rising Sun.

While he is still at his morning devotions, Duryodhana and Sakuni come to him and say, 'Dhritarashtra is in his sabha, with all the Kurus headed by Bhishma, and all the kings of the Earth. They request your presence, Krishna, with as much yearning as the Devas desire Indra's.'

Krishna greets them both with courtesy, and when the Sun has risen a little higher into the sky he calls for a number of Brahmanas and presents them with gold, clothes, cattle and horses. After he has made generous gifts he sits down; his sarathy Daruka come and salutes him; at Krishna's word, the sarathy fetches his master's dazzling chariot adorned with rows of tinkling bells and harnessed to the superb horses. Seeing his ratha, which rumbles like massed thunderheads, ready, Krishna walks in pradakshina around the sacred fire and the Brahmanas present, puts on the jewel Kaustubha and, blazing in beauty, surrounded by the Kurus and escorted by the Vrishnis, climbs onto the chariot.

Vidura follows Krishna, foremost of all the living and most brilliant among men, on his own chariot. Duryodhana and Sakuni follow in one Kuru chariot; Satyaki, Kritavarman and the other Vrishni Maharathas follow Krishna in chariots, and on horses and elephants. Rajan, those exotic chariots, adorned with gold and drawn by wonderful horses, flash and rumble as they move along.

In the lead, Krishna, radiant in beauty, comes to a broad avenue that has been swept and watered, and made fit for the most kingly of kings. As he approaches cymbals clash, conches sound and other instruments pour out their music in homage. Many young Kshatriyas, the most heroic in the world and lionish in their strength, surround Krishna's chariot as his escort. Thousands of soldiers, attired in a variety of uniforms and carrying swords, lances and axes, march in front of Krishna. Five hundred elephants and thousands of chariots follow that unconquered hero as he proceeds in majesty.

All the citizens of the city, men and women of all ages, come out onto the streets to catch a glimpse of him. The terraces and balconies of houses are so crowded by women that they look as if they will collapse. Worshipped by the Kurus as he comes down the king's highway, Krishna looks around, his eyes seeing everyone, he hears their adulations and responds to each one's greetings, individually, magically.

When at last he reaches the Kuru sabha his attendants blow their conches and trumpets, shaking the skies. And all the great kings assembled in the Kuru sabha shiver in excited anticipation of seeing Krishna. Hearing the rumble of his chariot, deep as the roll of thunderclouds, they know that he is near and the hair on their bodies stands on end.

Krishna reaches the lofty gates and, alighting from his chariot that is like the summit of Mount Kailasa, he enters the sabha, which glimmers like newly risen clouds and is as splendid as Indra's own court. He walks in with Vidura and Satyaki on either side; and he overshadows the splendour of the Kurus with his own, like the Sun dimming the lesser lights of the heavens.

Karna and Duryodhana face Krishna, and the Vrishnis with Kritavarman are behind him. Bhishma, Drona, the blind Dhritarashtra and his courtiers rise to honour Krishna. When Dhritarashtra stands the thousands of kings who surround him also rise. Krishna accepts the exquisite golden throne that has been prepared for him at Dhritarashtra's command. He smiles and greets the king, Bhishma, Drona and all the other kings, according to each one's age. All the kings and all the Kurus worship him in return. Through a vast window Krishna sees at the great palace gates the Rishis he saw in the sky on his way to Hastinapura.

Seeing them here, with Narada at their head, Krishna calmly says to Santanu's son Bhishma, 'These Devarishis have come to this earthly conclave of ours. Invite them in and offer them the finest seats and your gracious courtesy, for none of us can sit until they do. Without delay, offer worship to these Rishis who have mastered their souls.'

Bhishma sees the Rishis at the palace gate and orders the servants to fetch the finest seats for them, inlaid with gold and gem-set. Only after the Rishis are seated and have accepted the arghya offered to them does Krishna sit, and then so do the other kings. Dusasana assigns an excellent seat to Satyaki, and Vivimsati gives another golden one to Kritavarman. Not far from Krishna that illustrious and wrathful pair, Karna and Duryodhana, sit together on the same wide couch. Subala, the king of Gandhara, surrounded by the chiefs of his country, sits with his son beside him. The high-souled Vidura sits on a jewelled armchair covered with a white deer-skin, so close to Krishna's that it touches it.

All the kings gaze at Krishna for a long time but, just as people who drink amrita are never satisfied, even after imbibing cup after cup of it, their eyes remain unfulfilled. Krishna, clad in pitambara robes and his skin like the dark atasi flower, sits in the midst of the sabha, like a sapphire set in gold. A profound silence descends, for no one stirs, or speaks a word, why, they hardly breathe."

CANTO 95

BHAGAVAD-YANA PARVA CONTINUED

Vaisampayana said, "Finally, Krishna, master of silence, of the perfect teeth and deep voice speaks. Although his words are addressed to Dhritarashtra, his words resound through all the sabha like thunderheads rumbling, and all the assembly hears him.

He says, 'I have come here to bring about peace between the Kurus and the Pandavas, to prevent a slaughter of Kshatriyas. I have nothing new to say, as you, Rajan, know everything there is to be known in this world. Because of its gyana and dharma, and because it is adorned with every accomplishment, your vamsa is the most distinguished of all royal dynasties. Joy in the happiness of others, grief at the sight of another's suffering, desire to alleviate distress, abstention from injury, sincerity, forgiveness and truth: all these prevail amongst the Kurus. Your dynasty is so noble that it would be sad indeed if anyone born into it did anything to break dharma, and tragic if it were you, King, who did so. For, you should be the first to restrain the Kurus if they sin against strangers or even their own people.

Know that your sons, led by Duryodhana, have abandoned dharma and artha and, deprived of their good sense by greed, now treat their own cousins despicably, most viciously. What your sons do is the cause of the terrible danger which threatens us all. If you ignore it, their deeds will result in a massacre past imagining. If you so will, you can prevent this calamity even now, Bharatarishabha; peace is not difficult to achieve.

The establishing of peace depends on you and me, Rajan. You correct your sons and I will pacify the Pandavas. Your sons and their followers must obey your command, whatever it is. Indeed, their best course is to obey you. If you strive for peace by controlling your sons, it will be to your benefit, as well as to that of the Pandavas.

O great king, reflect carefully over this and do the proper thing. Let the Pandavas be your allies, and with their support seek dharma and artha. You cannot have better allies than them. With them as your protectors, Indra himself could not vanquish you. How can mere kings of the Earth withstand your might?

If you have the support of Bhishma, Drona, Kripa, Karna, Vivimsati, Aswatthama, Vikarna, Somadatta and Bahlika, of the rulers of the Sindhus and Kalingas, of Sudakshina the king of the Kambojas, of Yudhishtira, Bhimasena, Arjuna and the twins, of the mighty Satyaki and Yuyutsu, what man is there who is so misguided that he would dare challenge you? If you have both the Kurus and the Pandavas at your side, you will be invincible, and the sovereignty of the whole world will be yours.

All the rulers of the Earth, your equals as well as your superiors, will want an alliance with you. Protected on all sides by sons, grandsons, fathers, brothers and friends, you will live in unalloyed felicity. With all of them around you, and treating them affectionately, as you once used to, you will enjoy lordship over all this Earth. With your sons, allies and the sons of Pandu to support you will easily subdue all your enemies. Dhritarashtra, this is the most advantageous course for you to take. In unity with your sons, kinsmen and counsellors, you will be lord of the whole world, which they surely win for you.

O great king, nothing but death lies in war. What good can you see in the annihilation of both sides? Tell me, Bharatarishabha, if the

Pandavas are killed in battle or if your own sons fall, what happiness will you enjoy? All of them are brave and skilled warriors; all of them want war. Save them from the terrible danger that threatens them. After the war you will not see all the Kurus or all the Pandavas; Maharathas will kill each other and you will see both sides decimated.

All the rulers of the world are gathered here. They will exterminate the very population of the Earth in their anger. Save the world; do not let the people of this sacred Bhumi be destroyed. If you regain your natural goodness, the world will continue to be peopled as it is now. Rajan, save these kings from the horrible danger that threatens them; they are all of pure descent, modest, generous and devout, and related to one another by blood or marriage.

Let go of your wrath and enmity; let these kings embrace one another in peace. Let them eat and drink together; let them return to their homes in joy, dressed in rich clothes, decked with garlands and paying kind courtesies to one another.

Let the affection you had for the Pandavas be revived in your heart and let it lead to peace. They lost their father while they were mere boys, and you raised them. Now cherish them as befits you, as if they were your own sons. It is your duty to protect them, especially when they are in distress. Do not abandon dharma and artha.

The Pandavas have greeted you reverently and said, "At your command, we have suffered great misery. For twelve years we lived in the forests, and we lived unknown in the thirteenth year. We never broke our sworn pledge and believed that our father, too, would keep his word. The Brahmanas who were always with us will testify that we never once broke our word.

We have kept our side of the agreement; now you must abide by yours. Our travail has been long and great; now let us have our share of the kingdom. Knowing dharma and artha as you do, it falls to you to rescue us. We have endured our suffering in silence because we owed you obedience. Be a father and elder brother to us now.

A guru should behave with his sishyas in ways that befit a teacher;

and being your disciples, we regard you as our guru. So, treat us a guru should treat his sishyas. If we go wrong, it is the duty of our father to set us right. Therefore, set us on the right course and you, too, take the high path of dharma."

Your sons, the Pandavas, said this to the kings who have come here: "If the men in a sabha know dharma, they will not allow any impropriety to occur in their hallowed court. When, in the presence of men of dharma, sinners overpower the righteous and subvert truth by deceit, it is the evil ones who are vanquished. When, struck through by the arrow of adharma, good men seek the protection of a noble court, those who occupy that sabha are themselves pierced through by the arrow, if they do not extract it. Indeed, in that case, dharma will fell the men of that assembly, even like a river eating away the roots of trees on its bank."

Bharatarishabha, be your own judge. The Pandavas have kept peace, with their hearts set firmly in dharma, and deeply reflecting on all things. Whatever they have said is in keeping with dharma and nyaya. Rajan, what can you say to them except that you will restore their kingdom to them? Let these kings who are here tell you what your answer to the Pandavas should be.

If you think that what I say is dharma and true, save all these Kshatriyas from certain death. Make peace, and do not give in to anger. Give the Pandavas their rightful share of their father's kingdom; then enjoy happiness and prosperity with your sons; and have all your hopes fulfilled, Parantapa.

You know that Yudhishtira always walks the path of dharma. You know how he has conducted himself with you and your sons. Although you tried to have him burnt him alive in the house of lac, he fled into the wilderness, he returned and put his faith in you, only to be banished by you to Khandavaprastha. Ruling from Indraprastha, he brought all the kings of the Earth under his sway and yet looked up only to you, to honour you. In spite of the noble manner in which he conducted himself, Subala's son robbed Yudhishtira of his kingdom and wealth, at a deceitful game of dice. And despite being reduced to absolute penury, and having to watch Krishnaa dragged brutally into this sabha, Yudhishtira of the immeasurable soul did not swerve from Kshatriya dharma.

I want both your good and theirs. For the sake of dharma and artha, for happiness, Rajan, do not mistake evil for good or good for evil and, thereby, allow the Earth's population to be razed. Restrain your sons, whose greed has made them cross every limit. The sons of Pritha are as willing to wait upon you dutifully as they are to fight. Do what you think is best, Parantapa.'

In their hearts, all the kings in the sabha laud what Krishna says, but none of them dares speak out for dharma in Duryodhana's presence."

CANTO 96

BHAGAVAD-YANA PARVA CONTINUED

Vaisampayana said, "All in that sabha fall silent on hearing Krishna, the hair on their bodies stands on end. All the kings think that there is no man who would dare respond to what Krishna has said.

Seeing that all the kings sit silently, Parasurama addresses Duryodhana but speaks to the entire gathering of Kurus. He says, 'Listen to what I have to say and to the story I will tell to illustrate it; if you are convinced by me, do what will benefit you all.

There was a king named Dambhodbhava, who ruled all the world. They say that his kingdom covered all this Bhumi. Every morning, when he rose, he would call his Brahmanas and Kshatriyas to him and ask them if they knew of anyone—a Sudra, a Vaisya, a Kshatriya or a Brahmana—who was better than, or even equal to him in battle. The king wandered over the face of the Earth asking this question, and he became drunk with vanity.

High-souled Brahmanas, who knew the Vedas and who feared nothing, advised the boastful king to curb his pride. However, the king continued to ask his question day after day. Some great Brahmanas of immense tapasya became angry and spoke to the conceited king.

They said, "There are two men, who are the best of all men, and who are always victorious in battle. Dambhodbhava, you will be no match for either of them."

The king asked those Brahmanas, "Where might I find these two heroes? To what vamsa do they belong? What feats have they achieved? Who are they?"

The Brahmanas said, "We have heard that these two are Munis, named Nara and Narayana. They have both been born as mortals. Go and find them, O king. This illustrious pair practises the severest tapasya in a remote fastness of the Gandhamadana mountains."

The king could not bear to hear of the greatness of Nara and Narayana. He mustered his vast army of six kinds of forces and hastened to the rugged Gandhamadana mountains, where those unvanquished Rishis lived. There, he began to search for them and finally discovered them hidden in a deep vana. He saw that they were emaciated from hunger and thirst; their veins were swollen and stood out; and extremes of cold and heat had debilitated them. He approached them, touched their feet and enquired after their welfare.

The two Rishis received the king hospitably, with fruits and roots, with a darbhasana and water. They enquired about the king's business, and then blessed him, saying, *Tathaastu*. Dambhodbhava asked them what he always asked everyone.

He said, "I have conquered the Earth with the strength of my arms, and killed all my enemies. I have come here because I want to do battle with you. Do me the courtesy of hospitality by granting my wish, for I have wished for this for a very long time."

Nara and Narayana said, "Best of kings, anger and covetousness have no place in this mountain asrama. How then can we do battle here? There are no weapons here, no adharma or malice. Look somewhere else for a fight; there are many Kshatriyas on Earth."

Undeterred, the king tried to persuade them, but the Rishis ignored his repeated request and continued to try and placate him. Dambhodbhava, who was beside himself to fight them, would not relent.

Finally, Nara took up a handful of grass and said, "Since you are so eager for a fight, Kshatriya, take up your weapons and array your troops. I will rid you of your eagerness forever."

Dambhodbhava said, "Rishi, do you really think this weapon you hold is fit to be used against me? Nevertheless I will fight you, for I have come here expressly for that."

And with that, Dambhodbhava and his warriors shot arrows at the Muni from all sides. The Rishi, however, warded off those deadly banks of shafts that could mangle any enemy, with his blades of grass. The invincible Rishi directed his own astra, made just of the blades of grass, yet irresistible, at the king's army. Such was that weapon that it cut off the eyes, ears and noses of the troops.

The king saw the sky turned pale by those blades of grass, and he fell at the Rishi's feet and cried, "Bless me!"

Nara, who was always ready to grant refuge to anyone who asked for it, said to Dambhodbhava, "O king, always obey Brahmanas and live by dharma. Never again do what you have done today. The conqueror of hostile kingdoms, a Kshatriya who is mindful of his dharma, should never be as you are, even in his inmost heart. You must never, from pride in yourself, insult anybody at any time, be they inferior or superior to you. Conduct yourself in a manner that befits you.

Acquire wisdom, abandon covetousness and pride, control your soul, restrain your passions, be forgiving and humble, cherish your subjects and be well loved. Never slight anyone under any circumstances without first determining their true strengths and weaknesses. With our blessings, and by our leave, go now and change your ways from this day forth. We command you to ask sage Brahmanas what is good for you."

The king worshipped the feet of the two Maharishis and returned to his capital. And from that day on he began to live by dharma. This was the great feat that Nara achieved long, long ago.

The Rishi Narayana was superior even to Nara, for many more and greater qualities had their home in him. That is why the eight astras—Kakudika, Suka, Naka, Akshisantarjana, Santana, Nartana, Ghora and Asyamodaka—are integral to that best of bows, the Gandiva. Rajan, give up your pride and go humbly to Dhananjaya. His astras take lives.

These eight astras correspond with the eight sensual passions—lust, wrath, covetousness, vanity, insolence, pride, malice and selfishness. When these astras strike a man, he loses his senses and wanders about in bewilderment. Under their influence, men fall into a stupor, behave violently, vomit, pass urine and excreta, and weep and laugh uncontrollably.

Arjuna has Narayana—the Creator, the Lord of the Trilokas, the one who knows the destiny of every created being—as his ally beside him, and he is invincible in battle. Who is there in the three worlds who can vanquish that Kshatriya—Arjuna of the Vanara banner—who has no equal in battle? Countless are the virtues that reside in Arjuna, and Krishna is his superior. You know Kuntiputra Arjuna well. I say to you, the ancient Nara and Narayana are now Arjuna and Krishna. Great king, that is who these foremost of men are. If you believe this, and if you trust me, make peace of dharma with the sons of Pandu. Realise that it is for your good not to have discord within your clan, then do not set your heart on war but make sacred peace.

You are the foremost of the Kuru vamsa. The dynasty to which you belong has high honour through time. Let the vamsa continue to be worthy of that regard. Blessings be upon you; think of what is conducive to your own welfare.'"

CANTO 97

BHAGAVAD-YANA PARVA CONTINUED

Vaisampayana said, "The noble Rishi Kanva, who is present in the sabha, hears Parasurama and speaks to Duryodhana.

Kanva says, 'Loka Pitamaha Brahma is indestructible and eternal, as are the Maharishis Nara and Narayana; for, of all Aditi's sons, Vishnu alone is eternal. Only he is unconquerable and indestructible; he alone exists for ever; he is the Lord of all and the possessor of divine attributes. All others, the Sun and Moon, Earth and Water, Wind and Fire, Sky, the planets and stars, can be destroyed; when the end of the universe comes all these will cease to exist. They are destroyed and created over and over, again and again. Human beings, animals, birds and other living creatures that live in the mortal world have impermanent lives. Even kings, having enjoyed great prosperity, reach the hour of their death and are reborn to reap the fruits of their good and evil karma.

Therefore, it is essential that you make peace with Yudhishtira. Let the Pandavas and the Kauravas both rule this Earth together. Duryodhana, do not be vain about your strength, for there are always men more powerful than those who are considered strong. Mere physical strength is not regarded as true strength by the wise. The Pandavas are all blessed with prowess equal to that of the Devas and they live by dharma; they are truly strong.

There is an ancient tale told that illustrates this, of Matali's search for a husband for his daughter.

Indra, king of the three worlds, has a charioteer named Matali, whom he loves dearly. A daughter was born to Matali, and she came to be celebrated across the world for her beauty. The girl, named Gunakesi, was blessed with celestial beauty; and in loveliness of face and form she outshone other women. Knowing that the time for giving her in marriage had come, Matali and his wife became anxious, and he wondered what he should do.

He thought to himself, "Alas, the birth of a daughter in families that are noble and upright, that are respected and of great humility, brings evil in its wake. Daughters, when born into noble families, always endanger the honour of three families—their maternal and paternal families and the family into which they marry. In my mind's eye I have scanned the worlds of Devas and Manavas, but I have not found an eligible groom for my daughter."

Amongst the Devas, Daityas, Gandharvas, Manavas and Rishis, not one did Matali consider a suitable husband for his daughter. One night, after consulting his wife Sudharma, he decided to travel to Nagaloka, thinking that since he had not found an eligible groom for Gunakesi amongst the Devas and Manavas, he might find one amongst the Nagas.

Telling his wife this, he took her leave and, sniffing the head of his daughter in affection, Matali set out for the under-world.'"

CANTO 98

BHAGAVAD-YANA PARVA CONTINUED

"Kanva says, 'On his way, Matali saw Narada Muni going towards Varuna Deva's abode. Narada asked him, "Where are you going? Are you on some work of your own or is it at Indra's bidding that you journey?"

Matali told Narada about his quest, and the Muni said, "Let us go together. I am coming from Devaloka to visit Varuna. While we range through Nagaloka, we will seek out a suitable husband for your daughter."

The illustrious pair went into the underworld and there they saw Varuna, the Lord of the waters. Narada was worshipped in a manner befitting a Devarishi, and Matali received what would be offered to Indra. The two of them, pleased that they could get on with the business at hand, explained why they were there. With Varuna's leave, they began to wander about in Nagaloka and, while doing so, Narada, who knew all the inhabitants of that realm, described them in detail to his companion.

Narada said, "O Sarathy, you have seen Varuna with his sons and grandsons around him. Now see his kingdom, so enchanting and rich.

Varuna's son of great wisdom is distinguished for his conduct and saintly character. This beloved son has eyes like lotus leaves, is blessed with great beauty and is a joy to look at. Soma's daughter has chosen him for her husband. Her name is Jyotsnakali and she is as beautiful as Sree Devi. I remember that she once chose the eldest of Aditi's sons for her husband.

Matali, look at Varuna's dwelling, made of gold, where the wondrous wine called Varuni flows abundant. It is from having imbibed this wine that the Devas acquired their godly status. These blazing weapons of every kind that you see once belonged to the Daityas, who have since lost their sovereignty. These astras never decay and, when loosed at an enemy, return unerringly to the hand that cast them. The Devas obtained them as the spoils of war. Tremendous tejas is required for them to be used against enemies. Many tribes of Rakshasas and Daityas, who possessed all kinds of devastras, lived here long ago, but they were all vanquished by the Devas.

Look at that great fire in Varuna's lake; see where Vishnu's Chakra dazzles in the midst of those mighty flames. Look, there is that gnarled bow that was created for the destruction of the world. The Devas protect it constantly and vigilantly, and it is after this bow that Arjuna's Gandiva was named. It has the strength of a hundred thousand other bows, and the power that impels it in battle is indescribable. It quells all evil kings who are friendly towards the Rakshasas. Brahma, the first expounder of the Veda, created this fierce weapon, and Indra has declared it to be one of the most terrible of all weapons. This awesome astra obeys the command of Varuna's sons.

Look at Varuna Deva's sovereign parasol in that royal chamber. Like clouds, it showers cool water. The water that drops from it is as pure as the Moon and yet cloaked in such dense darkness that no one can see it.

Here, Matali, there are innumerable wonders to be seen. However, your mission will suffer if we spend more time in this palace of wonders. So let us go now," said Narada Muni,' says the Maharishi Kanva."

CANTO 99

BHAGAVAD-YANA PARVA CONTINUED

"Kanva says, 'Narada continued, "Here in the heart of Nagaloka is the city of Patala. It is celebrated across the universe and the Daityas and the Danavas worship it. Creatures that live on Earth cry out in terror if the ocean washes them to it. Here the fire, known as the Asura-agni, which is fed by water, burns continually. The Devas revere this fire, which does not move, being confined to this place.

It was here in Nagaloka that the Devas, when they had defeated and killed all their enemies, disposed of the Amrita that remained after they had drunk their fill. It is here that the waning and waxing of the Moon originate. It is here that son of Aditi, the horse-headed Vishnu, Hayagriva, rises and fills the universe with his lustre on festive occasions, to the accompaniment of Vedic hymns, at which times he is called Suvarna. This wondrous place is called Patala because the Moon and other forms of water shed blissful showers on it.

From here, the celestial elephant Airavata sucks cool water with which he fills the clouds for the nurture of the universe; and Indra pours the water down as rain. All kinds of aquatic animals of diverse shapes, the timingala and others, which get their nourishment from the Moon's rays, live here. Also living here are creatures that sunlight kills during the day and which are restored to life at night by the Moon. This is where the Moon rises every day and, with its rays, resuscitates the dead creatures with his touch. It is here that many demonic Daityas, whom Indra defeated and deprived of their prosperity, stay imprisoned. It was here that the lord and master of all creation, Bhutapati, sat in austere tapasya for their benefit.

Many Maharishis live here, who observe the vrata called *go*, who are emaciated from their arduous study and chanting of the Vedas, who have suspended their pranas and achieved Moksha by their tapasya. A man is said to live by the *go-vrata* when he can sleep wherever he chooses, and when he lives only on food and clothes that are given to him. Here were born all the best of elephants descended from the elephant Supratika of great renown—Airavata the king of his tribe, Vamana, Kumuda and Anjana.

Look around, Matali, and see if there is a bridegroom here who stands out because of his superior qualities. I will go to him and ask him to accept your daughter's hand.

Look at that dazzlingly beautiful Egg in the water. It has been here from the beginning of the creation. It does not move, nor does it hatch. I have never heard how it was born or what it is, and nobody knows who its father or mother is. It is said, Matali, that when the end of the world comes, a mighty fire will erupt from within it and consume the three worlds, with all their moving and rooted beings."

Matali heard all that Narada said and replied, "I do not see anyone here who is eligible. Let us leave this place."'"

CANTO 100

BHAGAVAD-YANA PARVA CONTINUED

"Kanva says, 'Narada continued, "Here is that great and most famous of cities, Hiranyapura. It belongs to the Daityas and Danavas who are skilled at one hundred types of maya. It was planned by the Danava Mayaa, and built by the divine architect Viswakarma. Many tejasvin Danavas, who obtained boons from Brahma long ago, live here, practising their thousand magical illusions. No one could vanquish them, neither Indra nor any other Deva, neither Yama, nor Varuna nor Kubera the Lord of treasures.

Also living here are the Kalakhanja Asuras, who sprang from Vishnu; and the Yatudhana Rakshasas, who came forth from Brahma's feet. All these violent beings have frightful fangs, are as swift and powerful as the wind, and have great powers of maya. Besides these, another invincible tribe of Danavas called Nivatakavachas also live here.

You know that Indra cannot vanquish them. Many times you with your son Gomukha, and Sachi's lord Indra Deva with his son, have had to flee before them. Look at their homes, Matali; they are all made of silver and gold, and grandly adorned. All these mansions are decked with vaiduryas and corals, and shine from the lustre of the jewels—arkasphatika and ajrasara. Many of these palaces seem as if they have been made of brilliant padmaragas, or of bright marble or of the most excellent wood. They dazzle like the Sun, or a blazing fire. Look how tall these jewelled edifices are, and they stand close together. They are of magnificent proportions and beauty, and it is impossible to determine exactly what materials they are built of, or to describe them. Indeed, they are lovely.

Look at these grounds that the Daityas use for recreation and sport; look at their bedsteads, their opulent utensils set with precious stones, their majestic thrones. Look at these hills of theirs that seem like massed clouds, these water fountains, these trees that move of their own will and yield all the flowers and fruit that they are asked for.

Matali, see if you can find a suitable groom here for your daughter. If you cannot, we will go elsewhere."

Matali said, "Devarishi, it is not wise or fitting for me to do anything that the Devas might disapprove of. The Devas and Danavas, though brothers, are always at war with each other. How can I make an alliance with our enemies? Let us go to some other place. I must not look among the Danavas for a husband for my child. Ah Muni, I know your nature and how you love instigating and fanning quarrels.""

CANTO 101

BHAGAVAD-YANA PARVA CONTINUED

"Kanva says, 'Narada said, "This region belongs to luxuriantly feathered birds that feed on snakes. They are tireless in their prowess, whether in flight or carrying loads. This avian tribe is descended from Garuda's six sons—Sumukha, Sunaman, Sunetra, Suvarchas, Surucha and that prince of birds Subala. These best of avians, born of Kasyapa's line, have multiplied and increased to create a thousand dynasties of birds. They are all of noble lineage and bring glory to Vinata's dynasty.

These birds are blessed with great prosperity; they all bear the auspicious Srivatsa mark; they are wealthy; and they are mighty. Their deeds are like a Kshatriya's, but living as they do on snakes, they are without compassion. And because they also prey on their own kind, they can never attain Brahman.

I will tell you their names, Matali. Listen well; these birds are respected because of the grace that Vishnu showers on them. They all worship Vishnu, who is their protector. He is always in their hearts and he is their refuge.

These are their names—Suvarnachuda, Nagasin, Daruna, Chandatundaka, Anila, Visalaksha, Kundalin, Pankajit, Vajraviskambha, Vainateya, Vamana, Vatavega, Disachakshu, Nimisha, Animisha, Trirava, Saptarava, Valmiki, Dwipaka, Daityadwipa, Saridwipa, Sarasa, Padmaketana, Sumukha, Chitraketu, Chitravara, Anagha, Meshahrit, Kumuda, Daksha, Sarpanta, Sahabhojana, Gurubhara, Kapota, Suryanetra, Chirantaka, Vishnudharman, Kumara, Parivarha, Hari, Suswara, Madhuparka, Hemavarna, Malaya, Matariswan, Nisakara and Divakara.

These descendants of Garuda all live in one province of this subterranean realm. The names I have recited are only of those who are distinguished by their power, fame and achievements. If you do not find one to your liking here, I will take you to another region, where you might find an eligible groom for your daughter," said Narada,' says Kanva."

CANTO 102

BHAGAVAD-YANA PARVA CONTINUED

"'Narada said, "This, now, is called Rasatala: the seventh stratum below the Earth. Here Surabhi lives, the mother of all bovine species, who was born of Amrita. She continuously yields milk that is the essence of all the best things of the Earth; its unique, unmatched taste is an amalgam of the six tastes.

Surabhi, the embodiment of perfection, sprang in that ancient time from Brahma Pitamaha. When he was satiated with Amrita the best of everything flowed out of his mouth. A single jet of Surabhi's milk fell on the Earth and created the Kshirasagara. The shores of that ocean are always covered with white surf that looks like a flower garland. The best of ascetics, who are known as Fenapas, foam-drinkers, live by this ocean and subsist only on its surf, and so their name. They practise the most austere tapasya and even the Devas fear them.

Surabhi gave birth to four calves, who stand one each at each of the four cardinal points and support them. They are called the Dikpalis. Surupa supports the east and Hansika the south; Subhadra, of the wonderful nature and universal form, supports the west, which is ruled by Varuna; and Sarvakamadugha supports the north, where dharma reigns supreme and is named after Kubera, the lord of treasures.

The Devas and Asuras, with the Mandara Mountain as their rod, churned the waters of Kshirasagara to obtain the wine called Varuni. Devi Lakshmi, Amrita, the prince of horses Uchchaisravas, and that most precious of jewels the ruby Kaustubha emerged from it as well. Matali, those waters that yielded these precious things are mixed with the milk of these four cows. As for Surabhi's milk, it becomes Sudha for those that live on Sudha, Swadha for those that live on Swadha and Amrita for those that live on Amrita.

Even today, learned men recite the verse that the dwellers of Rasatala sang in days of old: Neither in Nagaloka, nor in Swarga, nor in Vimana nor in Trivishtapa is one as happy as in Rasatala," says Kanva.'"

CANTO 103

BHAGAVAD-YANA PARVA CONTINUED

"Kanva says, 'Narada said, "This best of cities that you see now, which is like Indra's Amaravati, is Bhogavati. Vasuki, the king of the Nagas, is its ruler and he lives here. He supports the vast Earth by dint of having performed the most austere tapasya. His body is the size of Swetachala, the White Mountain; he is decked in celestial ornaments; he has a thousand heads; his tongues are like flames; and he is immeasurably strong.

Countless Nagas of varied forms and adorned in all kinds of ornaments, all sons of Surasa, live here happily. They are adorned with the marks of gems, swastikas, chakras and kamandalas. All of them are fierce and mighty; some have a thousand heads, some five hundred and some three; some have two heads, some five and some seven; all of them have mountainous bodies. There are perhaps millions of Nagas of each dynasty, or even tens of millions; they cannot be counted. Listen now as I name a few of the more famous amongst them.

They are Vasuki, Takshaka, Karkotaka, Dhananjaya, Kaliya, Nahusha, Kambala, Aswatara, Bahyakunda, Mani, Apurana, Khaga,

Vamana, Elapatra, Kukura, Kukuna, Aryaka, Nandaka, Kalasa, Potaka, Kailasaka, Pinjaraka, Airavata, Sumanomukha, Dadhimukha, Sankha, Nanda, Upanandaka, Apta, Kotaraka, Sikhi, Nishturika, Tittiri, Hastibhadra, Kumuda, Malyapindaka, the two Padmas, Pundarika, Pushpa, Mudgaraparnaka, Karavira, Pitaraka, Samvritta, Vritta, Pindara, Bilvapatra, Mushikada, Sirishaka, Dilipa, Sankhasirsha, Jyotishka, Aparajita, Kauravya, Dhritarashtra, Kuhura, Krisaka, Viraja, Dharana, Subahu, Mukhara, Jaya, Badhira, Andha, Visundi, Virasa and Sarasa. There are these as well as many other sons of Kasyapa. Matali, see if there is anybody here whom you can choose.'"

All this time Matali was gazing intently at one who stood before them, at a small remove, and when Narada stopped speaking, the celestial sarathy, looking very pleased, asked Narada Muni, "What vamsa does that handsome, radiant youth belong to, who stands in front of Aryaka of Kauravya vamsa? Who are his parents? Of which line of Nagas is he, who stands tall and erect like a flagstaff? His intelligence, patience, beauty and youth make my heart lean towards him. He will make an excellent husband for my Gunakesi."

Narada saw how delighted Matali was at seeing the young Sumukha and told him of his noble parentage and feats.

He said, "This prince of Nagas is Sumukha. He is born in Airavata's line; he is Aryaka's favourite grandson, and his maternal grandfather is Vamana. His father was the Naga Chikura, whom Vinata's son Garuda killed not so long ago."

Matali was delighted to hear this and said to Narada, "Lord, I would like to have this best of Nagas for my son-in-law. I beg you, try to make this match, for I am extremely pleased at the thought of bestowing him on my precious daughter,'""

CANTO 104

BHAGAVAD-YANA PARVA CONTINUED

"Kanva says, 'Narada said to the great Naga Aryaka, "This is Indra's sarathy Matali, and Sakra's dear friend. His conduct is pure; he has an excellent character and has many virtues; he has strength of mind, great tejas and might. He is Indra's companion, advisor and charioteer. In every battle, one sees that there is very little difference between him and Indra, in strength and prowess. In all the wars between the Devas and Asuras it is Matali who, with his mind, drives Indra's glorious and ever-victorious chariot, drawn by a thousand horses. The enemies of the Devas are defeated by Matali's expert handling of those unworldly steeds and by the might of Indra's arms: Matali first outmanoeuvres them and then Indra kills them.

Matali has an excellent daughter, of unrivalled beauty. She is truthful and accomplished; and her name is Gunakesi. Matali has searched all the trilokas for a suitable husband for her.

O Aryaka of godlike splendour, he finds your grandson Sumukha to be a suitable match for his child. If you think his proposal acceptable, decide quickly to receive his daughter as a gift to your grandson. As

Lakshmi does Vishnu's, or Swaha Agni's, let the slender-waisted Gunakesi grace your vamsa. Accept her for Sumukha, for they are born for each other, like Sachi and Indra.

Although this youth has lost his father, we chose him for his good qualities and for the honour of being related to Airavata and yourself. Sumukha's virtues, his disposition, purity, self-restraint and other qualities have persuaded Matali to offer his daughter to him. Do Matali the honour of accepting her."

Aryaka was filled with delight and sorrow, at once, on hearing Narada's words—delight to see his grandson being chosen as a bridegroom and sorrow at the memory of his son's death.

He said to Narada, "How, Devarishi, how can I have Gunakesi for a daughter-in-law? That I do not approve is not for lack of reverence for you, for who is there who would not want an alliance with Indra's own sarathy? Mahamuni, I hesitate only because I feel that the alliance will not be a lasting one. Effulgent one, this boy's father—my son—was devoured by Garuda, and we are in deep mourning. Worse still, when he left Nagaloka, Garuda swore that, in a month's time, he would devour Sumukha as well. Suparna will surely do as he said. His parting words have plunged us in grief."

Matali then said to Aryaka, "I have a solution for your fear. I have chosen your grandson as a son-in-law. Let him come with Narada and me to Indra, lord of Devas. I will do everything in my power to make Garuda desist from doing as he has sworn. If he does not agree, I will ascertain the life span allotted to Sumukha. Blessings upon you, O Naga; let your grandson come with me to Indra."

Saying this, Narada, Matali and Aryaka took Sumukha with them and these radiant ones went to Indra, in Devaloka. Vishnu, who happened to be there at that time, heard Narada's account of Matali's search and his eventual choice.

Vishnu said to Indra, "Give this youth Amrita; let him be immortal like the Devas. By your grace, let Matali, Narada and Sumukha have everything they wish for."

Thinking about Garuda's awesome might, Indra agreed and commanded that Sumukha be given Amrita. To this, Vishnu said, "You are the lord of all mobile and unmoving creatures. Who would refuse a gift from you?"

Indra then granted the young Naga the boon of longevity, that he become a Chiranjeevi even without having to drink any Amrita. Sumukha's face was suffused with radiant joy, making him truly *sumukha*! He married Matali's daughter and returned home. Narada and Aryaka, delighted with the success of their venture, departed after worshipping Indra, lord of the Devas.'

CANTO 105

BHAGAVAD-YANA PARVA CONTINUED

Kanva says, 'Meanwhile, Garuda heard about Indra's boon of longevity to Sumukha. Inflamed with rage the sky-ranger flapped his wings furiously and punished the three worlds with a hurricane.

He came to Indra and said, "Illustrious one, why have you deprived me of my food? Having granted me a boon of your own will, why do you now withdraw it? From the very beginning the Supreme Lord has ordained what my food is to be. Why do you now obstruct that divine decree?

I had chosen this great Naga and had appointed a time to kill him, for I wanted to offer the meat of his body as sustenance for my numerous young ones. Now your boon has made him immortal, how can I kill another of his species? How can you do as you please, so frivolously? I, my family and my servants will die of hunger; perhaps that will gratify you, Indra. Indeed I deserve this and worse because although I am powerful enough to be lord of the Trilokas, I agreed to become the servant of another. O Trilokapati, Vishnu is not the only cause of my inferiority. I am your equal, yet the sovereignty of the three worlds is yours.

Like you, I have Daksha's daughter for my mother and Kasyapa for my father. Like you, I can untiringly bear the weight of the three worlds. I have immeasurable and irresistible strength; no creature can withstand me. In the war with the Daityas I, too, achieved wondrous feats. I killed Srutasri and Srutasena, Vivaswat, Rochanamukha, Prasrura and Kalakaksha and other sons of Diti.

I perch on the flag-staff of your younger brother Vishnu's chariot and protect him in battle; I sometimes carry him on my back. Perhaps this is why you disregard me. Who else in the universe can bear such heavy burdens? Who is stronger than me? In spite of my superiority, I carry your younger brother and his companions on my back. By interfering with my prey, my sustenance, you insult me, just as your brother does when he makes me carry him.

As for you, Vishnu, of all the mighty and strong ones that Aditi has given birth to, you are the most powerful. Yet I can carry you, without feeling any fatigue, on just one of my feathers. Think then, brother, which of us is stronger."

Hearing the Bird's haughty words, Vishnu, wanting to forestall the crisis he saw looming, provoked Garuda further, saying, "How do you think of yourself as being strong when in fact you are a weakling? It does not become you to brag like this in our presence. The three worlds together cannot bear the weight of my body. The truth is that I carry my own weight and yours as well. Come now, lift my right arm. If you can, I will consider your boast to be true."

Saying this, Lord Vishnu placed his arm on Garuda's shoulders, and the golden Eagle fell down unconscious. To Garuda the weight of Vishnu's arm felt as great as that of the entire Earth with her mountains. Compassionate Vishnu did not submit him to more suffering, and spared his life.

Crushed by the immense weight of the Lord's arm, Garuda gasped for breath and shed his feathers. His limbs were weak and terror confounded him. He bowed his head low before Vishnu and spoke to him.

Garuda said feebly, "Illustrious Lord, the power that sustains the universe dwells in you. It is no wonder that one arm of yours, stretched out but lightly, crushes me. Divine One, forgive this worthless winged creature that perches on your flag-staff, this fool intoxicated with pride in his own strength, for, O Lord, I am entirely helpless. I did not know how great your strength is and, so, thought my own unrivalled."

Vishnu was gratified and, affectionately saying to Garuda, "Never yield to such arrogance again," with his toe he cast Sumukha onto Garuda's breast.

From that time, Rajan, Garuda has always lived in friendship with that Naga, and that is how that mighty and illustrious kings of birds, the son of Vinata, was crushed by Vishnu's might and cured of his pride.

In the same way, Duryodhana, you will live as long as you do not confront the heroic Pandavas in battle. Who is there that Vayu's son Bhima, and Indra's son Arjuna cannot slay in battle? Your enemies are verily the gods themselves—Vishnu, Dharma, Vayu, Indra and the two Aswins. You are not worthy of even looking at them on the field, let alone face them in battle. Rajan, do not set your heart on war; with Krishna's help, make peace. It is your duty to save your very race by doing this.

Mahamuni Narada saw with his own eyes the incident I have just narrated; it should tell you how great is Vishnu. Krishna is that Vishnu, the wielder of the discus and the mace,' says Kanva.

Hearing what Kanva Muni says, Duryodhana's face darkens; frowns and breathes heavily. Then he looks at Karna and bursts into loud mocking laughter and slaps his thigh that is like the trunk of an elephant.

He says to the Rishi, 'Maharishi, I am what the Creator has made me. What will be must be. Whatever is ordained for me must happen; and I cannot prevent it. Of what use then are your futile sermons?'"

CANTO 106

BHAGAVAD-YANA PARVA CONTINUED

Janamejaya said, "Why did Duryodhana's friends not try to dissuade him from taking the path that led surely to doom, knowing that he was wedded to evil, blinded by avarice, addicted to sin and determined to bring ruin upon himself, thereby filling his kinsmen with grief, afflicting his friends and well-wishers with sorrow and making his enemies joyful. And why did neither Krishna nor Pitamaha Bhishma say anything out of affection?"

Vaisampayana said, "Krishna and Bhishma both advise him. Narada, too, says much. I will tell you what they all say.

Narada says, 'Rare is the man who takes his friends' advice; and rare, too, is the friend who gives honest advice. The man who needs advice is never where the man who is willing to offer it is. Kurunandana, I think you ought to listen to what your friends say. Do not be obstinate; the path you choose for yourself is fraught with evil and danger. I will tell you an ancient story to illustrate this, of how Galava disgraced himself because of his unyielding disposition.

In an ancient time, Dharma Deva assumed the form of the Rishi

Vasishta and came down to Earth to test Viswamitra, who sat in austere tapasya. In this form—of one of the Saptarishis—and pretending to be hungry and in dire need of food, he came to Kausika's asrama. Viswamitra was awestruck and prepared charu—rice and honey boiled in milk—for him. He cooked with such careful concentration that he could not properly wait on his guest; and it was not until after his guest had eaten what some other hermits gave him that he was able to offer the charu that he had made, which was still hot.

The holy one said he had already eaten and, telling him to wait there, went away. The Mahatapasvin Viswamitra waited, standing as still as a post, holding the food on his head with his arms raised, and subsisting on air. As he stood there, a muni named Galava began to wait upon him out of reverence and affection for him, and in order to please him.

A hundred years passed and Dharma Deva assumed the form of Vasishta once more, and came to Viswamitra to ask for food. Seeing the wise Maharishi still standing there with the food on his head, living all the while on air alone, he accepted the still warm and fresh charu from him. After eating, Dharma Deva expressed his gratification and went away.

At Dharma Deva's word, Viswamitra, once a Kshatriya, was, to his great joy, elevated to being a Brahmana. Pleased with the services and devotion of his disciple Galava, Viswamitra gave him leave to go wherever he liked.

Galava was happy with his Guru's command and affectionately said to the radiant Viswamitra, "Exalted one, what shall I give you as Gurudakshina? Bestower of honours, any spiritual deed becomes successful only when accompanied by this final gift, and the giver attains Moksha. Gifts are the fruit of one's actions, which one enjoys in heaven, and they are the embodiment of peace. Tell me what I should give to you, my Guru?"

Viswamitra knew that he had been won over by Galava's devotion and repeatedly tried to dismiss him, but Galava kept asking him what he should give as Gurudakshina. Annoyed with Galava's persistence,

Viswamitra finally said, "Give me eight hundred horses, all of them as white as the Moon's rays and each with one black ear. Galava, go now!"'"

CANTO 107

BHAGAVAD-YANA PARVA CONTINUED

"Narada says, 'Viswamitra's words filled Galava with such consternation that he could not sit, sleep or eat. He became a victim of anxiety and regret and, lamenting bitterly and burning with remorse, Galava grew pale and skeletal.

Duryodhana, smitten with sorrow, he cried, "O where will I find rich friends? Where will I find money? Have I any savings? Where will I find eight hundred moon-white horses? How can I enjoy food or the things I like? The very love of life is extinguished in me. Why do I need to live? I will go to the opposite shore of the great ocean, or to the furthest part of the Earth and give up my life. What is the use of living? What happiness can there be, without extreme exertion, for one who is poor, unsuccessful, deprived of all the good things of life, and burdened with debt? The man who has, from friendship, enjoyed a friend's wealth and cannot repay him is better dead than alive.

When he fails to keep his word, a man's good deeds lose their punya and become stained with falsehood. One who is tainted in this way cannot be beautiful, have children, or acquire power or influence. How can such a man attain bliss? What ungrateful man has ever earned fame? What is his proper place and where is his happiness? An ungrateful man can never win esteem or affection; neither can salvation ever be his. The wretched man who has no wealth is barely alive; he cannot support his relatives or his friends. He is unable to repay favours, he will certainly be ruined.

I am this ungrateful wretch, destitute of resources and tainted with falsehood, for I have got what I wanted from my Guru but cannot do as he asks. I will do my best and then lay down my life.

I have never before begged the gods for anything, and they respect me for this in yagnas. I will seek the protection of Vishnu the divine lord of the Trilokas; I will place myself in Krishna's hands; he is the refuge of all who deserve protection. I will bow down and ask to see Krishna, that most exalted of ascetics, the Eternal One from whom all blessings flow to the Devas and the Asuras."

While Galava was thus lamenting, his friend Garuda, the son of Vinata, appeared before him and, wishing to help him, cheerfully said to him, "You are my dear friend. It is the duty of one who is prosperous to fulfil the wishes of his friends. Brahmana, Indra's younger brother Vishnu has blessed me with good fortune. I have spoken to him on your behalf and he is pleased to grant my wish to help you.

Come, we will go together wherever you like. I will carry you comfortably to the other shore of the ocean, or to the farthest end of the Earth. Come, Galava, do not linger.'"

CANTO 108

BHAGAVAD-YANA PARVA CONTINUED

"Narada says, 'Garuda said, "God, who is the source of all knowledge, has commanded me. In which direction shall I take you first, to show you what there is? Shall I go east, south, west or north, Dvija?

That cardinal direction where Surya, the illuminator of the universe, rises; where the ascetics practice their evening tapasya; where the Primeval Intelligence that pervades the universe was born; where the two eyes of Dharma are positioned to guide the universe; where ghee was first offered in sacrifice and from where it then flowed: that direction is the gateway of day and time, Dvijottama.

There in time out of mind the daughters of Daksha gave birth to their children; and there the sons of Kasyapa first multiplied. That quarter is the source of all the prosperity of the Devas, for it was there that Indra was first anointed as their king. It was there that Indra and the other Devas performed tapasya. That is why this cardinal quarter, the East, is called Purva, or the First; and also because in the earliest times it was the home of the Devas and said to be owned by the oldest inhabitants of the universe.

The Devas performed all their religious ceremonies here. It is here that the Creator first sang the Vedas. It is here that the Devi Savitri was born from Surya's mouth to live as a sacred mantra. It is here that Surya presented the Yajur Veda to Yagnavalkya. It is here that the Gods first drank sanctified Soma during yagnas. It is here that the Homa—the sacrificial fire—first accepted ghee and milk; and it is here that Varuna became prosperous when he left for the netherworld.

Here the ancient Rishi Vasishta was born, grew famous and died. Here *Om*, the mystical beginning of every mantra, was born and developed its one hundred branches. Here the smoke-imbibing Munis live as the smoke of sacrificial fires. Here Indra killed boar and other wild animals and dedicated them as sacrificial offerings to the Devas. Here the thousand-rayed Sun rises and in anger consumes all ungrateful and evil Manavas and Asuras.

This is the gateway of the three worlds, of Swarga and of happiness. This cardinal quarter is called Purva. If you like, we will go there. I will do whatever pleases you, my friend. Galava, tell me if there is any other direction to which you wish to go, and we will fly there. Listen, I will tell you about another cardinal quarter.""'

CANTO 109

BHAGAVAD-YANA PARVA CONTINUED

"Narada says, 'Garuda said, "Long, long ago Vivaswat performed a yagna and gave this quarter away as Dakshina to his Guru, which is why this region, the South, is known as Dakshina.

It is here that the Pitrs of the three worlds live; the Devas who live on smoke and the Devas known as Viswadevas also live here. They are worshipped in sacrifices in all the worlds and partake equally of the sacrifices with the Pitrs.

This cardinal direction is known as the second door of Dharma. It is here that the span allotted to man is calculated in periods of time known as trutis and lavas. It is here that the Devarishis, Pitrlokarishis and Rajarishis live, beyond the reach of pain. Here reside Dharma and Satya; here man's deeds bear fruit.

This quarter is the ultimate resting place of the deeds of the dead, and it is where everybody must eventually come. However, as all of them are shrouded by ignorance, they cannot be happy here, for thousands of Rakshasas have been created to obstruct the paths of men, and those who have not brought their souls under perfect control see them as obstacles.

Here, Brahmana, in Mount Mandara's glades and in the asramas of Rishis, Gandharvas chant hymns that entrance the heart and mind. Here the Daitya Raivata heard the hymns of the Sama Veda sung so sweetly that he left his wife, friends and kingdom and retired to the forest. Here the son of Savarna and Yavakrita set a boundary which Surya cannot cross. Here illustrious Ravana of the Pulastyas, the king of the Rakshasas, performed austere tapasya and asked the gods for a boon of immortality.

It is here that Vritrasura brought Indra's hostility upon himself by his evil ways. It is here that the lives of all beings come, to be broken up into their five elements. It is here that men of evil deeds rot in agony. It is here that the river Vaitarani flows, filled with the bodies of those who cannot cross it to obtain Moksha. People who come here are subject to the extremes of joy or sorrow.

When it arrives here the Sun drops sweet water on the Earth and then, continuing towards the cardinal direction named Vasishta, sheds dew. Once when I was hungry, in this realm, I found for food a huge elephant battling with an enormous tortoise.

It is here that Maharishi Chakradhanu was born from Surya. That Devarishi later came to be known as Kapila and it was he who made ashes of Sagara's sixty-thousand wild sons. It is here that a class of Brahmanas known as Sivas, who mastered the Vedas, were crowned with the fruit of their tapasya and finally attained eternal Moksha.

In this region is the city called Bhogavati, ruled by Vasuki, the Naga Takshaka and Airavata. Those who come here after they die encounter a heavy gloom that is so dense that neither Surya nor Agni can penetrate it.

Worthy as you are of worship, you still have to pass this way. Tell me now if you wish to go in this direction. Otherwise, listen while I tell you about the West.'"

CANTO 110

BHAGAVAD-YANA PARVA CONTINUED

'Garuda said, "The cardinal quarter, the West, is the favourite of Varuna, the lord of the ocean. He was born here and rules over it. Because it is here that the Sun sends his rays at paschata—the end of the day—it is called Paschima.

The divine Kashyapa installed Varuna as the king here to rule over all marine creatures and to protect the waters themselves. Here the Moon, the dispeller of darkness, drinks all six of Varuna's juices and renews himself at the beginning of every bright fortnight. It is here that Vayu defeated and captured the Daityas, who fled, panting, before a mighty tempest and finally laid themselves down to die.

Here, everyday, the mountain Asta lovingly embraces the Sun in welcome and dispels the evening twilight. It is from here that Ratri and Nidra—Night and Sleep—emerge at the close of day and spread themselves over the Earth to steal half the life-span of all living beings from them. It is here that Indra, seeing his pregnant stepmother Diti lying asleep, cut up the foetus in her womb into forty-nine parts, from which the forty-nine Maruts were born.

It is towards this cardinal direction that Himavat Parvata's base stretches to touch the immortal Mandara Parvata who is sunk in the ocean, and even if one travels for a thousand years one cannot reach it. It is here that Surabhi, the first cow, goes to the shores of the sea that is adorned with golden lotuses and pours forth her milk. Here, in the midst of the ocean, is the headless torso of radiant Svarbhanu, Rahu, who is always intent on devouring the Sun and the Moon.

Here the invincible and ever youthful Suvarnasiras, of the immeasurable tejas, loudly chants the Vedas. It is here that Muni Harimedha's daughter Dwajavati was transfixed in the sky by Surya's command to stop and stay. Here wind, fire, earth and water are all deprived of their inherent capacity to inflict pain. It is from here that the Sun's course starts its deviation; it is here that all luminous bodies enter the solar sphere, and after travelling for twenty-eight nights with the Sun they leave the Sun's orbit and move with the Moon. It is in this region that the rivers which always feed the ocean have their sources.

In this, the abode of Varuna, dwell the waters of the three worlds, Ananta—the king of snakes, Vishnu, who is without beginning and without end, and Maricha's son Maharishi Kashyapa.

I have told you now about Paschima. Tell me, where shall we go?"'"

CANTO 111

BHAGAVAD-YANA PARVA CONTINUED

"Narada says, 'Garuda said, "O Brahmana, the cardinal quarter of the North saves a man from sin, and it is here that one attains salvation. The power to do both these is called Uttarana and hence this direction is called Uttara. It is sometimes called Madhyama, central, because the repository of all its treasures stretches in a straight line from east to west.

Dvijarishabha, this quarter is the best of all—no one who is unfriendly, of uncontrolled senses or unrighteous can live here. In a refuge known as Badari live Krishna who is Narayana, Arjuna who is Nara, that most exalted of men, and Brahma the Creator. Here on the slopes of the Himavat Mountain dwells Maheswara, blazing in effulgence like the fire at the end of a yuga, like Purusha with the universal mother Prakriti. Only Nara and Narayana can see him, and not all the different classes of Munis, or the Devas with Indra at their head, or the Gandharvas, Yakshas and Siddhas. Vishnu, of the thousand heads and thousand eyes, which appear as one by the power of his maya, lives here.

It is here that that Chandramas, the Moon, was crowned king of all twice-borns. It is here that Siva first received Ganga on his head and afterwards let her flow from heaven into the world of men. It is here that the Devi Uma performed tapasya from her desire to have Siva as her lord. It is here that Kama, Siva's anger Rosha, Himavat and Uma were born and shone in unity. It is here that Kubera was vested with sovereignty over Rakshasas, Yakshas and Gandharvas.

Kubera's gardens, named Chitraratha, and the asrama of the Vaikshana Munis are here; the celestial river Mandakini and the mountain Mandara are here. The gardens called Saugandhi Kanaka are here, constantly guarded by Rakshasas. There are grassy, verdant plains, plantain forests and the celestial trees called sautanakas in this realm.

This is where the Siddhas, who have their souls ever under control and who wander as they please, have their luxurious and heavenly homes. This is where Arundhati and the Saptarishis reside, and where the constellation Swati rises. This is where Pitamaha Brahma lives, near the embodied Yagna. This is where the movements of the Sun, Moon and other stellar bodies are visible.

O Brahmanottama, here those illustrious and utterly truthful Munis called Dhamas guard the source of the Ganga; and no one knows where they came from, or how they look, or even what tapasya they perform. Indeed, the thousand dishes they use to serve food to those who go there, as well as how they prepare the food are all a mystery. Anyone who crosses the line of their protection is sure to meet with death; only the divine Narayana and the eternal Nara, Arjuna, can pass and remain unharmed.

It is in this cardinal quarter that Kailasa Parvatam lies and where Kubera lives. It is here that the ten Apsaras known as Vidyutprabhas were born. It is this quarter that Vishnu covered with three strides when he accepted the three worlds at the Asura king Bali's sacrifice; and one of his footprints is marked by a spot named Vishnupada.

Here, by the shore of the golden lake named Jambunada, is a place called Usirvija, where Raja Maruta performed his yagna. Here the lustrous gold mines of Himavat made themselves visible to Rishi Jimuta, who gave all their mined wealth away to Brahmanas and asked that it be named after him. That gold is called Jaimuta. Here, every morning and evening, the guardians of the four cardinal points call out and ask each other which person's affairs they should attend to.

O Brahmanottama, it for all these and many other reasons that the North is superior—uttara—to all the other cardinal quarters, and that is another reason for its name Uttara. I have described all four realms to you in detail. To which direction would you like to go? I am ready to show you all four quarters and all the Earth, so climb on to my back."'"

CANTO 112

BHAGAVAD-YANA PARVA CONTINUED

"Narada says, 'Galava said, "O Garuda, slayer of the king of serpents, you of the beautiful feathers, Vinataputra, carry me to the east, on which the two eyes of Dharma are focused. Take me to that region you described first, where the Devas are always, where Dharma and Satya reside. I want to meet all the Devas; so take me there."

Narada continues, 'Accordingly, at Garuda's prompting, Galava climbed onto the Bird's back and said to him, "Devourer of snakes, your beauty as you fly is as radiant as that thousand-eyed maker of day, the morning Sun. Sky-ranger, you are so swift that the trees break in the storm of your flapping wings and seem to fly behind you in your wake; why, you seem to tow Bhumi with all her waters, mountains and forests in the airs you stir. The tempest that your wings blow lifts the waters of the oceans with all their fish, snakes and crocodiles into the air.

The fish, the timis and timingalas, that look alike, and snakes with human faces are all dashed about by your wing-storm. And I am so deafened and stunned by the roar of the oceans that I seem to forget the reason for my journey. Slow down; remember that you may be endangering a Brahmana's life.

O Garuda, I can no longer see the Sun, the cardinal points or the sky. I see only a thick gloom all round me. I cannot see my body, but only your eyes, shining like two brilliant gems. I cannot see your body, but at every wing-beat I see fire spewing from it. Put out this fire and extinguish the dazzle from your eyes; I beg you, slow down! I do not need to go on this journey with you. Blessed one, I cannot bear your speed. I have promised to give my acharya eight hundred moon-white horses with one black ear each. I do not see how I can make good my word.

The only course open to me is to lay down my life. I have no wealth of my own, nor a wealthy friend; indeed, no wealth, however immense, can give me what I need."

Laughingly, and without slackening his speed, Garuda said to Galava, "Your wish to end your life shows that you are a man of little wisdom, O twice-born Rishi. Death can never be brought about by one's own effort. Death is God himself. Why did you not tell me what your intention was before we set out? There are many excellent ways by which your goal can be accomplished.

Here is the mountain Rishabha, on the seashore. We will rest here for a while and refresh ourselves with some food before we turn back.""'

CANTO 113

BHAGAVAD-YANA PARVA CONTINUED

"Narada says, 'The Brahmana and the Eagle landed on the summit of Rishabha and there they saw a Brahmana woman named Sandili in tapasya. Galava and Garuda bent their heads in respectful greeting and worshipped her. The devi asked after their welfare and invited them to sit. Seated, they accepted the food she offered, having first dedicated it with mantras to the Devas. After eating, they lay down on the ground and fell into a deep sleep. Garuda woke up, wanting to leave, but discovered that his wings had fallen off and that he had become a ball of flesh with only a head and legs.

Galava, seeing him in that plight, said, "What has staying here done to you? O how long will we have to remain here? Did you have any evil thoughts in your mind, for it cannot be a trivial sin that has taken your wings from you."

Garuda replied to the Brahmana, saying, "Actually, Dvija, I did think about carrying this Brahmani, of the tapasyashakti, away from here to where Mahadeva the Creator, Vishnu, and both Dharma and Yagna dwell, for I thought she ought to live there. For my own good, I will prostrate before this holy devi and pray to her.

Garuda said to the Brahmani, "With a sore heart, I confess that I entertained the idea of carrying you away. Whether I acted rightly or wrongly, my intention, of which you evidently disapprove, was prompted by my regard for you. I beg you, from the nobility of your heart forgive me."

Pleased with the prince of birds and the Brahmana, she said to Garuda, "Do not be afraid, beautiful-feathered one. Here, have your wings back and cast off your fear. You insulted me, and I do not forgive insults. The sinner who insults me will quickly fall from Swarga. I bear no inauspicious signs at all and, being blemishless in my purity, I have achieved exalted tapasyashakti. Dharma and artha are the fruits of pure conduct, which removes all that is inauspicious.

Go from here where you wish, prince of birds, and take care never to insult a woman, even in thought, even if she is not chaste. You shall regain your strength and energy as they were before."

At these words Garuda had back his splendid wings, and they were more powerful than before. Taking leave of Sandili, Garuda flew away with Galava on his back. They could not, however, find the kind of horses they were looking for.

On their way, they met that most eloquent of men, Viswamitra, and in Garuda's presence he said to Galava, "Brahmana, the time has come for you to give me what you promised. I do not know what you will do to get me the horses but, since I have waited so long, I will wait a little longer. Find a way of making good your solemn word."

Hearing this, Garuda said to the downcast Galava, who was plunged in sorrow, "I have now heard what Viswamitra said to you earlier. Come, Brahmanottama Galava, we will think about it together. You cannot rest until you have given your Guru what you swore.""

CANTO 114

BHAGAVAD-YANA PARVA CONTINUED

"Narada says, 'Garuda said to the cheerless Galava, "This wealth is called Hiranya because Agni created it in the bowels of the Earth, which is also named Hiranmaya, and then Vayu increased it. Because this wealth supports the world and sustains life it is called dhana; indeed that has been its purpose in the Trilokas from the beginning.

On the particular Friday, when either the constellation Purvabhadra or Uttarabhadra rises, Agni creates more wealth by his will and confers it on mankind in order to add to Kubera's store of treasures. Deities called Ajaikapats and Ahirbudnas guard the wealth created in the Earth's core, making it rare and well nigh impossible to obtain. This wealth is your only chance to acquire the horses; beg some king born into a vamsa of Rajarishis to help you, without harming his own subjects.

I have a friend who is a king born into the Chandra vamsa. Let us go to him for, amongst all who live on Earth, he has the greatest wealth. This Rajarishi Yayati is the son of Nahusha, and has irresistible prowess. If you plead with him and I endorse your plea with my commendation, he will give us what we need; he is immensely wealthy, as wealthy as Kubera the lord of treasures. Learned one, by accepting this king's gift, we can pay your debt to your Guru."

Talking together in this way and thinking about the best thing to do, Garuda and Galava went to King Yayati in his capital. The king received them hospitably and offered them arghya, and padya to wash their feet. Then he asked them why they had come.

Garuda said to him, "O Son of Nahusha, this ocean of tapasya is my friend Galava, who has been Viswamitra's sishya for several thousand years. This devout Brahmana, whom Viswamitra commanded to go wherever he chose, told his Guru that he wanted to give him gurudakshina. Viswamitra knew he was poor and did not ask for anything, but then, annoyed by his persistence, he asked for eight hundred moon-white horses with one black ear each. The Rishi told Galava that since he insisted, this is what he should give. The great tapasvin Viswamitra spoke in anger and it is this that grieves the Brahmana so painfully.

Unable to fulfil his Guru's command, he has come to you for refuge. Purushavyaghra, when he has accepted this favour he asks of you, he will pay his gurudakshina and happily devote himself to tapasya once again.

A Rajarishi such as you, endowed as you already are with great punya, will be even more enriched when this Brahmana gives you a share of his own tapasya. Lord of men, giving a horse as a gift entitles you to as much bliss as there are hairs on a horse's body.

This man is as worthy to accept the gift as you are to make it. Give it to him, as you would pour milk into a conch shell.""

CANTO 115

BHAGAVAD-YANA PARVA CONTINUED

"Narada says, 'Yayati, ruler of all the Kasis, performer of a thousand sacrifices, that most generous of men, reflected deeply on Garuda's words of truth.

He saw his friend Garuda and Galava's request for alms as an auspicious omen; he thought about Galava's tapasya, and he pondered the fact that these two had passed over all the other kings of the Surya vamsa and come to him.

Yayati said, "I and the vamsa into which I was born are blessed today. Sinless Garuda, you have blessed my kingdom. My friend, there is one thing that I wish to say to you. I am not as rich now as before, for my wealth is greatly reduced. Regardless, I cannot render your visit fruitless, nor can I disappoint this Rishi.

I will give him enough to allow him to accomplish his purpose. If a man who comes for alms leaves unfulfilled, he might destroy my entire race with a curse. There is nothing more sinful than to say, *I have nothing*, and dash the hopes of one who comes in need. The disappointed man can ruin the sons and grandsons of the one who fails to help him.

O Galava, take this daughter of mine, who will be the perpetuator of four dynasties. In beauty, she is like a daughter of the Devas; she will promote every virtue; and for her beauty, Devas, Manavas and Asuras are always me asking for her hand. The kings of the Earth would give entire kingdoms for her, let alone eight hundred horses with a black ear each. Take my daughter Madhavi. My only wish is to have a grandson by her."

Galava accepted the king's gift and left with Garuda, saying to the king, "We will see you again," and taking the maiden with them.

Then Garuda said to Galava, "We finally have the means to obtain the horses," and took his leave and went home.

After the prince of birds had gone, Galava, with the maiden beside him, began to think about going to a king who would give him a fitting dower for her. He first thought of that best of kings Haryaswa of the Ikshvakus, who ruled in Ayodhya, who was endowed with great tejas, who possessed a great army consisting of the four kinds of forces, who had a well-filled treasury and an abundance of corn, whose subjects loved him and who respected all Brahmanas. Wishing to have children, he lived quietly, performing austere tapasya.

Galava went to Haryaswa and said, "Rajadhiraja, this maiden will increase her husband's family by bearing many children. Accept her from me as your wife, Haryaswa, by giving me a dower. Listen to what dower I expect and then decide what you will do.'"

CANTO 116

BHAGAVAD-YANA PARVA CONTINUED

"Narada says, 'Raja Haryaswa reflected for a long time, breathing deep and fervent sighs at the thought of having a son. At last he said, "The six parts of the body that ought to be raised in one's body are well elevated in this maiden. The seven parts of the body that ought to be slender are indeed so in her. The three that ought to be deep are deep in her; and the five that ought to be reddish are flushed in her. It seems that her beauty is worthy of being gazed upon by Devas and Asuras, and she is accomplished in all the arts and sciences. With all these auspicious signs, she will certainly bear many children, and indeed one of them might become an emperor.

As for the wealth you seek, Brahmanottama, what should her dower be?"

Galava said, "Give me eight hundred horses of a lofty pedigree, which are all moon-white and with one black ear each. This blessed and large-eyed maiden will then become the mother of your sons, as the fire-stick gives birth to fire."

Hearing this, Rajarishi Haryaswa was filled with sorrow, but blinded by passion, he said, "I have only two hundred horses of the kind you want, but there are many others which roam in my kingdom. Galava, I want only one son with this maiden. Grant me my wish."

At this, the maiden said to Galava, "One who had attained Brahman once granted me a boon that I would, after the birth of every son, regain my maidenhood. Give me away to this king and accept his horses. In this way, you will get eight hundred horses from four different kings, and I will have four sons, as well. Collect the wealth that you want to give your Guru like this. This is what I think, but you may do as you think fit."

Galava said to Haryaswa, "O Haryaswa, best of men, accept this maiden for a fourth of the dower that I have asked for, and have only one son with her."

Haryaswa worshipped Galava and took the princess. In due time, she gave the king the son he so longed for, and the boy was named Vasumanas. He became richer than the wealthiest kings of the Earth and looked like one of the Vasus; and he came to be a great and generous king.

After some time had passed, Galava came back to the delighted Haryaswa and said to him, "O Rajan, you have had a son, a child who is as splendid as the Sun. The time has come for me to go to another king for alms."

Haryaswa, being truthful and honourable in all that he said and did, and remembering the balance of six hundred horses that he had been unable to give the Brahmana Galava, gave Madhavi back to him. Madhavi left that radiant and prosperous king and, becoming a virgin once more, she followed Galava.

Galava said to Haryaswa, "Let the horses stay here with you," and went with Madhavi to Raja Divodasa.'"

CANTO 117

BHAGAVAD-YANA PARVA CONTINUED

"Narada says, 'Galava said to Madhavi, "The ruler of the Kasis is the illustrious king Divodasa, who is Bhimasena's son. He is an immensely powerful king. Blessed one, we are now going to Divodasa; follow me slowly and do not worry. This king is virtuous and devoted to truth, and has his passions under control."

Muni Galava came before the king, who received him with due reverence and hospitality. Galava urged the monarch to have a child.

Divodasa said, "I have already heard about your quest, so you need not tell me much, Brahmana. As soon as I knew what you would come for, my heart was set upon it. I am honoured that you have passed over all other kings and come to me. What you want will be yours, but my wealth is like Haryaswa's, reduced. I shall, therefore, have only one royal son with this maiden."

The Brahmana gave the girl to the king, who duly married her. Rajarishi Divodasa enjoyed his time with Madhavi like so many illustrious couples: Surya with Prabhavati, Agni with Swaha, Vasava with Sachi, Chandra with Rohini, Yama with Urmila, Varuna with Gauri, Kubera with Riddhi, Narayana with Lakshmi, Sagara with Jahnavi, Rudra with Rudrani, Pitamaha Brahma with Saraswati, Vasishta's son Saktri with Adrisyanti, Vasishta with Akshamala, Chyavana with Sukanya, Pulastya with Sandhya, Agastya with princess Lopamudra of Vidarbha, Satyavan with Savitri, Bhrigu with Puloma, Kasyapa with Aditi, Richika's son Jamadagni with Renuka, Kusika's son Viswamitra with Himavati, Brihaspati with Tara, Sukra with Sataparva, Bhumipati with Bhumi, Pururavas with Urvasi, Richika with Satyavati, Manu with Saraswati, Dushyanta with Sakuntala, the eternal Dharma with Dhriti, Nala with Damayanti, Narada with Satyavati, Jaratkaru with Jaratkaru, Pulastya with Pratichya, Urnayus with Menaka, Tumburu with Rambha, Vasuki with Satasirsha, Dhananjaya with Kumari, Rama with Sita the princess of Videha, Janardana with Rukmini.

And to Raja Divodasa, who delighted in her, Madhavi bore a son named Pratardana. After the child's birth, Galava came to Divodasa and said to him, "Let the maiden come with me, but let the horses that you are giving me remain here. I need to go to another kingdom to obtain more dowry."

The virtuous Divodasa, who was devoted to dharma, gave Madhavi back to Galava.'"'

CANTO 118

BHAGAVAD-YANA PARVA CONTINUED

"Narada says, 'Madhavi was faithful to her promise and, abandoning prosperity and becoming a virgin once again, followed Galava. Galava, whose heart was set upon the accomplishment of his own business, had reflected on what he should do next and went to the city of the Bhojas, to King Usinara.

When he arrived before that king of the unrestrainable prowess, Galava said to him, "This maiden will bear you two royal sons, who will be like the Sun and the Moon. With these two princes you will be able to attain all that you hope for in this world and in the hereafter. O you who are knowledgeable about dharma, in exchange you must give me four hundred horses of moon-white splendour with one black ear each. My effort to obtain the horses is only for my Guru's sake; I myself have no need of them. If you accept my terms, do as I tell you, without hesitation.

Rajarishi, you are childless. Have two children, for children are like a life-saving raft, who will rescue you and your Pitrs. The man who enjoys the punya of having had a son never falls from heaven, nor will he ever have to go to that frightful hell, Naraka, to which the childless are doomed."

Raja Usinara said to him, "I have heard your words, Galava, and my heart is inclined to do as you say. However, only the Supreme Lord has ultimate power over all things. I have only two hundred horses of the kind you want, but I have thousands of other kinds in my kingdom. I will do as Haryaswa and Divodasa did and have only one son by Madhavi.

My wealth is for all my subjects, in the city and in the country, and not for my own comfort and pleasures. The king who gives away, for his own benefit, the wealth that belongs to others can never earn virtue or fame. Give this divinely radiant girl to me. I will accept her to bear me only one child."

Hearing these and other things that Usinara said, Galava approved of him. He gave Madhavi to him and went away into the forest. And as any man of dharma enjoys well deserved happiness that his good deeds have earned him, Usinara enjoyed Madhavi, and they sported in valleys and dales of the mountains, beside fountains and waterfalls, in charming mansions, in gardens, forests and woods, in other places of delight, and on palatial terraces beneath the stars. In due time, a son was born to them, who shone like the morning Sun, and who later became the great king Sibi.

After the birth of this boy, Galava came to Usinara, took Madhavi from him and went to Garuda.'"

CANTO 119

BHAGAVAD-YANA PARVA CONTINUED

"Narada says, 'Garuda saw Galava and said to him, "How happy I am to hear of your success."

Galava, however, informed him that a fourth part of his task was still unfinished, at which Garuda said, "Do not try to get the remaining two hundred horses, for you will not succeed. Long ago, Richika wanted to marry Satyavati, the daughter of Gadhi of Kanyakubja.

Gadhi said to Muni Richika, *Holy one, give me a thousand horses, all as brilliantly white as the Moon and each having one black ear.*

Saying, *So be it*, Richika went to Aswatirtha, the great home of horses in Varuna's abode, and found what he wanted, which he promptly gave the king. The king performed a yagna named Pundarika and gave those horses away as dakshina to deserving Brahmanas. The three kings, whom you made agreements with, each bought two hundred of those horses from the Brahmanas. The remaining four hundred were claimed by the river Vitasta, while they were being led across it.

You can never have that which is not there to be had. Virtuous one, give this girl as a gift to Viswamitra, along with the six hundred horses you have acquired. You will be freed from your grief and crowned with success."

Saying "*Tathaastu,*" Galava went with Garuda to Viswamitra, taking Madhavi and the horses with him. On arriving, he said, "Here are six hundred horses of the kind you asked for. I offer you this maiden in place of the remaining two hundred. I beg you, accept what I offer as gurudakshina. This girl has had three virtuous sons by three Rajarishis; let her fourth, and best, son be yours.

Let these six hundred horses be the complete discharge of my debt to you, so that I can be free to practice tapasya as I like."

Viswamitra saw Galava with the Bird and the maiden, and he said, "O Galava, why did you not give this girl to me before? All four sons, sanctifiers of my race, would have been mine. I accept this maiden, to give me one son. The horses can graze in my asrama."

Viswamitra lived happily with Madhavi, and she bore him a son, named Ashtaka. As soon as the child was born, Mahamuni Viswamitra instructed him in dharma and artha, and gave him the six hundred horses. Ashtaka went to live in a city, bright as the city of Soma; and Viswamitra gave Madhavi back to Galava and went away to the deepest forest.

The happy Galava who, with his friend Garuda's help, had succeeded in giving his Guru the dakshina he had asked for, said to Madhavi, "You have given birth to one son who is most charitable, to another who is very brave, to a third who is devoted to dharma and satya, and to a fourth who is a performer of great yagnas. Lovely Madhavi, through your sons you have saved not only your father but four kings and me, as well. Go to your father now, slender-waisted one."

Saying this, Galava bid farewell to Garuda that devourer of snakes, and after restoring the maiden to her father, went to live in the forest.'"

CANTO 120

BHAGAVAD-YANA PARVA CONTINUED

"Narada says, 'King Yayati wanted to give his daughter in marriage by way of a swayamvara. He took Madhavi, decked in flower malas, in his chariot to a sacred asrama at the confluence of the Ganga and Yamuna, with his sons Puru and Yadu following him. Gathered in that place were innumerable Nagas, Yakshas, Manavas and Gandharvas; animals and birds; dwellers of mountains, trees and forests; and many inhabitants of that particular province. The vanas that surrounded the asrama were home to many Rishis, who were like Brahma himself.

The swayamvara began, and that loveliest of maidens passed over all those assembled there and chose the vana as her lord. Descending from her chariot and greeting all her friends, Yayati's daughter went into the sacred forest and devoted herself to a life of tapasya.

She emaciated herself by fasting, performing religious rites and rigid vratas; and she took to living the life of a deer. She ate soft, green grass whose tender stems looked like lapis lazuli and tasted bitter-sweet; she drank the cool, sweet, crystalline water of sacred mountain streams. She roamed with other deer through forests where no lions or tigers lived, in deserts where there was no danger from forest fires and in dense forest, leading the life of a wild doe. She earned great spiritual punya because of her life of austere tapasya and brahmacharya.

King Yayati lived for many thousands of years and, like many before him, eventually succumbed to inexorable Time. The progeny of his sons Puru and Yadu multiplied, thereby earning great reverence for Yayati in this and the other worlds. Yayati lived in Swarga, like a Maharishi; he was greatly honoured and respected, and enjoyed the best of those regions.

One day, after many thousands of years had passed in great joy, when Yayati sat amongst illustrious Rajarishis and Maharishis, he mentally ignored all the Devas, Rishis and Manavas who were there, from folly, ignorance and pride. Indra immediately saw into his heart. The Rajarishis, too, saw this and disapproved.

Everyone began to ask, "Who is this man? What king's son is he? Why is he in Swarga? What has he done to deserve this honour? Where did he practice tapasya and earn punya? What is he known for? Who knows him?"

The Swargavasis questioned each other about Yayati and asked hundreds of heaven's charioteers, gatekeepers and those who were in charge of the seats in heaven; but all replied that they did not know. Their minds were suddenly clouded so that none of them recognised the king, who immediately lost his heavenly splendour.""'

CANTO 121

BHAGAVAD-YANA PARVA CONTINUED

"Narada says, 'In this state—deprived of his place in Swarga and cast out, his trembling heart consumed by fear and burning with remorse, his unfading garlands withered, his senses in turmoil, shorn of his crown and ornaments, his head reeling, his limbs weak and his body unadorned and unclothed—no one recognised Yayati. In the bewilderment of the fog that blanketed his mind, the Swargavasis swam in and out of his vision as Yayati fell headlong towards the Earth.

As he fell, the king thought, "What sinful thoughts did I think that lost me my place in Devaloka?"

All the kings, the Siddhas and the Apsaras laughed to see Yayati fall. At Indra's command, came a Duta whose task was to remove from Swarga those whose punya had run out.

He said to Yayati, "Intoxicated with pride, there is no one whom you have not disregarded. It is because of your vanity that Swarga is no longer for you. You do not deserve to live here, Rajaputra. We do not recognise you here, so fall you must."

At the Devaduta's words, Yayati, the son of Nahusha, said three times, "If I must fall, let me fall amongst the righteous," and this king, who was the best of all who had attained Swarga, thought about where he should fall.

As he plunged down, Yayati saw the four mighty kings, Pratardana, Vasumanas, Sibi and Ashtaka, in a forest, and he fell toward them. At the time, those kings were performing the Vajapeya yagna to gratify Indra, and the smoke that rose from their fire had reached the gates of Swarga, looking like a river that flowed between heaven and Earth. It resembled the sacred Ganga during her descent to Earth. It was the smoke that guided Yayati as he fell toward the Earth and brought him to those four lions among men, all blessed with great splendour, the foremost of all sacrificers, who were in fact his own kin, who resembled the four Lokapalas, and who blazed in glory like four mighty sacrificial fires. Having exhausted his store of punya, Yayati fell toward them, and hung in mid-air above the kings, and he was still dazzlingly beautiful.

Seeing him and how he shone, the kings asked, "Who are you? What race, country and city are you from? Are you a Yaksha, a Deva, a Gandharva or a Rakshasa? You do not appear to be a human being. Why are you here?"

Yayati answered, "I am Rajarishi Yayati. I have fallen from Swarga because my punya was exhausted. I wanted to fall amongst men of dharma and have fallen amidst you."

The kings said, "Purushottama, may your wish come true. Accept as yours our punya and the fruits of all our sacrifices."

Yayati said, "I am not a Brahmana but a Kshatriya, and I cannot accept charity; nor do I want to take others' punya from them."

Just at this time, Madhavi, in course of her wandering, came there. The four kings greeted her and said, "What brings you here? What would you command us to do for you? You have the right to command us, for we are your sons, O Tapasvini."

Madhavi was filled with delight when she heard this. She came before her father with reverence and greeted Yayati; and she touched the heads of all her sons.

She said to her father Yayati, "Rajadhiraja, these are my sons, your grandsons. They are not strangers. They will save you. This practice is not new; it has its origins in antiquity. I am your daughter Madhavi, and I have been living in the forest like a deer. I have earned punya, and you must accept half of it because all men have the right to enjoy a portion of the punya earned by their children. That is why men want their daughters to have sons. That is what you wished for when you gave me to Galava."

At their mother's words, the four monarchs paid homage to her and to their grandfather. They reiterated what their mother had said, as clearly and affectionately as she had; and the whole Earth resounded with their wish to save their fallen grandfather.

Galava too came there and said to Yayati, "Accept an eighth of my tapasya from me and go back to Swarga.""

CANTO 122

BHAGAVAD-YANA PARVA CONTINUED

"Narada says, 'No sooner was Yayati recognised by those virtuous ones, than he rose once more into Swarga, without having touched the Earth at all. He regained his celestial form and shed his grief. Once again he was adorned in celestial garlands, raiment and ornaments; sprinkled again with celestial perfumes and vested with heavenly attributes; all this without having actually set foot on the Earth's surface.

Vasumanas, whose generosity was renowned through the worlds, announced to Yayati, "I hereby give you the punya that I have won on Earth by my blemishless conduct towards men of all varnas. Let it all be yours King. I have acquired the punya that one gains from generosity, and redemption from my sins through the yagnas I have performed; let those, too, be yours."

Then Pratardana said, "My devotion to Kshatriya dharma has earned me fame and a heroic name. I hereby give you this punya."

Sibi, the intelligent son of Usinara, affectionately said, "I have never spoken an untruth to children, to women or in jest, to those in danger, in a crisis or during a game of dice. I can give up all objects of desire and pleasure, my kingdom and my life itself, but I cannot give up satya. By virtue of this and of us having gratified Dharma, Agni and Indra, you will ascend to Swarga.

Lastly, Rajarishi Ashtaka—Madhavi and Kusika's son, said to Yayati, "I have performed hundreds of Pundarika, Gosava and Vajapeya yagnas. Take the punya of these. I have spared nothing for their performance, not jewels, gold or other treasures. By that truth, ascend to Swarga."

Immediately, Yayati left the Earth and began to soar towards Swarga, higher and higher as his grandsons said what they were doing for him, one after the other. That is how those kings saved Yayati, who had been cast down from heaven, and how these royal grandchildren of Yayati's, those perpetuators of their dynasties, made their grandfather rise again into Swargaloka by means of their dharma, yagnas and dana.

The four kings said in unison, "We are your daughter's sons, O Rajan, endowed with nobility and every virtue. By our dharma and punya, ascend again into heaven.""'"

CANTO 123

BHAGAVAD-YANA PARVA CONTINUED

"Narada says, "Restored to his place on high by his grandsons, distinguished by the largesse of their sacrificial gifts, Yayati blazed in beauty, adorned by his own great deeds, showered with fragrant flowers and enveloped in scented, balmy breezes. He was welcomed back with the joyful clash of cymbals and entertained with songs and dances by diverse clans of Gandharvas and Asuras. Devarishis and Rajarishis paid homage to him, and the Devas worshipped him with arghya and other honours.

After he had returned to Swarga and, free from anxiety, regained tranquillity of heart, Brahma Pitamaha spoke words of approbation to him, saying, "You had earned the full measure—four padas—of dharma by your deeds on Earth. You had attained Swargaloka and renown for eternity. Rajarishi, you nullified all this punya by your vanity, which cloaked the hearts of Swargavasis in darkness so impenetrable that they could not recognise you, and you were cast down. You have been saved by the love and affection of your daughter's sons and returned, regaining this eternal, sacred, wonderful and deathless realm you won earlier by your own deeds."

Yayati said, "Holy One, I have a doubt, which only you can dispel. My punya was vast, augmented by my reign of dharma over my subjects for thousands of years, and won by innumerable sacrifices and gifts. How could such immense punya become exhausted, and I be cast down from here? You know that the place created for me was eternal. Why was it destroyed?"

The Pitamaha said, "Your merit, earned by countless yagnas and increased by your rule of dharma, perished because of a single fault: your vanity, and it made you the object of contempt of all the Swargavasis. Vanity, pride of strength, malice, deceitfulness or deception will all reduce your time in Swarga. Never disregard those that are inferior, superior or equal to you. There is no greater sinner than the man who is consumed by the fire of vanity. Those who tell of your fall and re-ascension will be protected from all calamities."

Rajan, this is the story of how vanity brought Yayati's downfall, and the distress that Galava suffered because of his obstinacy. Those who want their own good should listen to their well-wishers. One must never be stubborn, for it is the root of ruin.

O Son of Gandhari, forsake vanity and wrath; make peace with the Pandavas. Abandon anger; let go of what you have once given away, that which is done, austerities that you have practised and libations that you have poured on fire. These are indestructible and cannot be diminished. Also, no one other than their doer enjoys their fruit.

The man who understands this greatest and best of stories, which is praised by those who know the scriptures and who are free from anger and greed, gains knowledge of dharma, artha and kama, and sovereignty over the world.'"

CANTO 124

BHAGAVAD-YANA PARVA CONTINUED

"Dhritarashtra says, 'Holy one, it is as you say. I, too, want to do exactly as what you tell us to, but I am powerless.'"

Vaisampayana continued, "The Kuru monarch then addresses Krishna and says, 'O Kesava, you have spoken about the path that leads to Swarga, which is for the world's good, full of dharma and wise. However, being blind, I cannot act independently, and Duryodhana never pays heed to me. Krishna, you must persuade my foolish, unprincipled and disobedient son. He never listens to the advice of Gandhari, Vidura or other true friends, or Bhishma the chief of them, all of whom want his good.

Counsel my dishonest and evil prince, for by so doing you will have acted nobly, as a friend should.'

Krishna, all-knowing about dharma and artha, says to Duryodhana, 'Kurusattama, listen to what I say, which is good for you especially, as well as for your followers. You are born into a vamsa that is distinguished for its great wisdom, and you are honour-bound to keep dharma.

You are learned and possess so many excellent and qualities. Only low-born, evil, shameless and cruel men do what you mean to. Men of dharma are always inclined towards virtue while sinful men lean the opposite way. Everything you are thinking of doing is against dharma. Insisting on going to war is nothing but sinful, vicious and evil, and will lead you to death. Abandon this dangerous path you have chosen to tread; it is unworthy of you and will only lead to untold suffering and doom.

You will do yourself, your brothers and your followers a great service if you make peace with the Pandavas instead. The sons of Pandu are wise, courageous and learned; they have immeasurable tejas and perfect control over their souls. If you do what I ask, that will please Dhritarashtra, as well as Pitamaha Bhishma, Drona, Kripa, Somadatta, Bahlika, Aswatthama, Vikarna, Sanjaya, Vivimsati and many of your kinsmen and friends. The whole world will benefit from that peace.

You are blessed with modesty, noble birth, learning and kindness. Listen to what your father and mother tell you; a good son always obeys his father's command, knowing it will benefit him. When calamity strikes, men remember their father's advice, which they once ignored. Making peace with the Pandavas will please your father; so let peace recommend itself to you and your advisors.

The man who hears the counsel of his well-wishers but does not heed it will be consumed by the consequences of his disregard, even as if he has eaten the poisonous kimpaka fruit. The fool who rejects sage advice and procrastinates will fail to achieve his objective and then repent. On the other hand, the man who heeds wise counsel and accepts it, setting aside his own opinion, will always be happy.

He who discards the words of well-meaning friends, deluded that what they say is not in his best interest, will be crushed by his enemies. The man who ignores the views of the righteous and clings only to those of the sinful, who flatter his vanity, will sink into misery and make his friends weep for him. He who turns away from superior advisors and seeks out inferior ones will fall into distress, from which he will not be able to extricate himself. The Earth will abandon the man who befriends sinners, who behaves deceitfully, who ignores what his friends say, who honours strangers but hates his own people.

Bharatarishabha, you have chosen to make enemies of the Pandavas and look to incompetent, foolish and sinful men for support. What other man is there on Earth besides you, who would disregard kinsmen who are all Maharathas, each like an Indra, and instead seek refuge and help from strangers? You have persecuted the sons of Kunti from the time they were born, but because they are virtuous they were not angry with you. Indeed, although you have been deceitful to them since their birth, those noble men have always been noble and generous to you. You ought to reciprocate their magnanimity in like measure.

Do not yield to anger. Wise men's energies are always focused on dharma, artha and kama. If all three cannot be attained, men pursue at least dharma and artha. Even if these three are followed separately, superior men, who have their senses under control, choose dharma as their priority; those who have a position between good and evil choose artha, which is subject to dispute; while those whose minds are darkened by tamas concentrate on gratifying their desires, however base.

The fool who abandons dharma to pursue artha and kama by sinning is soon destroyed by his own senses. The man who seeks artha and kama should first practice dharma, because all three are inextricably linked. Rajan, the wise say that dharma is the primary source, and so he who seeks all three purusharthas will, by practicing dharma alone, flourish, like fire when it touches a hayrick.

Bharatarishabha, you want to employ sin to obtain sole sovereignty over this vast and flourishing empire. The man who deals falsely towards those who live by dharma cuts himself down, like a forest felled by the axe. One seeks to destroy the very mind of the man one wants to defeat, for with his mind in chaos he cannot devote his attention to his true welfare.

The man who has his soul under control is never heedless of anyone, not even the most common of creatures, far less those bulls among men, the Pandavas. He who gives in to anger loses his sense of right and wrong. Evil must not be allowed to grow; look at the proof of this.

Solidarity with the sons of Pandu is far better for you than union with sinners. If you make peace with them, you will make peace with yourself, and have everything that you wish for. You now enjoy the kingdom that the Pandavas founded, but you ignore them and go to others for friendship and protection. Wanting the undiminished continuance of your prosperity, you have vested the care of your kingdom with Dusasana, Durvisha, Karna and Subala's son, men far inferior to the Pandavas in knowledge, in dharma, in their ability to garner wealth and in prowess.

Let alone these four men, all these kings together, with you at their head, cannot even look at an angry Bhima on the battlefield. This army of so many kings of the Earth is at your command. Also with you are Bhishma, Drona, Karna, Kripa, Bhurisravas, Somadatta, Aswatthama and Jayadratha. All of them together cannot face Arjuna, whom even the Devas, Asuras and Gandharvas cannot quell. Do not set your heart on war, Duryodhana.

Have you seen any man who has encountered Arjuna in battle and come away unscathed, let alone victorious? What can you gain from a universal slaughter? Show me one man who will defeat Arjuna, whose defeat alone can ensure your victory. Who will face that son of Pandu in battle, who vanquished all the Devas, Gandharvas, Yakshas and Nagas at Khandavaprastha? There is also that marvellous account of the encounter in Virata's city, of one against many, which should convince you.

Do you hope to vanquish an enraged Arjuna, invincible, irresistible, ever-victorious and unfading, that hero who gratified even Mahadeva Siva in fight? When, with me as his sarathy, that son of Pritha storms on to the battlefield, like Indra himself, who will dare challenge him? He who would vanquish Arjuna in battle could lift up the Earth in his arms, consume in his rage the entire population of the world and cast the very gods out from heaven.

Look at your sons, brothers, cousins and other relatives. Let them not die because of you. Let the Kaurava vamsa not horribly dwindle or even become extinct. Rajan, let the people not call you the exterminator of your dynasty and the destroyer of its noble achievements. If you make peace with them, the Pandava Maharathas will install you as Yuvaraja and your father Dhritarashtra as the king of this vast empire.

Do not dismiss the prosperity that awaits you, which is sure to come if you tread the path of dharma. Give half the kingdom to the sons of Pritha and win great prosperity. Listen to your well-wishers. By making peace with the sons of Pandu and living with them in harmony you will be blessed for eternity.'"

CANTO 125

BHAGAVAD-YANA PARVA CONTINUED

Vaisampayana said, "After listening to Krishna, Bhishma says to the angry Duryodhana, 'Krishna has spoken to you out of a desire to establish peace between cousins. Follow his advice; do not give in to vindictiveness. If you do not do as Krishna says, you will never gain prosperity, happiness or your own welfare.

What Krishna said to you is in keeping with dharma and artha. Do as he says and you will achieve your every objective; do not obliterate the Earth's population. Do not destroy this resplendent prosperity of the Bhaaratas amongst all the kings of the Earth, even while your father Dhritarashtra is still alive. If you disregard Krishna, your father and the wise Vidura, your stubborn arrogance will take you to your death and, with you, all your counsellors, sons, brothers and kinsmen will also die. What your true well-wishers counsel is dharma and will benefit you greatly.

Do not become the extinguisher of your vamsa; do not cleave to evil; turn your heart away from sin; do not tread the path of adharma; do not drown your parents in a sea of grief.'

When Bhishma has spoken, Drona says to Duryodhana, who by now is panting with rage, 'Rajan, what Krishna said is consistent with dharma and artha, and Bhishma has said the same. Accept their counsel. Both of them are wise, learned, of superior intelligence, have their souls under control and want only what is good for you. What they say is salutary; listen to them. Wise king, do as Krishna and Bhishma say; do not disregard Krishna, who counsels you gravely out of your vain delusion.

The men who have been blithely encouraging you cannot give you victory. They will deny their responsibility and cast the burden of war onto others. Do not slaughter the Earth's population nor slay your sons and brothers. The army which has Krishna and Arjuna in it is invincible. If you reject what Krishna and Bhishma have said, you will have cause to repent. Arjuna is even greater than Bhishma describes, and as for Devaki's son Krishna, not the gods can withstand him.

Bharatarishabha, there is no use in continuing to tell you what is good for you. Everything that needed to be said has been said. Now do as you wish; I have nothing further to add.'

After Drona has spoken, Vidura looks at Duryodhana and says, 'Duryodhana, I have no sympathy for you. I do grieve, however, for your elderly parents Gandhari and Dhritarashtra. With an unprincipled protector like you, whom they will soon lose, they will be left to wander the Earth like beggars and, deprived of their friends and counsellors, as well, they will be like a pair of birds whose wings have been shorn.

Having a sinful son, who will cause the extermination of the human race as we know it, they will sorrowfully roam the Earth, living on alms.'

Now the king turns to Duryodhana, who sits among his brothers and all the other kings. Dhritarashtra says, 'Listen, Duryodhana, to what Krishna Mahatman advises. Do as he says, for his words are eternal, auspicious and will lead to your salvation. With the help of blemishless Krishna we, of all the kings, are sure to achieve our most cherished goals.

Join Krishna and reconcile your differences with Yudhishtira; give this the same importance you would a mahayagna, for the weal of all the Bharatas, the Pandavas and Kauravas as one. With Krishna's help, bind yourself closely with the Pandavas, in love. This is the time to make peace; do not let the opportunity pass.

If you choose to disregard Krishna, who wants your welfare as much as that of the sons of Pandu, and who urges you to make peace for your own good, you can never win the war that will be and ruin will overtake us all.'"

CANTO 126

BHAGAVAD-YANA PARVA CONTINUED

Vaisampayana said, "Dhritarashtra's impassioned words prompt Bhishma and Drona, who sympathise with the old king, to speak to the recalcitrant Duryodhana.

They say, 'While the two Krishnas are not yet clad in their armour; while the Gandiva is still quiet; while Dhaumya has not yet begun to burn his enemies in the fire that he will light and feed for the war; and while that mighty archer Yudhishtira, who wears modesty like a garment, has not yet begun to look on your army with anger, let all hostilities cease.

While Bhimasena has not yet positioned himself in the midst of his troops, let enmity end. While Bhima has not yet entered the battlefield with his mace in hand and begun to smash down his enemies, make peace with the Pandavas. Before Bhima with his deadly gada makes the heads of elephant-warriors roll on the field like ripe palmyra-fruit, make peace. While Nakula and Sahadeva, Dhrishtadyumna of Prishata's vamsa, Virata, Sikhandin and Sisupala's son, all seasoned warriors versed in the astra shastra, have not yet donned their armour or penetrated your army, like crocodiles cutting through helpless waters, and showered you with fusillades of burning arrows, put a stop to this insane enmity.

As yet, fierce-winged barbs do not fall upon the vulnerable bodies of the assembled kings; as yet, iron shafts, shot by mighty bowmen who unerringly find any target at whatever distance, do not pierce the breasts of your warriors, who sit here smeared with sandalwood and other fragrant pastes and adorned with golden necklaces and jewelled ornaments. Let hostilities end before they do.

Let that elephant among kings, Dharmaraja Yudhishtira, receive you with an embrace while you salute him with your head bowed down. Bharatarishabha, let that king, renowned for the munificence of his sacrificial gifts, place his right hand marked with the signs of banner and hook on your shoulder. Let him set his gem-adorned and red-palmed hands on your back when you are seated before him.

Let Mahabaho Vrikodara, his shoulders as broad as the sala tree, embrace you with goodwill for the sake of peace. When Arjuna and the twins greet you with respect, sniff their heads in affection and speak lovingly to them.

Let all these kings who have gathered here shed tears of joy on seeing you united with your heroic cousins. Let the news of this happy union be proclaimed in their cities. Rule the Earth with brotherly affection in your heart and let her forever be freed from the fever of envy and anger.'"

CANTO 127

BHAGAVAD-YANA PARVA CONTINUED

Vaisampayana said, "In the Kuru sabha, Duryodhana is not pleased to hear this, and he says to Krishna, 'O Kesava, it is indeed just that you speak as you have after reflecting on all the circumstances. Yet you speak harshly and, without reason, find fault only with me, whilst always speaking kindly to the Pandavas. Have you weighed the strength and weaknesses of both sides before censuring me?

You, Vidura, the King, the Acharya and the Pitamaha all reproach only me and none other. I do not find the least fault in myself, yet all of you, including my own father, despise me. Parantapa, even after reflection I cannot find any shortcoming in me, grave or insignificant.

At the game of dice, which the Pandavas happily accepted, Sakuni defeated them and won their kingdom. How can I be blamed for that? On the other hand, I commanded that the wealth I won from the Pandavas be returned to them. It cannot be any fault of mine that the invincible Pandavas lost again at dice and had to go into exile in the forest. What fault do they lay at my door and make me their enemy?

Krishna, why do the weakened Pandavas so confidently choose to have war with us, as if they were as strong as they were once? What have we done to them? For what injury do the sons of Pandu, as well as the Srinjayas, seek to slaughter the sons of Dhritarashtra? Neither their fierce deeds nor their intimidating words will deprive us of our good sense and make us bow in fear, to them or even to Indra.

I do not see any Kshatriya who can conquer us in battle. Let alone the Pandavas, the Devas themselves cannot vanquish Bhishma, Kripa, Drona and Karna. If, Madhava, we die while keeping our Kshatriya dharma in battle, we will still go to Swarga.

Our highest duty as Kshatriyas is that we lay ourselves down on the field of battle on a bed not of down but arrows. If we do this without bowing to our enemies, that sharp bed will not injure us. Is there a Kshatriya who lives by his dharma, who would bow to an enemy out of fear and the wish to save his own life? Warriors who seek their own good honour what Rishi Matanga said: *a Kshatriya should always keep himself erect and never bow down, for effort is manliness; he should rather break than bend.*

A Kshatriya like me should only bow to Brahmanas, out of piety, and not to anyone else; and with all others, I must conduct myself as Matanga said. This is Kshatriya dharma, and I have always been true to it.

The portion of the kingdom that my father gave the Pandavas can never be theirs again, not as long as I live. As long as Dhritarashtra lives, both we and they must put away our weapons and live under his command as his dependents. The kingdom was given away from ignorance and fear when I was a callow youth and a dependent. It will never be given away again, and the Pandavas will never have it.

As long as I live, I shall not give the Pandavas even as much of our land as may be covered by the point of a needle!'"

CANTO 128

BHAGAVAD-YANA PARVA CONTINUED

Vaisampayana said, "Krishna is thoughtful for a moment and then, his eyes reddening ominously, he addresses Duryodhana in the presence of all who have come to the Kuru sabha.

Krishna says, 'You wish for the bed of heroes, and you shall have it, and your counsellors as well. For a great slaughter will soon happen. Does your small intelligence truly make you believe you have not committed any sin against the Pandavas? Let the kings who are assembled here be your judges.

Piqued by the prosperity that the noble sons of Pandu enjoyed, you and Subala's son conspired to arrange the game of dice. Why would those virtuous, honest and noble cousins of yours otherwise play such a vile game with the deceitful Sakuni? Gambling robs even the best of their intellect; as for the evil, it fetches disputes and other problems. It was you who, with your evil confederates, planned that disaster in the form of a game of dice, without consulting any men of dharma.

Who else could shame his brother's wife in the way that you shamed Draupadi by dragging her into the sabha and speaking as coarsely to her as you did? She is of noble birth and of pure conduct, and dearer to Pandu's sons than their lives; yet you treated Panchali despicably.

All the Kauravas know what Dusasana said that day in the sabha to Kunti's sons when they were about to set out for the forest. Who could behave so disgracefully towards honourable kinsmen, who are always virtuous, untouched by greed and cleave to dharma? Karna, Dusasana, and you, too, used words that only the most cruel and contemptible men use.

You took great pains, albeit without success, to immolate the Pandavas and their mother at Varanavata, when the princes were just youths. They escaped and were forced to hide in the home of a Brahmana in the town of Ekachakra. You tried again to kill them with poison, with snakes and by strangling; indeed you used every means to have the Pandavas killed, but none of your plans succeeded. When you have always behaved so malignantly towards the noble sons of Pandu, how can you say you have not offended them?

O sinful one, you are not willing to give them their rightful share of the kingdom, although they beg you for it. But you will be forced to give it to them when you are vanquished in battle and forcibly stripped of your prosperity. Having wronged the Pandavas so cruelly and so grievously, you now want to present yourself in a different light.

Repeatedly, your parents, Bhishma, Drona and Vidura tried to persuade you to make peace, but you did not. Peace would be advantageous to both you and Yudhishtira, but you fail to see the good in it. What else can be said of you than that you are ignorant? Going against the advice of your well-wishers, your true friends, can never bring you felicity. What you are about to do is fraught with disgrace, sin and danger, and will fetch a doom you cannot begin to imagine.'

Now Dusasana speaks to Duryodhana. In the Kuru sabha he says, 'My brother, if you do not willingly make peace with the Pandavas, the Kauravas will bind and surrender you to Kunti's son; Bhishma, Drona and your own father will hand Karna, you and me to the Pandavas.'

His heavy breath hissing like a great snake's, Duryodhana rises in rage. He ignores Vidura, Dhritarashtra, Bahlika, Kripa, Somadatta, Bhishma, Drona and Krishna, indeed, all those present, and stalks out of the sabha, followed by his brother, his counsellors and all the other kings loyal to him.

Bhishma says, 'The enemies of the man who abandons dharma and artha to follow his greed and anger rejoice when he falls into distress. This evil son of Dhritarashtra, this foolish Duryodhana who knows nothing of dharma, who is undeservingly vain of his sovereignty, obeys only the dictates of wrath and avarice. Alas Krishna, I see that the end of all these Kshatriyas has come, all these deluded kings who follow Duryodhana.'

Lotus-eyed Krishna says to those that remain, chief among them Bhishma and Drona, 'This is the great sin that all the Kuru elders are guilty of: that they do not stop this evil king from enjoying sovereignty. The time has come to stop him, for that may still do some good. Listen to me, sinless ones. What I say will benefit you.

During the lifetime of the old Bhoja king, his son, who was evil and a slave to his passions, usurped his father's throne and was eventually killed. It was I who killed Ugrasena's son Kansa, whom his friends and relatives abandoned, in a great battle for the weal of the world. My kinsmen and I then paid homage to Ugrasena, son of Ahuka, and re-installed him on the Bhoja throne. All the Yadavas, Andhakas and Vrishnis found prosperity and peace by abandoning a single evil one: Kansa.

Rajan, when the Devas and Asuras were arrayed for battle with their weapons raised and ready to strike, Paramesthin, the lord of all creatures, said something which is pertinent to the situation in which we now find ourselves.

When the peoples of the worlds were divided into two sides and were about to be slaughtered, the divine Creator and Protector of the universe said, "The Asuras, Daityas and Danavas will be vanquished, and the Adityas, Vasus, Rudras and other Swargavasis will be victorious. The Devas, Asuras, Manavas, Gandharvas, Nagas and Rakshasas will massacre one another in this war."

With this in mind, Paramesthin commanded Dharma, saying, "Tie up the Daityas and Danavas securely and hand them over to Varuna," which Dharma accordingly did. Varuna bound them again, fastening his knots over Dharma's and even now keeps them in the depths of his watery kingdom, guarding them carefully.

Even so, secure Duryodhana, Karna, Sakuni and Dusasana and give them up to the Pandavas. For the sake of a family, an individual may be sacrificed; for a village a family may be sacrificed; for a province a village may be sacrificed; and for the sake of one's soul, the very Earth may be sacrificed.

Rajan, restrain Duryodhana and make peace with the Pandavas. Do not be the instrument by which the entire race of Kshatriyas is annihilated.'"

CANTO 129

Bhagavad-yana Parva continued

Vaisampayana said, "Dhritarashtra turns to Vidura, who knows all aspects of dharma.

He says, 'Go to the wise, far-seeing Gandhari and bring her here. Together with her, I will plead with my black-hearted son. If she can pacify him, we may yet be able to do as Krishna says. By speaking for peace, she might bring my greedy, foolish son, influenced by his evil friends, back to the path of dharma. If she can avert the calamity that Duryodhana is about to cause, we might be able to preserve peace and enjoy happiness for ever.'

Vidura brings Gandhari into the sabha, and Dhritarashtra says to her, 'My queen, with utter disregard for my commands, and greedy for power, your son is about to sacrifice the kingdom and his very life. Like some rough peasant, showing contempt for his superiors and the advice of his well-wishers, he walked out of our court with his sinful friends.'

Gandhari says, 'Have that sinful son of mine fetched here. The man who has a coarse soul and sacrifices dharma and artha does not deserve to rule a kingdom. Arrogant, envious and greedy, obtained a kingdom by the vilest means. Indeed, Dhritarashtra, you who are so fond of your son, are to blame for this, for, knowing his evil heart, you did as he wanted. Lust and wrath have seized this son of yours and he is a slave to delusion. You cannot force him to change his ways, Rajan; it is too late for that. Now you reap the fruit of having given charge of the Kuru kingdom to an ignorant, selfish and evil prince, and one with unscrupulous advisors.

Are you not affected by the imminence of the war that will be fought between such close relatives? Your enemies will rejoice at your discord with the Pandavas, who are as your own sons. What sane man would use force to overcome a calamity that can be resolved by conciliation and generosity?'

At Dhritarashtra and Gandhari's command, Vidura brings Duryodhana into the sabha. His tread is heavy, his angry breath hisses snake-like and his eyes glitter coppery as he comes back into the sabha to hear what his mother has to say. Gandhari rebukes him and speaks to him in an attempt to make him see reason and to secure peace.'

Gandhari says, 'Duryodhana, my son, listen to what I say; it is for your good and that of your followers as well. What I say is easy for you to do, and it will bring you prosperity and happiness. Duryodhana, do as your well-wishers tell you, those Bharatottamas: your father, Bhishma, Drona, Kripa and Vidura. If you make peace, you will pay homage to Bhishma, to your father, to me and to all the others who love you with Drona at their head.

Nobody succeeds in acquiring, retaining or enjoying a kingdom by his own effort alone. The man who does not have his passions under control can never enjoy a throne for any length of time. Only the restrained man, one endowed with great intelligence, can rule a kingdom. Unbridled lust and wrath make a man lose his possessions and enjoyments. It is after first conquering these enemies within himself that a king brings the Earth under his subjection.

Sovereignty over men is a great thing. Evil men may want to win a kingdom, but they cannot rule it when they do acquire it. He who desires to acquire an empire must firmly tether his senses to dharma and artha, for, if the senses are restrained, intelligence increases, like a fuel-fed fire. If uncontrolled, his senses can even kill him, like unbroken, wild horses can kill an unskilled rider.

The man who tries to win over his counsellors without first conquering himself, and who tries to conquer his enemies without subduing his counsellors, is soon vanquished and ruined. He who masters himself first, taking himself for his worst enemy, will later succeed in conquering his confederates and outside enemies. Prosperity worships the man who commands his senses and his advisors, who metes out punishment to transgressors, who acts after deliberation and who is calm and wise.

Lust and wrath, which live within a man, are like two small fish caught in the net of wisdom and restrained. These two, when they manage to escape and grow, make the gods shut the doors of heaven against a man who has shed his worldly desires and who is, otherwise, qualified to enter. The king who understands how to conquer lust, wrath, greed, boastfulness and pride can indeed rule the whole world.

The king who wants to acquire artha and dharma, and who wants to vanquish his enemies, should always restrain his passions. The man who, influenced by lust or anger, behaves deceitfully towards his kinsmen or others can never win true allies. By uniting with the heroic sons of Pandu, who are all blessed with great wisdom, you can happily enjoy the Earth, my son. What Santanu's son Bhishma and Maharatha Drona tell you is true—Krishna and Arjuna are invincible. So, seek the protection of this Mahabaho, to whom any exertion is as nothing, for if Krishna decides to be gracious, both sides will be happy.

The man who does not obey wise and learned friends, who want his prosperity, will gladden only his enemies. My son, there is no good in battle, no dharma, no artha. How then can it bring felicity? Besides, child, victory is far from certain. Do not set your heart on war. Bhishma, your father and Bahlika gave the Pandavas their share of the kingdom from fear. Parantapa, never even think of going to war against Pandu's sons. The peaceful state of your sovereignty over the Earth is the result of their rule, during which they removed all obstacles to harmony.

Give the Pandavas what is only their due. If you wish to enjoy, with your friends and advisors, your half of the empire, give them their share. Half the Earth is enough to support you and yours. By doing as your well-wishers say, you will win great fame, Bhaarata. A war with the sons of Pandu will result only in the loss of everything you now have, for they are all blessed with prosperity; they have their souls under control; they are vastly intelligent and they have conquered their passions. Dispel the anger of your elders and rule your kingdom in a manner that becomes you: by giving the Pandavas back their rightful share.

My son, for thirteen years you have made the Pandavas suffer; it is enough. Douse the fire that your lust and anger have fed. Neither you who covet their wealth, nor the always angry Sutaputra nor your brother Dusasana is a match for them. The fury of Bhishma, Drona, Kripa, Karna, Bhimasena, Dhananjaya and Dhrishtadyumna can obliterate the Earth's very population. Do not let your anger become the cause of the end of the Kurus. Do not let the world be destroyed for your stubbornness.

Your limited intellect deludes you into thinking that Bhishma, Drona, Kripa and all the rest will fight whole-heartedly for you. That will never happen, for these men, who have Atmagyana, are just as fond of the Pandavas as they are of you. Even if they are willing to give up their lives in gratitude for the care that Dhritarashtra has given them, they could never be angry with Yudhishtira.

Men never acquire true wealth through greed. Give up your avarice and desist, my son, O Bharatarishabha.'"

CANTO 130

BHAGAVAD-YANA PARVA CONTINUED

Vaisampayana said, "Duryodhana ignores his mother's words and, again, angrily walks away to be with his evil friends. Now the prince conspires with Sakuni, the crafty player of dice, and, together, he, Karna, Sakuni and Dusasana alight on a foul plan.

They decide, 'Krishna is always quick to act and, with Dhritarashtra and Santanu's help, he will want to seize us. So we must take him captive first, even as Indra did Bala. When the Pandavas hear of his being our prisoner they will lose heart and become hapless, like snakes without fangs. Mahabaho Krishna is their protector and their refuge. If we imprison this granter of wishes, this bull of all the Sattvatas, the Pandavas and the Somakas will despair and become impotent to fight.

We will ignore Dhritarashtra and take Krishna captive, even here in Hastinapura, and then go to war against the enemy.'

The intuitive Satyaki, who can read men's intentions by what he sees around him, soon realises what Duryodhana is plotting. He comes out of the sabha with Kritavarman.

Satyaki says to Kritavarman, 'Array our troops now! Wait with your armed men at the entrance to the sabha, while I speak to Krishna.'

He walks back into the sabha, like a lion into a mountain cave, and informs first Krishna, then Dhritarashtra and Vidura of the conspiracy.

Then he laughs, 'What these evil men have plotted violates dharma, artha and kama. Besides, they will never be able to achieve what they plan. Overwhelmed by their passions and yielding to their wrath and greed, these sinners want to commit the most heinous sin. These despicable men, who want to seize lotus-eyed Krishna, are like children who want to hold a blazing fire in their hands.'

Vidura says to Dhritarashtra in the Kuru sabha, 'O Rajan, the hour of all your sons' deaths is at hand for what they are plotting, however incapable they might be to actually accomplish this unspeakable plan. Alas, they are united in their wish to vanquish Indra's younger brother and make him their prisoner. When they encounter this Purushavyaghra they will all perish like insects in a fire. Even if they fight as one, if Krishna wants he can send all of them to Yama, like an angry lion dispatching a herd of deer.

However, he will not do anything so sinful. This best of men, of everlasting glory, will never leave the path of dharma.'

Krishna looks at Dhritarashtra, who sits in the midst of so many good men, all heedful of sage counsel, and he says to the Kuru king, 'Rajan, if these men of anger want to use violence against me, allow them to. As for me, easy though it may be for me to kill all of them, I will not commit any sin. Because of their greed for what belongs to the Pandavas, your sons will lose even what is rightfully theirs. And if they try to take me their prisoner, Yudhishtira will accomplish his purpose without fighting a war, for I will seize them and all their followers and make them over to the Pandavas. I tell you, it will not be difficult for me.

However, Bhaarata, I will not be driven by anger or evil, nor commit this offence in your presence. Let Duryodhana do as he likes; I give him and all your sons my leave to do as they plan.'

Dhritarashtra says to Vidura, 'Bring sinful Duryodhana, with his friends, counsellors, brothers and followers into my presence. I will make one last attempt to set him on the right path.'

Again, Vidura fetches the reluctant Duryodhana into the sabha with his brothers and the kings who follow him. Dhritarashtra says to Duryodhana, who stands haughty and defiant, surrounded by Karna, Dusasana and all those other kings, 'O, you wretch of accumulated sins, how do you even dream of doing what you and these sinful allies of yours have plotted? O, you disgrace to your race, only you could think of committing this impossible crime. You want to make the invincible and inexorable lotus-leaf-eyed Krishna you prisoner! Like a child wanting the Moon, you want to do what even all the Devas led by Indra cannot achieve.

Do you not understand that no one can withstand Krishna in battle, not the Devas, Gandharvas, Asuras, Uragas or Manavas? As impossible as seizing the wind, as reaching for the Moon with one's hand or as supporting the Earth on one's head is taking Krishna by force.'

Vidura looks at Duryodhana and says to Dhritarashtra's malignant son, 'Duryodhana, listen to what I have to say. At the gates of Saubha, the great Vanara Dwividha, who fought beside Rama at the gates of Lanka in the Treta yuga, covered Krishna with a thunderous shower of rocks, wanting to capture him. He did not succeed. And you want to apprehend Krishna by force?

When Sauri went to Pragjyotisha, Narakasura with all the Danavas could not overcome him. And you want to seize him by force? He slew Naraka, rescued a thousand women from his city and married them all, by law.

In the city of Nirmochana, six thousand awesome Asuras could not capture him with their sorcerous nooses. And you think you can take him by force? When he was a child he slew Putana and two other Asuras who took the shape of birds. He held up Govardhana on his little finger to protect the herd from Indra's deluge. He slew Arishta, Dhenuka, the powerful Chanura, Aswaraja and the evil Kansa. He vanquished Jarasandha eighteen times in battle, and killed Vakra and Sisupala, Bana and countless other kings.

His strength is limitless, immeasurable. He vanquished Varuna and Agni, and when he brought the Parijata tree down from Devaloka, he routed Lord Indra himself, along with all the gods. While floating on the Ekarnava, the single infinite ocean, he slew Madhu and Kaitabha; and in another birth he killed Hayagriva. He is the Creator of everything but is himself uncreated. He is the origin of all power. Whatever he wishes, he accomplishes without effort.

Don't you know that sinless Krishna is permanent and undecaying? Like an angry cosmic snake, he is the never ending source of energy. By trying to use violence against Krishna, you and all your followers will perish, like insects that fall into a great fire.'"

CANTO 131

BHAGAVAD-YANA PARVA CONTINUED

Vaisampayana said, "When Vidura has spoken passionately, Krishna says mildly to Duryodhana, 'You are under the delusion that I am alone, which is why you think of overpowering me and taking me captive. But look, foolish prince, here are all the Pandavas and all the Vrishnis and Andhakas. Here are all the Adityas, the Rudras and the Vasus, with all the great Rishis.' And throwing back his beautiful head, he laughs ringingly.

As the divine one laughs, from his body emerge myriad gods, each flashing like brilliant lightning and no bigger than a man's thumb. On his brow Brahma appears, on his breast Rudra, on his arms the Lokapalas, and from his mouth issue Agni, the Adityas, the Sadhyas, the Vasus, the Aswins, the Marutas, Indra, the Viswadevas and hosts of Yakshas, Gandharvas and Rakshasas, all in miniature forms.

From his two arms Balarama and Arjuna appear. Arjuna stands on his right with his bow in hand, and Baladeva on his left armed with the plough. Behind him are Bhima, Yudhishtira and the two sons of Madri, and before him are all the Andhakas and the Vrishnis with Pradyumna and other chieftains, with mighty weapons raised. In his countless other arms, now in view, flash the conch, the discus, the mace, the bow called Saranga, the plough, the javelin, the Nandaka and every other weapon, all shining with lustre and ready to strike. From his eyes, nose, ears and every part of his body burst forth dazzling sparks of fire and smoke; and from his pores flames spring, like the rays of the Sun.

Beholding the magnificence of this form of Krishna, all the kings shut their eyes in fearful awe, except Drona, Bhishma, the wise Vidura, the blessed Sanjaya and the saintly Rishis imbued with their profound tapasya, for the Lord has revealed this divine form to them before. While this wondrous vision is manifested in the Kuru sabha celestial drums beat in the sky, flowers rain down upon Krishna, the Earth trembles and the oceans churn turbulently. And, O Bharatarishabha, all living things on Earth are filled with uncanny wonder.

Krishna withdraws his divine and auspicious form and, taking the Rishis' leave, and his arms linked with Satyaki's and Kritavarman's, he leaves the Kuru sabha. An uproar breaks out, during which the Rishis, Narada and others, vanish from sight to return to their sacred abodes. And this, too, is marvellous to see.

Seeing Krishna leave the sabha, the Kauravas and all the kings follow him, like the Devas behind Indra. However, without a thought for any who walk behind him, Krishna of the fathomless soul emerges into the open, like a fire. At the gate his sarathy Daruka waits for him with his white chariot of the tinkling moonbells and golden embellishments, of untold speed, whose wheels rumble like thunderheads, its seats covered with white tiger-skins, and to which Saibya and his other horses are harnessed. Mounted and ready to ride with Krishna is that favourite of the Vrishnis, Hridika's son, Maharatha Kritavarman.

Krishna is about to leave when Dhritarashtra calls after him:

'O Parantapa, Janardana, you have seen how powerless I am to control my sons. You know everything now. Having seen how fervently I try to bring peace between the Kurus and the Pandavas, and knowing that I am blind and helpless, it is not fitting for you to doubt me.

Kesava, I have no ill-will towards the Pandavas. You heard what I said to Duryodhana. The Kauravas and all the kings of the Earth also know that I have done everything in my power to make peace.'

Krishna now says to Dhritarashtra, Drona, Pitamaha Bhishma, Vidura, Bahlika and Kripa, 'You have all witnessed what transpired in the hallowed Kuru sabha. You have seen how Duryodhana, like some lout, walked out of the court in anger, and how Dhritarashtra describes himself as being powerless. Now with leave from you all, I will return to Yudhishtira.' And, saluting them, Krishna climbs into his chariot and departs.

Those Bharatarishabhas, those maharathas Bhishma, Drona, Kripa, Vidura, Aswatthama, Vikarna and Yuyutsu follow him. And as the Kurus look on, Kesava turns his great white ratha of the tinkling bells toward the home of his aunt Kunti."

CANTO 132

BHAGAVAD-YANA PARVA CONTINUED

"Vaisampayana said, 'After entering Kunti's house and worshipping her feet, Krishna tells her briefly about all that happened in the Kuru sabha.

He says, 'The Rishis and I spoke in many ways and reasonably to persuade Duryodhana, but he would not heed anything we said. The time of his and his followers' end has come. Let me go now to the Pandavas. What message would you send them? Wise Matuli, speak to me, I want to hear what you have to say.'

Kunti says, 'Krishna, say to virtuous Yudhishtira: "My son, your dharma has diminished. Your mind is afflicted and you are like a man who vainly reads the Vedas without understanding their inner meaning, and who, thus, remains ignorant. You choose to take the Vedas literally while only your own intellect can see the truth. Think about your svadharma, for which Brahma created you. The Kshatriya was created from his arms, and by the strength of his arms he must live and perform the harsh deeds he may need to in order to protect his people. There is a story told in this connection, which I heard long ago.

In the days of yore, a gratified Vaisravana gifted the Earth to the Rajarishi Muchukunda. The sage refused the gift and said he wanted only to enjoy what he had won by his own prowess. The delighted Vaisravana marvelled at his response. In keeping with Kshatriya dharma, Muchukunda conquered the Earth by the strength of his arms and ruled over it.

Remember, Bhaarata, that a fourth of the punya gained by the subjects of a king who protects them accrues to the king himself, if a king keeps dharma that confers divine status on him, but if he sins, he finds Naraka, hell, for himself. Dandaneeti, the law of punishment, enforced by the king, ensures that the four varnas live by their inherent svadharma; and this leads to the king acquiring dharma, artha and moksha.

When the king fully upholds the Dandaneeti, the law, without discarding any part of it, the golden immaculate age, the Krita Yuga, sets in. Have no doubts about whether the king makes the yuga, or the yuga makes the king, do as he does. We know for certain that it is the king who ushers in the yuga. Indeed, it is the king who is responsible for ushering in all the yugas—Krita, Treta or Dwapara, and even the Kali yuga.

That king who ushers in a Krita yuga enjoys Swarga to the fullest. The king who causes a Treta yuga to set in does enjoy heaven but not fully. For fetching a Dwapara yuga, a king enjoys Swarga in proportion to his deeds. However, the evil king who causes a Kali yuga earns untold sin and lives in Naraka for countless years. This king's sins affect the world, and the world's sins affect him.

Observe your kingly duties as befits your lineage. The path you want to take is not the way of a Rajarishi. The man who, from faintness of heart, allows his compassion to shake him from his dharma does not find the punya that accrues from cherishing his subjects with love. When we blessed you, neither Pandu, nor your grandfather Vyasa or I ever wished on you the impulses which now prompt you. What we prayed for was sacrifice, charity, merit, courage, subjects and children, greatness of soul, and might and energy.

Brahmanas who wished you well worshipped and gratified the Devas and the Pitrs for life, wealth and children for you, whilst adding *Swaha* and *Swadha* to their mantras. As do the Devas, parents expect from their children generosity, tolerance, performance of yagnas, study and protection of their subjects. Whether this is virtue or not, you must perform these duties because of your birth. Though nobly born, my sons are destitute and persecuted. Hungry men can approach a brave and benevolent king and he will give them food and refuge. What can be more virtuous than for a man, who has acquired a kingdom, to make all the people of the world his own with his generosity, or establish his authority over them by the truth of his words?

A Brahmana's dharma is to be a priest or a mendicant, a Kshatriya's is to protect his subjects, a Vaisya's dharma is to earn wealth and a Sudra's is to serve the other three varnas. The life of a beggar is forbidden for you, and so is farming. You are a Kshatriya and, therefore, the protector of all who are in distress. You have to live by the prowess of your arms. Mahabaho, recover your rightful share of the kingdom, which you have lost, by conciliation, by argument, by giving gifts, by diplomacy or violently.

What can be sadder for me, who brought you into this world, than to be dependent on others for my sustenance? Fight, in keeping with your duty, the dharma of kings. Do not allow your Pitrs to sink into the disgrace of infamy. Do not exhaust your punya and, with your younger brothers, meet a sinful end.""'"

CANTO 133

BHAGAVAD-YANA PARVA CONTINUED

"Kunti says, 'Krishna, there is an ancient story told of the conversation between Vidula and her son. You must tell Yudhishtira this story, or any other that you think better. Listen to the tale.

There was a noblewoman, a queen called Vidula, who was blessed with great wisdom and foresight. She was famous, prone to anger and devoted to Kshatriya dharma. She was well-educated, and all the kings of the Earth knew of her. Vidula would listen to discourses of all kinds given by eminent sages.

One day, she rebuked her son, who lay prostrate with grief and despair after having been defeated in battle by the king of the Sindhus. She said, "You are not my son, making your enemies joyful as you do. You are not born from your father and me; from where have you come? You have no anger and cannot be called a man; and your unmanly body is a eunuch's and bears no sign of strength. Do you mean to spend your life in dejection and despair? For your own sake, be as a Kshatriya should and do your duty by your subjects.

Do not disgrace your soul; do not be satisfied with a little. Set your sights on great things and shed your fear. Rise, coward; you collapse like a woman after one defeat; do not be the source of delight to your enemies and grief to your friends; do not abandon honour and good sense.

Little streams are filled with only a little water. The palms of a mouse hold a very small quantity. It takes very little, small acquisitions, to satisfy a coward. It is better to die pulling out the fangs of a serpent than to die like a dog. Exercise your strength and risk your life. Like an intrepid hawk that ranges the skies, fearlessly wander the Earth, display your strength, silently watch your enemies and wait for an opportune moment.

You lie here like a man struck by lightning, a corpse. Rise, coward; shake off the memory of your defeat. Do not cower in hiding, so miserably. Let your deeds bring you renown. Eschew mediocrity; do not stand behind anyone, but proudly stand at the head of all. Blaze forth like a roaring fire. Even if for a moment, shine like a tinduka twig, rather than smoulder from unfulfilled desire like chaff. It is better to blaze for a single moment than to smoke impotently for ever.

It does not befit a Kshatriya to be either too fierce or inordinately mild. By achieving every possible feat on the battlefield, a brave man discharges his Kshatriya dharma and never disgraces himself. Whether he gains his objective or not, the man of good sense never wallows in grief. A true Kshatriya forges ahead to accomplish his next objective, without caring for even his life.

So, my son, show your strength or give up your life. What use is living like this, without honour, in shame, in disregard of Kshatriya dharma, and having lost the punya of all the yagnas you performed and nullified your past achievements? The basis of all your joy has been destroyed. Why, then, do want to live? If a man must fall, he should seize his enemy and fall with him. Even if his roots are severed, a man must not give in to despair. Think of the horse, which uses all its strength to pull carriages and chariots, or carry heavy burdens, and use your own strength and honour.

Understand what real manliness is, and work to redeem and elevate the honour of your race that has been lost because of you. The man who has failed to accomplish anything great or noteworthy only increases the human population by one. He is neither man nor woman. He whose fame is not based on charity, asceticism, truth, learning and the acquisition of wealth is only waste born of his mother's body; while, he who surpasses others in learning, asceticism, wealth, prowess and deeds is truly a man.

For you to adopt the idle and wretched life of begging alms is in no way noble but only cowardly. A man can never have joy from a weak friend, whom enemies are delighted to see, who is despised by others, who has neither possessions nor fine clothes, who is pleased with the smallest acquisitions, who is destitute, who has no courage and who is base.

Driven out of our home, exiled from our kingdom, deprived of all sources of enjoyment and wealth, we will soon die. I have given birth to Kali himself in the form of my son, who is a sinner among the virtuous, and who destroys our dynasty and family. O, let no woman ever have the misfortune of bearing a son like you, apathetic, weak, self-pitying and the joy of his foes. Do not smoulder sadly, but flare up like a great flame and show your prowess. Slay your enemies. Even if for a brief moment, blaze over your enemies' heads.

A real man nurtures his wrath and gives no quarter, whilst a man who forgives easily and has no anger is neither a man nor a woman but a eunuch. Contentment, softness of heart, fearfulness and the lack of effort destroy prosperity. The man who makes no effort does not win greatness. My son, exert yourself to undo the shackles of these failings that will lead to ruin. Steel your heart and go after your lost wealth.

A man is called a purusha because he can overcome his enemy. The man who acts like a woman does not deserve to be called a purusha. A brave and mighty king, who goes majestically through life like a lion, is subject to fate, like all other creatures, but his subjects are never unhappy. The king who disregards his own happiness and pleasure and seeks the prosperity of his kingdom is the source of great joy to his ministers and friends."

Hearing these words, the son said, "If you do not see me, of what use would the whole Earth be to you, of what use your ornaments, all objects of pleasure, and life itself?"

The mother said, "Let your enemies conquer regions that are the domain of the poor and low-born; let your well-wishers enjoy realms that are reserved for noble souls. Do not live the wretched life of a beggar, destitute and without servants, a weak and powerless life, lived on food given in charity. Our Brahmanas and your friends should depend on you for their sustenance, just as all the living depend on clouds for rain, as the Devas depend on Indra.

The life of a man, on whom all other beings depend for their well-being, is not in vain, but like the tree full of ripe fruit that birds flock to. Indeed the life of that brave man, by whose strength his friends attain happiness, like the Devas derive happiness through Sakra's prowess, is blessed. The man who lives on the strength of his arms wins fame in this life and bliss in the hereafter.'"

CANTO 134

BHAGAVAD-YANA PARVA CONTINUED

"Kunti says, 'Vidula said, "If, defeated, you choose to give up manliness, you will soon find yourself on the path that the lowly walk. A Kshatriya who does not exercise his might to the best of his ability, from fear of death, is like a thief.

Ah sadly, my grave words, which are for your good, and fitting and reasonable as well, fall uselessly on your ears, like medicine given to a dying man. What I say makes no impression on you.

It is true that the king of the Sindhus has many followers. Discount them, for they are weak and ignorant; but though discontented under his command, they can do nothing for themselves but wait for their master to be overtaken by some disaster to be free of him. As for his enemies, they will join their forces with yours when they see your strength. Unite with them and bide your time in the mountains, until fate strikes at your enemy, as it must, for he is old and not immune to disease or death.

Your name, Sanjaya, means victorious. I hardly see you living up to it. Be true to your name; do not prove it falsely given. A great Brahmana saw you when you were a child and predicted that you would fall into distress but rise to greatness again. Remembering his words, I feel some hope, and that is why I repeat myself over and over, my son.

The man who pursues his objectives prudently, and with determination, and who has others working with him towards the same end, will surely be successful. Whether I stand to gain, or lose what I have, Sanjaya, I will not stop fighting.

Sambara said that there is nothing more miserable than not to know where one's next meal will come from. It is worse than losing a husband or a son. Poverty is only another form of death.

I was born into a noble family and have been taken from one great lake to another. I am much blessed; my husband respects and cherishes me and I wield authority over so many. My friends have seen me living amongst well-wishers, my body bathed and adorned in rich clothes, garlands and ornaments. When you see me and your wife emaciated by hunger, you will not want to live, Sanjaya. Of what use will life be to you when you see our servants, our Acharyas and our Brahmanas leave us from want of sustenance?

What peace can my heart have if I do not see you following your dharma again, to reach for mighty achievements in the way you once used to? My heart will burst if I have to turn away a Brahmana, for my husband and I have never done so in the past. We were the protectors of others and never had to ask for protection ourselves. I will die if I have to be dependent on someone else.

My son, be our means of crossing this stormy ocean; be our raft. Make lavish room for us where now there is none. Bring us back to life. If you have a lust for life, you will be able to face any enemy. But if you insist on behaving like a eunuch and wallowing in self-pity, it would be better to end your life.

A brave man wins fame by killing even a single enemy. By killing Vritra, Indra achieved greatness; he acquired sovereignty over the Devas, the cup for drinking Soma and the lordship of all the worlds. When a Kshatriya declares himself in battle and challenges his mail-clad foes, when he slays the best of the enemy warriors, when he wins renown in fair fight, his enemies feel pain and bow to him. Men who are not brave contribute their own wealth to his cause and fight his fight, uncaring of their lives. Whether kingdoms are overtaken by ruin, or whether life itself is endangered, noble men do not give up until they destroy the enemy who is within reach.

Sovereignty is either Amrita or the gate of Swarga. Think of it as such and, bearing in mind that it is now shut against you, fall like a burning torch amongst your enemies. Rajan, slay your foes in battle; do your duty as a Kshatriya; let me not see you downcast. Enhancer of your enemies' fears, let me not see you dejected and miserable, surrounded by us who also grieve, while your enemy exults.

Rejoice in your wealth, and with the Sauvira daughters; do not be weak and ruled by the daughters of the Sindhus. If a handsome, educated, noble young man of renown, like you, yields in this unbecoming manner, like an angry bull with its yoked burden, life is like death itself.

How can my heart know peace if I see you eulogise other men or walk submissively behind them? Never has there been anyone in our race who walked behind another. My son, it is not fitting for you to live as a dependent.

I know what the essence of Kshatriya dharma is, as declared by our elders and sages of antiquity. Eternal and constant, Brahma himself ordained it. He who has been born into this world as a Kshatriya of a noble family, and who has studied Kshatriya dharma, will never be anxious about his sustenance, or bow to anybody on this Earth. You must stand erect with courage and honour and put forth your effort to vanquish your enemy, for effort is manliness. One should rather break in the joints than bend his will to another's. A noble Kshatriya should always walk like an infuriated elephant. He should, my Sanjaya, bow only to Brahmanas, for the sake of dharma. He should rule over all other varnas, destroying every evil-doer. Whether or not he has allies, this is how he should live, all his life."'"

CANTO 135

BHAGAVAD-YANA PARVA CONTINUED

"Kunti says, 'Hearing his mother's words, the son said, "O cruel and wrathful mother, you value heroism on the battlefield so highly, it seems as if your heart is made of stone. Fie on Kshatriya dharma, with which you urge me to battle, as if I were a stranger to you and not your only son, as if you were not my mother. If you do not recognise me, if you disown me, of what use will all the Earth be to you, of what use your jewels and riches, indeed, of what use your life itself?"

The mother said, "My son, wise men always base their actions on dharma and artha. I urge you to focus on these virtues and go to battle. This is time to show your prowess. If you do not fight, you will earn general contempt and my disapproval. If I say nothing when you are about to be tainted with dishonour and ridicule, my love for you would be as worthless a donkey's for her young.

Do not take the path that the wise disapprove of, which fools would take, for it is a base and ignorant way, in which innumerable common creatures of the world take refuge, with neither honour nor glory. However, if you choose the way of the Kshatriya, the way of war, you will endear yourself to me. If you tread the high path of dharma and seek artha, while using only ways of the godly and the honest, and relying on your own effort, you will be dear to me indeed. Real joy comes from sons and grandsons who are well taught and brave; while one who is happy with a son who is apathetic, immodest and without dharma might as well not have a son.

The base man, who never performs his duty but cleaves to cowardice and sin, does not find happiness here or in the hereafter. A Kshatriya is born to do battle and win victory. Whether he wins or dies, he will attain Swarga. The joy that a Kshatriya experiences by conquering his enemies has no equal even in the realms of Indra. If a great Kshatriya meets with defeat many times, he would still wait, burning with anger, for a chance to avenge himself and vanquish his enemy. How can he have peace of mind other than by killing his enemy or dying himself in the attempt?

The wise man considers pettiness distasteful. Insignificant things will eventually become the source of great pain to the man who finds them attractive. The man who does not have what is worthy soon becomes unhappy. He becomes needy and is overwhelmed, like the Ganga when she enters the ocean."

The son said, "Mother, you should not be saying such things to your son. Be loving and stand by him silently."

The mother said, "I am pleased to hear this. You have the right to remind me of my duty. And so, I will urge you even more to do yours. I will honour you only when I will see you crowned with success after slaughtering all the Saindhavas."

The son said, "With no wealth or allies, how can I have success or victory? Knowing this, I have relinquished the desire for kingdom, as a sinner does his wish for heaven. If, in your wisdom, you can see how I can succeed, tell me of it, and I will do as you command."

The mother said, "My son, do not disgrace yourself by anticipating failure. In the past, you have had victories as well as losses. You should never try to attain your goals using anger and foolhardiness. Success is never certain, yet men still act. Sometimes they succeed and sometimes do not. However, those who do nothing will never succeed. How can anyone dream of success without effort?

Effort can have one of two results—success or failure. The man who already believes that he will fail will never have success or prosperity. With firm belief in yourself, and with alertness, put all your energy into everything you do. Prosperity comes to the wise king who acts with valour and forethought, after having performed all auspicious rites to propitiate the Devas and Brahmanas. As the Sun does to the east, the goddess of fortune comes to him.

You have heard what I want you to do; now show me your manliness. It is your dharma to do your utmost to achieve your goals. Gather to you others who have enmity towards your enemy, men who are also hungry for victory and prosperity, men whom your enemy has weakened, who are jealous of him, whom he has humiliated. With their help you can break the ranks of the Saindhava, even as a violent storm does clouds.

Give your allies their share of wealth before it is due, be active and speak pleasantly, respectfully, to them; and they will stand by you in battle. When the enemy realises that you care little for your life, he will be as fearful of you as of a snake living in his house.

If a man does not try to kill in war an enemy he knows is powerful, he should at least conciliate him with friendly overtures and gifts, which is almost a victory. You can find artha through diplomacy, and if your wealth increases, your friends will adulate you and look on you as their refuge. If you lose your wealth, your friends and relatives will abandon you and, worse still, mistrust and despise you.

However, the man, who befriends his enemy, can never regain his kingdom.'"'

CANTO 136

BHAGAVAD-YANA PARVA CONTINUED

"Kunti says, 'The mother said, "Whatever calamity may strike a king, he must never betray his fear. Seeing a frightened king, the whole kingdom, his army and ministers will also be afraid and his subjects will become disunited. Some will defect to the enemy; others will abandon the king; some, whom he has humiliated, will try to finish him. His close friends might stay loyal to him and want his welfare, but will wait helplessly, like a cow for her tethered calf.

Well-wishers grieve for their king when he is plunged in distress, as true friends will. There are many, whom you have honoured in the past, who still bear friendship for you; and you have many true friends, who grieve over your loss of the kingdom and who want to share your troubles. Do not make them abandon you at seeing how frightened you are.

I tell you all this because I want to see your strength, manliness and intelligence; and to encourage and awaken your strength. If you understand that I speak the truth, gather courage and set your mind on victory, Sanjaya. We have a number of treasure-houses that you are unaware of; only I know they exist. I will place all these at your disposal. You also have many sincere friends who will share not only your joys but your troubles, and will not turn away from battle. Parantapa, such men are fitting allies and advisors of a king who wants victory."

Although he was not greatly intelligent, his mother's words melted away the despair that had gripped Sanjaya's heart; and he said to her, "With you, who are so devoted to my welfare, for my guide, I will lift my kingdom out of the depths into which it has sunk, or die in the attempt. I stayed mainly silent while you spoke, because I wanted to hear more. Just as a man's thirst for amrita is never slaked, I am not yet satiated with your love and wisdom.

Mother, I swear to you, I will win the support of my friends, and rouse myself to crush my enemy and be victorious!"

Stung by what his mother said, Sanjaya reared up like a proud horse of high pedigree and soon achieved everything she had urged him to.

When enemies beleaguer a king and he is overwhelmed by despair, his minister should tell him this excellent tale, to arouse his courage and infuse him with strength. Indeed, this story is called Jaya, and everyone who desires victory should hear it. And, having listened to it, a Kshatriya may vanquish his enemies and conquer the whole world.

A pregnant woman who hears it will give birth to a son, and repeatedly hearing it will ensure that a hero is born to her. The Kshatriya woman who listens to it will have a son of irresistible prowess, deeply learned and the most generous of men; who practises the severest tapasya and is utterly devout; who blazes with tejas and is the best of men; who is mighty and greatly blessed; who is a Maharatha, highly intelligent, irresistible in battle, ever victorious and invincible; and who suppresses the sinful and protects the righteous.""

CANTO 137

BHAGAVAD-YANA PARVA CONTINUED

"Kunti says, 'Say to Arjuna, "When you were born and I was in the asrama surrounded by my sakhis, a celestial voice spoke from the sky, saying, *Kunti, this son of yours will rival the thousand-eyed Indra. He will vanquish all the assembled Kurus in battle. With Bhima, he will conquer all the Earth and his fame will reach into the heavens. With Vasudeva as his ally he will slay the Kurus in battle and recover his lost kingdom. He will be blessed with great prosperity and, with his brothers, he will perform three mahayagnas.*

Ever-glorious one, you know how devoted to truth Arjuna is, and how irresistible. Let it be as that asariri said. If dharma exists, those words will prove true, and you will fulfil them. I do not doubt what the voice said. I bow to dharma, which supersedes everything else. Tell my Dhananjaya all this.

To Bhima, who is always ready for battle, say these words, "The time has come to fulfil the reason for which a Kshatriya woman gives birth to a son. The best men never grieve when a war has to be fought." You know Bhima's heart. That Parantapa will not rest until he has exterminated his enemies.

Krishna, speak next to the beloved Draupadi of great renown, noble Pandu's daughter-in-law, who knows every detail of dharma. Say to her, "Panchali, you are of noble descent and endowed with great fame. You are an exemplary wife to my sons and I bless you."

You must say to the sons of Madri, who always live by Kshatriya dharma, "Treasure that which you acquire by prowess more than life itself. Objects thus won fill the heart of a true Kshatriya with joy. Even while you lived a virtuous life, before your very eyes the Kurus spoke cruel and abusive words to Panchali. Will any Kshatriya worth his name forgive such an insult?

The loss of the kingdom did not distress me nor did the defeat at dice; but to see the noble, beautiful Draupadi weeping in the sabha broke my heart. Alas, she, who is ever devoted to Kshatriya dharma, found no protector then, though her husbands are such powerful men."

O Mahabaho, tell Purushavyaghra Arjuna, that best of warriors, that he should always do as Draupadi says. You know that, when angered, Bhima and Arjuna can send even the Devas to Yamaloka. Was it not an unbearable torment for them to see their wife being dragged into the sabha? Kesava, remind them of the vile things that Dusasana said to her in the presence of all the Kuru warriors.

Ask after the welfare of the Pandavas, Draupadi and their children for me. Tell them that I am well. Now go on your auspicious mission and, precious Krishna, protect my sons,' says Kunti.

Krishna pays homage to her by walking around her in pradakshina, and then the mighty-armed one walks in leonine majesty out of Pritha's apartments. He dismisses the Kurus, who follow him with Bhishma at their head, and, taking Karna with him in his chariot, leaves the Kuru capital accompanied by Satyaki.

And after he leaves, the Kurus gather and discuss what Krishna said and the wonderful vision he showed them. They say, 'Overcome by ignorance, the Earth is caught in death's meshes. Through Duryodhana's folly, everything is doomed.'

Krishna leaves the city and goes on his way, talking at length with Karna, before letting him go and urging his horses to greater speed. With Daruka holding their reins those horses fly with the speed of the mind and flash across the sky, devouring it as they go. Covering the long distance like swift hawks, they arrive at Upaplavya, bearing the wielder of the Saranga," said Vaisampayana.

CANTO 138

BHAGAVAD-YANA PARVA CONTINUED

Vaisampayana said, "When they hear of Kunti's message to her sons, Bhishma and Drona say to the defiant Duryodhana, 'Naravyaghra, did you hear the fiery words that Kunti said to Krishna? Her sons will do as she says, especially as Krishna approves. They will not be pacified until they have their share of the kingdom.

You inflicted untold pain on Draupadi and the sons of Pritha in the sabha. Bound by dharma, at the time they swallowed your savage insults. Now that Yudhishtira has Arjuna, master of the astra shastra, the determined Bhima, the Gandiva and its inexhaustible quivers, Arjuna's chariot that flies the Vanara banner, Nakula and Sahadeva, both blessed with brilliant tejas and awesome might, and Krishna and his allies by his side, the Dharmaraja will be unforgiving.

Duryodhana, you saw for yourself how Arjuna vanquished us in battle outside Virata's city. Dhananjaya, who flies the emblem of Hanuman on his flag, singly annihilated the dreaded Nivatakavachas. Have you forgotten the incident with the cattle, when the Gandharvas routed Karna and seized you and your brothers, whilst you wore armour and rode in your rathas? It was Arjuna who rescued you. Is all this not proof enough for you of what will happen if you go to war against Kunti's sons?

Bharatottama, you and your brothers must make peace with the Pandavas. O save this mother Earth from the apocalypse that looms. Yudhishtira is your elder brother; he is virtuous, affectionate, sweet-spoken and learned. Give up your evil plans and unite with that tiger among men.

If the Pandava sees you put away your bow, and wipe the angry frown from your face and look cheerful, it will bode well indeed for your vamsa. Go to him with your ministers and embrace him as a brother. Pay your respects to him as a king, as you used to, and let Yudhishtira hold you lovingly in his arms.

Let that most terrible warrior Bhima, of the lionish shoulders, mighty thighs and long, powerful arms embrace you. Then let Dhananjaya, of the lotus-petal eyes, wavy hair and conch-like neck greet you respectfully. Let those Purushavyaghras the twins, their beauty unrivalled on Earth, wait on you as their guru, affectionately and reverently. Let all the Kshatriyas with Krishna at their head shed tears of joy.

Divest yourself of pride and reunite with your brothers. Rule the whole Earth with them. Let all the kings embrace one another and joyfully return to their homes. There is no need for war, Duryodhana. Listen to your friends' sage advice, for they warn you that a complete decimation of Kshatriyas will be the only outcome of the war you mean to fight.

The stars are not propitious: animals and birds of ill omen, and all kinds of ominous signs can be seen, particularly in our kingdoms, which portend an unprecedented massacre of Kshatriyas. Meteors fall on your forces; our animals are listless and seem to weep; vultures wheel above our troops. The city and the palace have lost their old appearance and seem sinister. Jackals howl and run in all directions, and fires blaze up everywhere of their own accord.

Listen to your parents and to us, who want only your good. Mahabaho, war and peace both lie within your control. If you ignore the advice of your friends, you will repent when your army is shredded by Partha's arrows. You will remember these words when you hear mighty Bhima's terrible battle cry and the twang of the Gandiva. If you cannot find it in yourself to return to dharma, what we say will inexorably come to pass.'"

CANTO 139

BHAGAVAD-YANA PARVA CONTINUED

Vaisampayana said, "Duryodhana frowns, his eyes glitter and he averts his gaze from his elders, saying not a word in reply. Bhishma and Drona look at each other and address him once more.

Bhishma says, 'What can be sadder for us than to have to fight against Yudhishtira, who is devoted to serving his elders, who has no envy, who knows himself and is truthful?'

Drona says, 'I love Arjuna more than I love my son Aswatthama; and that hero who flies the ape-emblazoned banner reveres me more than my son does. Alas, out of loyalty to the Kuru House, I will have to fight him, who is dearer to me than my son. Fie on Kshatriya dharma. By my grace, there is no archer to equal Arjuna on Earth.

He who hates his friends, he who is sinful, he who denies God and he who is crooked and deceitful never receives the worship of the righteous, like a sacrifice performed by an ignorant man. Though dissuaded repeatedly, a sinful man will still want to continue sinning, while a righteous man will never abandon dharma, even if he is tempted to sin. Though you have been deceitful and vicious to the Pandavas, they still want to do the right thing by you.

O Duryodhana, your sins will bring you to disaster. The Kuru Pitamaha, Vidura, Krishna and I have all spoken to you, but you have not understood what is good for you. Like the Ganga flowing into the ocean, which abounds with sharks, crocodiles, timingalas and giant tortoises, you want to penetrate the Pandava host, which teems with heroes. You enrobe yourself in Yudhishtira's wealth as if it was discarded by him, and you think of it as your own.

Though Pritha and Pandu's son lived twelve years in the forest with Draupadi and his brothers, who, even amongst kings, can vanquish him? Yudhishtira shone in splendour even in the presence of Kubera, to whom all the Yakshas and their kings are servile. The Pandavas went to Kubera's court and obtained immense wealth from there, and now they want to attack your swollen kingdom and take back their sovereignty.

Both Bhishma and I have given gifts, poured libations on the fire, studied the scriptures and gratified Brahmanas by gifts of wealth. Our life on Earth has come to an end. Our work is done. You, however, have much to lose—happiness, your kingdom, friends and wealth—and great will be the catastrophe you face, if you go to war against the Pandavas.

How can you vanquish Yudhishtira when Draupadi, who is ever truthful and devoted to stern vratas and tapasya, prays for his success? How will you overcome that son of Pandu who has Krishna for his mentor, who has Dhananjaya for a brother? How will you defeat that son of Pandu, of the austere tapasya, who has on his side so many greatly intelligent Brahmanas who have mastered their senses?

In the way that a well-wisher would when he sees his friend drowning in an ocean of distress, I tell you again—there is no need of war. Make peace with those heroes for the sake of the prosperity of all the Kurus. Do not court defeat and death, with your sons, allies and our army.'"

CANTO 140

BHAGAVAD-YANA PARVA CONTINUED

"Dhritarashtra says, 'O Sanjaya, in the presence of all the princes and vassals Krishna left the city, taking Karna with him in his chariot. What did he of the immeasurable soul say to Radheya? What pacifying words did Govinda speak to the Sutaputra? Tell me, Sanjaya, whatever Krishna, of the voice as deep as newly formed monsoon clouds, said to Karna, mild or stern.'

Sanjaya says, 'Bhaarata, I will repeat the very words, both intimidating and mild, full of dharma, fraught with truth, beneficial and pleasing to the heart, that Krishna spoke to Radha's son.

Krishna said, "Radheya, you have worshipped many Brahmanas who have perfect knowledge of the Veda. With dhyana, and a mind free of envy, you have frequently sought knowledge from them, and thus you know the eternal truth of the Vedas and the subtleties of the Shastras.

Those who know the Shastras say that sons are of two kinds—kanina and sahoda. Both are born before her marriage to an unwed maiden who later marries their father. You were born in this way, Karna; you are Pandu's son. Be a king, as the Shastras dictate you should. On your father's side you have Pritha's sons for kin, and on your mother's, the Vrishnis. Bharatarishabha, both these families are your own.

Come with me today and let the Pandavas know that you are Kunti's son, born before Yudhishtira was. The five Pandava brothers, Draupadi's five sons and Subhadra's invincible son will all worship at your feet. All the kings and princes, who have gathered for the Pandava cause, all the Andhakas and all the Vrishnis, will do the same. For your investiture, queens and princesses will bring water in gold, silver and earthen jars, aromatic herbs and all kinds of grain, jewels and flowers. Draupadi will be a wife to the six of you.

Let Dhaumya, of the restrained soul, pour ghee on the sacred fire, and let the Pandavas' Brahmanas, for whom the Vedas are the final authority, perform your investiture. Let the Pandavas' family priest, who is devoted to Vedic rites, the five sons of Pandu, all bulls among men, Draupadi's five sons, the Panchalas, the Chedis and me join in installing you as sovereign lord of the Earth.

Let Dharma's son Yudhishtira, of the great soul and stern vows, be your heir apparent and rule the kingdom under your authority. Let him stand behind you in your chariot, holding the white chamara fan. Let Bhimasena hold the royal white parasol over your head. Arjuna will drive your chariot drawn by white horses, adorned with a hundred tinkling bells, its sides covered with tiger-skins. Nakula and Sahadeva, Draupadi's five sons, the Panchalas and that Maharatha Sikhandin will all follow. I with all the Andhakas and the Vrishnis will walk behind you. All the Dasarhas and the Dasarnas will be your kinsmen.

O Mahabaho, enjoy the sovereignty of the Earth with your brothers the Pandavas, with japas and homas and auspicious rites being performed in your honour. Let the Dravidas, the Kuntalas, the Andhras, the Talacharas, the Chuchupas and the Venupas, all walk ahead of you. Let vabdhis and magadhis sing hymns in your praise. Let the Pandavas proclaim, *Victory to Vasusena*!

O Kuntiputra, rule the kingdom surrounded by the Pandavas, like the Moon by the stars, and gladden Kunti's heart. Let your friends rejoice and your enemies tremble. Even today, let there be a union between you and the sons of Pandu, your brothers.'"

CANTO 141

BHAGAVAD-YANA PARVA CONTINUED

"Sanjaya says, 'Karna said, "O Kesava, I have no doubt that you speak out of love, affection and friendship for me, and also because you wish me well. I already know and understand everything you have said.

By descent, as well as by the laws of the Shastras, I know that I am Pandu's eldest son. Before she married Pandu, my mother, while still a virgin, conceived me through intercourse with Surya Deva, and, at his command, abandoned me as soon as I was born. Yes, by dharma I am indeed the firstborn son of Pandu.

Kunti abandoned me without a thought. The Suta, Adhiratha, saw me floating down the river, took me home and gave me to Radha. Her breasts filled with milk out of a mother's love, and she adopted and raised me as her own. How can we, who know dharma and are always listening to scriptures deprive her of her pinda?

Adhiratha, too, looked upon me only as a son and I loved him as my father. It was he who, with a father's love, performed all the samskaras for me from my infancy, as prescribed in the shastras. He had the Brahmanas name me Vasusena. When I grew to be a young man I married the girls my father chose. Through them all my sons and grandsons were born. My heart is bound to them by love. Neither from joy nor fear, neither for all the Earth nor mountains of gold will I break those bonds.

For thirteen years I have enjoyed lordship, without a thorn in my side, under Duryodhana's patronage. At the same time, I have performed the yagnas that being a Suta demands; and all my family rites and marriages were performed in accordance with Suta customs. Knowing that I am loyal to him, Duryodhana has made preparations for war and taken an openly hostile stand against the Pandavas. This is also why I have been chosen to fight Arjuna in the war that will be. O Krishna, I could never be disloyal to Duryodhana, not from fear of death, nor for ties of blood or any temptation at all. If I now withdraw from meeting Arjuna in battle, I will disgrace both myself and him.

I know that you said whatever you did out of love for me. The Pandavas are obedient to you and will do as you say. However, you must keep our conversation to yourself. If Yudhishtira comes to know that I am Kunti's first-born son, he will never accept the kingdom; and if this mighty and burgeoning empire becomes mine, I will give it to Duryodhana.

Let Dharmaraja Yudhishtira become king. He, who has Krishna for his mentor, Dhananjaya and Bhima for his warriors, and Nakula, Sahadeva and the sons of Draupadi by his side, is fit to rule the Earth. The Panchala prince Dhrishtadyumna, that mighty Maharatha Satyaki, Uttamaujas, Yudhamanyu, the prince of Somakas who is devoted to dharma, the ruler of the Chedis, Chekitana, the invincible Sikhandin, the Kekaya brothers whose skin is the hue of indragopaka insects, Bhimasena's uncle Raja Kuntibhoja who has rainbow coloured horses, Maharatha Syenajit, Virata's son Sanka and you yourself, Krishna, are on his side. This assemblage of Kshatriyas is like an ocean. Yudhishtira has as good as already won this radiant kingdom, celebrated among all the kings of the Earth.

Duryodhana is about to perform a great astra yagna, a sacrifice with weapons, of which you, Krishna, will be the Yajaman, as well as the Adhvarya, the head priest. Clad in his coat of mail, Arjuna, who flies the Vanara-emblazoned banner, will be the Hotri, the giver of offerings. His bow Gandiva will be the sruva, the sacrificial ladle, and the prowess of his warriors will be the ghrita he pours. The Aindra, Pasupata, Brahma and Sthunakarna astras he invokes will be the sacrificial mantras. Arjuna and Subhadra's son Abhimanyu, who is equal to, if not more powerful than, his father, will be the hymn that is sung. Mighty Bhima who roars in battle, that destroyer of elephant legions, that Naravyaghra will be the Udgatri, who chants the Veda, and the Prastota, who makes all the preparations, at this yagna. Dharmatma Yudhishtira, who is devoted to the performance of japa and homa, will be the Brahmana of that sacrifice.

The sounds of conches, tabors and drums, and the leonine roars rising into the heavens will be the gong that announces the meal. Madri's two sons Nakula and Sahadeva, of the great renown and strength, will be the slayers of the sacrificial animals. Rows of shining chariots, flying flags of all colours, will be the stakes to which the yagnapasus are tied. Karninas, nalikas, narachas and arrows with heads like calf-teeth will be the spoons used to distribute the Soma rasa; tomaras will be the vessels holding the Soma, and bows will be the pavitras—kusa leaves for pouring ghee.

Swords will be the papalas—the chalices, the heads of slain warriors will be the purodasas—the oblations, and their blood the ghrita. Lances will be the paridhas—the kindling, and bright maces will be the saktis—pokers used to stir the fire. Drona and Kripa's disciples and Saradwat's son will be the Sadasyas—the guests and assisting priests. The arrows shot by Arjuna, by other mighty warriors, by Drona and Drona's son will be the ladles for serving the Soma.

Satyaki will be the chief assistant to you, Krishna, the Adhvarya. Duryodhana will be the Dikshita—performer of this yagna, and his vast army will play the role of his wife. When the evening rites of this yagna begin with the animal sacrifices, mighty Ghatotkacha will be the slayer of the animals. Dhrishtadyumna, who was born from a sacrificial fire, will be the Dakshina—the fee paid to the priest—of the yagna.

I am consumed with remorse for my sin of speaking harsh words to the Pandavas in order to please Duryodhana. Krishna, the moment of my death at Arjuna's hands will mark the commencement of the punaschiti, the second part of the yagna of war. When Pandu's second son Bhima drinks the blood of the roaring Dusasana, only then the part of the yagna when the Soma rasa is drunk will occur.

When the two Panchala princes Dhrishtadyumna and Sikhandin overthrow Drona and Bhishma the yagna will be paused for a while; and when mighty Bhimasena kills Duryodhana the yagna will end. When the wives of Dhritarashtra's sons and grandsons stream onto the battlefield haunted by dogs, vultures and other birds of prey, and weep loudly in mourning with Gandhari for their slain husbands, sons and protectors, then the avabhrita snana, the final bath at the conclusion of the yagna, will take place.

Krishna, I pray you, for your own sake, do not let the old and learned Kshatriyas die miserable deaths. This vast host of Kshatriyas must die honourably by weapons on Kurukshetra, that most sacred of all places in the three worlds. Lotus-leaf-eyed one, somehow enable us to achieve our goal, so that the Kshatriya race may attain Swarga. As long as mountains stand and rivers flow the fame of this sacrifice in blood will last. Brahmanas will recite the Mahabharata, this great war of the Bhaaratas. The fame that they achieve in battle is Kshatriyas' true wealth.

O Krishna, bring Kuntiputra Arjuna before me to fight; and keep our conversation a secret forever."'"

CANTO 142

BHAGAVAD-YANA PARVA CONTINUED

"Sanjaya says, 'Krishna smiled and said to him, "Karna, do you not wish to have the empire in the way I have shown you? Do you not want to rule over the Earth, which I am giving you? The victory of the Pandavas is certain; there is no doubt of that. Arjuna's triumphal banner with the fierce Vanara on it seems to be flying already. The divine illusionist Bhaumana has created it with such enchantment that it stands high, like Indra's banner, and displays on it celestial creatures of forms that symbolise victory. Rising upwards and across for a Yojana, unobstructed by mountains or trees, it blazes like fire. When you see Arjuna in battle on his chariot drawn by white horses, with Krishna as his sarathy; when he looses the astras Aindra, Agneya and Maruta; and when you hear the twang of Gandiva splitting the air like thunder, then all signs of the Krita, the Treta and the Dwapara yugas will disappear. Only the wrath of the Kali will remain.

When you see in battle the invincible Yudhishtira, who is devoted to japa and homa, and who dazzles in brilliance like the Sun, protecting his mighty army and burning the army of his enemies, then all signs of the Krita, the Treta, and the Dwapara yugas will disappear.

When you see in battle the mighty Bhimasena, having drunk Dusasana's blood, dance like a fierce elephant with rent temples that has killed a fearsome antagonist, then all signs of the Krita, the Treta and the Dwapara yugas will disappear.

When you see in battle Arjuna contain Drona, Bhishma, Kripa, Duryodhana and Jayadratha of the Sindhus, all of whom rush to attack him, then all signs of the Krita, the Treta and the Dwapara yugas will disappear.

When you see in battle the two mighty sons of Madri, those Maharathas who shatter enemy chariots into shards, wreak havoc on the armies of Dhritarashtra's sons from the very moment that weapons begin to clash, like a pair of maddened elephants, then all signs of the Krita, the Treta and the Dwapara yugas will disappear.

Karna, go back and tell Drona, Bhishma and Kripa that this month is a delightful one, with an abundance of food, drink and all things salubrious. Plants and herbs are in a season of vigorous growth; the trees are full of fruit, and the flies are gone. The roads are free of slush, the water is sweet and the weather is pleasant, neither hot nor cold.

Seven days from now will be Amavasya, the day of the new moon. Let the battle begin then, for it is Indra's day. Tell all the kings who have come to fight that I will fulfil their cherished desires. All the kings and princes who are with Duryodhana, and who are killed by weapons, will attain Moksha.""'"

CANTO 143

BHAGAVAD-YANA PARVA CONTINUED

"Sanjaya says, 'Hearing Krishna's auspicious words, Karna worshipped him and said, "Knowing everything, why do you still want to confuse me? The destruction of the whole world is at hand because of Sakuni, Dusasana, Duryodhana and me. Certainly, Krishna, a great and fierce war will soon be fought between the Pandavas and the Kurus, which will soak the earth with blood. All the kings and princes who follow Duryodhana will be consumed by the fire of weapons and go to Yama.

Frightful visions and omens appear, making the people's hair stand on end; and they all portend Duryodhana's defeat and Yudhishtira's victory. That fierce planet of dark effulgence, Sanaischara—Saturn—is in opposition to the star Prajapatya, and will bring untold suffering on Earth. The planet Angaraka—Mars—wheels towards the constellation Jyeshta and approaches Anuradha as if seeking friendship, foretelling a great slaughter. Without doubt, Krishna, a terrible calamity for the Kurus is at hand, especially as all the planets oppose the nakshatra Chitra. The Sun spot has changed its position and Rahu approaches Surya to devour him. Meteors, thundering and shaking, fall from the sky.

Elephants trumpet loudly, the horses shed tears and shun food and water. Mahabaho, these omens forecast a great and universal slaughter. In Duryodhana's army the horses, elephants and soldiers, eat little but excrete a lot. Wise men say that these conditions are harbingers of defeat.

The elephants and horses that belong to the Pandavas are all in good spirits and the animals all wheel to the right. These signs augur success. In Duryodhana's army, all the animals move to the left while disembodied voices speak overhead, warning of doom. Auspicious birds—mayuras, hamsas, kraunchas, chatakas, jivajivas and sankhas—follow the Pandavas, while kazhukas, lankas, vakas, hawks, pisachas, jackal packs and swarms of bees follow the Kauravas. The Pandava drums boom without being struck, while those in Duryodhana's camp stay silent even when they are beaten.

Many other signs of defeat manifest themselves in Duryodhana's encampment: water tanks roar like bulls; soldiers are drenched in rains of flesh and blood; misty, ethereal edifices with high walls, deep trenches and imposing entrances suddenly appear, shimmering in the skies over the Kuru camp; and a black ring encircles the Sun. Sunrise and sunset are macabre, and jackals howl hideously at these sandhyas. These omens all foretell defeat.

Bizarre birds, all one-winged, one-eyed and one-legged, screech horribly, also portending defeat. Other ferocious birds with black wings and red legs hover over the Kuru camp at nightfall. Duryodhana's soldiers show hatred for Brahmanas, for their gurus and for all their loyal servants. From Duryodhana's camp the eastern horizon appears red; the south has the hue of weapons; and the west the colour of the Earth; and all the four directions seem ablaze. I know that all these omens augur grave danger.

I had a vision, Krishna, in which I saw Yudhishtira and his brothers climbing to a palace built on a thousand pillars. They all wore white robes and crowns and sat on white thrones. I saw you wrap the blood-dyed earth in an uncanny cover of weapons. Yudhishtira climbed upon a heap of bones and happily ate payasa and ghrita out of a golden cup.

I saw him swallow the Earth, which you handed to him. He will surely rule this Bhumi.

I saw Vrikodara, of fierce deeds, standing on the summit of a mountain with his mace in his hand, and he looked as if he was devouring this world. For sure, he will slay us all in savage battle. I know that victory follows dharma.

I saw Dhananjaya, wielder of the Gandiva, riding with you on the back of a white elephant, and he shone with lustre. I have no doubt, O Krishna, that you will kill all the kings led by Duryodhana in the war that will be.

I saw Nakula and Sahadeva, and that Maharatha Satyaki, adorned with white bracelets, white necklaces, white garlands and wearing white robes. Those tigers among men sat on grand palanquins borne on men's shoulders, with great royal parasols held over their heads. I saw three of Duryodhana's warriors—Aswatthama, Kripa and Kritavarman of the Sattvatas—also clad in white turbans, while all the other kings wore red turbans.

I saw the Maharathas Bhishma and Drona climbing into a carriage drawn by camels, and they rode past Duryodhana and me towards Agastya's kingdom. We shall soon find Yamaloka for ourselves. I have no doubt that all the kings and I, and indeed the entire assemblage of Kshatriyas, will enter the Gandiva fire and die."

Krishna said, "Yes, Karna. If you spurn my advice, the Earth will soon be destroyed. When a pralaya is at hand, adharma assumes the appearance of dharma and lodges itself in the heart."

Karna said, "Krishna, if we emerge alive from this great battle, which will raze numberless heroic Kshatriyas, we might meet here again. Otherwise we shall meet in Swarga and, O Anagha, to me this latter seems the only possibility."

Saying this, Karna clasped Krishna to him in a fervent embrace. With that, he alighted from Krishna's chariot and, riding in his own gold-decked one, the dejected Karna returned here to Hastinapura,' says Sanjaya."

CANTO 144

BHAGAVAD-YANA PARVA CONTINUED

Vaisampayana said, "When Krishna's mission for peace in Hastinapura fails, and after he leaves the Kurus and sets out for the Pandava camp, Vidura comes to Kunti and speaks to her, slowly, in grief.

He says, 'O Jivaputri, mother of living children, you know that I am always inclined to peace, but, although I cry myself hoarse, Duryodhana pays no heed to what I say. Yudhishtira has as allies the Chedis, the Panchalas and the Kekayas; he has Bhima, Arjuna, Krishna, Satyaki and the twins. Despite this he remains in Upaplavya, and out of his love for his kinsmen, still looks to dharma, seeming weak though he is in fact so powerful. Dhritarashtra, though he is old, does not care for peace and, intoxicated with pride in his sons, walks a sinful path.

The evil-mindedness of Jayadratha, Karna, Dusasana and Sakuni has caused this strife between cousins. Their sins against Yudhishtira Dharmaraja will soon fetch nemesis upon us all. Is there anyone who would not be filled with sorrow to see the Kurus persecuting dharma? When Krishna returns without having been able to make peace, the

Pandavas will prepare for war, and the sins of the Kurus will lead to the very race of Kshatriyas being annihilated. My mind is filled with these thoughts and I get no sleep by day or by night.'

Kunti listens to Vidura, who has always wished her sons well and, sighing deeply in grief, she thinks to herself, 'Fie on wealth, for the sake of which this great slaughter of kinsmen is about to take place. In this war friends will slay friends and kinsmen their own blood. What can be sadder than to see the Pandavas, the Chedis, the Panchalas and the Yadavas assembled to fight the Kurus? Ah, I see no benefit whatever in war. On the other hand, if we do not fight, we face poverty and humiliation. Death is preferable to poverty, but the extermination of one's kinsmen is not victory.

As I reflect on this my heart wells with sorrow. That Pitamaha Bhishma, Acharya Drona and Karna are on Duryodhana's side sharpens my fear. Surely Drona will never fight willingly against his pupils. Why does the Pitamaha not show any affection for the Pandavas? That leaves the sinful Karna, who follows the deluded Duryodhana who hates the Pandavas.

Single-mindedly pursuing the ruin of the Pandavas, Karna is powerful indeed. This thought is what most burns me now. I will meet him today and disclose the truth of his birth to him, and try to draw his heart towards the Pandavas.

When I was a maiden in my father Kuntibhoja's antahpura, Durvasa Muni was pleased by the way I looked after him and gave me a boon of mantras. With a trembling heart, I thought of the power of those mantras and what Durvasa said: that they were incantations to summon any Deva I chose. I was just a girl then, and had not attained puberty; and I thought constantly about the mantras. Watched over by my nursemaid and surrounded by my sakhis, not wanting to incur any reproach and wanting to keep my father's honour, I thought long about how I could use the secret mantras without sinning.

Finally, I bowed to the Muni in my mind, and from curiosity and childish folly, I spoke the mantras to invoke Surya Deva into my maidenhood, and that is how Karna was born. Why should this child that I held in my virginal womb not obey me, when what I will say to him is both dharma and beneficial to himself and his brothers?'

After reflecting in this way, Kunti makes a decision. She sets out for the sacred Bhagirathi, and arrives on the banks of the Ganga. There she hears her son chanting slokas from the Veda. Karna stands facing the east with his arms raised above his head. Kunti stands behind him and waits for him to complete his prayers. In the noonday heat Kunti begins to wilt, like a faded lotus garland; she comes closer and stands in the shade cast by awesome Karna's great body.

Karna continues his prayers until his back burns from the Sun's heat and his body radiates lustre. At last, he finishes his worship, lowers his arms and turning round, he is startled to see Kunti. He greets her respectfully, folding his hands together; he bows and speaks gently to her."

CANTO 145

BHAGAVAD-YANA PARVA CONTINUED

"Karna says, 'I am Karna, son of Radha and Adhiratha. Devi, what brings you here? What can I do for you?'

Kunti says, 'You are Kunti's son, not Radha's, and Adhiratha is not your father. Karna, you are not a Suta; believe what I say to you.

You were born to me when I was a girl; I carried you in my womb. My son, you were born in Raja Kuntibhoja's palace. Resplendent Surya Deva, who makes everything visible, is your father. You were born in my father's house, wearing ear-rings and armour that were a part of your body, and you were radiantly beautiful. It is not right that you remain ignorant of who your brothers are and serve Duryodhana. It is a sin. The laws of dharma state that a man's highest duty is to obey and please his father and his mother. His mother is the one who most loves her child.

Evil men have, from avarice, taken Yudhishtira's wealth, which Arjuna won for him. Retrieve it from Dhritarashtra's sons and enjoy that prosperity. Let the Kurus see Karna and Arjuna uniting today in brotherly love; and let the evil ones bow to you. Let yours and Arjuna's names be spoken of in the same breath as Krishna's and Balarama's. If you two are united, what is there in this world that is unattainable?

O Karna, surrounded by your brothers, you will blaze in glory, even like Brahma surrounded by the Devas at a mahayagna. Endowed with every virtue, you are my first born. Let the world no more call you a Sutaputra; you are a Partha—a son of Pritha, and you are a great tejasvin.'"

CANTO 146

BHAGAVAD-YANA PARVA CONTINUED

Vaisampayana said, "When Kunti has finished speaking, Karna hears a voice redolent with love coming from the Sun above. The far away voice is Surya Deva's.

The voice says, 'What Pritha says is true. Karna do as your mother tells you; great good will come of it.'

Though his mother and his natural father have spoken to him, Karna's heart is resolute, for he is devoted to the truth.

He says, 'O Kshatriya Devi, I cannot accept what you say, that to obey you is my highest dharma. Mother, you abandoned me as soon as I was born. This grievous injury not only put my life at risk, but has been detrimental to my achievements and fame. If indeed I am a Kshatriya, you have deprived me of all my rightful samskaras. An enemy could not have done me more harm.

You mercilessly robbed me of the rites of passage that are my birthright, and now you come to demand my obedience. Never until now have you cared about my welfare, as a mother should; and you have come to me today only for your own good. Who is there who would not be afraid of Dhananjaya, who has Krishna as his sarathy? If I go to your sons now, everyone would think that I do so because I am afraid. Nobody knows I am their brother. If this becomes known on the eve of battle, and I join the Pandavas, what would all the Kshatriyas say?

Dhritarashtra's sons have given me everything I want, and they have worshipped me purely from a desire to make me happy. How can I make a mockery of this friendship and render it futile? Even though they have initiated hostilities with others, they have always honoured me and bowed to me, even as the Vasus do to Vasava. They base their confidence that they can conquer their enemies on my might. How can I betray their cherished hope? With me as their boat, they would cross the impassable ocean of war. How can I abandon them, when I am their only refuge?

This is the time when all those who have received patronage and support from Dhritarashtra's sons should show their gratitude and loyalty. I, surely, will fight for them, uncaring of even my life. Sinful, faithless men who, at the time to repay the kindness done to them, turn traitors to those who have fed them and met their every need, are like thieves who steal their master's food. They will not prosper in this world or in the next.

I will not lie to you. For Duryodhana's sake I will fight against your sons, putting forth all my strength and might. At the same time, I will be compassionate, and I will observe my dharma. Therefore, however benevolent your words may be, I cannot obey them. Yet, your pleas shall not be in vain. Other than Arjuna, I will not kill your other sons—Yudhishtira, Bhima and the twins; I will spare their lives even when I hold them in the palm of my hand.

Of all the warriors in Yudhishtira's army, it is with Arjuna alone that I will fight. If I kill Arjuna, I will achieve great renown, and if he kills me, I will yet be covered in glory. Devi, you will always have no less than five sons. Five they will number, either including me, or Arjuna, if I am killed.'

Kunti trembles in grief and embraces her son, who remains resolute, and she says, 'Karna, even if what you say is true, the Kauravas will certainly be killed. Destiny rules supreme. You have sworn you will not harm four of your brothers. Remember this oath when you are in the midst of battle. Be blessed with good health, my son.'

Karna says *Tathaastu*, and they both leave, each in a different direction."

CANTO 147

BHAGAVAD-YANA PARVA CONTINUED

Vaisampayana said, "Krishna returns to Upaplavya from Hastinapura and tells the Pandavas all that has transpired. He confers with them for a long time, and then goes to his own apartments to rest. The Pandavas give leave to Virata and the other kings, and at sunset they say their evening prayers.

With their hearts set on Krishna they think worshipfully of him. At last, they bring Krishna into their midst and deliberate again on what they should do.

Yudhishtira says, 'O you of the eyes like lotus-petals, tell us what you said to Duryodhana in the Kuru sabha when you went to Nagapura.'

Krishna says, 'What I said to Duryodhana in Nagapura was honest, reasonable and benign. But that evil one paid me no heed.'

Yudhishtira says, 'When Duryodhana declared his intention to take the path of sin, what did the Kuru Pitamaha say to the vindictive prince? What did the noble Acharya, the son of Bharadwaja, say? And what did Duryodhana's parents Dhritarashtra and Gandhari say? What did our uncle Vidura, who is the best of all those who know dharma, who grieves for us whom he loves as his own sons, say to Duryodhana? What did all the kings who sat in that ancient court say? Krishna, tell us everything, exactly as it happened.

You have already told us all that Bhishma and Dhritarashtra, as well as the others in that sabha, said to Duryodhana, who believes himself wise, while he is ruled only by lust and greed. But I wish to hear everything again. Lose no time, Krishna, you are our refuge, our lord, our guide.'

Krishna says, 'Rajan, listen to what was said to Duryodhana in the Kuru sabha, and remember the words.

After I had spoken, Duryodhana laughed aloud, at which Bhishma grew incensed and said, "Duryodhana, listen to me for the sake of our vamsa. Then do whatever you think is best for your family.

My father Santanu was famed throughout the world. At first, I was his only son, but he began to wish for another because the wise say that an only son is as good as not having any. He wanted his vamsa to live and his fame to spread. Knowing what he wished for, I made the dark Satyavati my step-mother and swore the most difficult vow, of lifelong celibacy: for my father's sake and for the continuance of our royal line. You know how I could not be king and remain celibate, without breaking my solemn vow. I have no regret; I have lived contentedly, keeping my vrata. My step-mother bore my younger brother Vichitravirya, mighty-armed and handsome supporter of Kuru vamsa.

When my father attained Swarga I installed Vichitravirya as ruler of the kingdom and served him as his subject. Later, I defeated several monarchs at the swayamvara for the daughters of the king of Kasi, and I brought home suitable wives for him. You have heard all this many times.

Sometime after, I fought a duel against my guru Parasurama Bhargava, and my brother fled from fear of Rama and because his subjects deserted him. During this time, he indulged himself entirely in his wives and, because of the time he spent with them, was afflicted by consumption and died. There was anarchy in our kingdom.

Indra did not send us a drop of rain, and the subjects, plagued by fear of hunger, came to me and said, 'Your people are on the point of extinction. Be our king for our good. End this drought, and be blessed, O perpetuator of Santanu's dynasty. Your subjects suffer from fearsome diseases, and very few are left alive. It is incumbent on you to save them, Gangaputra. Put an end to our suffering and rule your subjects with dharma. Let your kingdom not be destroyed even while you live.'

I remained unmoved by their tearful pleas. Remembering dharma, I wanted only to be faithful to my vow. Then, Rajan, the citizens, my stepmother Kali, our servants, priests, acharyas and many learned Brahmanas, all beset with sorrow, begged me to take the throne.

They said, 'While you still live will this ancient kingdom that was once ruled by the illustrious Pratipa go to ruin? Generous one, be the king for our sake.'

I joined my hands together and, filled with anguish, I told them about the vow I had sworn for my father's sake. I told them that it was for the sake of our kingdom, and especially for my step-mother, that I had taken the vow of celibacy and renounced the throne. I begged them not to place the burden of kingship on me.

I joined my hands once more and pacified my step-mother, saying repeatedly, 'Mother, as Santanu's son, and a Kuru, I cannot break my word. I took this vow especially for your sake; and I am your servant and yours to command, my loving mother.'

I placated her and the people, and then she and I begged Mahamuni Vyasa, who was also Satyavati's son from the Rishi Parasara, to father children on my brother's widows. He granted our prayers. The Rishi fathered three sons, Bharatottama: Dhritarashtra, Pandu and Vidura. Your father Dhritarashtra was born blind and he could not be king. Instead, the noble, mighty and celebrated Pandu ruled the Kuru kingdom; he expanded its boundaries immeasurably and the people flourished under his golden reign.

Since Pandu was the king, his sons must rightfully inherit their father's kingdom. Rajan, do not go to war; give them half the kingdom. While I am alive, what other man is fit to reign? Do not disregard what

I say. My only wish is for peace amongst you. I make no distinction between you and them, and love all of you equally.

What I have said to you now is also the opinion of your father, Gandhari and Vidura. One must always pay heed to one's elders; do not ignore what I say. Do not destroy all that you have and the very Earth as well."'"

CANTO 148

BHAGAVAD-YANA PARVA CONTINUED

"Krishna says, 'After Bhishma spoke, Drona, always eloquent, says to Duryodhana in the midst of the assembled kings, "May you be blessed, Duryodhana. Pandu was as devoted to the Kuru vamsa as Pratipa's son Santanu was, and as Devavrata Bhishma is. Pandu was devoted to truth, had his senses under control, was virtuous, practised excellent vratas and was attentive to all his duties in dharma. Although he was king and conqueror, that perpetuator of the Kuru vamsa made over the sovereignty to his elder brother Dhritarashtra, of deep wisdom, and to his younger brother Vidura. After installing Dhritarashtra on the throne, Pandu went to live in the forest with his two wives.

Vidura, in great humility, placed himself under Dhritarashtra's command and waited on him like a servant, fanning him with palm leaves. All the subjects of the kingdom took his lead and submitted to Dhritarashtra just as they had to Pandu.

Having handed the kingdom over to Dhritarashtra and Vidura, Pandu, conqueror of hostile cities, wandered the Earth. Vidura, ever devoted to dharma, took charge of the treasury, and of administering the kingdom and the welfare of its subjects. Bhishma, of the mighty tejas, took charge of the army, of making war and peace, and the giving or withholding of gifts to other kings. All the time that Dhritarashtra has sat on the throne, the noble Vidura stayed near him.

How could you, who have been born in Dhritarashtra's dynasty, even think of creating a rift in the family? Unite with your brothers the Pandavas and enjoy every pleasure. Rajan, I do not say this to you from cowardice or for the sake of wealth. Best of kings, the wealth I enjoy is what Bhishma, and not you, gave me. I do not desire any means of sustenance from you. Where Bhishma is, there Drona must be.

Do what Bhishma has told you. Parantapa, give the sons of Pandu half the kingdom. I was their teacher as much as yours. Indeed, Arjuna is as much a son to me as Aswatthama. But, ah, of what use are speeches? Victory and dharma go together."

Now the virtuous Vidura turned to his uncle Bhishma and, looking him in the face, said, "O Devavrata, pay heed to what I say. When Kuru vamsa was threatened with extinction you revived it. That is why you are now indifferent to my pleas. Duryodhana is a blot on our royal house; and you follow his inclinations, although he is evil, ungrateful, and a slave to greed and lust.

Duryodhana disregards his father's command, which is in keeping with dharma and artha, and the Kurus must face the dire consequences of war. O Maharajan, do what needs to be done so entire house of Kuru is not extinguished. Even as an artist creates a painting, you brought Dhritarashtra and me into this world. The Creator creates beings and destroys them; do not do as he does, for you are not Him. Do not turn away in indifference from the coming extinction of your vamsa, which you see plainly before your eyes. If the imminence of a pralaya of blood has robbed even you of your vision, then take sannyasa in the forest, and take Dhritarashtra and me with you. Otherwise, this very day restrain Duryodhana, who uses deceit as wisdom, and rule this kingdom yourself with the sons of Pandu guarding its boundaries.

Relent, O tiger among Kshatriyas. A great slaughter of the Pandavas, the Kurus and of other mighty kings is about to happen," Vidura said, and he stopped and sighed deeply, his heart overflowing with sorrow.

Then, alarmed at the prospect of the destruction of an entire race, King Subala's daughter Gandhari spoke in anger to her sinful son Duryodhana in the Kuru sabha, words of dharma and artha.

She said, "Let all the kings present in this ancient sabha, the twice-born Rishis and others who have gathered here listen to me proclaim your guilt for the sins that you and your companions have committed. The kingdom of the Kurus is inherited in the proper order of succession. This has always been the custom of our royal line, but you, of evil soul and inhuman deeds, seek to destroy the kingdom. The wise Dhritarashtra now rules the kingdom, with the far-sighted Vidura as his advisor. Why do you want the kingdom for yourself? What is your right to pass them by?

Indeed, Dhritarashtra mahatman and Vidura should both be subordinate to Bhishma while he is alive. Gangaputra Bhishma has foresworn sovereignty for the sake of dharma. That is how Pandu became the king. And only his sons are the true kings today. This vast kingdom rightfully belongs to the Pandavas, and to their sons and grandsons, as their inheritance by the laws of succession.

We must all do as Pitamaha Bhishma says, in accord with Kshatriya dharma and for the sake of our kingdom. In obedience to Bhishma's command, Dhritarashtra and Vidura must declare the same thing, as must everyone who wishes us well, setting dharma above all else. I say let Dharmaputra Yudhishtira, guided by Dhritarashtra and with Bhishma for his mentor, rule this kingdom of the Kurus for many long years.""

CANTO 149

BHAGAVAD-YANA PARVA CONTINUED

"Krishna says, 'Then Dhritarashtra addressed Duryodhana in the midst of the assembled monarchs, saying, "Duryodhana my son, listen to what I say, and may you be blessed. Obey me if you have any respect for your father.

Soma Deva, the lord of creatures, was the original progenitor of the Kuru vamsa. Nahusha's son Yayati was sixth in descent from Soma; and Yayati had five sons who were all Rajarishis. The eldest of them was tejasvin Yadu and the youngest was Puru, from whom we are descended. Puru's mother was Vrishaparva's daughter Sarmishta, and Yadu's mother was Devayani, and thus he was the grandson of Sukra of the immeasurable tejas, who is also called Kavya.

Our ancestor Yadu was mighty, but also arrogant and seized by evil. Intoxicated with his prowess, he humiliated all the Kshatriyas of the world; and disobeyed his father, and insulted his younger brother. Yadu became all-powerful on Earth and, suppressing everyone, he established himself in his capital city, which he named Hastinapura. His enraged father cursed him and expelled him from the kingdom. The furious

Yayati cursed his other sons, too, who were obedient to their arrogant eldest brother. He set his youngest son Puru, who was obedient and devoted to him, on the throne. Thus the eldest son may be passed over and deprived of the kingdom, and younger sons may, because of their reverence towards their elders, inherit the kingdom.

Then there was my great-grandfather Pratipa, who was devoted to dharma and celebrated through the three worlds. This narasimha, this virtuous king, had three sons, all of great renown and like three Devas. Devapi was the eldest, Bahlika was second and my grandfather Santanu, of the scintillating intellect, the youngest. Devapi, who suffered from an ailment to his skin, was endowed with prodigious energy; he was virtuous, truthful, and devoted to the service of his father. Respected and popular among his subjects, loved by young and old, in cities and villages, Devapi was generous, firm in his adherence to dharma, devoted to the good of all creatures and obedient to his father and the Brahmanas. His noble brothers Bahlika and Santanu loved him dearly.

In time, in accord with the shastras, Pratipa began to prepare for Devapi to inherit the throne, and all the arrangements he made were auspicious. However, the Brahmanas and the elders in the kingdom forbade him. Hearing this, the voice of the old king became choked with tears and he began to grieve for his son. Thus, though Devapi was liberal, virtuous, devoted to truth and loved by the subjects, he was deprived of his inheritance because of his sickly skin, for the gods do not approve of a king who has a physical disability. Those best of Brahmanas did not allow Pratipa to enthrone his eldest son as king. Devapi saw how his father grieved for him and took sannyasa in the forest.

Bahlika left his father's city and lived with his maternal uncle, whose rich kingdom he inherited. On Pratipa's death, Santanu took Bahlika's leave and became king. That is why, though I am the eldest, wisely, and after much thought, I was excluded from inheriting the Kuru throne, and, though he was younger than me, Pandu became king.

After his death, Parantapa, our kingdom must pass to his sons. When I could not have the kingdom, how can you want it? You are not the son of the true king and you have no right to this kingdom. Despite that, you want to take what rightfully belongs to another. Dharmatma Yudhishtira is the eldest son of the king and this kingdom is his in dharma. This magnanimous soul is the sovereign lord of our Kuru vamsa.

Yudhishtira is devoted to truth, clear thinking, heedful of the advice of his well-wishers, honest, loved by all his subjects, kind-hearted, master of his passions and a chastiser of criminals and sinners. All the kingly attributes dwell in him: forgiveness, renunciation, self-control, a deep knowledge of the scriptures, compassion and the ability to rule with dharma as his sceptre.

You are not the son of a king, and are always inclined to sin against your own blood. How can ever you appropriate this kingdom that lawfully belongs to another? Dispel this delusion and give away half the kingdom with the proper share of wealth, animals and other possessions and treasures. Then, Duryodhana, you can hope to live a long life with your younger brothers."'"

CANTO 150

BHAGAVAD-YANA PARVA CONTINUED

"Krishna says, 'Although Bhishma, Drona, Vidura, Gandhari and Dhritarashtra spoke to him, the evil one could not be made to see sense. Duryodhana ignored them all and left the sabha, his eyes red with anger. All the kings he had called upon followed him, prepared to lay down their lives for his cause.

Duryodhana said to those kings, "Today the Pushya nakshatra rises. Let us march at once to Kurukshetra!" And, inexorably propelled by destiny, those kings gladly set out with their armies, making Bhishma their Senapati, their Commander-in-chief.

Eleven akshauhinis of troops have assembled on the Kaurava side. At the head of that host, Bhishma shines, flying the flag with the palmyra emblem on his chariot.

In view of all that has happened, do what you think proper, Yudhishtira. I have told you everything that Bhishma, Drona, Vidura, Gandhari and Dhritarashtra said in my presence. I did my very best to establish brotherly feelings between yourselves and your cousins: for the preservation of the race of Kuru and for the survival and prosperity of the Earth's people. When conciliation failed, I used the art of dissent by creating disunity amongst his warriors, and I spoke about all your extraordinary powers and feats.

When Duryodhana showed no interest in my attempts at conciliation, I had all the kings gather together and tried to create dissension amongst them. I showed them strange and terrible manifestations. I rebuked those kings and ridiculed Duryodhana; I terrified Karna and upbraided Sakuni for contriving the game of dice. I tried once more to disunite the kings with intrigue; and again, I resorted to diplomacy. To unite the Kurus, and given the uniqueness of the circumstances, I spoke also of charity.

I said, "As subjects of Dhritarashtra, Bhishma and Vidura, the sons of Pandu will sacrifice their pride. You keep the kingdom; let them not have any power; let it all be as Dhritarashtra, Bhishma and Vidura decide. Let the kingdom be yours. Give just five villages to the Pandavas. Best of kings, the Pandavas deserve your father's support and protection."

That malevolent one would still not yield; Duryodhana said he would not give up even land that would cover the point of a needle. The only method one can use against this evil man is danda, punishment. Why, even as we speak, those kings have already marched to Kurukshetra.

I have told you everything that happened in the Kuru sabha. Pandava, they will not give you your kingdom without battle. Death awaits them, and they have chosen to become the cause of an apocalyptic war that will see the very race of Kshatriyas perish.'"

CANTO 151

SAINYA NIRYANA PARVA

Vaisampayana said, "Dharmaraja Yudhishtira now says to his brothers in Krishna's presence, 'You have heard all that happened in the Kuru sabha; you have understood what Krishna said. Purushottamas, array our troops for battle.

Seven akshauhinis of fighting men have gathered to give us victory. Listen to the names of the seven celebrated warriors who will lead these akshauhinis. They are Drupada, Virata, Dhrishtadyumna, Sikhandin, Satyaki, Chekitana and Bhimasena. These heroes are learned in the Vedas; they are valiant, and they have all practised excellent vratas. They are modest, conversant with politics, Maharathas and masters of mundane weapons and astras of the gods.

Tell us now, Sahadeva, my wise brother, which warrior will be our Senapati? Who will lead our seven akshauhinis in battle, who knows about all the divisions of our forces? And who can withstand Pitamaha Bhishma, who will be an unimaginable fire shooting arrows of flame. Tell us, Narashardula, who you think is capable of being our Commander?'

Sahadeva says, 'Mighty Virata, king of the Matsyas, is closely related to us; he sympathises with our cause; he is powerful, knows dharma, is skilled in weapons and irresistible in battle. We should rely on him to win our kingdom back, for he can surely withstand Bhishma and all the other Maharathas.'

The eloquent Nakula says, 'There is one, who is an elder, who is learned in the Shastras, whose family and birth are impeccable and who is widely revered. He is blessed with modesty, strength and prosperity; he is deeply-versed in all branches of learning; he has studied the astra shastra under Rishi Bharadvaja; he is invincible; he is steadfast in dharma; he boldly challenges Drona and Bhishma; he belongs to one of the foremost royal houses; he is a renowned leader of armies; he resembles a tree of a hundred branches, so many sons and grandsons surround him. Impelled by wrath, this king, with his wife, performed the most arduous tapasya to effect the death of Drona; this Kshatriya is an ornament of any sabha; this bull among monarchs cherishes us as a father would. I speak of our father-in-law Drupada, and he should have full command of our army.

I believe that he will withstand Drona and Bhishma in battle, for he is Drona's peer and as much a master of the devastras as the Acharya.'

After the two sons of Madri express their opinions, Indra's son, Arjuna, his father's equal, says, 'There is a mighty-armed, celestial man, who was born from fire through austere tapasya and Rishis being gratified. He emerged full-grown from a sacrificial fire armed with bow and sword, clad in iron mail and mounted on a chariot, yoked to superb horses, the clatter of whose wheels was as deep as the roar of massed thunderclouds. This Kshatriya is endowed with lionish energy and strength, and leonine are his shoulders, arms and chest; even his voice is like the lion's roar. This splendid hero is handsome with a chiselled face, perfect teeth, round cheeks, long arms, sturdy thighs, large eyes, strong legs and a powerful frame.

This prince, who cannot be pierced by weapons of any kind, and who looks like an elephant with rent temples, is Dhrishtadyumna. He is truthful in speech and has his senses under control; he was born to kill Drona.

It is Dhrishtadyumna who will resist Bhishma's arrows, which look like snakes with fiery tongues and strike with the fierceness of thunderbolts, which are as swift as Yama's dutas and which fall like flames consuming everything they touch, and which so far only Parasurama Bhargava could bear in battle. Rajan, I do not see any man other than Dhrishtadyumna who will withstand Devavrata Bhishma.

Blessed with lightness of hand, a master of every vyuha of war, and accoutred in impenetrable mail, this brilliant Kshatriya is like the lord of a great elephant herd. Only Dhrishtadyumna is fit to be our Senapati.'

Bhima says, 'O king, Rishis and Siddhas have said that Drupada's son Sikhandin was born to kill Bhishma. On the battlefield, with his devastras, he looks like the illustrious Rama himself. I do not see the man who can cleave Sikhandin's kavacha when he stands in his chariot ready for battle. No warrior, other than Sikhandin, can kill Bhishma. I think that only Sikhandin is fit to be our Senapati.'

Yudhishtira says, 'Rajan, Krishna knows the strength and weakness of everything in the universe; he knows the mind of every man here. Be he a Maharatha or not, be he old or young, let Krishna choose the man who will lead my forces. Krishna is the bedrock of our victory or defeat. In him our lives rest, our kingdom, our prosperity or adversity, our happiness or sorrow. He is the Ordainer and Creator; in him dwells the fruition of our endeavours. Yes, let Krishna name the leader of our force.

And let him tell us his choice now, for night draws near. Once Krishna has chosen our Senapati, we will worship that man with offerings of weapons, flowers and perfumes, and then under Krishna's will, we will march into battle.'

The lotus-eyed Krishna looks at Arjuna and says, 'Rajan, I approve of all the powerful warriors that each of you has named to be your Senapati. All of them can withstand your enemies. They can affright Indra himself in battle, let alone the greedy and evil sons of Dhritarashtra.

Mahabaho, for your sake, I made great efforts to prevent the war and bring about peace. We have discharged our duty to dharma. Even the most critical man cannot fault us. Foolish Duryodhana has lost all good sense; he thinks that he is a great Maharatha, and, though weak with sins, imagines he is strong.

Array your troops quickly, for war is the only way to retrieve your kingdom. When they see Arjuna with Satyaki behind him, when they face Abhimanyu and the five sons of Draupadi, and Virata, Drupada and our other mighty kings, all of them lords of akshauhinis, Dhritarashtra's sons will not stand their ground.

Our army is great and invincible; it is inexorable. Our forces will raze Dhritarashtra's legions. And for our Senapati, I name Parantapa Dhrishtadyumna.'"

CANTO 152

SAINYA NIRYANA PARVA CONTINUED

Vaisampayana said, "When Krishna has spoken, all the kings are filled with joy and shout out their delight. The troops swiftly begin to array themselves, calling out *Draw up! Draw up!* The air is filled with the whinnying of horses, the trumpeting of elephants, the rumble of chariot wheels, the blare of conches and the booming of drums, making a tremendous din. The Pandava host teems with chariots, foot-soldiers, horses and elephants; and the invincible Pandava warriors bustle, putting on their armour and shouting battle-cries; and they look like the turbulent Ganga in spate, churning with fierce eddies and waves.

At the van of the army march Bhimasena, Madri's two sons, Subhadra's son, Draupadi's five sons and Dhrishtadyumna of the Prishata vamsa. Behind Bhimasena march the Prabhadrakas and the Panchalas. The joyous roar made by the marching hosts is like the boom of the sea at high tide on a new moon night. Such is the tumult that it seems to reach the heavens, as those warriors march in joy.

Kuntiputra Yudhishtira marches with them, accompanied by his chariots and other conveyances to transport food, fodder for the animals, tents, carriages, draught animals, treasury-chests, war-machines and weapons, surgeons and physicians, even invalids and weak soldiers, attendants and camp-followers.

Panchali remains in Upaplavya with the noblewomen of the household, and surrounded by her servants and maids. To protect them and safeguard their treasures, soldiers are posted in a circle around them and more men in a vigilant, mobile outer ring. The Pandavas are ready to set out with their awesome host. First they give gifts of cattle and gold to the Brahmanas, who walk around them and utter blessings; and then the sons of Pandu march, riding in jewelled chariots.

Behind Yudhishtira march the Kekaya princes, Dhrishtaketu, the prince of Kasi, Sreniman, Vasudana and the invincible Sikhandin, all men in their prime, wearing shimmering armour, bearing weapons and glittering with rich jewels. Bringing up the rear are Virata, Dhrishtadyumna the son of Yajnasena of the Somakas, Susarman, Kuntibhoja, Dhrishtadyumna's sons, forty-thousand chariots, five times as many horsemen, foot-soldiers numbering ten times as many as those, and sixty-thousand elephants[2]. Anadhrishti, Chekitana, Dhrishtaketu and Satyaki ride in formation around Krishna and Arjuna.

Those warriors arrive at the field of Kurukshetra in battle-array and, like a herd of bellowing bulls, the Parantapas blow their conches; Krishna and Dhananjaya sound theirs as well. The Pandava army hears the thunderous boom of the Panchajanya and rejoices. The Earth, the skies and the oceans resound with the leonine roars of those warriors, mingled with the blare of conches and drum beats.'"

---

[2] The actual numbers should far exceed these, given the composition of an akshauhini.

CANTO 153

SAINYA NIRYANA PARVA CONTINUED

Vaisampayana said, "Yudhishtira orders his troops to set up camp on a part of the field that is flat, cool and rich in fodder and fuel to burn. At this delightful, fertile and auspicious site, where no cemeteries, temples, shrines, asramas or other sanctified places will be violated, Yudhishtira establishes his camp.

After the animals have rested, the Pandava monarch rises and, surrounded by hundreds of thousands of kings, stands forth in joy that this hour is upon them. Krishna and Arjuna range the perimeters of the field, putting to flight hundreds of Dhritarashtra's soldiers posted there as sentries. Dhrishtadyumna and Satyaki supervise the measurement of the camp boundaries. Krishna orders the soldiers to dig a moat around the camp and to fill it by diverting the clear, pure water of the sacred lake Hiranvati, where a holy asrama is located, and whose bed is free of sludge and pebbles. He has soldiers stationed there as guards. Krishna instructs the other kings who are Yudhishtira's allies to establish their camps and erect their tents, exactly as the Pandavas have done.

Lakhs of rich and impregnable tents are put up, separately for each of the kings; and they look like palaces, replete with food, drink and fuel to cook and warm the nights. Hundreds of skilled and experienced workmen are engaged in creating and fortifying the camp; surgeons and physicians, experts in their fields, are provided with everything they might need. In special pavilions, veritable mountains of bows and bow-strings, armour, weapons, honey, ghee, powdered lac, water, cattle-feed, chaff, coal, heavy machines, spears, lances, battleaxes, breast-plates, swords and quivers are heaped. Countless war elephants covered in armour and spiked mail, giant tuskers that can crush lakhs of fighting men, are tethered to iron stakes and pillars.

O Bhaarata, when they learn that the Pandavas have camped on that field, numerous other kings arrive from their respective kingdoms, with their legions and animals, to support the sons of Pandu. Many of the kings who come to ensure the Pandavas' success have practised strict brahmacharya, imbibed consecrated Soma rasa and have given generous gifts to Brahmanas at yagnas."

CANTO 154

Sainya Niryana Parva continued

Janamejaya said, "What measures does Duryodhana take when he hears that Yudhishtira has come with his army and set up camp on Kurukshetra, ready for battle under Krishna's protection, supported by Virata and Drupada with their sons, surrounded by the Kekayas, the Vrishnis and numberless other kings, and by countless mighty Maharathas, and looking like glorious Indra surrounded by the Adityas?

O Mahatman, I want to hear in detail all that happened in Kurujangala on that horrific occasion. The son of Pandu, with Krishna, Virata, Drupada, the Panchala prince Dhrishtadyumna, the Maharatha Sikhandin and the mighty Yudhamanyu, whom even the gods cannot withstand, could strike fear into the hearts of all the Devas with Indra at their head. O you of tapodhana, tell me everything that the Kurus and the Pandavas did, just as it happened."

Vaisampayana said, "When Krishna leaves the Kuru sabha, Duryodhana says to Karna, Dusasana and Sakuni, 'Kesava has gone to the sons of Pritha, without fulfilling his goal. He is furious and will stir up the Pandavas. He is anxious to see a war between me and Pandavas, and Bhimasena and Arjuna are of the same mind. Yudhishtira, who has no animosity, is influenced by Bhimasena and, besides, I have indeed persecuted him and his brothers. Virata and Drupada, against whom I have fought, are obedient to Krishna, and both have become leaders of Yudhishtira's forces. The war will be savage and terrible.

With meticulous care and heedfulness, make preparations for war. Let all the kings who are my allies pitch their thousands of tents on Kurukshetra. Their tents must be large, well protected and within easy reach of plentiful water and fuel; their camps should be in positions where the enemy cannot sever communications and supplies between them; they must be stocked with a plenitude of all kinds of weapons and adorned with streamers and flags. Have the road from our capital levelled in preparation for the march of our armies. Make a proclamation today, at once, that we will set out tomorrow.'

Saying *Tathaastu*, those great warriors make arrangements for the kings, who hear Duryodhana's command and rise from their thrones, now focusing their Kshatriya wrath on the enemy.

The kings massage and flex their mace-like arms that dazzle with gold bracelets and are smeared with sandalwood paste and daubed with fine perfumes. With their lotus-like hands, they tie their turbans, fasten their upper and lower garments and put on their ornaments. Maharathas supervise the equipping of their chariots; syces harness the horses; mahouts prepare the elephants. The warriors don kavachas made of gold and arm themselves with every sort of weapon. Foot-soldiers pick up their weapons and put on their gold-inlaid armour. And, O Bhaarata, Duryodhana's capital city Hastinapura, filled by these jubilant warlike millions, looks festive.

With the excitement of impending battle, the city swells like the ocean at high tide; the vast crowds of the people are its current; the chariots, elephants and horses are its fish; the tumult of conches and drums is the ocean's roar; the treasure chests are the jewels on the ocean floor; the warriors' ornaments and armour are its waves and their shining weapons are its surf; the rows of houses are the mountains on the shore;

and the masses of chariots are the lakes on the sea bed.

His warriors shine on Duryodhana like the Moon over the ocean, making him look like the ocean at moonrise."

CANTO 155

SAINYA NIRYANA PARVA CONTINUED

Vaisampayana said, "Yudhishtira remembers what Krishna said, and says to him, 'O Krishna, how could Duryodhana say what he did? Ever glorious one, what should we do? How shall we conduct ourselves so we do not swerve from Kshatriya dharma?

You know how Duryodhana, Karna and Sakuni think, and you know my brothers' and my mind as well. You have heard what Vidura and Bhishma said, as well as Kunti's wise message to us. But set all that aside, and you tell us unequivocally, Krishna, what is best for us.'

In a voice that booms as deeply as thunderclouds, or great drumbeats, Krishna says, 'What I said to Duryodhana in his sabha was to his advantage and in keeping with dharma and artha, but I got no response from the Kuru prince, whose wisdom has been replaced by delusion and deceit. That sinner does not pay the slightest heed to Bhishma, Vidura or to me. He relies just on Karna, and assumes he has already won the war.

Black-hearted Duryodhana even wanted to make me his captive, but he did not succeed. Neither Bhishma nor Drona said anything about that; and all, except Vidura, follow Duryodhana's lead.

Subala's son Sakuni, Karna and Dusasana, all equally foolish, constantly give Duryodhana evil counsel about what he should do. Is there any use in my repeating everything that Duryodhana said? Suffice it to say that the wretch bears you nothing but ill will. More sinfulness resides in Duryodhana's black heart than in all the kings and all the men in your army put together. As for us, we do not want to make peace with the Kauravas at the cost of losing what is ours. Yudhishtira, war is the only course open to you.'

All the kings hear Krishna and wordlessly look at Yudhishtira, who understands their silence and quietly tells Bhima, Arjuna and the twins to see that their forces are arrayed for battle. His command passes around like light, and a great tumult rises in the Pandava host and fills the warriors with joy. Yudhishtira, however, sighs, seeing in his mind's eye the impending massacre of the undeserving.

He says to Bhima and Arjuna, 'I went into exile in the forest and suffered to avoid the very calamity that now overtakes us. The thing that we strove for so intensely slips out of our grasp even as if because of our striving for it. Instead, Kali Yuga comes to us uninvited. How are we going to fight against our revered elders, whom we must not kill for any reason whatever? What kind of victory shall we achieve by slaying our acharyas?'

Seeing Yudhishtira's mood, Arjuna repeats everything Krishna has said, and he says to his brother, 'Rajan, you know and understand what Kunti and Vidura said, which Krishna also affirms. I am certain that neither Vidura nor Kunti would say anything that is adharma or sinful. Kuntiputra, we cannot turn away from war.'

Krishna vouchsafes what Arjuna says, and then, O Rajan, with their soldiers, Pandu's sons pass the night in some hope, and even happiness, their minds now resolved on war."

CANTO 156

Sainya Niryana Parva continued

Vaisampayana said, "When the night has passed, Duryodhana deploys his army of eleven akshauhinis, in proper order. He divides men, elephants, chariots and horses into three classes, superior, medium and inferior, and sets them in the front, middle and rear of his ranks.

Well equipped and cared for is Duryodhana's army: it has timber and wooden planks for repairing damage to the chariots in the battle; large containers of tiger-skins and other stiff leathers to encase the sides of the chariots; and barbed javelins. Elephants and horses carry quivers full of iron spears, and foot soldiers carry heavy wooden clubs. Flagstaffs fly vivid banners; long, heavy arrows for bows are heaped in hillocks, as are all sorts of nooses and lassoes, armour of many kinds and in every size, and short, sharp clubs made of wood. Oil and sand; earthen pots filled with poisonous snakes, pulverised lac and other inflammable materials; short spears with tinkling bells; weapons of iron and machines for hurling hot oil, water and stones; whistling hardwood clubs, wax, heavy mallets, spiked clubs, plough-poles and poisoned arrows: all these are stocked in plenty. Long syringes for spraying hot oil over the enemy, planks of cane, battle-axes, forked lances, spiked gauntlets, axes and pointed iron-spikes; chariots whose sides are covered with tiger- and leopard-skins; razor-sharp discs, horns and every other weapon imaginable; kuthara axes, spades, cloths soaked in oil and ghee: these, too, are stocked in endless store.

Handsome warriors glitter in their gold embroidered battle-dress; they are radiant in jewels and gemstones. Kshatriyas of noble birth, in glittering kavacha, all master horsemen, swordsmen and archers, ride in splendid chariots, which carry stores of potent medicaments for wounds and are drawn by horses that have rows of bells and pearls on their heads; they fly fine banners on towering, richly ornamented flagstaffs; they bear loads of shields, swords, spears, slender javelins that can be flung far and spiked maces. Each ratha is yoked to four pedigreed horses; each carries a hundred bows; and each has one sarathy for the pair of horses in front, and two for the horses yoked to the wheels on either side; and all three charioteers are men of the highest skill. These chariots, numbering thousands, protected even like fortified towns and unassailable, are positioned on all sides.

The elephants, too, are decked with rows of bells, pearls and other ornaments; on their backs each mighty beast carries seven warriors and, so, look like jewelled hills. Two of the warriors are armed with hooks, two are archers, two are expert swordsmen, and one is armed with a lance and trident. Duryodhana's army teems with countless war-elephants, which bear loads of weapons and quivers filled with arrows, and all the great beasts are devastating in battle.

Thousands of richly caparisoned horses fly their heroic riders' flags. Hundreds of thousands of these well-broken and superbly trained steeds stand patient and docile before the war, neither restive nor whinnying in any excitement, though knowing full well why they are here.

Hundreds of thousands of foot-soldiers of diverse races, wearing golden ornaments and armour of diverse hues and kinds, armed with a variety of weapons, have all come as part of the eleven teeming akshauhinis. Every chariot is protected by ten elephants, every elephant by ten horses and every horse by ten foot-soldiers. A large force is kept to regroup broken ranks, and this reserve force has countless chariots each with fifty elephants surrounding it; one hundred horsemen, and seven foot-soldiers follow each horse.

One sena consists of five hundred chariots, five hundred elephants, one thousand five hundred horses and two thousand five hundred foot-soldiers. Ten senas make a pritana, and ten pritanas make a vahini. In common parlance, however, the words sena, vahini, pritana, dhwajini, chamu, akshauhini and varuthini are used in the same sense.

The brilliant Duryodhana arrays his force in this manner, and, between the two sides there are eighteen akshauhinis, with seven in the Pandava army and eleven for the Kauravas.

Two hundred and fifty men make a patti. Three pattis make a senamukha or gulma. Three gulmas make a gana. In Duryodhana's army, there are hundreds and thousands of such ganas of able warriors, all impatient for battle. Duryodhana selects from among them the bravest, most intelligent men and makes these the leaders of his troops. He places an akshauhini of troops under each of those Purushottamas—Kripa, Drona, Salya, Jayadratha the king of the Sindhus, Sudakshina of the Kambojas, Kritavarman, Drona's son Aswatthama, Karna, Bhurisravas, Subala's son Sakuni and the mighty Bahlika. The king summons them every day and at all hours, looks after them himself, talks to them and honours them personally, making them and their followers eager to please him."

CANTO 157

SAINYA NIRYANA PARVA CONTINUED

Vaisampayana said, "With all his allied kings gathered round, Duryodhana, with folded hands, says to Bhishma, 'Without a great Senapati, even the mightiest army can be crushed in battle like a swarm of ants. Two intelligent men will have different opinions and are often jealous of each other's prowess.

Wise one, I have heard the story of how, once, the Brahmanas, fighting under a banner of Kusa grass, clashed with the mighty Kshatriyas of the Haihaya clan. Pitamaha, the Vaisyas and the Sudras followed the Brahmanas, so that three varnas were on one side with the Kshatriyas alone on the other. In the battles that ensued, the Kshatriyas vanquished the combined force of the three varnas. The Brahmanas asked the Kshatriyas to explain how this had happened.

The truthful ones among the Kshatriyas said to them, "In battle we obey the orders of one man blessed with great intelligence, while your forces are not united, but each follow different paths."

The Brahmanas made one amongst themselves as their Senapati, a man who was brave, a skilled tactician and diplomat, and they vanquished the Kshatriyas. Those who appoint a seasoned, courageous, wise and sinless man, devoted to the good of his men, always win battles.

You are equal to Usanas himself, and always look to my welfare; you are invincible and devoted to dharma. Pitamaha, you be our Senapati. You shine amongst us like the Sun among the planets, like the Moon over fragrant herbs, like Kubera among the Yakshas, like Indra among the Devas, like Meru among mountains, like Suparna among birds, like Kumara among the Devas, like Havyavaha among the Vasus. If you protect us, as Sakra protects the Devas, even the gods will not be able to defeat us. Ride at the head of our forces, as Agni's son Kumara leads the Devas; we will follow you like calves behind a mighty bull.'

Bhishma says, 'Mahabaho, what you say might be true, but the Pandavas are as dear to me as you are and, although I will fight on your side because I have given you my word, I must be mindful of their welfare as well. There is no warrior on Earth who is my equal, except Arjuna. He is brilliant, and is a great master of the devastras, but he will never engage me in open war.

With all the astras I command I can destroy this universe of Devas, Asuras, Rakshasas and Manavas in an instant, but Pandu's sons are invincible, even by me. But every day I will kill ten thousand enemy warriors and denude the Pandava forces, as long as I am not killed in battle.

Then, there is one more condition that you must fulfil before I accept the command of your forces. Either Karna or I shall fight, but not both together. The Sutaputra always boasts and compares his prowess with mine.'

Karna says, 'O king, as long as Gangaputra Bhishma lives I will not fight. After he is killed, I will fight Arjuna.'

Duryodhana makes Bhishma the Senapati of all his army and distributes generous gifts all round. Installed in his command, Bhishma blazes in splendour. The king orders musicians to joyfully beat drums and sound the conches in their hundreds of thousands. Loud roars of soldiers and the sounds of their animals fill the air. From the cloudless sky bloody showers rain down, soaking the ground; whirlwinds and earthquakes shake the Earth; horses whinny in fear, elephants trumpet, and the soldiers' hearts tremble in dread. Ethereal voices are heard, and falling meteors flash across the sky; jackals howl hideously, foretelling a great cataclysm. A hundred other dreadful omens appear at Bhishma's installation as the Senapati of Duryodhana's army.

Duryodhana gives an abundance of cattle and gold to Brahmanas and asks for their blessings. Basking in their benedictions and surrounded by his troops, with Bhishma in front and his brothers alongside him, Duryodhana marches to Kurukshetra with his immense host. He inspects the plain with Karna and decides to camp on a level field, a pleasant and fertile place, rich in grass and firewood, and it dazzles with that awesome force of men, their armour, ornaments, gold and weapons, like Hastinapura."

CANTO 158

SAINYA NIRYANA PARVA CONTINUED

Janamejaya said, "When Yudhishtira hears that Ganga's mahatman son Bhishma, first among Kshatriyas, Pitamaha of the Bhaaratas, foremost of all regents, and Brihaspati's equal in wisdom, deep as the ocean in character, calm and unshakable as Himavat, like Brahma himself in nobility, like the Sun in tejas; Bhishma who razes whole armies single-handedly, even as Indra does, has been made Senapati of the Kaurava army on the eve of the horrific war to be, the prospect of which makes the hair on men's bodies stand on end, until death strips him of the command, what did Pandu's mighty-armed son, Yudhishtira Dharmaraja say? What did Bhima and Arjuna say? And what did Krishna say?"

Vaisampayana said, "When the news reaches him, Yudhishtira calls his brothers and Krishna to him.

He says calmly, 'Make your rounds among the men and take precautions by putting on your armour. Our first encounter will be with our Pitamaha. Inform the leaders of our seven akshauhinis.'

Krishna says, 'Bharatarishabha, let it be as you say. I approve. Let us summon the seven lords of our akshauhinis'

Yudhishtira summons Drupada, Virata, Satyaki bull of the Sini vamsa, Dhrishtadyumna prince of the Panchalas, Dhrishtaketu, Sikhandin, and Sahadeva lord of the Magadhas, all of whom are eager for battle. Dhrishtadyumna, born from a sacrificial fire, is Senapati of the Pandava forces, the Panchala prince born to kill Drona. Yudhishtira sets Arjuna, of the curly hair, at the head of the other seven commanders, and gives Krishna charge of being Arjuna's sarathy and guide.

Upon learning that the war of the age is at hand, many other kings come to the Pandava encampment to support them: Halayudha with Akrura, Gada, Samba, Uddhava, Rukmini's son Pradyumna, Ahuka's sons, Charudeshna and more. Mighty-armed and handsome Balarama arrives, surrounded by the foremost Vrishni warriors, who resemble a herd of mighty tigers, and he looks like Indra in the midst of the Maruts. He arrives in his lion's gait, wearing his customary blue silken robes, the corners of his eyes red from drink, and looking like the peak of Mount Kailasa.

Dharmaraja Yudhishtira, Krishna of matchless effulgence, Vrikodara of terrible deeds, Arjuna wielder of Gandiva and all the other kings there rise from their places and offer worship to Balarama; and Yudhishtira touches his hands lovingly in greeting. Rama, in return, greets them all, with Krishna at their head and, respectfully saluting Virata and Drupada, he sits beside Yudhishtira on the same seat.

After the other kings have resumed their seats, Rohini's son Rama looks at Krishna and begins to speak.

He says, 'This great and brutal slaughter is inevitable. It is fate's decree, and it cannot be averted. I hope to see all of you, with your friends, come safely and uninjured out of this war. Without doubt, all the Kshatriyas of the world who are assembled here have reached the end of their days. This war without precedent, this war like no other will cover the Earth with flesh and blood.

Many times I said to Krishna, "Madhusudana, be impartial to all that are related to us in the same way. As are the Pandavas to us, so is Duryodhana. Give Dhritarashtra's son the same help you do Yudhishtira.

Indeed, he always asks for it."

However, for your sake, Krishna ignored what I said. For Arjuna's sake, he has devoted himself entirely to your cause. I am certain that a Pandava victory is what he wants. As for me, I dare not face the world without Krishna by my side. That is why I aspire to whatever Krishna seeks to achieve. However, Bhima and Duryodhana are both my disciples and I love them equally. Hence, I will go to the tirtha of the Saraswati to bathe, for I cannot be indifferent to the slaughter of the Kauravas.'

Mahabaho Balarama takes leave of the Pandavas and, preventing Krishna from following him, sets out on his journey to the sacred river."

CANTO 159

SAINYA NIRYANA PARVA CONTINUED

Vaisampayana said, "At this time, there comes to the Pandava camp Bhishmaka's son Rukmi, one of the most truthful men in the world. The Rajarishi Bhishmaka, also named Hiranyaroman, is Indra's friend; he is the most illustrious of the descendants of Bhoja; and he is the ruler of the whole southern country. Rukmi was a disciple of that lion among the Kimpurushas, Drona, who lived on Gandhamadana Mountain. He learnt the entire astra shastra of four divisions from his guru, and also obtained the celestial bow Vijaya, which once belonged to Indra, and which is as powerful as the Gandiva and Krishna's Saranga.

Three celestial bows were owned by the lords of heaven: Varuna owned the Gandiva, the Vijaya belonged to Indra, and Vishnu the Saranga; all of them struck fear in the hearts of enemy warriors. Indra's son Arjuna had the Gandiva from Agni after he burnt down Khandava Vana, and Rukmi had the Vijaya from Drona. Krishna obtained the Saranga when he baffled the Asura Mura's paasas, deadly nooses, slew that demon, and then vanquished Bhumi's son Naraka Asura to recover Aditi's jewelled earrings, sixteen thousand exquisite women and various jewels and gems of beauty and power.

Rukmi, who has the Vijaya, whose twang is like the roar of thunderclouds, comes to the Pandavas, and fills the universe with dread.

The heroic Rukmi was arrogant of his might and, unable to tolerate Krishna's abduction of his sister Rukmini during her swayamvara, he set out in pursuit, swearing that he would not return to his city without killing Krishna. With a large army of four kinds of forces, clad in beautiful mail and armed with every kind of weapon, and looking like the swollen Ganga, Rukmi went after Krishna.

When he overtook Krishna, despite the power of every punya that tapasya can possibly confer, Rukmi was routed. In shame, he did not to return to his capital Kundina, but built a great new city for himself in the very place where Krishna vanquished him, and he called it Bhojataka. He filled the city with innumerable soldiers, elephants and horses, and it became renowned throughout the world.

Now, this great Kshatriya and tejasvin enters the Pandava camp clad in mail, bearing many bows, lances, swords and quivers, and with an akshauhini of troops. He marches with his vast army under a flag as bright as the Sun, and comes haughtily before the Pandavas, expressing his wish to serve under Krishna's command. Yudhishtira comes forward and pays his respects, and the Pandavas worship him and praise him. He salutes them in return and rests for a while with his troops.

Then he addresses Arjuna grandly in the presence of the assembled Kshatriyas, saying 'If, Panduputra, you are afraid, I am here to support you in battle. Your enemies will not withstand me. No man in this world is my equal in prowess. I will slay whichever of your enemies you ask me to. I will kill Drona, Kripa, Bhishma or Karna. Let all the kings who are here step aside; I will annihilate all your enemies myself and make a gift of the Earth to you.'

When Rukmi says this in the presence of Yudhishtira, Krishna, their allied kings and all the others in the camp, Arjuna looks at Krishna and Yudhishtira and replies, smiling, 'Having been born into the Kuru vamsa, and especially being a son of Pandu; having had Drona for my guru and having Krishna for my ally; and having the bow Gandiva for my weapon, how can I be afraid?

O Kshatriya, when I fought the mighty Gandharvas to free Duryodhana, who was there to help me? When countless Devas and Danavas united against me in Khandava vana, who fought by my side? When I fought the Nivatakavachas and the Kalakeyas, who was my ally? When I fought countless Kurus outside Virata's city, who helped me in battle?

I, who have paid due obeisance to Rudra, Sakra, Vaisravana, Yama, Varuna, Pavaka, Kripa, Drona and Krishna before going to war; I, who wield the Gandiva; I, who have twin quivers that well with inexhaustible arrows and all the devastras to command, how can a man like me say to my father Indra, who wields the Vajra, words of shame: that I am afraid? Mahabaho, I am never afraid, nor have I any need of your help. Go away or stay; do as you please.'

Rukmi takes his ocean-like army and goes to Duryodhana. He says the same thing to Duryodhana, but that proud king spurns him scornfully, as the Pandavas did. Thus, two great Kshatriyas take no part in the war on Kurukshetra—Balarama and Rukmi.

After Rohini's son Rama has set out on his tirtha-yatra, after Bhishmaka's son Rukmi has left, the sons of Pandu sit together once more in consultation. Yudhishtira presides over this meeting attended by many kings, and that conclave dazzles like the sky spangled with stars with the Moon in their midst."

CANTO 160

SAINYA NIRYANA PARVA CONTINUED

Janamejaya said, "O Brahmanarishabha, after the troops have been arrayed on Kurukshetra, what did the Kauravas do, impelled as they were by destiny?

Vaisampayana said, "O Bharatarishabha, when his troops have been arrayed, Dhritarashtra says to Sanjaya, 'Come, Sanjaya, and tell me in the fullest detail all that is happening in the Kuru and Pandava camps. I am convinced that destiny reigns over effort, for, although I understand that this war will lead only to ruin, I cannot restrain my son, who rejoices in gambling and considers deceit to be wisdom. I understand all this, yet I can do nothing to prevent the slaughter that will be.

O Suta, I clearly see my son's defects, but when I am with him my mind turns away from dharma. Sanjaya, what will be must be. To sacrifice of one's body in battle is the duty of every Kshatriya, and it is praiseworthy.'

Sanjaya says, 'What you say is true, but you cannot blame Duryodhana entirely. Listen to me, O king.

The man who comes to evil because of his own sins can never impute the fault to either time or the gods. The man who perpetrates great evil deserves to die. The sons of Pandu silently bore all the injuries inflicted on them during the game of dice, looking only to you for refuge, which you denied them.

Let me tell you now, Rajan, of the general carnage that stalks us close, the bloody massacre of horses, elephants and kings of measureless tejas. Listen patiently, wise one, to the destruction of the world as we know it that this war of wars will inexorably fetch; and the only conclusion you can come to is that man is never the agent of what he helplessly does, right or wrong.

Like a wooden puppet, man is not the doer. However, there are three differing opinions about this. Some say that God ordains everything; some say that we act out of free will; and some say that all our actions are a result of our past lives. Now hear about the evil that is upon us.'"

CANTO 161

ULUKA DUTA GAMANA PARVA

"Sanjaya says, 'Rajan, after the great-souled Pandavas established their camp by the Hiranvati, the Kauravas too set up theirs. Duryodhana deployed his troops; he paid homage to all the kings on his side; he set up outposts and deployed soldiers in these to protect the camp. Then he summoned Karna, Dusasana and Sakuni. First he consulted with Karna and next with his brother Dusasana and Sakuni together. He summoned Uluka and spoke to him privately.

He said to Uluka, "O Uluka, you are the son of a master of dice. Go now to the Pandavas and Somakas and repeat what I say to Yudhishtira, in Krishna's hearing.

Say to him, 'The long awaited war between the Kurus and the Pandavas is at last upon us. The time has come, Kuntiputra, to make good the boasts you roared out with your brothers and Krishna, which Sanjaya repeated to me in the Kuru sabha. Now let us see you actually do everything you so glibly said you would.

How does your virtuous character allow you, with your brothers, the Somakas and the Kekayas, to fix your heart on a sinful war? How can you want the destruction of the very world when you should be the dispeller of all people's fears?

O Bharatarishabha, this is the sloka, which Prahlada chanted when the gods took his kingdom from him: *O Devas, the man who always flies the flag of dharma, whose sins are hidden, is like the cat in this story.* Listen to that excellent story Narada told my father.

O king, long ago, a wicked cat began to live on the banks of the Ganga, sitting still and with his arms raised above his head in the way of a tapasvin. Wanting to lull the other creatures there into trusting him, he announced that he had indeed begun to practice tapasya and had purified his heart. In time, the birds in that place trusted him and came to praise him. Seeing the feathered ones come to worship him, the cat, bird-eater that he was, considered the reason for his tapasya already accomplished.

Time passed, and mice began to come there as well, and they too saw him as a virtuous creature practising tapasya. Firmly convinced of the cat's virtue, they, who had many enemies, decided to make the cat their matulan, their maternal uncle, and ask his protection for the young and old of their kind.

They went to the cat and said, "With your grace, we want to live our lives happily and without fear. You are our friend, and we place ourselves under your protection. You are devoted to dharma and always engaged in acquiring punya. Wise One, protect us in the same way as Indra Vajradhari does the Devas."

The cat answered the mice, "I do not see how my tapasya and this protection you ask for are connected. However, I am your well-wisher and I cannot refuse what you ask. All of you must obey me and do what I say. My tapasya has weakened me I and cannot move from where I sit. Everyday, you must carry me to the river for my ablutions."

The mice agreed and sent all their old and young ones to attend on the cat. That sinful feline began feeding on the mice and became fat, healthy and strong. The mice reduced in numbers, while the cat grew fatter daily. One day, all the mice met together and remarked that their uncle grew fatter by the day, while their numbers decreased.

A wise mouse called Dindika told his entire tribe to go to the riverside together and said that he would follow with their uncle the cat. They did as Dindika said, for his words seemed grave and important to them. The cat knew nothing of this and ate Dindika that day.

When Dindika did not appear at the river, the worst suspicions of the other mice were confirmed. A very old mouse called Kilika said to them, "Our uncle, the cat, does not really want to acquire punya. He is a hypocrite, and pretends to be our friend while he is really our enemy. The excreta of a creature that lives only on fruit and roots never contains hair or fur; and look how he grows fatter by the day, and our numbers dwindle. We have not seen Dindika for eight days."

The mice fled in all directions and the cat went back to where he had first come from.

Sinful Yudhishtira, you are like that cat. You treat your kinsmen in the same way as the cat did the mice. You have honeyed words of dharma on your lips, but your actions are a sinner's. Your devotion to the shastras and your mildness is only for show. You are no Brahmana. Stop your hypocrisy, O king, and be a Kshatriya; and you might deserve to be called Dharmaraja.

Win the Earth through your prowess and give gifts to Brahmanas and offerings to your Pitrs, as you ought. Look to the welfare of your mother, whom you have distressed for many years; dry her tears and honour her with victory over your enemies in war. You have humbly asked for only five villages, and we refused even that. All we wanted was to anger you sons of Pandu and provoke a war.

Remember that we dismissed the cowardly, treacherous Vidura because of you; remember, also, how we tried to burn you alive in the house of lac; at least now, be a man and fight, as you told Krishna you would when he set out from Upaplavya for the Kuru sabha. You sent a message to us through him, telling us that you are prepared both for peace or for war. The time for war has come, Yudhishtira, and I am ready for it. What better way is there for a Kshatriya to acquire punya than battle?

You were born a Kshatriya; your fame has spread across the world; you have got weapons from Drona and Kripa; why then, Bharatarishabha, do you depend on Krishna, who is not in any way better than you by birth, as a Kshatriya, or in might?"

Uluka, in the presence of the Pandavas say to Krishna, "For your own sake, as well as for the Pandavas, face me in battle as best you can. Use your powers of maya and take the form which you took in the Kuru sabha and, with Arjuna, fight me. A conjuror's tricks can be frightening but only provoke rage in the man who stands ready for war. I, too, can use maya, sorcery, to fly into the sky, to plunge into the bowels of the Earth, to ascend into Indraloka and to assume many forms. However, it is not by terrifying another that a man attains his goal. The Creator brings all creatures under his control by the power of his will alone, and not by conjuring tricks.

You say that you will confer absolute sovereignty on the sons of Pritha by annihilating Dhritarashtra's sons in battle. Sanjaya brought me this message from you. You also said that when we declare war against Arjuna, it will also be against you. Keep your word now and put forth all your might for the Pandavas. Show us that you can be a man.

The man, who knows his enemy's faults and, using his manliness, makes them suffer, is truly a man. Your fame in the world is unjustified. The truth will soon be known that there are those in the world who appear to be manly but are really eunuchs. You were Kansa's slave, and it does not befit me as a king to don armour to fight you."

O Uluka, next give this message to that stupid, ignorant and gluttonous Bhimasena, who is like a bull without horns, a bullock even. Say to him, "Prithaputra, you became a cook and called yourself Ballava in Virata's city, because of what I did to you. Let the vow you swore before me in the Kuru sabha not be a lie. Drink Dusasana's blood if you dare. You have often boasted that you will kill all Dhritarashtra's sons in battle. The time has come to make good that boast. Bhaarata, you always deserve to be plied amply with food and drink, but there is a great difference between cooking food and fighting a war. Fight now; be a man. You will lay down your life and fall on the field, clutching your mace. And all your boasts in the Kuru sabha shall be proved vain, Vrikodara."

Then, Uluka, say to Nakula, "Fight us, Bhaarata; we want to see your manliness, your reverence for Yudhishtira and your hatred for me. Remember all the suffering that Draupadi has endured."

Next, say to Sahadeva in the presence of the assembled monarchs, "Fight now, to the best of your little prowess. Remember all your sorrows and meet us on the field."

Then say to Virata and Drupada, "Since the beginning of time, slaves, however accomplished, have never fully understood their masters; nor have wealthy kings been able to understand their slaves. Possibly, you pit yourselves against me assuming that I have done nothing praiseworthy. Unite now and fight to kill me; do your utmost to accomplish your goal, which is the same as the Pandavas'."

Say to Dhrishtadyumna prince of the Panchalas, "Your time has also come, and your end is near. When you face Drona in battle, you will discover the harsh truth. Yet, fight for your friends, your kinsmen, and die trying to accomplish the impossible."

Next, Uluka, say to Sikhandin, and emphasise these words, "Gangaputra Bhishma, foremost of all bowmen, will not kill you, since you became a woman once. So fight fearlessly and put forth your best in battle. We want to see your prowess."'

Duryodhana laughs aloud and continues, saying to Uluka, 'Address Arjuna once more, in Krishna's hearing. Say to him, "Kshatriya, either vanquish us and rule the world, or submit to us and lay down your life on the field of war. Remember how you suffered when you were banished from the kingdom; recall the sorrows you endured whilst you lived in the forest; remember Krishnaa's torment; and be a man, Pandava. The time has come to fulfil the purpose for which a Kshatriya woman gives birth to a son.

Display your might in battle; show us your tejas, your courage, your manliness, your dexterity and speed with weapons; appease your wrath. Is there a Kshatriya whose heart would not have broken had he been driven from his kingdom, as you have, tormented with grief and despondent in long exile? Is there a man born into a noble house, who is brave and not covetous of another's wealth, who would not be enraged when his ancient kingdom, handed down through the generations, is attacked and seized?

Translate your lofty speeches into deeds. Good men regard the man who boasts without doing anything as worthless. Recover your kingdom and your wealth, which are now in the hands of your enemies. These are the twin objectives of a Kshatriya who wants war; so, Dhanajaya, show us your might.

We defeated you at a game of dice and we dragged Krishnaa into the sabha. This alone should have been enough fuel to ignite the wrath of a real warrior. You have spent twelve long years in the forests, exiled from your home; and you have spent a year in Virata's service. Remember the pangs of banishment, the hardships of your life in the vana, the torment that Draupadi has suffered, and show yourself to be a man. Vent your righteous anger on those who spoke cruel words to you and your brothers, for this is the way of a Kshatriya.

Express your rage; display your might and your knowledge; show us your lightness of hand. Fight, Kaunteya, and prove your manhood. You have invoked your astras; the field of Kurukshetra has been cleared; your horses are strong and fleet; your soldiers have received ample wages. With Krishna as your sarathy, fight us.

Why do you brag even before you have encountered Bhishma in battle? You are like the fool who boasts of scaling the summit of Gandhamadana before beginning to climb it. How can you eye your kingdom without defeating the invincible Karna, or Salya, or Drona that mightiest of Maharathas, our Acharya who is Indra's equal in battle? How vain is your fond desire to conquer the effulgent Drona, commander of armies, teacher of the Vedas and archery, master of both bodies of knowledge, open and hermetic, foremost in the arts of war, unshakeable as a mighty tower, whose strength knows no diminution. It is like dreaming of the wind moving Mount Meru! If what you wish for does come to pass, the wind will blow Sumeru away, heaven will fall to the Earth and the yugas will change their order and duration.

Which man, Arjuna or anyone else, could hope to escape with his life if he dares fight Drona? What man who walks the Earth could escape alive after facing Drona and Bhishma's arrows in battle? Like a frog in a well, you do not see the vastness of the mighty armies of the countless kings who are with me, the armies that look like the celestial host, and which they protect just as the Devas do their forces. This army is ready for war and as difficult to ford as the Ganga; the kings of the East, the West, the South and the North lead it; as do the Kambojas, the Sakas, the Khasas, the Salwas, the Matsyas, the Kurus of the middle country, the Mlechchas, the Pulindas, the Dravidas, the Andhras and the Kanchis.

Foolish Arjuna, how can you dare fight against me when I, Duryodhana, stand in the midst of my elephant legion? We will test your inexhaustible quivers, your chariot that Agni gave you and your ape banner. Do not brag, Arjuna, come and fight. Why so much vaunting? Victory in battle comes from fighting, never from vainglorious boasting. If boastfulness could indeed garner success, all men would achieve their objectives, for who is there that cannot boast?

I know that you have Krishna for your ally. I know that your Gandiva is six cubits long. I know that there is no warrior equal to you. Yet, despite all this, I still hold your kingdom. A man can never win success merely by virtue of his lineage. It is Brahma alone who, if he wills it, can turn the tide of misfortune. For the past thirteen years, I have enjoyed sovereignty while you wept. I will kill you, your brothers and your kinsmen and continue to do so.

Where was your Gandiva when you were put up as a stake in the dice game and we won you for a slave? What happened to Bhima's might then? Your deliverance came neither from Bhimasena armed with his mace, nor from you with your Gandiva, but from the faultless Draupadi. It was the daughter of Prishata's house who rescued you all who had been bound in slavery to work as menials. You were all like de-husked sesame seeds, and covered by nothing but shame.

Partha, did you not later wear a woman's braid whilst living in Virata's city, and was Bhima not exhausted by cooking in Virata's kitchens? Is this what you call manliness or being a Kshatriya? Arjuna, you became a eunuch, covered yourself in hip- and waist-chains, braided your hair and taught young girls to dance. All from fear of fighting us. This is how Kshatriyas punish lesser Kshatriyas.

I will not give up my kingdom out of fear of you or of Krishna. Fight, with Kesava as your ally. Neither deception, nor conjuror's tricks, nor jugglery can frighten the Kshatriya who is armed for battle. Instead, these pretty tricks will only provoke his wrath. A thousand Krishnas and a hundred Arjunas will fly from me in panic and in all directions. Encounter Bhishma in war; you will find it is like butting the hill with your head or swimming across the vast, deep sea.

My army is like the ocean; Saradwata's son is its sharks, Vivimsati its huge snake; Bhishma is its immeasurably powerful tide, Drona as its unconquerable alligator; Karna and Salya are its fish and whirlpools, the king of Kambojas is the badavamukha, the horse-headed creature that spits fire from his mouth; Brihadbala is its fierce waves, Somadatta's son its whale, Yuyutsu and Durmarshana its waters, Bhagadatta its wind; Srutayus and Hridika's son is its gulfs and bays, Dusasana its current; Sushena and Chitrayudha are its hippopotami and crocodiles, Jayadratha its submarine rocks; Purumitra its deeps and Sakuni its shores!

Plunging into this surging ocean with its inexhaustible waves of weapons, you will see all your relatives and friends killed, and you will repent. Then your heart will turn away from the thought of ruling the Earth, like the heart of a sinful man turning away from hope of heaven. Indeed, for you to win a kingdom is as impossible as for one without tapasya punya to attain Swarga," said Duryodhana to Uluka,' says Sanjaya."

CANTO 162

Uluka Duta Gamana Parva continued

"Sanjaya says, 'The gambler's son Uluka went to the Pandava camp and, presenting himself to the Pandavas, addressed Yudhishtira and said, "You know full well the role of envoys and how they speak. So you must not be angry with me for repeating Duryodhana's words exactly as he told me to."

Yudhishtira said, "You have nothing to fear, Uluka. Tell us without any anxiety what the greedy and short-sighted Duryodhana thinks."

In the midst of the illustrious Pandavas, the Srinjayas, of Krishna of the great renown, of Drupada and his sons, of Virata and of all the kings, Uluka delivered Duryodhana's message.

Sakuni's son said, "This is what the noble king Duryodhana, in the presence of all the Kuru heroes, instructed me to tell you. Listen to what he said, O Yudhishtira.

'We beat you at dice and dragged Draupadi into the sabha. Any real Kshatriya would be enraged at this. You were exiled to the forest for twelve years, and then lived for a year in Virata's service. Remember the reasons for your wrath—your exile, and our shaming of Krishnaa—and be a Kshatriya, O Pandava. Despite his weakened state, Bhima made a vow; now let him drink Dusasana's blood. You have worshipped your weapons and invoked the deities who preside over each of them. The field of Kurukshetra is clear; the roads are smooth and your horses are well-fed. Begin the battle tomorrow, with Kesava as your ally.

Why do you boast glibly without having faced Bhishma in battle? Like the fool who brags of his intention to climb Gandhamadana, without having set foot on it, you want sovereignty without having vanquished invincible Karna and Salya the mightiest of men, who is equal to Indra in combat.

Salya is a preceptor of the Vedas and archery, having attained the ultimate levels in both branches of learning. You wish, in vain, to vanquish the illustrious Drona, who fights from the front. He is infinitely strong, unshakeable. We have never heard of the mountains of Sumeru being stirred by the wind! But the wind will blow away Sumeru; Swarga will fall down on Bhumi and the very yugas will be reversed if what you said to me comes to pass. Could any man escape with his life after facing Parantapa Drona in war, even if he fought from on the back of an elephant, a horse, or from a chariot?

What creature that walks on Earth could escape with his life, if Drona and Bhishma attack him in battle and pierce him with their terrible arrows? You are like a frog in a well, that you do not see the awesome massed armies of kings, like the very host of the gods. My legions teem with the kings of the East, West, South and North; with Kambojas, Sakas and Khasas; with Salvas, Matsyas, Kurus of the middle country, Mlechchas, Pulindas, Dravidas, Andhras and Kanchis. Indeed, so many nations ready for battle are uncrossable like the swollen tide of Ganga. O, foolish cousin, how will you fight me when I take the field with my legion of elephants?'"

Having repeated Duryodhana's words to Yudhishtira, Uluka turned to Arjuna and delivered the message Duryodhana sent to him:

"'Arjuna, why do you brag so much? Fight, instead. Victory comes from deeds. A war is never won by boasts. If enterprises could succeed just by boasting, then all men would achieve their goals, for who cannot brag? I know that you have Krishna for your ally. I know that your Gandiva is six cubits long. I know that there is no warrior equal to you. Knowing all this, I still hold your kingdom. A man never wins success merely because of his lineage. It is the Supreme Ordainer alone who, by his will, turns hostility into friendship and subservience.

For the past thirteen years have I enjoyed sovereignty, while you were sunk in grief. And I shall continue to rule, after killing you and your people. Where was your Gandiva when you were made a slave won at dice? Where, Phalguna, was Bhimasena's might then? Your deliverance came neither from Bhimasena with his mace, nor from you with the Gandiva, but from the faultless Krishnaa. It was she, the daughter of Prishata's house, who delivered you all, who were bound to us in slavery. I think of you as husks, sesame seeds without kernels, eunuchs. Did you not wear a braid while living in Virata's city? Bhimasena tired himself out, working as a cook in Virata's kitchens. Is this evidence of your manliness, Kuntiputra? To avoid facing me in battle, you braided your hair and taught girls how to dance. This is how Kshatriyas punish Kshatriyas.

I will not give up the kingdom, Arjuna, from fear of Krishna or of you. Fight us, with him as your ally. Neither deception, nor conjuror's tricks, nor jugglery can affright a Kshatriya armed for battle; on the contrary, these only ignite his wrath. A thousand Krishnas and a hundred Arjunas will fly from me in all directions. Encounter Bhishma in combat; it is like shattering the mountains with your head. Penetrate my army; it is like swimming across the vast and deep ocean. My army is a veritable ocean; Saradwata's son is its large fish, Vivimsati its smaller fish, Brihadbala its waves, Somadatta's son its whale, Bhishma its mighty current, Drona its unconquerable alligator, Karna and Salya its fish and whirlpools, Kamboja its horse's head vomiting fire, Jayadratha its submarine rock, Purumitra its depth, Durmarshana its waters and Sakuni its shores.

When, having plunged into this swelling ocean with its inexhaustible waves of weapons, you wilt from fatigue and have all your relatives and friends slain, then repentance will grip your heart. Then your heart will turn away, Partha, from the thought of ruling the Earth, like the heart of a sinner giving up hope of heaven. Indeed, for you to win a kingdom to rule is as impossible as for a man without any tapasya to attain Swarga,"' said Uluka,' says Sanjaya."

CANTO 163

Uluka Duta Gamana Parva continued

"Sanjaya says, 'O Rajan, Uluka repeated these words to Arjuna, provoking him who is like a venomous snake further. The haughty, scornful message Uluka brought goaded the already incensed Pandavas beyond endurance.

They began to flex their mighty arms and, truly like angry cobras, looked at one another, fire in their eyes. Bhimasena, with his head bent down and his breath hissing like a great hamadryad's, turned his blood-red eyes to look at Krishna. Krishna saw how Bhima suffered and spoke to Uluka.

He said, "Go now, Uluka, and tell Duryodhana that we have heard and understood his words. Let it be as he wishes."

Having said this, Krishna looked once more at the wise Yudhishtira. Then in the presence of all the Srinjayas, of Draupadi, of Drupada and his sons, of Virata and of all the other kings, Uluka yet again repeated what he had already said to Arjuna, like prodding a great and already furious serpent with a stick.

And he repeated the same message again to Krishna and the others.

Arjuna's mighty body quivered with rage, and sweat beaded his brow. The kings saw him like that and were afraid; and the Pandavas' Maharathas were greatly agitated to listen repeatedly to Duryodhana's mocking message. They were all men of firm equanimity, but now they burned with anger. Dhrishtadyumna, Sikhandin, Maharatha Satyaki, the five Kekaya brothers, the Rakshasa Ghatotkacha, the sons of Draupadi, Abhimanyu, Dhrishtaketu, Bhimasena and the twins jumped up from where they sat, their eyes crimson, swinging their splendid arms that were decked with red sandalwood-paste and golden ornaments. Knowing what was in their hearts, as Bhima sprang up he gnashed his teeth and wet the corners of his mouth with his tongue. Beside himself with anger, he clenched his huge fists and, turning his furious gaze on Uluka, spoke to him.

He said menacingly, "Fool, we have heard Duryodhana's vile message, sent to taunt us. Now listen to what I say, and, in the hearing of the Suta's son and your black-hearted father Sakuni, repeat it to Duryodhana, who stands protected in the midst of his many Kshatriyas. Say to that sinner from me:

'We always want to please our elder brother. That is why we tolerated everything you did to us. Do you not see this as being fortunate for you? It was for only the good of our entire vamsa that Yudhishtira Dharmaraja sent Krishna to the Kurus to try and make peace. But fate drives you to long for death. Come, fight us! Tomorrow, there will be war. I have sworn to kill you and your brothers. Sinful fool, do not have the slightest doubt that I will fulfil my vow.

Varuna's abode, the ocean, might suddenly flood the continents; and the mountains might split open, but what my oath will never prove false. Even if Yama, Kubera, or Rudra himself helps you, the Pandavas will still accomplish what they have sworn to do. I will drink Dusasana's blood as I have sworn. I vow that I will kill any Kshatriya who comes to me in anger, even if he comes with Bhishma himself before him. All I have said in the Kuru sabha will come to pass. This I swear by my very soul.'"

When Bhima finishes, Sahadeva, whose eyes have also turned red as plums, spoke before the assembled forces, in the ringing voice of a great, proud Kshatriya.

He said to Uluka, "Listen well, sinner, to what I say, and convey this message to your father:

'No difference would ever have arisen between us and the Kurus, if Dhritarashtra had not befriended you. You were born an embodiment of dissent and to be the instrument of the destruction of Dhritarashtra's vamsa and of the whole world.'

O Uluka, from the time we were born your evil father always tried to do us injury. I will cross the sea of malice and first kill you before his eyes, and then kill him in the sight of all the warriors."

Hearing Bhima and Sahadeva, Arjuna smiled and said to Bhima, "Bhimasena, those who have incited your enmity will not live. Even if they think they are safe in their homes now, they will surely be caught in death's meshes. My brother, Uluka does not deserve to be spoken to harshly. What is his fault, who is only a messenger, and merely repeats what he has been instructed to say?"

Then Arjuna Mahabaho addressed his allies and well-wishers, led by Dhrishtadyumna, saying, "You have heard the foul message of the sinful son of Dhritarashtra, sent to insult Krishna and especially me, and you are full of anger because you wish us well. Before Krishna's might and yours, all the Kshatriyas of the Earth together, count for nothing. With your leave I will give Uluka a response to his message, to take back to Duryodhana:

'When tomorrow comes, I will keep myself at the head of my legions, and answer to your vile message with the Gandiva, for it is only eunuchs who respond in words:'"

And all the kings applauded Dhananjaya. Now Yudhishtira Dharmaraja spoke respectfully to the friendly kings, to each according to his age and as befitted his rank; and, finally, to Uluka he gave this message for Duryodhana.

Yudhishtira said, "No good king should patiently bear an insult. I have heard what you had to say; this is my reply."

Uluka Duta Gamana Parva continued

Bharatottama, in response to Duryodhana's message Yudhishtira, eyes red with rage, breath hissing like a serpent's, tongue wetting the corners of his mouth, and trembling with anger, looked at Krishna and his brothers and spoke both gently and strongly to Uluka.

Flexing his great arms, he said to the gambler's son, "Go, Uluka, and say to Duryodhana, that ungrateful, evil embodiment of violence, that wretch of his race:

"Malignant one, you always hated us Pandavas and treated us with deceit. The man who relies on his own strength, calls his enemies to battle, displays his prowess and makes good his boasts is a true Kshatriya. Be a Kshatriya and face us in war. Do not come to battle with those whom we revere at your head. Kaurava, rely on your own might and on that of your servants when you summon the sons of Pritha to war; be a Kshatriya in every way. He who declares war on his enemies, counting on the might of others, is a eunuch.

You think highly of yourself, but you rely on the might of others. Being so weak and incapable yourself, why do you roar at us so grandly?"

Krishna said, "O Son of Sakuni, take my words, as well, to Duryodhana:

'When tomorrow the war dawns on you, show yourself to be a man, O evil one. You are foolish to think Krishna will not fight because the Pandavas have chosen him to be a charioteer; that is why you are fearless. But I say to you that if my anger is ignited, I will consume all the kings whom you have brought together, as fire burns a heap of straw. But since Yudhishtira commands me, I shall be a sarathy to Arjuna, and he alone will actually fight.

But hear me, sinner, even if you hide beyond the three worlds, or deep in the bowels of the Earth, you will, even there, see Arjuna's chariot flying at you tomorrow. You think that Bhima's boasts are empty, but know that Dusasana's blood is already as good as drunk. Know also that, although you have said a lot, and so haughtily and mockingly, not Arjuna, Yudhishtira, Bhimasena or either of the twins thinks much of you.'"

CANTO 164

Uluka Duta Gamana Parva continued

"Sanjaya says, 'Arjuna looked at Sakuni's son Uluka with angry red eyes, and then at Krishna and, raising his arms, he said to Uluka, "The man who challenges and fights his enemies fearlessly, relying on his own strength, is a Kshatriya. While the man who summons his enemies to battle, depending on the strength of others, is a disgrace to all Kshatriyas and is considered the lowest of men. Tell Duryodhana from me, again:

'Cowardice makes you use the strength of others as your own, and you depend on them to vanquish your enemies. You have given the command of your forces to Bhishma, who is the eldest of the Kshatriyas, who is devoted to dharma, who has his passions under control and who is wise; and by this you make him face certain death. And then you brag! We know that you assume that we Pandavas will not kill our Pitamaha. But, Duryodhana, Bhishma is the first man that I will kill, and in full view of both armies.'

Uluka, go back to the Bhaaratas and tell Duryodhana that I, Arjuna, say this to him: 'So be it. Tomorrow the great war will begin. Bhishma, of tireless might and devotion to truth, has already said to you that the task of destroying the Srinjaya and Salweya armies is his, and that he can kill anyone on Earth, excepting Drona; and that you need have no fear of the Pandavas. His assurances make you presume that the Pandavas will be easily vanquished and that you will become the undisputed sovereign of the world; and this fills you with pride. But what you will find is your own defeat and death.

First of all, I will slay Pitamaha Bhishma before your very eyes. At sunrise tomorrow come with your chariots and banners to protect your Senapati, who is firm in his resolve; and watch my arrows fell him, who is your refuge. Tomorrow, when you see our Pitamaha covered by my arrows, you will realise the difference between bragging and battle.

Duryodhana, very soon you will see Bhima fulfil the angry oaths he swore in the Kuru sabha to your bestial brother Dusasana. You will reap the terrible consequences of vanity, of wrath and cruelty, of arrogance and boastfulness, of vicious words and deeds, of adharma and sin, of speaking ill of others, of disobedience to elders, of prejudice and of all your vices.

O you scum of the Earth, how can you hope to live or keep the kingdom if I, with Krishna beside me, give rein to my anger? After Bhishma and Drona have been stilled, and after Karna is slain, you will have no hope of any kingdom, of your son's lives or your own worthless one. When you hear of the slaughter of your brothers and sons, and when Bhima strikes you a final, mortal blow, you will remember all your sins.'

Tell him, Uluka, that I make a vow only once. I swear that everything I have said will come to pass."

Now Yudhishtira said, "Repeat my words as well when you go to Duryodhana. Say to him:

'Do not judge me by your own dark nature and ways. We are as different as dharma and adharma. I never wish harm to even the smallest creatures, ants and other insects, let alone desire the massacre of my cousins. That is why I asked for just five villages. Why don't you see the horrific calamity that threatens you? Your soul is overwhelmed by greed and lust, and you boast from being deluded. And you ignore even

Krishna's counsel. But the time for words is past; fight us with all your allies.'

Uluka, also say to the pathetic Kuru prince: 'I have heard and understood what you said. Let it be as you wish.'"

Then Bhimasena said, "Uluka, take my message to Duryodhana, who is an embodiment of sin.

Say to him: 'You are destined to find a home either in a vulture's belly or in Hastinapura. I will fulfil the vow I swore in the Kuru sabha. I swear in the name of Truth: I will kill Dusasana in battle and drink his blood. I will kill all your brothers and then smash your manhood, and you will die in agony. Know, Duryodhana—I am the nemesis of all Dhritarashtra's sons, and Abhimanyu will be the scourge of your younger princes. I will gratify you all with my deeds.

Duryodhana, when I have killed you and your brothers, I will kick your stamp on your head with my foot in the sight of Yudhishtira Dharmaraja.'"

Nakula said, "Uluka, tell Duryodhana that I have heard and understood everything he has said. Tell him that I will do exactly as he has asked me to."

Sahadeva said, "Tell Duryodhana for me: 'Your fond hopes will all prove vain. You will repent, with your sons, kinsmen and your friends, that you bragged in joyful anticipation of killing us.'"

The two old kings, Virata and Drupada, said to Uluka, "We are glad to serve a good man. Tomorrow we shall see who is the servant and who the master, and who will prevail in battle."

Now Sikhandin said to Uluka, "You must say to Duryodhana, who is addicted to sin: 'Watch helplessly, O king, my fierce deeds on the field. I will kill your grandfather, on whose prowess you depend for victory. I was created by Brahma to kill Bhishma, and I will do what I was born to in the sight of all your bowmen.'"

Dhrishtadyumna said to Uluka, "Say to Duryodhana: 'I will kill Drona with all his followers; this task is mine and no one else's.'"

Yudhishtira spoke again, noble and compassionate words: "'Rajan, I do not want the slaughter of my kinsmen, and everything that is now sure to happen is your fault. I have no choice but to sanction what all these great men around me will do.'

Now either go from here without delay, Uluka, or stay with our blessings; for we too are your kinsmen."

Uluka took leave of Yudhishtira and went back to Duryodhana, taking with him all that had been said; and when he came before Duryodhana, he repeated everything that Arjuna had told him to say. He faithfully delivered the messages that Krishna, Bhima, Yudhishtira, Nakula, Virata, Drupada, Sahadeva, Dhrishtadyumna and Sikhandin had given him; and then what Arjuna and Krishna had said later.

Duryodhana listened to Uluka, and he ordered Dusasana, Karna and Sakuni to array their own and the troops of the allied kings for war before dawn broke. At Karna's command, messengers mounted their chariots, camels and horses and rode through the camp, calling out, *Into battle formations before sunrise!"*

CANTO 165

Uluka Duta Gamana Parva continued

"Sanjaya says, 'After listening to Uluka's messages from Duryodhana, Yudhishtira also deployed his army led by Dhrishtadyumna and the others: the vast army of the four kinds of forces—infantry, elephants, chariots and cavalry—as awesome and immovable as the Earth herself. The Pandava army was protected by mighty Maharathas led by Bhima and Arjuna, and was like the ocean, immense, still and calm.

At the head of that sea-like force was the invincible bowman Dhrishtadyumna, prince of the Panchalas; and he chose Drona as his particular adversary and target. As Senapati, Dhrishtadyumna picked individual warriors from the enemy ranks and told his own warriors which one they would fight. He gave his chariot-warriors battle instructions, each according to his strengths.

He assigned Karna to Arjuna, Duryodhana to Bhima, Salya to Dhrishtaketu, Kripa to Uttamaujas, Kritavarman to Nakula, Jayadratha to Satyaki, and Bhishma to Sikhandin. He pitted Sahadeva against Sakuni, Chekitana against Sala, and the five sons of Draupadi against the Trigartas. He set Abhimanyu against Karna's son Vrishasena as well as against the rest of the kings, for he considered Abhimanyu superior to Arjuna himself in battle. He allocated responsibilities to his warriors, individually and collectively, and finally this Maharatha, brilliant as a blazing fire, reserved Drona for himself.

And having arrayed the Pandava troops and its maharathas, Dhrishtadyumna waited coolly for the war to begin, his mind firmly fixed on victory for the sons of Pandu.'"

CANTO 166

RATHATIRATHA SANKHYANA PARVA

Vaisampayana said, "Dhritarashtra says, 'After Arjuna had sworn to kill Bhishma in battle, what did my evil sons, led by Duryodhana, do? Ah, I can already see the sure-handed Arjuna, with Krishna by his side, killing my uncle Bhishma. And what did that greatest Kshatriya Bhishma, who is immeasurably wise, say when he heard Partha's words? Having accepted the Kaurava command, what did that splendid warrior do?'

Sanjaya tells him everything that Pitamaha Bhishma said.

Sanjaya says, 'Rajan, having been given the command of the Kaurava force, Bhishma spoke words to Duryodhana that pleased him greatly.

Bhishma said, "I bow to Lord Kumara, Velayudha, bearer of the inexorable spear, Senapati of the armies of Devaloka and I gladly accept command of your army. I know about the affairs of state, about every kind of battle formation, and how to inspire fighting men to give their best efforts. I know as much about the deployment of the vyuhas of war and their strategic movements as Brihaspati himself. I know the methods of attack and defence that the Devas, Gandharvas and Manavas use; and with these I will confound the Pandavas. Dispel the fear in your heart. I will fight the enemy, whilst protecting your army, in keeping with the dharma of war. Cool the fever of your mind."

Duryodhana said, "O Gangaputra, Mahabaho, I do not fear the hosts of the Devas and Asuras combined; then how will I fear these Pandavas with you as my Senapati and with Drona beside you, fighting for me? With you both on my side I will surely win this war; why, I could I could even win sovereignty over the gods.

But tell me, Pitama, who amongst our warriors we count as a Ratha and who as an Atiratha. Pitamaha, you know the strengths of every warrior on both sides. I want to hear what you think with all these kings present."

Bhishma said, "Listen, Rajarajan, and I will tell you who the Rathas and Atirathas in your army are. In your legions are many millions of Rathas, but I will name the main ones. Firstly, there is you. Amongst your brothers, including Dusasana, you are the foremost of all the Rathas. All of you are skilled fighters, experts at attacking and destroying chariots. You are all great charioteers when you take the reins of the sarathy, and expert elephant-riders, as well. You are all doughty mace-fighters, excellent archers and swordsmen; you also wield impenetrable shields. You are learned in the astra shastra and ably discharge your duties. You are all Drona's and Kripa's disciples in archery and at others weapons. In the coming war, the mighty sons of Dhritarashtra will put forth their prodigious energy to destroy the irresistible Panchalas.

Next come I, the Senapati of your troops. I will vanquish the Pandavas and extirpate the enemy forces. It does not become me to speak of my own strengths, but I believe you know me well.

One of the finest among all warriors is Raja Kritavarman of the Bhojas. He is an Atiratha, and he will accomplish your goal in battle. No man, not the most skilled warrior, can overcome him. Shooting or hurling his weapons to great distances, and a master swordsman in close combat, he will raze the enemy ranks, just as Indra did the Danava hordes.

The lord of the Madras, the mighty Salya, is an Atiratha. He considers himself equal to Krishna in every battle he fights. He has deserted his sister's sons to take your side. In this war he will decimate the Maharathas of the Pandava army with tidal waves of arrows.

The great archer Bhurisravas, the son of Somadatta, is an Atiratha and one of your sincerest friends. He has overall command of the heads of all our chariot divisions. He will wreak havoc among the enemy and swiftly reduce their numbers.

Jayadratha king of the Sindhus is, in my opinion, equal to two Rathas. That best of chariot-warriors will display his prowess in battle. He still smarts from the humiliation the Pandavas meted out to him when he abducted Draupadi. He practised severe tapasya and obtained a boon most difficult to acquire, one he will use while fighting the Pandavas themselves. Harbouring his old hatred, he will fight, reckless of his life, which is well nigh impossible to take anyway."'"

CANTO 167

RATHATIRATHA SANKHYANA PARVA

CONTINUED

"Sanjaya says, 'Bhishma said, "Sudhakshina, king of the Kambojas, is equal to one Ratha. He wants your victory, and he will fight boldly against your enemies; and the Kauravas will see that the prowess of this lion amongst Maharathas as he fights for you is equal to Indra's. His Kamboja force of fierce chariot-warriors will swarm over the battlefield like locusts.

Then there is Nila of Mahishmati, clad in blue mail; he is one Ratha. With his chariot army he will bring bloody havoc to your enemies. He detests Sahadeva and will fight loyally for you. The princes Vinda and Anuvinda of Avanti are powerful and seasoned warriors; they are two Rathas. These two will consume the enemy's troops with maces, feathered arrows and swords, with spears and javelins. Lusting for battle, these Kshatriyas will range across the battlefield like bull elephants sporting in the midst of a herd, each of them looking like Yama.

The five princely Trigarta brothers are, in my judgment, the best of

Rathas. Pritha's sons provoked enmity with them outside Virata's city. Like great crocodiles churning the stream of the Ganga into high crested waves will they agitate the ranks of the Pandavas in battle. All five are Rathas, with Satyaratha being the first among them. They still remember the shame that Arjuna inflicted on them, many years ago, when he swept through the land with his white horses, on his campaign to subjugate all the kings of the Earth. They will give their all and, having already fought many of the leading Pandava warriors in the past, they will surely slay them now.

Your son Lakshmana and Dusasana's son are both tigers among men and unwavering in battle. In the prime of youth, of lithe limbs, and endowed with powerful energy, these two princes are expert warriors and could well lead all the Kuru chariots. I believe they are our two best Rathas and devoted to Kshatriya dharma. They will achieve great feats.

Dandadhara is equal to a single Ratha. Guarded by his own soldiers, he will fight for you. Raja Brihadbala of the Kosalas, who is blessed with mighty tejas and strength, is equal to one Ratha. A fierce fighter, this great bowman is devoted to the Dhartarashtra cause, and will exert himself powerfully in battle, to the joy of his friends.

Saradwata's son Kripa is a commander of leaders of chariot forces. Uncaring of his life, he will consume your enemies at will. Kripa, who was born in a clump of heath as the son of Mahamuni Saradwata, also called Gautama, is as invincible as Kartikeya. Burning numberless warriors with all kinds of astras, he will rage across the field like a blazing fire."'"

CANTO 168

RATHATIRATHA SANKHYANA PARVA

CONTINUED

"Sanjaya says, 'Bhishma said, "Your uncle Sakuni is equal to one Ratha. Being the cause of the hostilities with the sons of Pandu, he will definitely fight. His troops are irresistible when they charge the enemy and are armed with arsenals of all kinds of weapons; and they are as swift as the wind.

Drona's son Aswatthama is superior to all other archers. He is a profound knower of the astra shastra and his weapons are inexorable. He is a great Maharatha. Like Arjuna's arrows shot from the Gandiva, Aswatthama's shafts fly in an unbroken line, touching one another. This best among Rathas, whom I cannot laud enough, can consume the three worlds, if he sets his mind to it. He has performed austere tapasya and augmented his fury and energy. Brilliant is his intellect, and Drona has favoured his son with the gift of devastras.

However, Aswatthama has one great defect, and for that I do not consider him a Ratha or an Atiratha: he loves his life too much, and holds it too dear. Yet, there is not a man amongst the warriors of both armies who is his equal.

From a single chariot he can put the army of the Devas to rout. So powerful is his powerful body, that he can rive mountains merely by slapping his bowstring on the leather sleeve of his arm. Blessed with countless exceptional qualities, Drona's son of fierce effulgence will range over the battlefield, as irresistible as Yama with his mace. Lustrous Aswatthama of the lion's neck will extinguish your enemies like the fires of the pralaya do at the end of a yuga.

His father Drona is endowed with great tejas, though old, he is superior to any younger man. He will perform great deeds in battle; of this I have no doubt. Standing immovable on the field, he will burn Yudhishtira's troops with many fires. The Pandava army will be the dry grass and fuel in which those fires will be sparked, and the power of Drona's weapons will be the wind that fans it into mighty flames. This bull among men is a leader of Maharathas. The son of Bharadwaja will achieve astounding feats for you.

The venerable Acharya Drona, guru of all the royal Kshatriyas, will exterminate the Srinjayas. However, he loves Dhananjaya and, remembering the remarkable virtues Arjuna has acquired, and remembering that Arjuna is his most beloved disciple, he will never be able to bring himself to kill him. Indeed, Drona always prides himself on Arjuna's accomplishments, and looks on him with more affection than on his own son. Otherwise, such is his prowess that he can, from a single chariot, vanquish all the Devas, Gandharvas and Manavas united together, with his devastras.

Narashardula Paurava is one of your finest Maharathas, and he can shatter the ranks of enemy chariots. He will attack the enemy from the front of his own large force and consume the Panchalas like fire burns dry grass.

Satyasravas, the son of Brihadbala, is equal to one Ratha. He will sear through your enemy's troops like Death himself. His men, wearing motley armour and armed with all manner of weapons, will spread across the field, killing all that stand against them.

Karna's son Vrishasena is one of your best chariot-warriors and is a Maharatha. He will devastate your enemy's forces.

Then there is the great tejasvin Jalasandha, and he is among your foremost Rathas. Born in Krishna's vamsa, he is always willing to give his life in battle. He is a true warrior and will scatter the enemy before him, whether from his chariot or elephant back. That best of kings is, in my judgment, a Ratha. He will fight a brutal battle, ready to surrender his life for your sake, and among his mighty legions, expert in all types of warfare, he will be fearless.

Brave and like Yama himself, Bahlika is an Atiratha. He rushes headlong into any encounter and never retreats. He will blow away any enemy in his path even like Vayu Deva.

Another router of hostile chariot divisions, Maharatha of wonderful feats in battle, is Satyavan. He knows no fear of war. He will fall like a blood-storm on those that stand on his way; and in the fierce press of battle he will achieve all that a Kshatriya should.

The lord of Rakshasas, the feral Alambusha, is a Maharatha. Remembering his old hatred of the Pandavas, he will kill a countless enemy fighters. He is the best of Rathas amongst all the Rakshasa warriors and, with his magical powers and his uncompromising enmity, he will be merciless on the field.

The great sovereign of Pragjyotisha, the powerful Bhagadatta, is the best of all elephant-warriors. Once, he and Arjuna fought for days on end, each avid for victory. Then, for the sake of his friendship with Indra, Bhagadatta made a treaty of peace with Indra's son. And during this war, that king will fight from his formidable elephant's back like Indra mounted on Airavata and fighting for the Devas.""''

CANTO 169

Rathatiratha Sankhyana Parva

CONTINUED

"Bhishma said, "The brothers Achala and Vrishaka are Rathas. They are invincible in battle and will raze your enemies. These Naravyaghras are the best of Gandharvas and never relinquish their anger. They are young, handsome and of unworldly prowess.

This brings me to your dearest, most devoted friend Karna, always so proud of his battle skills, and who constantly goads you into fighting the Pandavas. You have taken this braggart as your advisor, guide and friend and elevated him to too high a position. The arrogant fellow is neither a Ratha nor an Atiratha. Yet he is generous and, deprived of good sense, he gave away his natural coat of mail and his divine earrings, which made him invincible. Without his kavacha and kundala, because of his guru Parasurama's curse, as well as that of another Brahmana, he is merely an ardharatha, half a Ratha. When he faces Arjuna in battle, he will not escape with his life."

Hearing this, Drona said, "I agree with Bhishma. Karna boasts on the eve of every battle, and he has fled from every encounter. I judge him to be only half a Ratha because his generosity in giving away his kavacha and kundala was reckless and because of his brash and unrestrained ways."

Karna heard all this and his eyes widened in anger. He glared at Bhishma and said, "O Pitamaha, I am innocent, but your dislike for me makes you malign me as you please, with words like arrows at every step. I tolerate it for Duryodhana's sake. You calling me an ardharatha makes plain how worthless you think I am, why, as if I were a coward!

You, Gangaputra, are an enemy of the whole universe, especially of all the Kurus. But the king is unaware of this. What man but you, Bhishma, would seek to create envy and discord among us, to sap the united purpose and energy of these kings, all equals in rank and courage, as you do from your contempt for their great accomplishments?

Neither years, nor wrinkles, nor wealth, nor possession of friends would entitle a Kshatriya to regard himself as a Maharatha! It has been said that a Kshatriya acquires greatness only through might proven on the field, just as Brahmanas acquire eminence through superiority in their knowledge of mantras, Vaisyas through wealth and Sudras with age. Influenced by hatred and envy, and speaking loosely from malice and ignorance, you list Rathas and Atirathas, capriciously, according to your whim.

May you be blessed, Mahabaho Duryodhana; you be the true judge of this. Abandon the evil Bhishma, who wrongs you. Once seeds of discord are sown it is difficult to reunite warriors who have been divided by cunning comparisons. With some effort, your own army can be reunited in spirit, but it will be far more difficult to do the same with the armies from outside. Look how doubt has already raised its head in the hearts of your warriors. Bhishma subtly weakens us, even as we stand here, before the first arrow has been loosed in war. Besides, judging the true merits of Rathas is beyond Bhishma of the limited intellect.

Alone, I, Karna, will withstand the Pandava army. My every arrow is unerring and deadly; when they face me, the Pandavas and the Panchalas will fly in all directions, like oxen before a tiger.

Bhishma is old and twisted; he is not the one who should speak of battle or the dangers of war; he should not be the one to rely on for sage advice. Indeed, he is fated to be the first victim of destiny. He challenges the whole world, and deludes himself that no one else is a man or a warrior. It is true the shastras teach us to heed the elderly. But they do not mean those who are far too old, for they become children again.

Alone, I would extinguish the Pandava army. However, the fame of that feat will go to Bhishma. You have made him your Senapati, and recognition always belongs to the leader and not to those who fight under him. Rajan, as long as Bhishma lives I will not fight. After Bhishma falls I will fight all the enemy Maharathas together, and kill them all for you."

Bhishma said, "I am about to assume the onerous burden of fighting Duryodhana's war against the Pandavas. I have thought of this day for many years and now the time for this dreadful battle is upon us, I still would not have conflict between the Bhaaratas. It is you, Sutaputra, who were born for that vile task. It is fated; otherwise, old though I am and you young, I would quell your lust for war by taking your life .

Your guru, Jamadagni's son Parasurama, could not do me the least injury with his unearthly astras; so what could you do? Good men do not approve of self-praise. O wretch of your vamsa, I speak like this because I am angry and I am sad.

From my lone chariot, I vanquished all the assembled Kshatriyas of the world at the swayamvara of the king of Kasi's daughters and carried away those princesses. Alone, on so many fields, I stopped the charge of countless kings with their soldiers.

With you as an embodiment of violence, a great carnage is about to overtake the Kurus. Yes, Karna, strive to vanquish our enemies; be a man and fight Arjuna, whom you envy so much and never tire of challenging. Evil one, I want to see how you come out of that encounter alive."

Duryodhana said to Bhishma, "Look at me, Gangaputra. The task we have at hand is dire and grave. Think earnestly of what is best for me. Both of you will render me great services. I want to hear now of the best of the enemy's chariot-warriors, of their Rathas and Atirathas. I want to hear of the strengths and weaknesses of my enemies. When this night is over our great war will begin."'"

CANTO 170

RATHATIRATHA SANKHYANA PARVA
CONTINUED

"Sanjaya says, 'Bhishma said, "I have told you who your Rathas, Atirathas and Ardharathas are. Listen now to who the Pandavas' Rathas and Atirathas are. If you truly wish to know, hear, with these kings, of the Rathas in the army of the Pandavas.

Yudhishtira himself, the son of Pandu and Kunti, is a mighty Ratha. Without doubt he will course unimpeded through the battlefield like a blazing fire.

Bhimasena is equal to eight Rathas; none can remotely match him with the mace or with arrows. With the strength of ten thousand elephants, and with his enormous pride, his might and energy are superhuman.

The two sons of Madri are both Rathas. In beauty they are like the twin Aswins, and they are blessed with mighty tejas. Stationed at the head of their divisions, they will remember the torment you inflicted on them and range the field like many Indras.

All the Pandavas have noble souls; they are tall like Sala trees, taller than other men by half a cubit; they are brave as lions and blessed with awesome prowess. Rajan, all of them have practised brahmacharya and other stern austerities; they are modest; they have tigerish strength; in speed, in smiting and crushing foes, they are more than human. During their campaign of universal conquest before the Rajasuya yagna, each of them vanquished many great kings. No other men can wield their weapons; no other men can even string their bows or heft their maces, let alone shoot their arrows.

In speed, in aim, in eating and in every sport they used to excel all of you even when you were all boys. With their prodigious might, they will exterminate this army. War with them is not desirable. Each of them, by himself, can slay all the kings of the Earth. You saw for yourself, Rajan, what happened during the Rajasuya yagna. Now they will remember Draupadi's sufferings and the abusive, vicious words you spoke after the game of dice, and they will come to war like so many Rudras.

As for Arjuna Gudakesa, of the reddish eyes, with Krishna as his sarathy, there is no warrior in either army who is remotely his equal. Let alone men, I have not heard of any among the Devas, Asuras, Uragas, Rakshasas and Yakshas, who has been born already or yet to be born, who can compare with him.

His chariot flies the banner of Hanuman; Krishna is his sarathy; Dhananjaya himself is the Kshatriya who fights from it; his bow is the Gandiva; his horses are as fleet as the wind; his unworldly coat of mail is impenetrable; his two quivers are inexhaustible; he has obtained his astras from Indra, Rudra, Kubera, Yama and Varuna; and his chariot bears maces of dread and all sorts of other astras, including the Vajra.

What warrior can equal Arjuna, who killed a thousand Danavas in Hiranyapura from his lone chariot? Inflamed with wrath, his prowess beyond your imagination, this Mahabaho will raze your army even as he protects his own legions.

Dronacharya and I, with no third warrior, can stand against Dhananjaya's arrow storms for a time. Yet, when this son of Kunti comes to war, with Krishna seated before him, his gales of astras will not cease, but blow like monsoon winds. He is masterly and young, while Drona and I are both old and worn; we will not last against Nara and Narayana."

Listening to Bhishma, and now vividly remembering, with a trembling heart, the valour of Pandu's sons, and thinking of the war as if it was already happening before their eyes, the kings' great arms, decked with bracelets and smeared with sandal-paste, seemed to hang limp, sapped of their strength,' says Sanjaya."

CANTO 171

RATHATIRATHA SANKHYANA PARVA
CONTINUED

"Bhishma said, "Draupadi's five sons are Maharathas. Virata's son Uttara is among the best Rathas. The mighty-armed Abhimanyu is a commander of the leaders of their chariot divisions; this youthful Parantapa is Arjuna or Krishna's equal. Gifted with marvellous lightness of hand, and steeped in the ways of the astra shastra and every kind warfare, he has untold energy and is firm in his vratas. He will remember his father's agonies and put forth all his valour.

Brave Satyaki of the Madhu vamsa is also a commander of leaders of chariot divisions. Foremost among the Vrishnis and of towering wrath, of fear he knows nothing. Uttamaujas is also a magnificent chariot-warrior, as is Yudhamanyu. All the kings own many thousands of chariots, elephants and horses, and they will fight, uncaring of their lives, to please Kunti's sons. They will unite with the Pandavas and sweep through your troops like fire and wind, burning through and scything down all warriors that confront them.

Virata and Drupada, bulls among men, are both blessed with awesome prowess. Both are Maharathas. Though old, they are devoted to Kshatriya dharma, and will give their utmost in battle. Because of their relationship to the Pandavas, the energy of these two great bowmen will only swell in tide. Men become heroes or cowards by the righteousness of their cause. Motivated by a singleness of purpose, both these aged kings will lay down their lives to destroy your troops. Fiery in battle, leading great akshauhinis, these most noble Kshatriyas will accomplish great and terrible feats, and justify both the confidence that the Pandavas have placed in them and their relationship with them.""""

CANTO 172

RATHATIRATHA SANKHYANA PARVA

CONTINUED

"Sanjaya says, 'Bhishma said, "Sikhandin, scion of the Panchalas, is a subjugator of hostile cities and is among the foremost of Yudhishtira's Rathas. He will fight your troops to win great fame. He has a vast legion of Panchala and Prabhadraka troops to support him. With his hosts of chariots he will achieve dreadful feats.

Dhrishtadyumna, Senapati of Yudhishtira's army, disciple of Drona, is a Maharatha. He is an Atiratha. He will harry his foes and, by himself, sweep the field clean, as Mahadeva does the worlds with his Pinaka at the Pralaya. Great warriors will speak in awe of his oceanic chariot forces, which are like those of the Devas.

Dhrishtadyumna's son Kshattradharman is young and inexperienced, and so I consider him only half a Ratha. Sisupala's heroic son Dhrishtaketu, who is kin to Pandavas, is a mighty bowman and a Maharatha. This king of Chedis and his son will perform deeds of valour in battle that are difficult even for a Maharatha.

Kshattradharman is a conqueror of enemy cities, and he is devoted to Kshatriya dharma; and his son Kshattradeva is one of the best of the Pandavas' Rathas. Then there are the dauntless Panchala warriors—Jayanta, Amitaujas and the Maharatha Satyajit. They are all noble Maharathas and will fight like angry elephants. Aja and Bhoja are both Maharathas and will fight for the Pandavas. Both are gifted with uncanny lightness of hand; they use every manner of weapon and are exceptional warriors.

Five Kshatriya brothers, related to the Pandavas by blood, are almost impossible to defeat. They, too, fight with diverse weapons, and are skilful, fierce and unshakeable. These five who fly blood-red banners, Kasika, Sukumara, Nila, Sankha, also called Madiraswa, and Suryadatta, are incomparable Rathas.

Vardhakshemi is a Maharatha. Raja Chitrayudha is a superlative Ratha and, besides being an asset in battle, he is utterly devoted to Arjuna. The two Maharathas, Chekitana and Satyadhriti, are tigers among men and two of the Pandavas' unrivalled Rathas, as are Vyaghradatta and Chandrasena.

Senabindu, also named Krodhahantri, is a warrior equal to Krishna and Bhimasena; he will fight with formidable audaciousness. That best of kings is proud of his achievements in battle. You should think of him as you do of Drona, Kripa and me. Then there is Kasya, who is truly praiseworthy for his dexterity with every weapon. This subduer of hostile cities is equal to one Ratha.

Drupada's son Satyajit, though young in years, shows great prowess in battle, and he is equal to eight Rathas. He is Dhrishtadyumna's equal and, thus, an Atiratha. He will also accomplish great and savage deeds in battle in his eagerness to spread the fame of the Pandavas.

Devoted to Pandu's sons and brave beyond common ken is another great Ratha—Pandya, bowman of scintillating tejas. The superb archer Dhridadhanwan is a Maharatha; and Kurusattama Srenimat and Raja Vasudeva are both Atirathas.""'

CANTO 173

RATHATIRATHA SANKHYANA PARVA

CONTINUED

"Bhishma said, "Rochamanas is another Maharatha in the Pandava army. He will fight against us like a Deva. Bhima's uncle Kuntibhoja is an Atiratha. He will fight with the same might as Indra did against the Danavas, and his renowned warriors are all accomplished and fearless. Devoted to his nephews, he will achieve extraordinary feats for their sakes.

Bhima and Hidimba's son, the Rakshasa prince Ghatotkacha is gifted with powerful magical powers. He is a commander of the leaders of chariot-divisions. He revels in battle and, using maya, he and his feral Rakshasa legion will also fight without fear.

All these and many other kings, with Krishna at their head, have gathered to fight Yudhishtira's cause. I have listed the main Rathas, Atirathas and Ardharathas of the Pandava army, and these will lead Yudhishtira's fearsome legions, protected by Kiritin Arjuna. I will confront these warriors in battle, some of whom will fight with sorcery, and all of whom are fired by a consuming will to win the war; and I, too, am prepared for victory or for death.

I will ride against Krishna and Arjuna who, with the Gandiva and the Chakra, are like the Sun and the Moon shining together in the evening sky. I will face Yudhishtira's other Maharathas and their swarming troops.

Duryodhana, I have named for you, in their order of importance, the Rathas, Atirathas and Ardharathas in your army and theirs. I will fight Arjuna, Krishna and all the other lords of Earth whom I encounter, but I will neither strike nor kill Sikhandin, prince of Panchalas, not if I see him rushing at me with his weapons raised.

The world knows how, to please my father, I renounced the kingdom I inherited and have lived as a brahmachari. I made Chitrangada king of the Kurus and the child Vichitravirya the Yuvaraja. I swore a pledge in the presence of all the kings of the Earth that I will never kill a woman or one who was once a woman. Sikhandin was a woman once. Born as a girl child, he later changed himself into a man. I will not fight against him.

Also, Rajan, although I will strike down all the other kings I meet on the battlefield, I could not kill the sons of Kunti.'"

CANTO 174

AMBOPAKHYANA PARVA

"Sanjaya says, 'Duryodhana said, "Why will you not kill Sikhandin even if you see him riding at you to take your life? You once told me that you would destroy the Panchalas and the Somakas; why now this reluctance, Gangaputra?"

Bhishma said, "Duryodhana, I will not kill Sikhandin, even if I meet him in battle. Hear why, you and all these other kings.

My father Santanu was renowned throughout the world. When that virtuous king died I crowned my brother Chitrangada king of the vast Kuru kingdom. On Chitrangada's death, in keeping with dharma and with Satyavati's acquiesance, I made Vichitravirya king. Vichitravirya was a mere boy then, and though I had invested him with sovereignty, I ruled in his name and he looked to me in all things.

When the time came, I wanted to him to wed and began to look for princesses from a royal house equal to our own. I heard that the three daughters of the king of Kasi, Amba, Ambika and Ambalika, of unrivalled beauty, were to hold a swayamvara, and that all the kings of the Earth had been invited. Amba was the eldest, Ambika the second and Ambalika the youngest. On a chariot, I rode on my own to the city of Kasi and saw the three girls clad in finery and bejewelled, and I saw all the kings who had been invited there.

Bharatarishabha, I seized the three princesses, lifted them into my chariot and said to the kings, *I, Bhishma, son of Santanu, abduct these young women! O kings, do your best to rescue them. I am taking them away by force, with all of you as witnesses.*

The kings sprang up and shouted to their sarathies to fetch their chariots. Those Kshatriyas rode after me in their rathas, with weapons unsheathed—chariot warriors looking like dark clouds massed; those mounted on elephants, and others on horseback. They surrounded me with countless chariots, but I vanquished them all, as Indra does Danava hordes.

Laughing, and easily, I cut down the kings' many-coloured flags embroidered with gold thread. I felled their horses, elephants and sarathies, each one with a single arrow. Seeing my lightness of hand, they stopped fighting and yielded. I returned victorious to Hastinapura and brought the young princesses to Satyavati, as brides for my brothers, telling her everything I had done."'"

CANTO 175

AMBOPAKHYANA PARVA CONTINUED

"Sanjaya says, 'Bhishma said, "Coming before my mother Satyavati, a daughter of the dasa clan, I saluted her, the mother of heroes.

I said to her, *I defeated all the kings and took these daughters of Kasi, who have their beauty as dowry, to be Vichitravirya's brides.*

Rajan, Satyavati's eyes streamed tears as she sniffed my head in affection and she was joyous at my triumph. With Satyavati's approval the nuptials approached, when Amba, the Kasi king's eldest daughter spoke bashfully to me.

She said, 'Bhishma, you know dharma well and the shastras. Hear what I have to say and then do what you think is just. I had already chosen the king of the Salvas to be my husband before when you took me away from the swayamvara. He proposed to me privately, without my father's knowledge. Can you, O Bhishma of the Kuru vamsa, go against dharma by forcing someone who longs for another to live in your household? Bear this in mind and decide what you will do.

The king of the Salvas waits for me, and you must let me go to him.

Be merciful to me, O most righteous of men. All the world knows of your devotion to dharma."'"

CANTO 176

AMBOPAKHYANA PARVA CONTINUED

"Sanjaya says, 'Bhishma said, "I shared what Amba told me with my mother Kali, otherwise called Gandhavati, as well as with our ministers and our priests, and we allowed the eldest princess Amba to leave. She went to the city of the Salva king with an escort of Brahmana elders and her own maid.

She went before the king and said, 'Mahabaho, I have come to you, take me for your wife.'

But the king of Salva laughed and said to her, 'Princess, you have already been taken by another, and I will not marry you. So, go back to Bhishma. He abducted you and I no longer desire you. When he defeated the other kings and took you away, you went happily. He humiliated and vanquished all the kings of the Earth, and I do not want another man's leavings. I am a king and a lawmaker, who knows the shastras; how will I take a woman already given into my home? Devi, go wherever you wish; do not waste your time here.'

Amba, who was struck by Kama Deva's subtle arrows, cried to Salva, 'Ah, do not say this, Rajan, for it is not true. Parantapa, I did not go happily with Bhishma. He seized me by force, defeated all the kings, and I wept the whole time. Accept me; I am innocent.

The shastras do not approve of a man abandoning one who loves him. I told Bhishma about our love, begging him to release me, and I have come to you with his leave. Besides, Bhishma does not want me for himself; it is for his brother that he abducted me. He has given my two sisters Ambika and Ambalika to his younger brother Vichitravirya. O lord of the Salvas, I swear on my very life that I have never thought of any man but you as my husband. I do not come to you as a betrothed woman. I speak the truth, Salva; I swear it on my soul.

Take me as a maiden who comes to you on her own, as one who is not promised to another, as one who asks for your grace.'

Although she spoke in this vein, Salva rejected the princess of Kasi, like a snake sloughing off his old skin. Although she entreated him repeatedly, the king of the Salvas would not relent. Then rage filled Amba and, her eyes streaming, she cried, 'You may have cast me out, Rajan, but righteous people will protect me wherever I may go, for truth is indestructible.'

This is how the lord of the Salvas spurned the princess, who pleaded with him and sobbed so piteously in grief.

The king of Salva said, 'Go, go! I am in terror of Bhishma, you of the lovely hips, and you are Bhishma's prize.'

Thus evicted by Salva, the princess Amba left his city, crying like an osprey."'"

CANTO 177

AMBOPAKHYANA PARVA CONTINUED

"Bhishma said, "As she left the city, sobbing, Amba thought, 'There is no woman in the world in as miserable a plight as me. Without family or friends and cast out by Salva, I cannot return to Hastinapura after begging Bhishma to let me leave. Who can I blame—myself, or the invincible Bhishma, or my father who held a swayamvara for me?

Perhaps it is my own fault. I could have leapt off Bhishma's chariot when he fought the other kings, and gone to Salva then. My turmoil and anguish are because I did not do that. I curse Bhishma. I curse my own wretched and misguided father, who fixed valour as my bride price, as if I were a commodity to be sold. I curse myself. I curse the king of Salva. I curse my Creator too. I curse them all, who have been the cause of my terrible misery.

Human beings suffer what they are destined to; but the cause of my suffering is Bhishma, and I will avenge myself on him, either through tapasya or by battle. But is there a king who would dare face Bhishma in battle, to fight my cause?'

Deciding that she would have revenge on Bhishma, she set out for an asrama of virtuous Munis, where she stayed the night, protected by them. The once sweet-smiling devi told them all that had happened to her, to the smallest detail, of how Bhishma abducted her and how Salva betrayed her love. She begged their help.

There lived in that asrama a Brahmana of great tapasya called Saikhavatya, who was a teacher of the shastras and aranyakas. This Muni said to the suffering princess, from whom pitiful sighs came like her very breath, 'Princess, how will we Rishis, who perform tapasya in the forest, help you?'

Amba said, 'Be merciful to me. I have renounced the world and wish to live in the forest. I will practise the severest of tapasya. My suffering is the result of the sins I committed in ignorance. I have no desire to return to my family, and grief has its way with me after Salva humiliated me. You are a godly man, who have washed away your sins; teach me how to perform tapasya. Be merciful to me.'

The Muni comforted her with examples and explanations from the scriptures, and he and the other Brahmanas promised to help her."'"

CANTO 178

AMBOPAKHYANA PARVA CONTINUED

"Sanjaya says, 'Bhishma said, "Those Munis then went about their daily chores, study, penance and worship, thinking all the while about what they could do for that devi.

Some amongst them said that she should be taken back to her father; some said she ought to blame me; some thought that they should go to the king of Salva and persuade him to accept her; some disagreed with this for he had shamed her in his court.

After some time had passed in such deliberations, Saikhavatya Muni said to her, 'Devi, what can sadhus of self-restraint do for you? Do not renounce the world and devote yourself to a life in the forest. Listen to me; I speak for your good. Go from here to your father's palace. Your father, the king, will do what needs to be done. You can live there happily, in luxury. You are a woman and, so, your only protector is your father.

Fair child, a woman's protector is either her father or her husband. Her husband is her protector when she is happy, but when she is plunged in grief it is her father she goes to. A life in the wilds is very difficult, especially for one who is delicate. You are a princess by birth and you are fragile. Devi, a life in the forest entails many hardships and tribulations, none of which you have known in your father's house.'

The other Munis looked at the helpless girl and said, 'Seeing you alone in the deep and lonely forest, wild hunters, bandits or even kings may seek to ravish you. Do not set your heart on a life of sannyasa.'

Amba said, 'I cannot go back to my father's house in Kasi, for I am certain to be shunned by all my relatives. Rishis, I spent my childhood there, but I cannot return to my father's city. With your protection, I want to practise penance, so that someday I can be rid forever of suffering. Maharishis, I want to be a tapasvin.'

Whilst the Brahmanas deliberated on what to do with her, there came to that forest the mighty sage, Rajarishi Hotravahana. The Munis paid their homage to him and welcomed him courteously, offering him padya, arghya and a darbhasana. After he was seated and had rested a while, the Munis began to talk to the devi once more, in his hearing.

Hearing the story of Amba and the king of Kasi, Hotravahana grew distraught. He heard how she spoke and saw how distressed she was, and that Rajarishi was moved to pity. In fact, Hotravahana was her grandfather, and he stood up suddenly, tears springing in his eyes; and, taking her onto his lap, he comforted her lovingly. He asked her in detail about her sorrows from the beginning, and she told him everything that had happened. He was filled with sadness when he had heard it all and decided what she should do.

Trembling in some agitation, he said to the tormented girl, 'Do not go back to your father's house. Devi, I am your mother's father. I will remove your grief; rely on me, child. Your suffering must be great that you are so wan and thin. You must go to Jamadagni's son Parasurama Bhargava. He will rid you of your deep sorrow. He was Devavrata's guru and will kill Bhishma in battle if the Kuru does not obey him. Go to that greatest of all the Bhrigus, whose tejas and urjas are like the flames of the pralaya. That Maharishi will set you on the right path.'

The girl, who wept on while he spoke, bowed her head reverentially to Hotravahana and said to him, 'I will go to that greatest of sages, but will I succeed in even catching a glimpse of Parasurama, whose renown echoes through the world? How will the Bhargava dispel my torment? How will I find him? Tell me, O my grandfather.'

Hotravahana said, 'You will find the mighty Parasurama in the great tapovana on the mountain Mahendra, where he sits in tapasya with many Rishis learned in the Vedas, many Gandharvas and Apsaras. Go with my blessings and tell the Mahamuni what I said, after first bowing your head to him in worship. He is a sage of strict vratas and fathomless ascetic punya. Tell him whatever you wish for. If you name me, Parasurama will do anything for you, for he is my devoted friend and always wishes me well.'

Even as Hotravahana was speaking to the princess, Akritavrana, a close companion of Parasurama's, arrived there. All the hundreds of Munis and the Srinjaya king Hotravahana rose, and together they performed all the rituals of welcome and hospitality and then sat down around him. Delighted to have him amongst them, they spoke with him on many profound and wonderful subjects. When silence fell on the sacred gathering, Hotravahana asked Akritavrana where Parasurama was at the time.

Akritavrana said, 'Lord, Parasurama always speaks of you as his dear friend, and I believe he will arrive here tomorrow morning, for he comes even to see you.

But why has this maiden come to the forest? Whose is she, and what is she to you? I wish to know all this.'

Hotravahana said, 'She is the favourite daughter of the king of Kasi, and her mother is my daughter. She is Amba, the eldest daughter of the king of Kasi. She and her two younger sisters Ambika and Ambalika were in their swayamvara in Kasi, for which all the Kshatriya kings of the Earth had come. Great festivities were underway there, when Santanu's son, Bhishma of mighty valour, brushed aside all the kings and abducted the three princesses. Bhishma of Bharata vamsa took them to Hastinapura and to Satyavati. He asked his brother Vichitravirya to marry the princesses he had brought.

Seeing arrangements for the wedding being made, this devi Amba said to Bhishma, 'O Kshatriya, in my heart I had already chosen the lord of the Salvas to be my husband. Knowing dharma as you do, you know that your brother must not marry me, when my heart is given to another.'

Bhishma consulted his ministers and after deliberation, and with Satyavati's consent, gave Amba leave to go to Salva. She went to that king and told him that she had come with Bhishma's permission; that she had not done anything to break adharma and that she had chosen him, Salva, for her husband.

But Salva rejected her, suspecting her purity. Now she has come to these sacred forests, fervently wanting a life of tapasya. I recognised her from what she told me of her parentage. She blames Bhishma for her sorrow.'

Then Amba said to Akritavrana, 'Holy one, what my grandfather says is true. I cannot go back to my own city for fear of disgrace and shame. I have decided to obey whatever Parasurama tells me to do.'

CANTO 179

AMBOPAKHYANA PARVA CONTINUED

Akritavrana said, 'Devi, for which of your two problems do you seek a remedy? Do you wish that the king of Salva should be persuaded to marry you? Parasurama Mahatman will certainly urge him to do so for your sake. Or, if you want to see Gangaputra Bhishma defeated in battle by Parasurama, Bhargava will gratify even that wish of yours. Let us hear what Hotravahana has to say further, and what you say as well, and decide today what should be done for you.'

Amba said, 'Holy one, Bhishma abducted me without knowing that I had given my heart to Salva. Bear this in mind, and dharma, when you decide what I should do. Do what is just, towards both Bhishma and Salva. I have told you honestly about the root of my grief; now you must decide what is best for me.'

Akritavrana said, 'Lovely Devi, what you say is imbued with dharma, and worthy of you. If Bhishma had not taken you to Hastinapura, Salva would have married you on Parasurama's asking him to. It is because Bhishma carried you away by force that Salva is suspicious of you. Bhishma is proud of his valour and is crowned with success. Your vengeance should be directed at him.'

Amba said, 'Dvija, I too dearly want to kill Bhishma in battle. Mahabaho, be it Bhishma or Salva, punish the man you think guilty, the one who has made me suffer.'

With a delicious, balmy breeze blowing, that day passed, and the night as well, while they discussed Amba's plight. In the morning, awesome, splendid Parasurama arrives in that asrama, his matted hair in jata, clad in deer-skin and carrying his bow, sword and battle-axe.

He came to Hotravahana, and that Rajarishi, all the Munis and the distressed princess stood up and waited on him with joined hands. They worshipped Bhargava with offerings of honey and curds, and he sat down in their midst, and Hotravahana and the great Bhargava began to speak of many profound and mysterious matters.

Finally, at an opportune moment, Hotravahana said, 'Rama, this girl is the daughter of my daughter and the king of Kasi. She needs your blessing from you. You are the lord of all things; I beg you, listen to what she has to say.'

Now Parasurama asked the princess to tell him what she wanted to say. Amba approached Parasurama, who blazed with tejas, like a fire. She laid her head at his feet in worship, touched them with her two lotus-like hands, and then stood silently before him. Overwhelmed by grief, and her eyes bathed in tears, she asked for his protection, for he was the refuge of all those in distress.

Parasurama said, 'Tell me what grief you hold in your heart, and I will do what needs to be done.'

Encouraged, Amba said, 'O holy one of the great vratas, I seek refuge with you. Free me from my suffering and raise me out of this ocean of sorrow.'

Seeing her beauty and her youthful, tender body, Parasurama sat silently in thought for a time, filled with pity, wondering what she would ask. Then he asked Amba to tell him everything, and she told him all that had happened.

Parasurama heard her out and, having first resolved what he should do, said to the exquisite girl, 'Beautiful devi, I will send word to Kurusattama Bhishma. He will do whatever I ask, and if he does not, I will consume him in battle. Or, if you prefer, I can speak to the heroic king of the Salvas and tell him to marry you.'

Amba said, 'O Bhargava, Bhishma allowed me to leave Hastinapura as soon as he heard that I had already given my heart to the lord of the Salvas. I went to Salva and spoke to him in forthright words. Doubtful of my purity, he refused to accept me. O great one, reflect on all this, and in your wisdom, do what you think is best.

However, Bhishma is the root cause of my distress, for he assumed control over my life by carrying me away in his chariot. Ah, kill Bhishma for me, Mahabaho; it is because of him that I suffer so grievously. Bhishma is covetous, mean and proud of his victory. Anagha, you must punish him. In my heart I wished for Devavrata Bhishma's death even while he was abducting me. Sinless Parasurama, gratify this desire of mine; slay Bhishma, as Purandara slew Vritra.""'

CANTO 180

AMBOPAKHYANA PARVA CONTINUED

"Sanjaya says, 'Bhishma said, "O Rajan, Parasurama said to the weeping girl, who repeatedly urged him to kill Bhishma, 'Daughter of Kasi, I do not take up arms on any account now except on behalf of Brahmanas. Tell me what else I might do for you.

Both Bhishma and Salva are implicitly obedient to me. Do not grieve, I will accomplish what you wish for. But I will not take up arms, unless I am asked to by a Brahmana, for this is the law I live by.'

Amba said, 'Ah, holy one, somehow dispel my misery, which Bhishma has caused. Do not delay, kill him!'

Parasurama said, 'Princess of Kasi, you have only to ask and I will have Bhishma set your feet on his head.'

Amba said, 'Parasurama, slay Bhishma, who roars like an Asura. If you want to allay my torment, let him call you to a duel and kill him there. You have given me your word that you will help now; you must not break it.'

Now Rishi Akritavrana intervened, 'Mahabaho, you should not break your word to this child, who seeks your protection. If, when you summon

Bhishma, he comes and does what you ask, or you humble him in battle, if he does not, Amba's wish will be fulfilled and you will not forswear yourself.

Mahamuni, you swore an oath that after you have conquered all the Kshatriyas, you would kill any man, be he a Brahmana, a Kshatriya, a Vaisya or a Sudra, who is an enemy of us Brahmanas. You also swore that as long as you lived you would not forsake anyone who sought your protection in fear. You also said that you would slay the arrogant warrior who vanquished all the Kshatriyas of the Earth.

Lord, Bhishma, scion of Kuru vamsa, has achieved such a victory. Go to him now, O Bhargava, and humble him.'

Parasurama said, 'Best of Rishis, I remember that vow I once took. However, in this instance, I must first use the way of conciliation as best I can. What the princess of Kasi wants is grave indeed, Brahmana. I will take her with me and go to Bhishma. If he does not do what I ask, I will kill that arrogant one. The arrows I shoot do not glance off the bodies of my enemies, but pass through them. You know this when I fought the Kshatriyas of the Earth and spilled their blood in rivers.'

Parasurama and the Brahmanas decided to set out from the asrama. They spent the night there and duly performed their homas and recited their prayers the next morning; then they set out, intending to kill me.

Rajan, Parasurama came to Kurukshetra with the young princess and his followers. With the Bhargava at their head, those great Munis arrived on the banks of the Saraswati," said Bhishma.'"

CANTO 181

AMBOPAKHYANA PARVA CONTINUED

"Sanjaya says, 'Bhishma continued, "On the third day, Parasurama sent a message to say that he had come to help me.

Hearing that this Rishi of tejas, vast as the ocean had entered our kingdom, I went to him at once, and in joy. A cow led my retinue, and many of our family priests went with me, as also other great Brahmanas, whom we employed for special occasions such as this.

Parasurama accepted the worship that I offered and said to me, 'Bhishma, having cleansed yourself of desire, what were you thinking when you abducted the king of Kasi's daughter during her swayamvara, and then later when you let her leave? You have sullied her virtue; and, since you have touched her who will marry her now? Salva spurned her because you abducted her. Take her for yourself, Narapumgava, and let this princess fulfil a woman's dharma. It is not dharma that she be humiliated like this.'

I saw Parasurama's anguish at the princess' plight and said to him, 'O my guru, there was no way that I could bestow this girl on my brother once she herself told me that she belonged to Salva; and so I let her go to him. As for me, I cannot break my vrata and abandon Kshatriya dharma; not for fear, pity, wealth or lust.'

Parasurama's eyes rolled, and he said to me, 'Bharatarishabha, if you do not do as I say, I will kill you and all your followers this very day,' and he repeated this again and again in his fury.

I pleaded with him, but to no avail. I bowed my head before that Brahmanottama and asked him why he wanted to fight me.

I said, 'When I was a child it was you who instructed me in all four parts of the Dhanurveda. I am your sishya, O Bhargava.'

His eyes still red, he retorted, 'Bhishma, you acknowledge me as your guru, but you refuse to please me by taking this princess of Kasi for your wife. I will not be satisfied unless you do what I ask. Take this devi and safeguard the dharma of your vamsa; you abducted her forcibly from her swayamvara, and now she cannot find a husband. You must marry her yourself.'

I said, 'That I cannot do. I am eager to please you because you were once my guru. I refused this princess before I was aware of the great evil that the frailties of women can bring. No man will welcome into his household a woman whose heart belongs to another, and who is, thus like a venomous snake. I would never forsake my dharma by breaking my solemn oath, not even for fear of Indra. Be gracious, or do to me now what you think is just.

There is a sloka from the Puranas, which Maruta Mahatman once told me of: A man may disobey the command of even a guru who is filled with vanity, who does not know right from wrong and who walks a path of adharma.

You are my guru and I have revered you out of my love for you. However, you do not know the dharma of a guru, and I would fight you. But I could never kill a guru in battle, especially if he is Brahmana, and more so, one who is blessed with boundless tapasya. And so I forgive you.

It is a well known scriptural truth that no guilt attaches to a man who kills a Brahmana who has taken up arms as if he were a Kshatriya, and who fights in anger without trying to escape. I am a Kshatriya, and I am devoted to my dharma. One does not sin, neither does one do any harm, by treating a person as he deserves. When a man, who is aware of the timeliness of things, and versed in dharma and artha, is doubtful about anything, he should, without misgivings, follow his svadharma, for that will give him the most punya.

O Bhargava, you have violated dharma by asking me to break my vow, and I have no qualms about fighting you. You know that my prowess is superhuman, and I will give my all when I face you on the field of Kurukshetra. Effulgent one, prepare yourself for single combat; take your position.

My arrows will purify you and you will attain the regions to which your tapasya has entitled you. I will come to fight you, who so love battle, on Kurukshetra, where long ago you propitiated your ancestors with sea-like offerings of Kshatriya blood. There, Bhargava, I will propitiate those slain Kshatriyas by killing you.

Come, do not delay. On Kurukshetra I will curb your pride, of which the Brahmanas speak. For long years you have boasted that you single-handedly slew all the Kshatriyas in the world. And well you could boast, for in those days Bhishma was not yet born, nor were there any Kshatriyas like him. Only later did the truly valiant Kshatriyas come into this world.

All your vaunted conquests were against men of straw. The man who can quell your pride has since been born. I, Bhishma, am that man: the conqueror of enemy kingdoms. I will crush your pride of old conquests.'

Parasurama said to me, laughing, 'I am glad that you will do battle with me, Bhishma. I will come to Kurukshetra with you even now. Yes, I will do what you want. Come there, and let your mother Jahnavi see you lying dead on the battlefield, pierced by my arrows and become carrion for vultures, crows and jackals. Let that Devi, whom the Siddhas and Charanas worship, Bhagiratha's blessed daughter who took the form of a holy river and who gave birth to you, weep today when she sees you lying lifeless on Kurukshetra, although she does not deserve the grief of such a sight.

Come, Bhishma; follow me, arrogant Kshatriya always hungry for battle, and bring your chariot and weapons.'

I worshipped Parasurama with my head bent and answered him by saying *Tathaastu*.

He strode away toward Kurukshetra, and I went to our city to inform Satyavati of what had happened. I performed propitiatory rites for victory, took my mother's blessings, and made the Brahmanas utter their blessings over me. I mounted a superb silver chariot yoked to white horses. It was finely crafted, spacious and covered on all sides with tiger-skin; it had many great weapons in it. My sarathy was a brave nobleman, an expert horseman and charioteer, and one who had seen many battles.

I wore a white coat of mail and carried my white bow; and I set out, Bharatottama. A royal white parasol was held over my head and white chamaras waved over me. Clad in white silk and with white head-gear, all my adornments were also white. I rode out of Hastinapura to songs of praise and to the sound of Brahmanas wishing me victory, and I rode to Kurukshetra.

Spurred by my sarathy, the steeds, fleet as the wind or the mind, bore me swiftly to the great encounter. Upon Kurukshetra, Parasurama and I, both keened for battle, would display our prowess. When I came within sight of Parasurama I blew a loud blast on my conch. Many Brahmanas and sadhus who lived in the forest had come to watch our duel. Divine garlands, celestial music and canopies of clouds were all around and above us, and the Rishis who had come with Bhargava stood on the periphery of the field.

Suddenly, my divine mother Ganga, who washes the sins of men in her sacred waters, appeared before me in her human form and said, 'What is this that you are about to do? I will go to Jamadagni's son and beg him not to fight Bhishma, who is his disciple. My son, you are a Kshatriya; you must not fight Parasurama; he is a Brahmana.'

She continued to reproach me, 'My son, Parasurama Bhargava is as powerful as Mahadeva himself; he once exterminated the entire Kshatriya varna. You do not know this as I do, who saw it all, and you want to face him in battle!'

I saluted the Devi reverentially and with folded hands recounted the events that had taken place at the swayamvara; I told her everything that happened with the princess of Kasi, and how I had tried to dissuade Parasurama from fighting me.

My mother Ganga went to Parasurama and beseeched him to desist since I was his disciple. He said to her that she ought to urge me to obey him, and that he had challenged me because I refused to do what he wanted."

Out of her love for him, Ganga came back to persuade Bhishma to relent, but the angry Bhishma refused. And just then, Parasurama of the Bhrigu vamsa came to Bhishma and said they should begin their duel,' says Sanjaya."

CANTO 182

AMBOPAKHYANA PARVA CONTINUED

"Bhishma said, "Smiling, I said to Parasurama, 'You stand on the ground and I do not want to fight you from my chariot. Mount a chariot and put on a coat of mail, if you wish to fight me.'

He also smiled and said, 'The Earth is my chariot and the Vedas are the steeds that pull me; the wind is my sarathy and the mothers of the Vedas are my coat of mail—Gayatri, Savitri and Saraswati. With their protection, I will fight.'

With that, he covered me with a barrage of arrows; and indeed I saw him, standing on a supernal chariot equipped with weapons of every kind. Wondrous was his chariot, created by his will, and great and beautiful, like a town. Celestial horses were yoked to it, and it was armoured on all sides. It was decked with ornaments of gold, covered with tough skins, and it bore the symbols of the Sun and the Moon. Parasurama was armed with a bow and quiver of arrows, and his fingers were encased in leather gloves. His friend Akritavrana was his sarathy.

Parasurama repeatedly summoned me to battle, crying, *Come, come, make me a happy man!* And so that invincible exterminator of Kshatriya kind, resplendent like the rising Sun, became my adversary in battle.

He showered me with three bursts of arrows, curbing my horses; I alighted from my chariot, set aside my bow and walked up to him. I paid reverent homage to him.

I said, 'My lord, whether you are equal or superior to me, I will fight you, my virtuous guru. Bless me and wish me victory.'

He said, 'The man who desires victory should do as you have. Those who fight with warriors elder and more eminent than themselves must perform such homage. Kshatriya, I would have cursed you if you had not come to me in this way. Go; fight carefully and call on all your patience. I cannot, however, wish you victory, for I am here to vanquish you. Go, fight in dharma. I am pleased with you.'

Bowing to him, I quickly returned and, climbing onto my chariot once more, I blew my conch. The fervid duel between us began. It lasted many days. Parasurama drew first blood, striking me with nine hundred and sixty vulture-feather-winged arrows, which covered my horses and my sarathy, although I myself was unscathed in my coat of mail.

Bowing to the Devas, and especially to the Brahmanas, I said to Parasurama, 'Although you have shown scant respect for me, I have paid you full reverence as my guru. There is another auspicious duty to be discharged if you want to earn punya. I do not loose my arrows at the Vedas you have absorbed, or at you as a Brahmana or at your great tapasya. I take aim at the Kshatriya warrior you have chosen to become. When a Brahmana takes up weapons he becomes a Kshatriya. Now witness the power of my bow and the might of my arms. Look how I sever your bow with my single arrow!'

I shot a sharp broad-headed arrow at him and cut off one of the horns of his bow, which fell on the ground. I then shot a hundred arrows at his chariot. They flew through the air like serpents and pierced him. Blood covered his body and poured out. And he shone in battle, like Mount Sumeru with molten lava flowing down its sides, or like an asoka tree in spring when it is covered with red flowers, or the kinsuka tree in bloom.

Angrily, he took up another bow and inundated me with keen, golden-winged arrows and, like snakes, fire or venom, these vicious barbs of terrific impetus flashed at me from all sides, piercing me deep and making me tremble. I gathered myself, and struck Parasurama with a hundred shafts that were like fire, or the Sun, and which also looked like snakes spitting venom, and he seemed to swoon away.

Pity surged in me and I lowered my bow, in disgust of battle and Kshatriya dharma. Grief quite overwhelmed me and I kept saying to myself, *Ah, great is the sin I have committed by observing my dharma. I have sorely wounded my own guru, who is a virtuous Brahmana, with arrows!*

Thousand-rayed Surya, having warmed the Earth, now sank away to his abode in the west at the close of day; and the duel between the Bhargava and me ceased."'"

CANTO 183

AMBOPAKHYANA PARVA CONTINUED

"Bhishma said, "After the day's battle ended, my sarathy skilfully drew out the arrows embedded in his own body, from the bodies of our horses and from mine as well. The next morning, at sunrise, we resumed battle.

My horses had been bathed, fed, given water and had rested, rolling luxuriantly in the grass, and they were re-invigorated. Seeing me come, in my coat of mail, Parasurama refitted his chariot with care. And when I saw him ride towards me, eager to fight, I put down my bow and got down from my chariot. I paid him worship, before climbing back on, and now stood fearlessly before him, ready for battle.

I overwhelmed him with a thick shower of arrows, and he mantled me with a barrage of shafts in return. His rage mounting, my guru loosed a storm of serpentine shafts with blazing mouths. I retaliated with lakhs of arrows, cutting off his barbs before they could reach me.

He now invoked devastras against me, which I repelled with greater astras of my own; the spirit of war risen in us absorbed both of us entirely. The thunder of astra fusing with astra rose into the sky. I cast the Vayavyastra at him, but he quelled it with his Varunastra. And so we fought, each of us subduing the astras of the other.

Suddenly, he wheeled to my right and struck me squarely through the chest, and I fainted in my chariot. My sarathy quickly bore me away from the field. Great was the joy of Akritavrana, Amba and all Parasurama's followers, who began to shout with joy when they saw me being borne away unconscious.

Regaining my senses, I ordered my sarathy to take me back into battle, for I was recovered. He flicked his reins over the superb windswift horses, which seemed to dance as they flew across the plain, and we were soon there.

In fury, and now determined to vanquish my adversary, I covered him with a deluge of arrows that fell from the sky. But the Bhargava shot three missiles for every one of mine and bisected my arrows in the air. His followers were joyous again, seeing my countless arrows cloven by his.

Now the urge to kill him seized me. I struck him with an arrow of blazing effulgence, with Death sitting at its head. He fell unconscious from his chariot. Exclamations of *Oh!* and *Alas!* arose on all sides, and everywhere was confusion and alarm, as might have been if the Sun were to fall from the sky.

All the gathered ascetics and the princess of Kasi rushed, in great anxiety, to where he lay. They embraced him and soothed him with the soft touch of hands cooled by having been dipped in water, and with assurances of victory.

Parasurama rose, fixed an arrow to his bow and roared at me, *Stay, Bhishma. You are slain!*

The arrow he shot at me pierced my left side and I began to tremble like a young tree in a gale. Calmly, he killed my horses and, with unearthly lightness of hand, shot locust-like swarms of winged arrows which enveloped me in darkness. I, too, loosed arrows beyond count to stem his tide. Our arrow clouds covered the sky, suspended there interlocked and not falling down. The Sun's rays could not penetrate them and the wind could not pass through them. From their vast friction a conflagration flared up in the sky. Every arrow burst into flames and fell to the Earth as ashes. Beside himself with fury, Parasurama loosed crores and crores of deadly barbs at me; and I shot them into fragments and they fell around us like snakes chopped up.

Finally, when the shadows of evening fell, my guru withdrew from the field.""

CANTO 184

Ambopakhyana Parva continued

"Sanjaya says, 'Bhishma said, "The next day, the duel was no less frightful. Day by day, that Mahatman, master of celestial weapons, invoked more devastras, of diverse kinds. With no thought for my life, so difficult to sacrifice, in the ferocity of that duel, I baffled all his weapons with astras of my own. And, Bhaarata, when his astras proved ineffectual, Jamadagni's mighty son cast a fierce and sorcerous lance at me, blazing like a meteor, with a flaming mouth, filling the whole world with its effulgence, and like Yama's very dart. But I cut that missile in three, that occult weapon which shone like the Sun that rises at end of the yuga.

At this, fragrant breezes began to blow around me. His anger burning higher, Bhargava loosed a ferocious astra at me. Their forms, Bhaarata, I cannot describe, but terrible was their lustre and speed. I saw those missiles flare at me from all sides, interminable tongues of flame, truly like the twelve suns that arise at the pralaya, and I was filled with fear. Holding my nerve, I doused the fire of those missiles with a great astra of water, and never pausing, shot down the twelve with twelve arrows of my own.

Undeterred, Parasurama showered a fusillade of golden-winged darts over me, with variegated handles chased with gold, which were like comets afire. I warded them off with my shield and sword so they fell impotent on the ground. I covered Parasurama's horses and charioteer with clouds of gold-shafted arrows. His wrath mounted further to see my barbs like snakes coming out of their nests, and once more he summoned the devastras.

Locust-like swarms of missiles overwhelmed me, my steeds, my charioteer and my chariot. Indeed, Duryodhana, my ratha, horses and sarathy were completely enmeshed by those arrow nets. The yoke, shaft, wheels and the wheel-spokes of my chariot broke.

When his arrow storm ceased, I, too, covered my guru with a heavy shower of weapons. That sage of Brahmic punya began to bleed copiously. I was also densely pierced by his barbs.

When, at last, the Sun set behind the western hills, our savage duel ended for the day.'"

CANTO 185

AMBOPAKHYANA PARVA CONTINUED

"Bhishma said, 'The next morning, Bhargava and I resumed our contention. From his chariot, he rained a downpour of arrows on me, as clouds do on a mountain. My sarathy was struck and fell unconscious to the ground; to my great grief, he succumbed to his injuries.

Rajan, fear gripped my heart, and while I was still numb Parasurama shot me with an arrow that pierced deep into my chest, and I fell to the ground with the arrow. Presuming that I was dead, Parasurama roared in triumph, like a thundercloud. All his followers rejoiced loudly with him, while the Kurus who had followed me, and all the rest who were watching, were stricken.

As I lay there, I saw eight ethereal Brahmanas, who shone like the Sun. They surrounded me and picked me up in their arms. My breathing was laboured as they held me; and, sprinkling me with water and still carrying me, they blessed and reassured me repeatedly. Soothed by their words, I got up, and I saw my mother Ganga standing embodied on my chariot.

O king of the Kurus, it was that great Devi who had held my horses' reins after my sarathy fell. I worshipped my mother's feet and my Pitrs, and I climbed onto my chariot with my weapons. I begged my mother to leave and took the reins myself and, restraining those steeds gifted with the speed of the wind, I resumed my duel with Parasurama and we fought until that day ended.

I shot him with an arrow that pierced his breast, so he lost his grip on his bow and fell onto his knees, and then out of his chariot, unconscious. Masses of clouds filled the sky and rained blood. Hundreds of meteors fell and thunder rolled across the sky, making everything tremble. Rahu covered the Sun, and violent winds blew. The Earth herself trembled, and vultures, crows and cranes began to alight in joy, in anticipation of a feast. The points of the horizon seemed to be on fire, and jackals howled. Drums rang out spontaneously in cacophony. When the great Parasurama embraced the Earth all these frightful omens of evil appeared.

All of a sudden, he arose and came towards me, more furious than ever and ready to fight again. That Mahabaho took up his bow of immeasurable power and shot a deadly arrow at me; but I struck it down in flight. The Rishis who watched were filled with horror and pity, but Bhargava felt only rage. I shot an arrow fulgurant as the fires of the pralaya, but Parasurama of the fathomless soul baffled my weapon. Clouds of dust obscured the splendour of the Sun as it moved to the western sky. Night came with its cool breezes, and both of us suspended our duel till the morrow.

In this way, stopping when dusk came and resuming at daybreak, we fought relentlessly for twenty-three days.'"

CANTO 186

AMBOPAKHYANA PARVA CONTINUED

"Sanjaya says, 'Bhishma said, "That night, after paying my respects to the Brahmanas, the Rishis, the Devas, the creatures of the night and the kings of the Earth, I lay down on my bed, and in the solitude of my chamber I began to reflect.

I thought to myself, *The battle between Bhargava and me has gone on for many days without my being able to defeat this tejasvin. If indeed I am going to overcome Parasurama, then let the gods appear before me tonight.*

As I lay asleep on my right side, my body fairly mangled by arrows, the same Brahmanas who had lifted me up when I fell from my chariot on the field, and who reassured me then, appeared in a dawn dream. They stood around me and said:

'Rise, Kurupravira. Gangaputra, have no fear; we will protect you, for you are our own body. Jamadagni's son Parasurama can never vanquish you in battle. Instead, you will conquer him. In another life you commanded the matchless Praswapastra, which belongs to the Lord of all creatures, and which Tvashtri forged; it shall be yours again to invoke. Neither Parasurama nor anyone else but you knows it. Think hard of it, Mahabaho, and it will come to you on its own.

With the Praswapa, you can vanquish the greatest tejasvins of the world. But you will not be able to kill Parasurama, so you will not sin by using it against him. Overpowered by the mighty astra, Parasurama will fall into sleep, and you will awaken him with the Sambodhanastra.

In the morning, from your chariot, do what we have said. We think of sleep and death as being the same; Parasurama will not actually die, but fall into a deathlike slumber. At the right moment, invoke the Praswapastra gladly and use it against the Bhargava.'

Saying this, those eight lustrous and identical Brahmanas vanished."""

CANTO 187

Ambopakhyana Parva continued

"Bhishma said, "When the night passed, I awoke and, thinking of my dream, was filled with joy. Then, Bhaarata, we took to the field again and fought with so far unprecedented ferocity, so the hairs of all those who watched stood on end.

Bhargava unleashed a deluge of arrows over me, but I checked it with a rising shower of my own. Then, filled with wrath at what he had seen the day before and what he now saw, he hurled an occult spear at me, as hard and as brilliant as Indra's Vajra, like Yama's very mace. It flew towards me, flaming, hungrily consuming the whole battlefield, before falling on my shoulder like a bolt of lightning.

Blood gushed from me like streams bubbling down a mountain after rain. Shaken, stung, I shot a naracha like a venomous snake at him. It struck him on the brow, ah, turning him so handsome, like a crested hill. He assumed a fresh archer's stance, drew his bowstring taut and shot a deathly shaft at me. It streaked through the air and took me in the chest. I fell on the ground, covered in blood.

Coming quickly awake, I cast a dazzling missile, another veritable thunderbolt, which pierced his breast, so he trembled and, his eyes glazing over, swooned. Akritavrana held him close and comforted him. Waking, his eyes now turned red as plums, and Parasurama invoked the Brahmastra. I called upon the same astra myself, and the two weapons fused high above us and broke into a conflagration that occurs only at the end of a yuga.

The sky was on fire; all the Earth's creatures were terrified; the Rishis, the Gandharvas and the Devas panicked; the Earth, her mountains, seas and trees shook violently; and every living being burned in the energy the fused astras radiated. As the sky blazed, all ten points of the horizon billowed with smoke, and sky creatures fell helplessly to the ground.

The whole world with the Devas, the Asuras and the Rakshasas cried out in terror, and I thought that the time had come for me to invoke the Praswapastra. At my very thought, the mantras for the astra flashed into my mind.""'"

CANTO 188

AMBOPAKHYANA PARVA CONTINUED

"Bhishma said, "A tumult of unearthly voices sounded in the sky, begging me not to invoke the Praswapastra. When I still aimed the astra at the Bhargava, Narada appeared there and said to me, 'In the sky, O Kaurava, are the Devas. They forbid you from what you are about to do. Do not loose the Praswapastra. Parasurama is a tapasvin of Brahma punya, and he is also your guru. Never humiliate him.'

As Narada spoke, I saw those eight Brahmanas in the sky. Smiling, they said to me, 'Bharatottama, do as Narada says, for it will benefit the whole world.'

I recalled that astra and invoked, instead, the Brahmastra. When Parasurama saw the Praswapastra being withdrawn, he exclaimed, *Bhishma, you have vanquished this wretch!*

Then he saw before him his father and his grandfathers. They stood around him and spoke words of consolation to him, 'Never again challenge Bhishma or any Kshatriya to a fight, Bhargava, for it is their dharma to fight and not yours. The study of the Vedas and practice of vratas are a Brahmana's greatest wealth. Once, we did indeed command you to take up arms, and you annihilated all the Kshatriyas of the world. Let this battle with Bhishma be your last, for you have done enough already. Retreat from battle, Mahabaho. Our blessings be upon you. Let this be the last time you pick up a bow. Throw your weapon away and return to your tapasya.

See how the Devas forbid Bhishma. They try to pacify him and make him desist from this battle; they try to prevent him from fighting against you, who are his guru, for, they say, it is not proper that he vanquishes you in battle. They tell him to do you every honour on the field. As his superiors they forbid him to humiliate you.

Bhishma is the greatest of the Vasus. You are fortunate to be alive. How can you defeat this son of Santanu and Ganga? Stop, Bhargava. Brahma has ordained that Indra's mighty son Arjuna will be the one to slay Bhishma.'

Parasurama answered his Pitrs, 'I cannot abandon a battle; that is my solemn vow. I have never yet given up a fight or left any battlefield. Pitamahas, if you so wish, tell Bhishma to stop, for I cannot.'

Hearing him, the Rishis with Richika at their head came to me with Narada and said, 'Bhishma, desist from battle. Honour your guru the Bhargava.'

I replied, 'In keeping with Kshatriya dharma I have sworn never to yield in battle, or turn my back, or allow arrows to strike me in the back. Not from temptation, distress, fear, or for any gain or wealth, renounce my dharma. In this I am resolved.'

All those tapasvins and Narada, as well as my mother Bhagirathi, stood on the battlefield before me. I stood quietly, with my bow and arrows as before, determined to fight on.

They turned towards Rama once more and said to him, 'The hearts of Brahmanas are soft like butter. Be pacified, Bhargava, give up this battle. You cannot kill Bhishma; and neither can he kill you.'

They stood between us as they spoke and made Bhargava set aside his weapons. Just then I saw those eight Brahmanas once more, irradiant, and like bright stars in the sky.

They said to me gently, with great love, 'Mahabaho, Parasurama is your guru; you must go to him first. Do what is good for the world.'

When I saw that the Bhargava restrained himself, I too, set aside my weapons, for the weal of the world. Although I was sorely wounded, I came before Parasurama and worshipped him.

The Maharishi smiled and, with great affection, said to me, 'There is no Kshatriya equal to you on Earth. Go now, Bhishma, for you have pleased me greatly in battle.'

He summoned the princess of Kasi into our presence and spoke to her with some regret in the midst of all those Mahatmans."'"

CANTO 189

AMBOPAKHYANA PARVA CONTINUED

"Sanjaya says, 'Bhishma said, "Parasurama said, 'Devi, in the presence of all these great ones, I put forth all my prowess and fought as hard as I could. Even by using the most formidable astras I could not prevail over Bhishma. Beautiful Amba, go wherever you wish, unless there is something else you want from me. Seek refuge with Bhishma, for you have no other now. He has vanquished me in battle.' The Bhargava sighed and fell silent.

Amba said, 'Holy one, it is true what you say: Bhishma of the great intellect cannot be vanquished, even by the Devas. You have done what I asked, as best you could. You used tejas that cannot be dimmed and weapons of all kinds. Yet, you could not conquer Bhishma. As for myself, I will not go to Bhishma a second time. Instead, I will go to the place where I might acquire the means to kill Bhishma in battle myself.'

Saying this, Amba left, wild-eyed in anger, my death her sole aim, and resolved to devote herself to tapasya. Bhargava bid me farewell and, with the tapasvins, departed for the mountains from where they had come. I also left on my chariot, praised by the Brahmanas, and when

I entered Hastinapura I told my mother Satyavati everything that had taken place; and she invoked blessings on me.

I sent forth trusted agents to discover where Amba had gone and what she did, and these loyal spies brought me regular reports of her, from day to day. When Amba went into the forest, resolved to perform tapasya, melancholy and heartache gripped me and I became unwell. No Kshatriya can vanquish me in battle, other than one who knows Brahman, and who observes perfectly austere and praiseworthy vratas.

O king, I humbly told Narada and Vyasa all about Amba, and they both said to me, 'Bhishma, do not yield to sorrow because of the princess of Kasi. Who would try to avert destiny by his own efforts?'

Meanwhile, Amba went to live near some asramas and began practising tapasya so stern that it was beyond human endurance and belief. Without food, emaciated, dry, with matted-locks and grimy, for six months she lived only on air, and stood immobile like a post. After this, that devi, now rich in tapasya, fasted for a year, standing in the waters of the Yamuna. The whole of the next year, her anger unabated, she stood on her toes, having eaten only one fallen leaf. In this way, for twelve years, she scalded heaven with her austerities, and though her relatives tried to dissuade her, she would not be moved.

She then went to Vatsabhumi tirtha, the retreat of lofty, pious Rishis, and where Siddhas and Charanas lived. There she bathed frequently in the sacred waters and wandered about as she pleased. In this way she went to many tirthas, one after the other. She went to Narada's asrama, then to Uluka's, then to Chyavana's, then to the place most sacred to Brahmanas, then to Prayaga the yagnashala of the gods, then to that forest sacred to the gods, then to Bhogavati, then to the Viswamitra's asrama, to Mandavya's, to Dilipa's, then to the sacred lake Ramahrida, and then to the hermitage of Garga. In the sacred waters of all these places the princess of Kasi performed ablutions, while constantly observing the most difficult of vratas.

One day, from the waters my mother Ganga asked her, 'Blessed devi, why do you torture yourself like this? Tell me truly.'

That faultless princess answered with folded hands, 'O you of the beautiful eyes, Bhishma vanquished Parasurama. What other Kshatriya king would venture to face Bhishma in battle when he has his weapons raised? I am performing the severest tapasya in order to kill Bhishma. I wander over the Earth with just one purpose—that I obtain the means to kill that Kshatriya. Devi, in everything I do this is my only goal.'

Ganga said, 'Devi, what you do is not wise. Weak girl, you will never achieve your end. If you observe these vratas for Bhishma's death, and if you lose your own life whilst doing so, you will become a river in your next birth, sourceless, its course crooked and filled only by rain water. All the bathing ghats along your course will be difficult to reach and filled only during the rainy season. You will be dry for eight months of the year. You will be full of terrible crocodiles and other frightful monsters. '

Speaking to Amba in this way, my mother Ganga, the thrice-blessed Devi, sent the princess of Kasi away. Amba renewed her tapasya, going without food and water, sometimes for eight months and sometimes for ten. She wandered here and there in her passionate quest of holy tirthas until she came back once more to Vatsabhumi. It is here that she became a river, filling only during the monsoon, abounding with crocodiles, her waters flowing a crooked course, and difficult to find or ford. But, O king, because of her tapasya only half of her turned into this river in Vatsabhumi, while her other half remained a woman.""'

CANTO 190

AMBOPAKHYANA PARVA CONTINUED

"Sanjaya says, 'Bhishma said, "All the Rishis living in Vatsabhumi saw how intent the princess of Kasi was in her tapasya, and they tried to dissuade her from it. The aged ascetics asked her what she wanted, to which Amba responded, 'Bhishma cast me out and deprived me of the dharma of living with a husband. I keep these vratas for his destruction, and not to gain Swarga. O you of tapasyadhana, I will find peace only with Bhishma's death.

I will not rest until I kill the son of Ganga in battle. All my grief is because of him; he has robbed me of the punya I would have gained by having a husband; because of him I am neither man nor woman. As a woman, I no longer have any desire. I want to be a man, for then I can take my revenge on Bhishma. So, you should not try to keep me from my penance.' And she kept repeating this to the munis.

Soon, the divine lord of Uma, the Trisulin, appeared before that tapasvini who lived amongst the Maharishis. Mahadeva Siva told her to ask for a boon; she begged for my death.

You shall slay him, were the words Siva said to that devi of the great strength of mind.

Amba was reassured but said again to him, 'How can I, a woman, defeat mighty Bhishma in battle? Umapati, as a woman, my heart is perfectly calm. However, you have promised me Bhishma's death. Vrishabdhvaja, do what you must to keep your word that I will kill Santanu's son in battle.'

The Devadeva said to Amba, 'The words I have uttered cannot be false. Blessed Amba, they will prove true. You will become a man and slay Bhishma. You will also remember everything about this life even when you inhabit a new body. You will be born in Drupada's house and become a Maharatha. You will be swift in the use of astras, and a fierce warrior; and you will be skilled in battle. O princess, all that I have said will be come to pass, in time.'

The god of gods, the Kapardin, who has the bull for his emblem, vanished while the Brahmanas looked on in awe. Without delay, that faultless and lovely princess, eldest daughter of the king of Kasi, gathered wood from the forest and, in the presence of those Maharishis, heaped a large funeral pyre on the banks of the Yamuna. She lit it, and eagerly entered the blaze, her heart yet another fire. As she walked into the flames, she repeatedly reminded herself of her purpose, *This I do for Bhishma's death.*"'"

CANTO 191

AMBOPAKHYNA PARVA CONTINUED

"Sanjaya says, 'Duryodhana said, "Tell me, Pitamaha, how Amba, having been a woman, later became a man."

Bhishma said, 'Duryodhana, the eldest and beloved queen of king Drupada of the Panchalas was at first childless. Drupada went into the vana and worshipped Lord Sankara with a fervid tapasya for the sake of sons, for he wanted to have a son who would kill me.

He begged Mahadeva, 'Let a son, and not a daughter, be born to me. I want a son to take revenge on Bhishma.'

Mahadeva said to him, 'You shall have a child who will be both female and male. Stop your penance, king, it will not be otherwise.'

Returning to his capital, Drupada said to his wife, 'Devi, I worshipped Siva and He said to me that my child would be a daughter first and then become a man.

And though I asked him repeatedly, all Siva said was, 'This is fate's decree. It will not be otherwise; that which is destined must come to be.'

Drupada's queen came to Drupada as her fertile time drew near. Purifying herself, she came to him and in due time she conceived. Narada told me this. And that lady, of eyes like lotus-petals, held the embryo in her womb, and Mahabaho Drupada saw to his beloved dear wife's every comfort. Kaurava, the queen of that childless lord of the Earth had all her wishes granted when she gave birth to a beautiful daughter.

The strong-minded queen announced that she had given birth to a son. King Drupada had all the samskaras prescribed for a male child to be performed for his daughter, as if she were a son. Drupada's queen guarded her secret closely; nobody in the city other than she and Drupada knew the sex of the child. With faith in what the ever-glorious Siva had said, the Panchala king also kept the secret, saying, *It is a son.*

Drupada named the child Sikhandin. But, through my spies and from Narada's news, I knew the truth, for I knew from my spies about Amba's tapasya and what Siva had promised her.""

CANTO 192

AMBOPAKHYNA PARVA CONTINUED

"'Bhishma said, "O Parantapa, Drupada paid careful attention to the education of his daughter. He taught her writing, painting and all the arts. In the astra shastra the child became a disciple of Drona. And when the time came, Sikhandin's lovely mother urged her husband to find a wife for their daughter, as if she were a son.

When the king saw that his daughter had reached puberty and her femininity become apparent, he spoke to his queen.

Drupada said, 'Our daughter, who fills me with sorrow, has attained maturity. On the strength of Mahadeva's word, I have so far kept the truth secret.'

The queen said, 'Great king, what Siva says can never be untrue! Why would the Lord of the three worlds say something that will not happen? If it pleases you, my husband, listen to what I have to say and then follow your own heart. Have our child married to a young woman, for Siva words can never prove false. Of this I am certain.'

The royal couple chose the daughter of the king of the Dasarnakas to be Sikhandin's wife. Drupada, lion among kings, made inquiries from all the kings of the world about the purity of her lineage before he chose this maiden. And Hiranyavarman of the Dasarnakas gave his daughter to Sikhandin.

Hiranyavarman was a powerful king, not easy to vanquish. He himself was irresistible and he had a large army. A while after the wedding, Hiranyavarman's daughter attained puberty. Sikhandin returned to Kampilya and his wife soon knew that her husband was a woman like herself. Shyly, Hiranyavarman's daughter told her sakhis and servant-maids about Sikhandin's secret.

The women who had come to Kampilya with the Dasarnaka princess were aghast and sent word to Hiranyavarman. When he heard about the fraud that had been perpetrated against him, Hiranyavarman was beside himself, and sent a messenger to Drupada's palace.

The king's messenger approached Drupada and said to him in private, 'Rajan, the king of the Dasarnakas is outraged at the deceit you have shown him. Sinless one, he is furious and he said these words to you:

Foolish Drupada, you have humiliated me by making my daughter your daughter's wife. Now reap the consequence of your vile deception; wait just awhile, and I will kill you with all your relatives and advisors!" said Bhishma.'"

CANTO 193

AMBOPAKHYANA PARVA CONTINUED

"Sanjaya says, 'Bhishma said, "Drupada, found out, was numbed by Hiranyavarman's message. He made every effort to pacify the Dasarnaka king; he sent messengers to him with instructions to speak sweetly and persuasively. King Hiranyavarman, however, having confirmed that the child of the Panchala king was really a daughter, left Kampilya immediately.

He sent messages to all his powerful friends about what Drupada had done. That best of kings mustered a great army to march against Drupada. Hiranyavarman consulted his ministers, and it was decided that they should bind Drupada and drag him out of his city; and after installing another king to rule over the Panchalas, they would kill both Drupada and Sikhandin.

Hiranyavarman again sent a duta to Drupada with the same message, *I will kill you, just wait.*

King Drupada was not naturally brave and, because he was guilty, he was filled with fear. He sent his own messenger again to Hiranyavarman to placate him; and panic-stricken by now, he went to his wife to discuss the matter with her.

The terrified king said to his favourite wife, Sikhandin's mother, 'The powerful Hiranyavarman has gathered a large force and is coming here in rage. My queen, we have both been fools; what are we to do now about Sikhandin? Hiranyavarman and his allies want to kill me for deceiving him.

O you of the beautiful hips, tell me what you think, and I will decide what to do. I am in grave peril and so is Sikhandin. Why, my queen, you are also in danger. For all our sakes, tell me where you think dharma lies.

Although you misled me about my duty towards our son, who is no son at all, I show you both mercy. So have no fear, and do not let our daughter be afraid either.

I have indeed deceived the king of the Dasarnakas. Tell me what I must do now so that everything turns out well?'

Drupada had always known the truth about Sikhandin, but now he spoke to his wife in the presence of others in this way, to proclaim his own innocence. And his queen answered him."'"

CANTO 194

AMBOPAKHYANA PARVA CONTINUED

"**B**hishma said, "Sikhandin's mother openly declared the truth about her daughter, keeping up the pretence that Drupada had not known the truth.

She said, 'I was childless, Rajan, and it was from fear of your other wives that, when she was born, I pretended that our daughter was a son. Out of your love for me, you did not question me and had all the samskaras for a son performed, for our Sikhandin. You had her married to the daughter of the king of Dasarnakas, and, remembering the words of Mahadeva, I approved of the wedding. I did not try to stop the marriage because Siva said, *She will be born a daughter, and she will become a son.*'

Thus, subtly, Drupada Yajnasena informed all his counsellors of the truth, and sought their advice on how to protect his subjects from Hiranyavarman's invasion. Although he had himself deceived the king of the Dasarnakas, he made it seem as if he had not known about Sikhandin's sex; and then he turned his undivided attention to the looming threat from Hiranyavarman.

King Drupada's city was already well-protected, but he now bolstered its fortifications. The king and his queen were, however, consumed by the thought of how to avoid a war. Drupada began to pay fervent homage and adoration to the gods, and his wife did as well.

Then she said to him, 'Paying homage to the gods has its benefits and is approved of by the righteous. What shall I say of those that are plunged in an ocean of distress? Pay homage to your elders and superiors and worship all the gods; making bounteous gifts to Brahmanas; pour oblations on the fire to pacify the ruler of the Dasarnakas. My lord, think of a way of pacifying Hiranyavarman without a war. The grace of the gods will help you make peace with him.

Take the counsel of your ministers for the protection of our city. Do everything they advise, for reliance on the gods, when supported by human effort, always leads to success. These two must go hand-in-hand; one by itself cannot be successful. So, consult your advisors and make every arrangement to defend our city, and also worship the gods.'

While husband and wife were conversing, both full of grief and fear, their hapless daughter Sikhandin was full of shame and guilt. Thinking that it was because of her that her parents were in such anguish, she decided to end her life. She left Kampilya, her heart breaking, and went into a dense and lonely forest that was the haunt of a formidable Yaksha called Sthunakarna, for fear of whom no-one ever entered that forest.

In that vana stood a mansion with high walls; it was plastered with clay and rich with smoke that bore the fragrance of roasted paddy. Sikhandini entered that mansion and began to emaciate herself by fasting for many days. The Yaksha named Sthuna, who was a kindly being, appeared before her.

He said to her, 'What is the purpose of your endeavour? I will accomplish it for you; tell me what it is.'

Sikhandini replied, 'You cannot.'

The Yaksha retorted, smiling, 'Accomplish it I will! I am a follower of the Lord of treasures and I can grant boons, princess. I will grant you even the impossible. Tell me what you want.'

Now Sikhandini told Sthunakarna everything that had happened, in detail. She said, 'O Yaksha, my father will soon meet his end. The king of the Dasarnakas marches against him in rage. Hiranyavarman in his golden armour is mighty and invincible. Yaksha, save me, my mother and my father! You have already said you will give me what I want. Through your grace, Yaksha, I want to become a man in all my parts. Be gracious to me, great Yaksha.'"

CANTO 195

AMBOPAKHYANA PARVA CONTINUED

"Bhishma said, "Bharatarishabha, the Yaksha heard Sikhandin's strange story and saw it was fraught with destiny, when she said, 'It was all pre-ordained, and it was ordained for my grief.'

The Yaksha said, 'Blessed princess, I will do what you wish. Listen, however, to the condition I have. For a specified time, I will give you my own manhood, and take your womanhood upon myself. But you must come back to me at the specified time. Promise me this, and you shall become a man. I am a ranger of the skies and wander at my pleasure; I have great powers and I can accomplish whatever I want. Take my boon, and save your city and all your kin. Swear in truth to return my manhood to me, and I will do what you want.'

Sikhandin said to him, 'Holy one of most excellent vows, I will return your manhood to you. Wanderer of the night, bear my womanhood for a short time only. After the king of the Dasarnakas, who wears golden mail, has left my city, I will become a woman once more and you will be a man again.'

Thus, the two made a pact with each other and exchanged their genders. The Yaksha Sthuna became a female, while Sikhandin obtained the resplendent form of the Yaksha.

Sikhandin of the Panchala vamsa entered Kampilya in great joy and approached his father. He told Drupada everything that had happened and Drupada heard it and was very glad; and the king and his wife remembered Mahadeva's words.

Forthwith, Drupada sent a messenger to Hiranyavarman saying that his Sikhandin was indeed a son. Meanwhile, the king of the Dasarnakas arrived suddenly outside Kampilya and despatched a messenger to the Panchala king, a man who was one of the foremost of Vedic scholars.

The king of the Dasarnakas said to his messenger, 'O duta, say to that worst of kings, the ruler of the Panchalas:

O evil-minded one, you chose my daughter as a wife for your daughter. Today, you will taste the fruit of deception.'

The Brahmana messenger went before Drupada. The king of the Panchalas, with Sikhandin, offered the duta a cow and honey. However, without accepting that worship, the Brahmana delivered Hiranyavarman's rough message.

The duta said, 'My lord Hiranyavarman says: *O vile Drupada, you have deceived me. I will kill you and all your counsellors, sons and kin!*'

Forced to listen to King Hiranyavarman's censure in the midst of his counsellors, Drupada assumed a mild and friendly manner and said, "My reply to my brother's words I will send to him with my duta."

Drupada sent a Brahmana, learned in the Vedas, to Hiranyavarman.

The messenger delivered this message: "Sikhandin is my son, you can have him examined. Somebody has lied to you; do not believe the liar."

King Hiranyavarman of the Dasarnakas was filled with sorrow. He sent some beautiful virgins to ascertain the truth about Sikhandin's sex. These maidens returned and told the king that Sikhandin was a powerfully built man. The king of the Dasarnakas was filled with great joy. He accepted Drupada's hospitality and stayed happily with him for a while.

In his joy, he gave Sikhandin much wealth, many elephants, horses, cows and bulls. For as long as he was there, Drupada treated him worshipfully, and, before leaving, Hiranyavarman rebuked his daughter for what she had done. Sikhandin rejoiced that Hiranyavarman left in joy and with his anger pacified.

Meanwhile, a while after Sikhandin became a man, Kubera, in the course of his wanderings over the world, borne as always on the shoulders of men, arrived at the home of the Yaksha Sthuna. From the sky, he looked down at the Yaksha Sthuna's palace and saw that it was adorned with beautiful garlands of flowers, and perfumed with fragrant extracts of fine grass and other sweet scents. It was decked with canopies, and incense wafted in the air. Beautiful flags and banners adorned the palace, which was filled with food and drink of every kind.

Kubera, lord of the Yakshas, saw Sthuna's glorious abode filled also with strings of jewels and gems, perfumed with the fragrance of many different kinds of flowers, well-watered and swept.

He said to the Yakshas in his train, "My mighty ones, grand indeed is this mansion of Sthuna's, but why does the wicked one not come out to greet me, though he knows I am here? He deserves some stern punishment."

The Yakshas said, "Lord, the king Drupada had a daughter born to him, named Sikhandini. Sthuna has given her his own manhood and become a woman in her place. He remains inside his palace because he is ashamed to come before you. Now do what you think is right."

Kubera ordered his chariot to stop there and Sthuna brought before him, still repeatedly vowing to punish Sthuna. Summoned by the lord of Yakshas, Sthuna came out and stood before his Lord, head bent in shame.

The Lord of treasures cursed him in anger, "Guhyakas, let this wretched Yaksha remain a woman!

Sinner, you have shamed all Yakshas by giving your manhood to Sikhandini and becoming a woman. You have done what no one has ever done before, and from this day you shall remain a woman and she a man."

Now all the Yakshas tried to pacify him for Sthunakarna's sake and begged him to limit his curse.

Kubera relented, "After Sikhandin's death, O Yakshas, this one will regain his own form. So, let the noble Sthuna not worry."

And the illustrious lord of the Yakshas received worship and departed with his colourful and wild people, who could travel great distances in short time. And, thus cursed, Sthuna continued living in his fine sanctuary.

When Hiranyavarman left, Sikhandin came at once to the Yaksha Sthuna, as he had promised. Sthuna was pleased that the prince had kept his word, and he told Sikhandin everything that had happened.

The Yaksha said equably, "O Kshatriya, because of you, Vaisravana cursed me. Go now and live happily amongst men as you please. Both your arrival and Kubera's visit were fated, and they could not be avoided."

Sikhandin went back to his city, full of joy. He worshipped the gods, the Brahmanas, the great ancestral trees and the crossroads with all kinds of garlands and costly gifts. Drupada, king of the Panchalas, his son Sikhandin whose wish had been crowned with success, and his kinsmen, all rejoiced. The king sent his son Sikhandin, who had once been a woman, to Acharya Drona as a sishya. With all of you, Sikhandin mastered all four parts of the astra shastra, as did his brother Dhrishtadyumna.

Rajan, I gathered all this information through my spies whom I set on Drupada, disguised as fools or blind men.

This is how Maharatha Sikhandin of the Panchalas was born as a girl, and later became a man. And it was the king of Kasi's eldest daughter, Amba, who was born into Drupada's royal house as Sikhandin.

If Sikhandin comes to fight me, bow in hand, I will not so much as look at him, let alone attack that prince. The world knows that I have vowed never to take up arms against a woman, or one who was once a woman, or one who has a woman's name, or one who looks like a woman. I will not kill Sikhandin. Now that I know about this prince's past, I will not slay him in battle even if he rides at me with his weapon raised. If I, Bhishma, kill a woman, the righteous will speak ill of me." When he heard this, Duryodhana, after a moment's reflection, agreed with Bhishma.'

CANTO 196

AMBOPAKHYANA PARVA CONTINUED

Sanjaya says, 'When night passed and morning broke, your sons, standing in the midst of their vast legions, asked their Pitamaha, "O Gangaputra, Yudhishtira's army is ready for war; it teems with men, elephants and horses; Maharathas throng its ranks and protected by these mighty bowmen—Bhima, Arjuna and others headed by Dhrishtadyumna, who are all like the rulers of the world—that great force is impregnable, invincible; it resembles the endless sea. Even the gods cannot perturb it in battle; how long will it take you to raze Yudhishtira's army? How long will Acharya Drona need, and Kripa, and Karna who loves battle? How long will that Brahmanottama, Aswatthama son of Drona, need? My army has you all, who have devastras at your command.

I am beset by curiosity. Mahabaho, tell me what I want to know."

Bhishma said, "First among Kurus, your question about the strength and weakness of your enemy is worthy. I will tell you of my prowess in battle, of my own strength and the power of my weapons. One should fight common soldiers in a simple, straightforward way, but one must use cunning with those who resort to deception. This is the dharma of a Kshatriya.

I can indeed raze the Pandava army. Every morning, I can mark ten thousand common warriors and a thousand chariot-warriors to kill, and accomplish my task by dusk. So, given time, donning my impenetrable kavacha and putting forth my tireless urjas, I can entirely destroy the vast enemy forces. However, if I loose my devastras, which consume thousands in moments, I can complete the massacre in a month."

Duryodhana then asked Drona, "Acharya, in how much time can you annihilate the legions of Pandu's son?"

Drona said, smiling, "I am old, Mahabaho. My tejas and urjas have both waned, but with the fire of my astras I can, like Santanu's son Bhishma, consume the Pandava army in a month."

Then Kripa declared that he could finish the enemy in two months. Drona's son Aswatthama swore that he would do the same in ten nights; and Karna, who commanded the most potent astras, claimed he would achieve that feat in five days.

Bhishma laughed aloud to listen to Karna, "Radheya, your vainglory will last until you encounter Arjuna, flying into battle on his chariot, with his conch, bows and arrows, and with Krishna beside him. You can say anything you like, for talk is cheap.'"

CANTO 197

Ambopakhyana Parva continued

Vaisampayana said, "When Yudhishtira hears what the Kuru commanders said, he summons his brothers and speaks privately to them.

Yudhishtira says, 'The spies I sent into Duryodhana's army brought me news this morning.

They told me that Duryodhana asked Bhishma how long it would take him to raze our army and Bhishma said he could do it in a month. Drona declared that he could achieve the same thing in the same time; Kripa indicated twice that period; so we have heard. Aswatthama, who has powerful astras, said he would take only ten nights; and Karna, who, also, can summon the most devastating astras, declared that he could complete the slaughter in five days.

Arjuna, I want to hear what you have to say. How long will you take to vanquish the enemy?'

Dhananjaya, of the curly hair, glances at Krishna and says, 'Bhishma and all these other warriors are Mahatmans, masters of arms and all the methods and vyuhas of war. They can, doubtlessly, destroy our forces as they have said. But, my lord, dispel the anxiety in your heart. With Krishna beside me, from a single chariot, I, Arjuna, can incinerate the three worlds, with even the gods, and indeed all living creatures that were, are and will be in the blink of an eye. This is my belief.

I still command the awesome astra which Mahadeva, Lord of all creatures, gave me when I fought him hand-to-hand, when he came as a Vetala; the Pasupatastra is still mine. O Naravyaghra, I have, besides, the astra that Mahadeva uses to destroy creation during the Pralaya at the end of a Yuga. Bhishma knows nothing of that astra, nor do Drona, Kripa and Drona's son. How can the Sutaputra Karna have any knowledge of it? However, it is adharma, and a great sin, to use such devastras against ordinary mortals in war. We will vanquish our enemies in a fair contention.

Then, Rajan, look at all these mighty kings, your allies. They are all masters of devastras and all eager for battle. After their initiation into the Vedas, they have all performed the final ritual bath in great yagnas. All of them are undefeated, and they can vanquish even the host of the Devas in battle.

You have for your allies these incomparable Kshatriyas: Sikhandin and Yuyudhana; Dhrishtadyumna of Prishata vamsa; Bhimasena and Madri's twins; Yudhamanyu and Uttamaujas; and Virata and Drupada who are Bhishma and Drona's equals in battle; Mahabaho Sankha, Hidimba's mighty son and his son Anjanaparva, whose strength and prowess defy description; Sini's descendant, Mahabahu Satyaki; and Abhimanyu and Draupadi's five sons.

And then, you, by yourself, Dharmaraja, can destroy the three worlds. O you who are blessed with the effulgence of Indra himself, I know, for it is manifest, that you can turn any man, whom you look upon in anger, to ashes.'"

CANTO 198

AMBOPAKHYANA PARVA CONTINUED

Vaisampayana said, "The next morning, under a cloudless sky, led by Duryodhana, all the kings in his army, prepare themselves for the great war, what will be the Mahabharata yuddha, against the Pandavas. They leave Hastinapura and go forth to Kurukshetra like a sea leaving its bed.

They take ritual baths of purification; they put on royal white robes and drape garlands around their necks. They pour ritual offerings onto sacred fires, and when they have received the blessings of their Brahmanas they take up their weapons and raise their standards. All these kings are knowers of the Vedas; they are courageous without exception, and have observed stern vratas. They are great warriors, and men of kingly generosity. Those mighty lords of the Earth, all of them equally confident of their own prowess and that of their companions, share the single-minded desire to attain mukti through battle: the greatest goal of any Kshatriya.

First, the Avantis, Vinda and Anuvinda, the Kekayas and the Bahlikas go forth with Bharadwaja's son, Drona, at their head.

Then come Aswatthama, Bhishma and Jayadratha of the Sindhus; the kings of the southern and the western countries and of the mountainous regions; Sakuni, king of the Gandharas, all the chiefs of the eastern and the northern regions, the Sakas, the Kiratas, the Yavanas, the Sibis and the Vasatis with their Maharathas at the heads of their respective divisions: all these great chariot-warriors ride in the second legion.

And next: Kritavarman, at the head of his swarming troops; that Maharatha—the king of the Trigartas; Raja Duryodhana surrounded by his brothers; Sala, Bhurisravas, Salya and Brihadratha the king of the Kosalas. All these, with Dhritarashtra's sons at their head, make up the rear; they are magnificent warriors, without exception, and, uniting together in immaculate formations, their armour shimmering like some vast lake of lustre, they make camp on one side of the hallowed field of Kurukshetra.

Duryodhana has his encampment adorned to look like a second Hastinapura. Indeed, even the citizens of Hastinapura could hardly distinguish their city from the sprawling cantonment. By order of the Kaurava king, there are hundreds of thousands of inaccessible pavilions, each one as grand as his own, for every king in his army. The tents for the troops occupy five yojanas of the field, and the lords of the Earth and their fighting men enter those countless pavilions and tents, all richly appointed and replete with every excellent manner of provender and comfort, even like some unimaginable pride of lions.

Rare and of the finest quality are the supplies and comforts Duryodhana orders for the kings, their footsoldiers, elephants and horses, and all their followers. He makes more than ample provisions for the engineers, bards, singers and panegyrists loyal to him, for the vendors and traders, for prostitutes, spies and the people who have come to witness the great war."

CANTO 199

AMBOPAKHYANA PARVA CONTINUED

Vaisampayana said, "Like Duryodhana, Yudhishtira, too, commands his heroic legions and warriors led by Dhrishtadyumna. He does this through his Senapati the Panchala prince, through Dhrishtaketu of the Chedis, Kasis and Karushas, as well as through Virata, Drupada, Yuyudhana and Sikhandin, and the two other Panchala princes, the peerless bowmen Yudhamanyu and Uttamaujas.

These warriors in their shining kavachas, adorned with golden kundalas, blaze like flames in a ghrita-fed yagna fire and are as resplendent as the great planets in the sky. Yudhishtira Dharmaraja honours all his warriors and then commands them to take the field. He, also, provides the best of food and drink for the Mahatman kings, as also for their footsoldiers, elephants and horses, their camp followers and engineers.

Yudhishtira first has Abhimanyu, Brihanta and Draupadi's five sons set, with Dhrishtadyumna at their head; he then sends Bhima and Arjuna with the second division of his forces. The din that the men make as they harness their horses and elephants and load the chariots with weapons and other battle equipment, and the excited shouts of the soldiers, rises into the heavens. And last of all, the king himself sets out, with Virata, Drupada and all the other kings come to fight for him.

And the army of fierce bowmen that Dhrishtadyumna leads, which until now was gathered in one place, now streams into interminable columns, and looks like the wide and turbulent Ganga. Yudhishtira sends forth his divisions in formations calculated to bewilder Duryodhana; and at this, he succeeds.

In Yudhishtira's first division ride the five sons of Draupadi, Maharathas; Abhimanyu, Nakula, Sahadeva and all the Prabhadrakas are part of this vast complement of warriors, as are ten thousand horses, two thousand elephants, ten thousand foot-soldiers and five hundred chariots. And Yudhishtira gives charge of this force to Bhimasena.

In the middle division of his army he places Virata and Jayatsena; the two Maharathas Yudhamanyu and Uttamaujas, those noble Panchala princes, both of great prowess and both armed with maces and bows; and Krishna and Arjuna, as well as countless other master warriors who seethe with rage and warlust. Countless are the valiant horsemen, five thousand the elephants, all these surrounded by fleets of chariots. A thousand fearless footsoldiers, armed with bows, swords and maces, march behind them and a thousand before them, all united in spirit and purpose like a single terrible Being.

In the oceanic division, in which Yudhishtira himself is, numberless great kings ride, along with thousands of elephants, tens of thousands of horses, and thousands upon thousands of chariots and footsoldiers.

Chekitana and the Chedi king Dhrishtaketu march with their own immense akshauhinis; with them rides the most brilliant Satyaki, best of the Vrishni Maharathas, whom hundreds of thousands of chariots surround. The Purusharishabhas Kshattradharma and Kshattradeva bring up the rear, where, also, are carts, stalls, wagons laden with battle-fatigues, other conveyances for immense stores of weapons and provisions, and draught animals, as well; here go thousands of elephants and tens of thousands of horses.

Yudhishtira goes forth slowly, majestically, his elephant divisions bringing all the sickly and women, all the emaciated and the weak to watch the great war; pack animals carry the Pandava king's treasures, and the contents of his granaries. The ever truthful and invincible Sauchitti follows him; and Srenimat, Vasudeva and the king of Kasi's son Vibhu, as well, with twenty-thousand chariots, and a hundred million mettlesome horses with bells on their legs. Twenty-thousand fighting elephants with curved tusks as long as plough-shares, all of the highest pedigree, and looking like dark, rolling cloud masses, bring up the rear, ambling behind the kings, in lordly gait.

Besides these twenty-thousand war-elephants in Yudhishtira's division, are seventy-thousand more, in his army of seven akshauhinis. The juice of musth trickles down their trunks and spills out of their mouths, and they are like moving mountains with spring water flowing down them.

Thus does Yudhishtira array his awesome army, upon which he relies in the war against his cousin Duryodhana. Besides these that I have named, there are others: lakhs of smaller legions of free men, who follow the main body of Pandava army, roaring as they march. Thousands of warriors infused with the joy of imminent battle upon them beat thousands of drums and sound tens of thousands of booming conches," said Vaisampayana.

The End of Udyoga Parva